Foundation
ActionScript 3.0 Animation
Making Things Move!

Keith Peters

friendsof

DESIGNER TO DESIGNER™

an Apress® company

Foundation ActionScript 3.0 Animation: Making Things Move!

ISBN-13 (pbk): 978-1-59059-791-0

ISBN-10 (pbk): 1-59059-791-5

Printed and bound in the United States of America 9 8 7 6 5 4 3 2

Distributed to the book trade worldwide by Springer-Verlag New York, Inc., 233 Spring Street, 6th Floor, New York, NY 10013. Phone 1-800-SPRINGER, fax 201-348-4505, e-mail orders-ny@springer-sbm.com, or visit www.springeronline.com.

For information on translations, please contact Apress directly at 2855 Telegraph Avenue, Suite 600, Berkeley, CA 94705. Phone 510-549-5930, fax 510-549-5939, e-mail info@apress.com, or visit www.apress.com.

The source code for this book is freely available to readers at www.friendsofed.com in the Downloads section.

Credits

Lead Editor Chris Mills	**Assistant Production Director** Kari Brooks-Copony
Technical Reviewer Todd Yard	**Compositor** Dina Quan
Editorial Board Steve Anglin, Ewan Buckingham, Gary Cornell, Jason Gilmore, Jonathan Gennick, Jonathan Hassell, James Huddleston, Chris Mills, Matthew Moodie, Jeff Pepper, Paul Sarknas, Dominic Shakeshaft, Jim Sumser, Matt Wade	**Artist** April Milne **Proofreader** April Eddy **Indexer** John Collin
Project Manager | Production Editor Laura Esterman	**Cover Image Designer** Corné van Dooren
Copy Edit Manager Nicole Flores	**Interior and Cover Designer** Kurt Krames
Copy Editors Nicole Flores, Ami Knox	**Manufacturing Director** Tom Debolski

To Kazumi and Kristine, who again put up with me doing this whole writing-a-book thing. Just a few dozen more, at most.

CONTENTS AT A GLANCE

CONTENTS

Chapter 12 Particle Attraction and Gravity 305

Chapter 13 Forward Kinematics: Making Things Walk 323

FOREWORD

There is a deepening chasm in the Flash world between those who understand and use ActionScript in their work and those who don't. We sometimes erroneously call this the difference between "designers" and "developers." The assumption is that "designers" do not understand code and "developers" do not understand design. This is, at best, a convenient oversimplification.

The labels "designer" and "developer" may have sufficed in the early days of the Web when we were all still trying to make sense of this new and exciting medium. More than a decade since, we have discovered that the medium is not entirely new and that it does *not* exist in a vacuum, separate from all that came before it and all that exists alongside it.

Today, the "designer" and "developer" labels do not tell you much about what a person is or what a person does. And yet they are frequently used to describe both.

As a description of job function, these labels are woefully inadequate in detail. What type of design work do you do? What is your function on the team? Do you do graphic design, or motion graphics design, or information design (architecture), or object design (modeling)? By lumping graphic designers, information architects, animators, and illustrators under the huge catch-all category of "designer," you strip that label of any meaning whatsoever.

The role of the "developer"—at least in a Flash context—appears to be somewhat better defined. You can assume to some degree of accuracy that the person's job involves building user interfaces and, more than likely, programming.

Where these titles lack the necessary granularity in describing job function, one thing is certain: They are overly restrictive when it comes to describing who a person *is*. "I am a designer," for example, is often used to justify time not spent learning to program. Similarly, "I can't draw a straight line" is an oft-used excuse by "developers" to rationalize a lack of invested time in learning the basics of graphic, motion graphics, and user interface design. (Contrary to popular belief, many of the best graphic and motion graphics designers in the world couldn't draw a very impressive straight line either if given an easel and brush; similarly, some of the most talented artists I know couldn't design a passable user interface layout to save their lives.)

No, at the personal level, you should accept no less than the title of "artist" and aspire to earn the right to carry the title. And earning this right is influenced not so much by your accomplishments as by your approach: a relentless pursuit of perfection, where the journey is the destination.

Like it or not, we are the artists of our era, and this crazy and wonderful conglomerate of digital media are our easels, palettes, and brushes. We can create beautiful things, thought-provoking things, things that can make a difference. And we can potentially reach more people in more ways than has ever been possible in the past.

Our medium is so broad that it encompasses, among so much else, graphic design, with a static emphasis on form, contrast, repetition, color, and typography; motion graphics design, where framing, editing, and composition come into play as well as the animator's toolbox of expectation and expressiveness and the art of the storyteller, director, and actor; user interface design and information architecture; and last, but definitely not least, that newest and most unrecognized of art forms: programming.

But *is* programming an art form? Only so far as photography or film are art forms and painting and puppetry and theater before them.

When photography was first developed, it was heralded as a wonderful technical achievement but nothing more. It was seen as the technical act of capturing reality. Over 150 years later, we can now read the photographic text as a subjective device and a means of artistic expression.

A mere century ago, we saw films as absolute, objective slices of reality—as documents, devoid of artistry. Today, we can appreciate their subjective nature and the many intricacies that separate a master work from a home movie. This was not always so. When Louis and Auguste Lumiere first showed their film of the arrival of an express train at Lyons station, the audience fled from the theater in terror, afraid for their lives at the sight of the oncoming train. Today, we know better. We know how to "read" film. We are film-literate. We cannot yet say the same thing about programming.

There is a magical line that separates artist from artisan: a line conceived by a spark of creativity but carved, laboriously, by boundless passion, energy, and dedication. The artist exudes an envious ability to simultaneously inspire awe, impart experience, and evoke emotion in others. Whereas once the title was reserved for the master painter, sculptor, and architect, we now have a wider appreciation of what composes art, and thus what composes the artist.

Today, we look upon programming as a purely technical pursuit. We talk of a divide between the creative and the technical, and lump programmers in the latter. The programmer is today as the filmmaker was early last century: an artist toiling in relative obscurity, awaiting a code-literate society to appreciate the nuances of her art. Will it take a century for this happen? I don't think so.

Thanks to programmer/artists like Keith Peters, we are seeing bridges being built between the realms of programming and the visual arts, leading to a growing social understanding and appreciation for the art behind programming. Keith's code is visual, alive, pulsing, breathing, growing, changing—many times in wholly unpredictable, unique, and wonderful ways. Variables, statements, loops, methods, and classes combine to create emotive, moving experiences that take us beyond our everyday experience to discover new worlds made entirely of light and sound.

The first version of this book covered ActionScript 2. Since then, the Flash platform has been revolutionized with the introduction of a new scripting language, ActionScript 3, and a new virtual machine in Flash Player 9. These improvements open up a new world of possibilities, and I am ecstatic that Keith has updated *Foundation ActionScript Animation: Making Things Move* to take advantage of this exciting new technology. But, exciting technologies and version numbers aside, don't forget the most important thing:

This is a book about art.

Programming is a new, exciting art form that is growing daily in audience, relevance, and recognition. And the best way to learn any art form is through apprenticeship—by sharing the invaluable experience of a skilled master. Within the covers of this book, you will find such a master to lead you on your own artistic journey of programming. This book is the next best thing to having Keith next to you, guiding you on your own journey of discovery.

So budding artist, prepare to join the ranks of the Flash masters. The knowledge within this book will provide you with the grounding to unlock your own creative potential. The rest, as they say, is 10% inspiration, 90% perspiration. Dreamers plan, artists create. Get cracking!

Your easel and brush await, and your journey begins . . .

Aral Balkan
January 8, 2007
San Francisco

ABOUT THE AUTHOR

Keith Peters has been working with Flash and ActionScript since 1999. He is currently a senior software engineer at Brightcove in Cambridge, Massachusetts. This book is the eleventh book on Flash or ActionScript Keith has written or contributed to. In addition, he has written several magazine articles on the subject, spoken at many conferences around the world, and contributed to several award-winning Flash sites. His personal site, www.bit-101.com, became famous for its hundreds of open source ActionScript experiments, and continues to be a source of open information in the Flash community. When he manages to pull himself away from the computer, he spends time with his wife, Kazumi, and daughter, Kristine.

ABOUT THE TECHNICAL REVIEWER

 **Todd Yard** is currently a senior software engineer at Brightcove in Cambridge, Massachusetts, where he moved early in 2005 in the middle of a blizzard. Previously, he was in New York City, New York, where he initially moved in 1996 in the middle of a blizzard, working with EGO7 on their Flash content management system and community software while freelancing with agencies, developing web applications for clients such as GE and IBM. Todd originally hails from Phoenix, Arizona, where there are no blizzards, and has written for a number of friends of ED books, of which his favorites are *Flash MX Studio* and *Flash MX Application and Interface Design*, though he feels *Extending Flash MX 2004: Complete Guide and Reference to JavaScript Flash* was the most useful. His personal site, which he used to update all the time, he fondly remembers, is www.27Bobs.com.

ABOUT THE COVER IMAGE DESIGNER

 **Corné van Dooren** designed the front cover image for this book. Having been given a brief by friends of ED to create a new design for the Foundation series, he was inspired to create this new setup combining technology and organic forms.

With a colorful background as an avid cartoonist, Corné discovered the infinite world of multimedia at the age of 17—a journey of discovery that hasn't stopped since. His mantra has always been "The only limit to multimedia is the imagination," and it keeps him moving forward constantly.

After enjoying success after success over the past years—working for many international clients, as well as being featured in multimedia magazines, testing software, and working on many other friends of ED books—Corné decided it was time to take another step in his career by launching his own company, Project 79, in March 2005.

You can see more of his work and contact him through www.cornevandooren.com or www.project79.com.

If you like his work, be sure to check out his chapter in *New Masters of Photoshop: Volume 2* (friends of ED, 2002).

ACKNOWLEDGMENTS

There are three groups of people I'd like to acknowledge. I'll avoid any specific names as there are so many, and I'm sure I'd miss someone.

First are all those in the Flash community who have shared their knowledge in forums, mailing lists, articles, tutorials, blogs, e-mails, and books. Without the spirit of open sharing of knowledge that has always been such a strong part of the Flash community, this book would never have even been a thought in my mind.

Second is every person at Apress and friends of ED who touched this book in any way. You guys are truly a professional group. You've made writing both editions of this book a very smooth experience, and the resulting book a top-quality product.

And finally, I want to acknowledge every person who bought the first edition of the book, wrote such great reviews of it, and said so many nice things about it to me in person or via e-mail. It is you who have made this book the success I knew it could be when I first envisioned it.

INTRODUCTION

This is a great book!

There, I said it again! In the introduction to the original version of this book, I went on to clarify that the book's greatness wasn't necessarily a reflection of my own greatness, but of the fact that the book covered some great topics. It answered all the questions about animation in ActionScript that I had struggled with over the years, the questions that I had seen others struggle with, and the questions that people still e-mail me with. Even the answers aren't things that I dreamt up on my own, but discovered by searching, reading, and asking people far wiser and more educated than myself. OK, I'll take a little credit for assembling it all in a logical order and explaining things in what people tell me is a pretty understandable way. At any rate, my rather conceited opening statement has proven to have some merit, if sales figures and the feedback that many of you have given me personally are any indication. So, thanks for buying it, and thanks for the nice comments.

This version of the book is essentially the same book, converted to ActionScript 3. The same basic formulas and techniques are covered that were covered in the first version, in roughly the same order. I would have liked to get into some new, additional techniques, but there was little that I could really cut out of the existing text, and in fact, even covering those same basics takes up a lot more space in ActionScript 3, as virtually every example here is contained in its own full class. But although the same basic topics are covered, it was still quite a bit of work, considering the massive changes this version of ActionScript has brought us.

Yes, if you plan to read this book, plan to learn a little object-oriented programming. I was able to largely avoid the subject in the first version of the book, but this time I decided to abandon the timeline and dive into ActionScript 3 the way it was meant to be written—with classes. Although you may find that a bit scary if you haven't used classes or OOP before, I guarantee you that by the time you finish Chapter 4, you will have gotten the hang of programming with classes, and by the time you are halfway through the book, it will be old hat to you. And if you are already familiar with ActionScript 2 classes, this book should serve as a nice transition into ActionScript 3.

Other than that, I'll briefly repeat a few of the things I said in the introduction to the first version. First, that the example and techniques I give here are not the only or even necessarily the best way of doing things. I will say that they all do what they are supposed to, and most of them are pretty darned good, but if you feel you can improve on them, go for it.

Second, there are no start-to-finish full game tutorials or anything of the sort in here. It's more of a catalog of individual techniques. It's my belief that if you understand and can apply these techniques, you'll have no problem dreaming up plenty of cool things to create with them.

And finally, a point I'll make a few more times throughout the book (and have even been criticized for making *too* often) is that although I cover a lot of mathematical formulas and physics in the following chapters, I take a lot of liberties with them. The resulting formulas are designed to *look* realistic and run at a decent speed within Flash Player. But don't be surprised if you find a lot of discrepancies between what you see in this book and your college physics text book.

But enough introduction. As I also said in the first edition, this is a *fun* book! So dive in and enjoy!

Layout conventions

To keep this book as clear and easy to follow as possible, the following text conventions are used throughout.

Important words or concepts are normally highlighted on the first appearance in **bold type**.

Code is presented in `fixed-width` font.

New or changed code is normally presented in **`bold fixed-width font`**.

Pseudo-code and variable input are written in *`italic fixed-width font`*.

Menu commands are written in the form Menu ➤ Submenu ➤ Submenu.

Where I want to draw your attention to something, I've highlighted it like this:

Ahem, don't say I didn't warn you.

Sometimes code won't fit on a single line in a book. Where this happens, I use an arrow like this: ➥.

```
This is a very, very long section of code that should be written all on ➥
the same line without a break.
```

Part One

ACTIONSCRIPTED ANIMATION BASICS

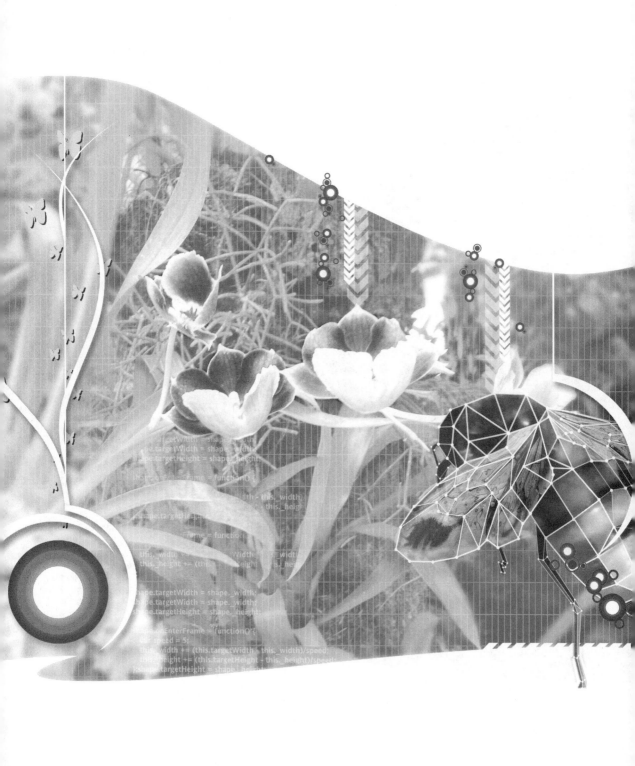

Chapter 1

BASIC ANIMATION CONCEPTS

What we'll cover in this chapter:

- What is animation?
- Frames and motion
- Dynamic vs. static animation

Flash, at its core, is an animation machine. From the very earliest versions, Flash has supported animation through tweens—where you create a couple of keyframes that are different and let Flash fill in what is in between. However, this book is not about tweens. This book is about the powerful language built into Flash, called ActionScript. This book covers programming, math, and physics techniques used to make things move with ActionScript. As you'll see, this gives you levels of power, control, and interactivity that you could never hope to match with tweening.

But before we dive into specific techniques and formulas for moving things around with ActionScript, let's take a quick look at exactly what animation is, some of the basic techniques behind it, and some concepts that you can use to make your Flash animations more dynamic and interesting.

Sure, you can skip this chapter if you are just dying to write some code. But I strongly suggest you come back to it at some point. If nothing else, you'll find some interesting insights into the subject.

What is animation?

First, the question of all questions: What is animation? Well, per the *American Heritage Dictionary of the English Language, Fourth Edition* (Houghton Mifflin Company, 2000), it means the following:

1. To give life to; fill with life
2. To impart interest or zest to; enliven
3. To fill with spirit, courage, or resolution; encourage
4. To inspire to action; prompt
5. To impart motion or activity to
6. To make, design, or produce (a cartoon, for example) so as to create the illusion of motion

While I could get philosophical with the first four definitions, what we are really talking about here are the fifth and sixth definitions. Animation means motion. I like to broaden that a bit and say that animation is change over time, specifically some type of visual change. Motion is basically the change in something's position over time. One minute it is over here; the next minute it is over there. Theoretically, it was also in the space between those two points, but I won't get metaphysical about it (not just yet anyway). It moved, and some time elapsed between the time it was at the first point and the time it was at the next one.

But an object doesn't necessarily need to change its location in order to be considered animated. It could just be changing its shape. Remember those photo-morphing programs that were all the rage in the late 1990s? You start with one picture of a girl and one picture of a tiger, and the program creates an animation between them. Or the object could be changing its size or orientation, such as a plant growing or a top spinning. Or it could even simply be changing its color. If you've been around long enough, you might remember some of the earliest animations on home PCs consisted of just cycling colors. You make a picture of a waterfall with a bunch of shapes in various shades of blue. You then cycle the colors of those shapes. If done right, the result gives the impression of falling water even though, technically, nothing is moving at all.

The connection of animation to time is an important one. Without any motion or change, there is no animation, of course, but also there is no sense of time. Sometimes you might see a webcam image of an empty room or a city skyline where nothing seems to be happening. It's impossible to tell if you are looking at a still image or a live video stream. Finally, you might notice some subtle change—a flickering light or a moving shadow. Just that slight flicker has reassured you that time is present, and maybe if you keep watching, something else will change. If you don't see any change after a while, you become convinced that it is a still image. There is no time, and you know nothing else will be happening in the picture.

That brings up another point: Animation keeps us interested in things. While the *Mona Lisa* is a wonderful piece of work and one of the most famous paintings of all time, I bet the average person gets bored after looking at it for 15 minutes tops, and then wanders off to see what else he can brag about having seen. But stick him in front of the latest high-budget Hollywood action film and he won't budge for a good two and a half hours. And if he does need to go to the restroom or to get a snack, he will wait for a "slow" part—one without so much action. That's the power of animation.

Frames and motion

Now, let's go back for a minute to that last definition of animate:

To make, design, or produce (a cartoon, for example) so as to create the *illusion* of motion.

Interesting that the definition writers should choose to throw that word *illusion* in there, yet entirely accurate. It happens that with just about every form of motion media, only an illusion of motion exists. Here's where we get to the concept of frames.

Virtually all visual animation media uses *frames*—a series of still images shown very rapidly to simulate motion or change. Anything you see on a computer, television, or movie screen is based on frames. This goes back to the earliest days of cartoon animation, where the individual pictures were drawn on sheets of cellophane and became known as *cels*, and the earliest motion pictures, where a similar technique was used with multiple photographs.

The concept is simple: You show a bunch of images that vary slightly from one to another, and the mind blurs them together as a single, moving image. But why do we insist on calling it an *illusion of motion*? If you see a man walk across the room on a movie screen, is that not motion? Of course it's only an image of a man, not the real thing, but that's not why we don't consider it to be real motion.

Remember when I talked about an object being over here and then later over there, and I said it moved through the intervening space? Well, that is real motion. Objects move through space smoothly, not in several jumps. (You quantum physicists in the audience, just be quiet.) But any and all frame-based motion does just that. It doesn't move from spot to spot; it disappears and reappears in another location in the next frame. The faster it's moving, the bigger jumps it takes.

If I showed you a picture of a man on the left side of a room and then a few seconds later another picture of the same man on the right side of the room, you'd say I showed you two pictures, not an animation. If I showed you half a dozen pictures of him in the process of crossing the room, you'd still say it was a series of individual photos. (See Figure 1-1 for an example of a series of still photographs.) If I presented enough photos fast enough, that wouldn't change the fact that they are still just a whole bunch of still photos, but you would no longer see it that way. Your mind would take it in as a man moving across the room. It is no more real motion than the original two photos were, but at *some point*, the mind gives up and buys into the illusion. As a matter of fact, that point has been well researched by the film industry.

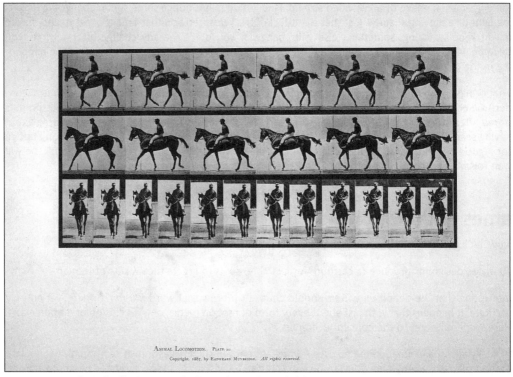

Figure 1-1. A series of still photographs by Eadweard Muybridge

Researchers have found that at a rate of 24 frames per second, people are perfectly happy to accept those frames as a single moving image. Go too much slower than that, and the jumpiness gets annoying and starts to break the illusion. And it seems that the human eye can't distinguish frame rates very much higher than that, so theoretically, going 100 frames per second isn't going to make your movie seem any more realistic (although higher frame rates in programmed animation can result in more responsiveness in interaction, and will seem smoother, especially for fast-moving objects).

Frames as records

The whole concept of frames makes three things possible: storage, transmission, and display. You can't really store, transmit, and display a man walking across a room. But you can store a picture, or many. And you can transmit them and display them. Thus you can show that animation almost anywhere, at any time, as long as you have or can receive the stored images and have a way to display them.

Now, let's get a little more general definition of what a frame is. So far, I've been referring to a frame as a still image or a drawing. Let's call it a record of a system at a specific point in time. That "system" could be your two-year-old daughter caught mid-grin, and the record would be that image. On the other hand, that system could be a collection of virtual objects, and the record could be their shapes, sizes, colors, positions, and so on at that particular moment in time. Thus, your movie would become not a series of still images, but rather a series of descriptions of images. Instead of just displaying the image, the computer would take that description, create the image from it, and then display it. You can even go a step further by using programmed frames.

Programmed frames

Since you have a computer that can calculate things on the fly, you don't really need a long list of descriptions for your frames. You can cut it down to a description of the first frame and some rules on how to build the subsequent frames. So, now the computer is not merely creating an image from a description. It's creating the description first, then creating the image based on the description, and finally displaying the image.

Consider how much file space you could save using this approach. Images take up a lot of hard disk space and bandwidth. And 24 images per second add up fast. If you can boil that down to one description and a set of rules, you've possibly reduced the file size by a factor of hundreds. Even a very complex set of rules for how the objects should move and react takes up less space than a single medium-sized image. Indeed, one of the first things people notice about scripted animation is just how small it winds up being.

Naturally, there is a trade-off. As your system gets larger and your rules get more complex, the computer must work furiously to calculate the next scene description, and then work overtime to render it. If you're trying to maintain a particular frame rate, that gives the CPU a limited amount of time (milliseconds) to think about it. If it can't calculate the scene in time, your frame rate will suffer. On the other hand, image-based animation doesn't care so much about what's in the scene or how complex it is. It just shows the next picture, generally right on time.

I've used prerendered animation to my advantage at least once. I was putting together a presentation of a number of complex Flash ActionScripted animations. File size was not a problem, since the animations were going to be played from a local machine. But timing was critical, and I had no idea how smoothly the ActionScript would render the images on this unknown, untested computer. So I brought the Flash movies into Director and exported the whole thing as a giant QuickTime movie. Since the movie was now just a series of prerendered images, it didn't really matter anymore how complex they were. As long as the computer was capable of displaying a QuickTime movie, I knew it would do so smoothly. The presentation went off without a hitch.

Dynamic vs. static animation

Another advantage to using coded animation goes far beyond simple file size. It's the fact that a coded animation becomes dynamic. Have you ever watched the movie *Titanic*? I hope I'm not giving away too much, but the boat sinks—every time. It sank in the theaters, it sinks on VHS, and it even sinks on DVD. Short of pressing the Stop or Pause button, you can't stop it from sinking. That's because a movie is a series of still images. The images near the end of this particular series show the boat sinking, and that's that.

Now let's move from the *Titanic* movie to a Flash website. Remember the late 1990s, when Flash was originally taking off? Everyone had to have a Flash website intro. Some shapes would slide in and grow or fade out. A cheap audio loop would play. Some trendy buzzwords would fade or slide in or out. Maybe a beam of light or some shadows would appear. Wow!

OK, I won't be too harsh. At least two or three I remember really were "wow" material—real works of art. The intros for the Gabocorp and Ray of Light sites, shown in Figures 1-2 and 1-3, were legendary. But when I think back on it, I recall actually sitting through them only a couple of times. They were a minute or two long, and I watched them two or three times. Was that because they weren't good? No, it was because after you saw them a couple of times, there wasn't much more to see. Just like the *Titanic* movie, the website intros did the same thing each time. I call that *static animation* (my own personal oxymoron!), because the animation never changes. Each frame, from start to finish, is predefined.

Now, a coded animation isn't necessarily dynamic. I could take an object and, using code, put it in a certain position and have it move across the screen. Each time you play the movie, the same code runs and causes the same movement. That's hardly dynamic.

But what if I take an object, and again using code, determine a random point to place it and a random direction and speed to move it? Now each time you play the movie, something different will happen.

Figure 1-2. The legendary gabocorp.com intro

Figure 1-3. Intro for rayoflight.com

Or what if, when the movie starts, I find out the time of day and month of the year, and use that data to create a scene—say a winter morning, a summer afternoon, or an evening in April?

Or how about if I have some factors in my movie that can be changed while the movie is running, via the keyboard and mouse? That would allow the user to interact with the objects on the screen. That's about as far from static as you can get. You could even save the *Titanic*!

Perhaps the most interesting aspect of dynamic animation, and what this book is mainly about, is the application of real-world mathematics and physics principles to the objects in the movie. You don't merely have some object move off in some random direction; you also give it some gravity, so that as it moves, it starts to fall down. When it hits the "ground," it bounces, but not as high as it started out. Then it eventually settles down and just sits there. Now you add some user interaction to that, allowing the user to "pick it up" with the mouse or move it around with the keyboard. As the user throws the object around, she starts getting the feeling that she is really handling a physical object.

With this type of animation, the user is no longer just sitting there watching some frames play out. She has entered into the environment you have created. How long is she going to stay there? She will remain as long as the environment keeps her interested. The more she can interact with the environment, the longer she will be interested. Make it interesting enough, and she will stay there a lot longer than she would sit through your intro (and sadly, probably longer than she would sit in front of the *Mona Lisa*). I have many e-mail messages from people telling me they spent their entire morning or afternoon playing with the experiments on www.bit-101.com. And not only will people stay longer, but they will also come back for more.

Summary

So, where is all this leading? In this opening chapter, I've gone over some of the basics of animation. But what do you actually do with this? Well, that's up to you.

In the following chapters, I'm going to put some tools in your hands and give you a quick lesson in how to use each one. What you build with these tools is entirely your decision. The most obvious use for much of what's in this book would be for game creation. Games are essentially interactive animations with some goals for players to achieve. But I really want to avoid this becoming simply a games book. I have used almost all of the techniques here in some kind of professional work other than games—from horrendous 3D menus and other not-so-bad navigation systems, to advertisements and educational applications.

A word of warning: Pick up any web design book, and you'll find a chapter telling you all about how too much animation is bad. I won't disagree, but I'm not going to say another word about it. If you want to hang yourself with animation, I'm going to spend the next few hundred pages giving you all the rope you need!

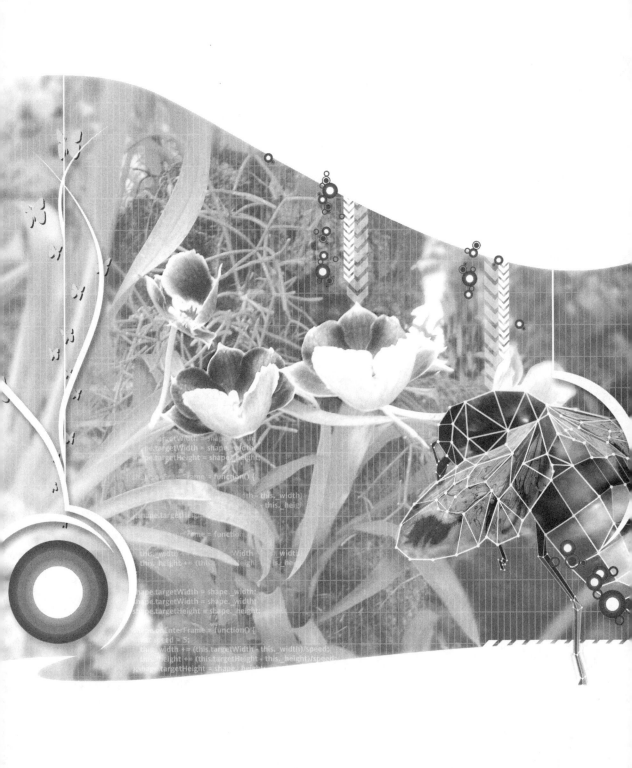

Chapter 2

BASICS OF ACTIONSCRIPT 3.0
FOR ANIMATION

What we'll cover in this chapter:

- Basic animation
- Sprites
- Classes and object-oriented programming (OOP)
- User interaction

If the first chapter was a somewhat philosophical overview of animation, this one is a sort of technical overview of what it takes to animate with ActionScript, and in particular, ActionScript 3.0 (AS 3). This chapter covers the essentials of loops for animation, movie clips and sprites, classes, and user interaction. It gives you the majority of the information you need to understand the ActionScript techniques used in the rest of the book.

Basic animation

To start off, let's quickly review what Chapter 1 covered.

- Animation is made with frames, with each frame slightly different to present the illusion of motion.
- Frame-by-frame or tweened animation contains an image or a description of an image for each frame.
- Dynamic animation contains an initial description of an image and rules that are applied to alter the description on each frame.

Most of the rest of this book will focus on the rules for dynamic animation, providing a catalog of techniques to change the image description, resulting in realistic motion. In this chapter, you'll see how to structure the initial description, how to apply those rules on each frame, and how to put the whole thing together. You'll be creating plenty of working examples as you go.

A note on ActionScript versions

The original edition of this book came out shortly after Flash 8 was released. Although it was designed with basic ActionScript 2 syntax in mind, I made the decision to avoid a lot of heavy OOP principles. Instead, most of the code was intended to be placed directly on the timeline. The result was a bit of a mishmash of ActionScript 1 and 2.

This edition of the book, however, is dedicated to Flash 9 and AS 3. As of this writing, there are at least three ways to create a Flash 9, AS 3 movie:

- The Flash CS3 IDE
- Flex Builder 2
- The free Flex/AS 3 command-line compiler and Flex 2 Software Development Kit (SDK)

While it is still possible to write AS 3 on the timeline in the Flash CS3 IDE, the other two methods absolutely require the use of at least one AS 3 class file. So to keep things consistent, I decided to leave the timeline behind. All the examples presented in this book will thus be presented in AS 3 classes.

In this chapter, I'm going to show you how to set up an AS 3 project for each of the development environments just mentioned (Flash CS3, Flex Builder 2, and the free SDK). In the rest of the book, only the applicable class code will be presented, and it should work in any of the three environments.

Occasionally, when describing a simple concept, I may give a small snippet of code to demonstrate the idea. Although it won't be explicitly shown, it is assumed that this snippet will be inserted into a skeleton class, which I will present in this chapter.

Given that classes will be such a vital part of the examples in the book this time around, I'll discuss them sooner, and a bit more in depth. Even so, this book is not meant to be an in-depth reference on OOP, and the material on classes will really only be the minimum amount needed to get you up and running and creating the examples in this book.

Classes and OOP

I imagine some readers might have no idea what a class or the term "object oriented" means, while others have been using classes in ActionScript (or other languages) for years. So as to not lose anyone, I'm going to try to cover all the basics. AS 2 OOP experts might want to at least skim this section, too, as there are quite a few changes in the way things work in AS 3.

If you think you do not have any familiarity with classes, you may be wrong. If you've written any code in Flash, chances are you used several classes. A *class* simply refers to a type of object. MovieClip is a class referring to—you guessed it—movie clips. Text fields, movie clips, buttons, strings, and numbers all have classes.

A class basically has two things associated with it: properties (data or information) and behaviors (actions, or things it can do). Properties are essentially variables that hold information relating to the class, and behaviors are just functions, though when a function is part of a class, we usually refer to it as a *method*.

A basic class

If you have used Flash for a while, you know that you can create a symbol in the library, and then create several instances of that symbol on the stage. Similar to the relationship between symbols and instances, classes are templates, and objects (also known as instances) are individual manifestations of a particular class. You can make a simple class like this:

```
package {
  public class MyClass {
    public var myProperty:Number = 100;

    public function myMethod() {
      trace("I am here");
    }
  }
}
```

Let's run through the code. First we have something that is new even to AS 2 class veterans: the package statement. *Packages*, simply put, are a way to group related classes together. I'll discuss packages more in a bit, but most of the examples in this book will not even use packages. Still, though, you'll need to include the package keyword and brackets as shown in this example. This is also known as the default package.

Next comes the class definition itself. Another change here for you old timers: Classes can now have access modifiers. An access modifier is a word that specifies what other code can access the code in question. The word public here means that this class is accessible by any code outside of the class. In all the examples in this book, the classes will be public. If you decide to study more about AS 3, you'll find out about nonpublic classes and even multiple classes within a single class file, but all that is beyond the scope of this book.

You can see the class has a name, MyClass, followed by another pair of opening and closing brackets that enclose the class.

Within the class are only two things: a variable named myProperty and a function named myMethod. These will become properties and methods of any instance of this class you create. Again, for properties and methods, the word public means that any code outside the object will be able to access that property or call that method. If you create properties or methods that are meant only for use within the class itself, you can label them private, which prevents them from being messed with by any code outside the class. AS 3 also adds the modifiers internal and protected. An internal property of a class can only be accessed by other classes in the same package, and protected means that a property can only be seen by classes that extend this particular class (which is pretty much what private was in AS 2).

Confused yet? Again, I'm filtering out a large portion of the more complicated stuff, and a lot of the stuff I am describing here won't be used all that much in the book. Most of the book's examples use a bare minimum class, and once you see a few classes in action, you'll get the idea.

A class is written and saved in an external text file named the same as the class, with the suffix .as, as in MyClass.as. You can create the file by using the ActionScript editor in the Flash CS3 IDE, Flex Builder 2, your favorite code editor, or any other text-editing program.

If you are using the Flash CS3 IDE, you'll also be creating an FLA. The class files you create must be in the same directory as your FLA file if you're using the default package. If you're using a package structure, the root directory of that structure should be in the same directory as your FLA. Alternatively, you can store these classes somewhere else, and add that directory to your class path. The *class path* is simply a list of directories. When you specify a class name in your code, Flash will search those directories for a class with that name. Again, for the examples in this book, you'll stick to the default package, and you can keep the classes alongside the FLAs.

Packages

Again, packages are mainly there to organize classes. Packages are structured according to the directories in which they are located, and they can be nested several layers deep. Each name in the package refers to an actual folder, with the names separated by dots. For instance, you could have a class named Utils in a set of folders: com/friendsofed/makingthingsmove/. (It is a common convention to use domain names as packages. This ensures the package will be unique.) This class would be referred to as com.friendsofed.makingthingsmove.Utils.

In AS 2, you would declare the class with its full package name, like so:

```
class com.friendsofed.makingthingsmove.Utils {
}
```

In AS 3, the package part goes with the package declaration, and the class part goes with the class declaration, like this:

```
package com.friendsofed.makingthingsmove {
    public class Utils {
    }
}
```

Imports

As you can imagine, typing com.friendsofed.makingthingsmove.Utils every time you wanted to use some utility function would get pretty old, pretty fast. Using *imports* can alleviate this problem. In this example, you can put the following at the top of the package, before the class itself: import com.friendsofed.makingthingsmove.Utils;.

You just have to write it the one time. From there on out, in that file, you can now just write Utils to refer to that class. Now, in AS 2 imports were a great convenience, but in AS 3 they have become necessities. The fact is that in AS 3, you *must* import any class you use from a different package, even if you do write out the full name each time, or your code will not compile. Flex Builder 2 actually has a neat feature that will automatically add the import statement whenever you type out the full package of a class. In any case, it is up to you to make sure that the import is there. This makes that class available to the compiler to use when creating your movie.

Constructors

You can set a *constructor* for the class, which is a method that has the same name as the class and is automatically called when a new instance is created. You can pass arguments to the constructor as follows.

```
First, create the class:
package {
    public class MyClass {
        public function MyClass(arg:String) {
            trace("constructed");
            trace("you passed " + arg);
        }
    }
}
```

Then, assuming you are working in the Flash CS3 IDE, create the instance right on the timeline:

```
var myInstance:MyClass = new MyClass("hello");
```

This should trace "constructed" and then "you passed hello". If you are working in Flex Builder 2 or the free SDK, you'll have to just take my word for it that this works for now. You'll get plenty of hands-on practice later.

Inheritance

A class can *inherit* from, or extend, another class. This means that it gets all the properties and methods that the other class has (unless the properties or methods are marked as private). The *subclass* (the one that is inheriting) can then add additional properties and methods, or change some of the ones from the *superclass* (the one that is being extended). This is done by creating two separate classes (in two separate .as files) like so:

```
package {
    public class MyBaseClass {
        public function sayHello():void
        {
            trace("Hello from MyBaseClass");
        }
    }
}

package {
    public class MySubClass extends MyBaseClass {
        public function sayGoodbye():void {
            trace("Goodbye from MySubClass");
        }
    }
}
```

Remember that each class must be in its own file named after the class name, with the .as extension, so you will have a MyBaseClass.as file and a MySubClass.as file. Again, using the Flash CS3 IDE, make a new FLA file and save it in the same directory as the two classes. Now, on the timeline you can make a couple of instances and see what happens:

```
var base:MyBaseClass = new MyBaseClass();
base.sayHello();

var sub:MySubClass = new MySubClass();
sub.sayHello();
sub.sayGoodbye();
```

The first instance has no surprises. But notice that the second one has a working sayHello method, even though MySubClass does not define sayHello. The class inherited it from MyBaseClass. Also notice that it added a new, additional method, sayGoodbye, that the base class does not have.

Next, say you want to change an existing method from the base class in the subclass. In AS 2, you could simply redefine it. In AS 3, you must explicitly override it by using the word override in the new definition:

```
package {
    public class MySubClass extends MyBaseClass {
        override public function sayHello():void {
            trace("Hola from MySubClass");
        }
        public function sayGoodbye():void {
            trace("Goodbye from MySubClass");
        }
    }
}
```

Notice that sayHello, when called from MySubClass, now has a totally new message, as the original method has been overridden. Realize, of course, that a private method could not be overridden, as it is only accessible from within its own class.

A MovieClip/Sprite subclass

You may or may not ever write a class and then write another class that extends that. But if you are working with AS 3 for anything beyond putting code on the timeline, you are going to wind up extending either the MovieClip or the Sprite class. The MovieClip class is the template for all the ActionScript properties and methods that are part of a movie clip object. It contains properties you are probably very familiar with, such as the x and y position of the clip, its scale, and so on, though many of these have changed slightly in AS 3. AS 3 also adds the Sprite class. For the most part, you can think of a sprite as a movie clip without a timeline. In most cases, when you are manipulating objects with code only, you aren't dealing with the timeline and frames. Therefore, it makes sense to use the more lightweight Sprite class.

If you write a class that extends MovieClip or Sprite, it will automatically inherit all the properties and methods inherent to that type of object. Then you can add specific behaviors or properties that apply only to the type of object you are creating. For example, say you wanted to make a spaceship object for a game. You might want it to contain some graphics, have a position on the screen, move around, rotate, listen for enterFrame events for animation, and listen for keyboard and mouse events for interaction. These are all things that movie clips and sprites can do, so it makes sense to extend one of them. You could then add custom properties such as speed, fuel, and damage, and custom behaviors such as takeOff, crash, shoot, and selfDestruct. The class might start out something like the following:

```
package {
    import flash.display.Sprite;

    public class SpaceShip extends Sprite {
        private var speed:Number = 0;
        private var damage:Number = 0;
        private var fuel:Number = 1000;

        public function takeOff():void {
            // . . .
        }
        public function crash():void {
```

```
        // . . .
    }
    public function shoot():void {
        // . . .
    }
    public function selfDestruct():void {
        // . . .
    }
}
}
```

Note that first you must import the Sprite class, which is in the flash.display package. If you decide to extend MovieClip instead, you still need to import the MovieClip class from the same package: flash.display.MovieClip.

Creating your document class

You now have enough information about classes to start writing one for actual use. A few times I've mentioned how important classes are in creating an AS 3–based SWF. This is because of a new concept introduced in AS 3, the *document class*. Basically, a document class is a class that extends Sprite or MovieClip, and is used as the main class for your SWF. When the SWF is loaded, the constructor of that class will be called. That will be your entry point for anything that you want to have happen in the movie, such as creating additional movie clips, drawing graphics, loading assets, and so forth.

If you are coding in the Flash CS3 IDE, using a document class is optional. You can always just go on writing code on the timeline. But if you are using Flex Builder 2, or the free Flex SDK, there is no time-line for you to write code on. The only way to get code into the SWF is to put it in classes. In those tools, everything revolves around that one mighty document class. Without it, there would be no SWF.

Here is the skeleton document class I promised you earlier:

```
package {
    import flash.display.Sprite;
    public class Example extends Sprite {
        public function Example() {
            init();
        }
        private function init():void {
            // sample code goes here
        }
    }
}
```

None of this should be new to you if you've followed along with the preceding sections, but here you have it all together in one place. I'm using the default package, and importing and extending the Sprite class. The constructor has one line that calls the init method. It would certainly be fine to put all of your code into the constructor, but it is usually considered a best practice to limit the amount of code in a constructor, so I shuffle it off to another method. So, throughout the book, if I give you a small snippet of code to try out, you should use the preceding class and insert the snippet right there inside the init method. When the movie is compiled and run, the constructor will call init, which will run your code.

Now all you need to know is how to link this document class to the SWF you will create.

Setting up an ActionScript 3.0 application

To review what I said earlier, there are three main ways to create an AS 3 SWF:

- The Flash CS3 IDE
- Flex Builder 2
- The free Flex/AS 3 command-line compiler and Flex 2 SDK

Each of these starts with a document class and ends up with a SWF, but how you set up and use each tool is quite different. We'll take them one at a time, from the easiest (Flash CS3 IDE), to the most complex (the free compiler and SDK). I'll use the following document class, which simply draws a red circle on the stage, as proof of its existence.

```
package {
    import flash.display.Sprite;
    public class Test extends Sprite {
        public function Test() {
            init();
        }
        private function init():void {
            graphics.beginFill(0xff0000);
            graphics.drawEllipse(100, 100, 100, 100);
            graphics.endFill();
        }
    }
}
```

Note that this is exactly the same as the skeleton class I just gave you, with a few drawing commands in the init method.

Using the Flash CS3 IDE

Again, the Flash CS3 IDE is the easiest tool to use to implement your document class. Simply save the previous class in the folder of your choice, with the name Test.as. Then, using Flash CS3, create a new FLA and save it in the same directory. Make sure that the FLA has the default publish settings of Flash Player 9 and AS 3. In the Properties panel, you should notice a new field called Document Class (see Figure 2-1). Simply enter the name of your class there: Test.

Figure 2-1. Setting the document class

Note that you enter the name of the class, not the name of the file, so there's no need to add the `.as` extension. However, if your class was within a package, you would enter the full path of the class—for example, `com.friendsofed.chapter2.Test`.

Now you simply test or publish your movie the same way you have for years. Flash will look for that class and compile it into your SWF. When the SWF is run, the constructor and `init` method will execute, and you'll get your lovely red circle.

When using a document class, avoid putting any code on the main timeline of the FLA—even comments—as this can cause a conflict with the code the compiler is adding in, and can prevent your movie from compiling or running.

Using Flex Builder 2

I said that the Flash CS3 IDE was the simplest way to create an AS 3 application. However, that is largely based on the fact that it is probably the most familiar tool to many Flash designers or developers, who may have been using it for years.

The truth is, though, that creating an AS 3 application with Flex Builder 2 is probably just as easy, once you've installed and gotten used to the tool itself. You don't even have to worry about creating multiple files (`.as` and `.fla`) and making sure they are in the right places. You basically just create your class and compile it.

Assuming you have installed Flex Builder 2 and have it up and running, start by creating a new ActionScript project. In the New ActionScript Project dialog, enter a project name and click Finish. Later when you become more experienced, you can explore the rest of the dialog, which offers you a lot of other ways to customize your project, but for now all you really need is the name of the project, which will become the name of your document class. (Note that the term "document class" does not actually appear in the Flex Builder 2 tool. I am simply using it across all three development environments for consistency.)

Flex Builder 2 will create a directory for your project (along with some other directories and subdirectories), and will even create most of the skeleton class for you. All you need to do is add in the `init` method and call it from the constructor, and then add whatever code you want to the `init` method.

Then click the run button on the toolbar; that's the green circle with the arrow in it. This will compile your class into a SWF, create an HTML file to hold it, and launch that in your default browser. Pretty simple, eh?

If you want to specify various parameters for your SWF, such as frame rate, size, and background color, right-click the project name in the Navigator view, and choose Properties. In the Properties dialog, choose *ActionScript Compiler*. On that page of the dialog, you will see a field labeled *Additional Compiler Arguments*. In this field, you can enter the following arguments to change the properties of your published SWF:

- `default-size` *width height*
- `default-frame-rate` *fps*
- `default-background-color` *OxRRGGBB*

Just put them all on one line, substituting the actual values you want, as shown in Figure 2-2.

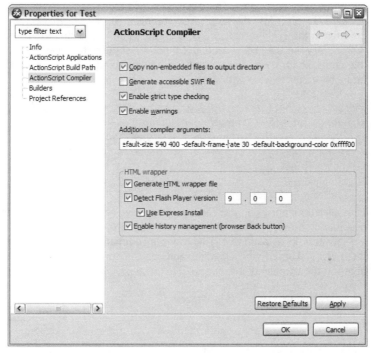

Figure 2-2. Adding compiler arguments

There are many other command-line arguments that you can add in here, all of which are covered in the Flex Builder 2 and AS 3 documentation. But these are the ones you will use most often for now.

You can also choose to set these values via metadata right in the document class itself. This method is covered at the end of the next section.

Using the free command-line compiler

Well, sorry to say I can't go back on my word and tell you that this method is even simpler than the others. It is very much the do-it-yourself method of compiling AS 3. But on the bright side, it's also completely free! As with most command-line tools, it also has the added benefit of being able to be called from other applications, so you can set it up to run as a shortcut from your favorite editor, as part of a build process using Apache Ant, and so on. In this section, I'm just going to outline the bare-bones process for how to get the compiler compiling. Hopefully once you get the hang of it, you can figure out how to integrate the compiler with your other development tools. As of this writing, the free ActionScript editor, FlashDevelop, available at www.flashdevelop.org, has begun to implement support for AS 3. By the time this book hits the shelves, there will undoubtedly be others.

The first thing you need to do is download the free Flex 2 SDK from www.adobe.com. It comes as a zipped archive of files that you can extract to wherever you like on your machine. It is best to put it in an easily accessible location, such as C:\flex_2_sdk on a PC, or /Applications/flex_2_sdk on a Mac.

There are actually three versions of the compiler itself. There is mxmlc.exe, the Windows executable compiler, and mxmlc, the Mac application. These are both in the bin directory within the main install directory. Finally, there is mxmlc.jar, the Java-based compiler, which will work on a Mac or PC. The Java compiler is located in the lib directory, which is on the same level as the bin directory. If you are really into Java, you can try out the Java version, but there are some differences in how it is called and how it handles file paths, so for ease of explanation, I'm going to stick to the applications in the bin folder, which I find a bit easier to work with.

> It's worth noting that Adobe did a very good job in making the Mac and PC versions work in pretty much exactly the same manner. Other than the PC version having the .exe file extension, they are largely indistinguishable, which makes my job of writing about them a lot easier!

Now that you've installed your compiler, you can create and save your class as already described. Since the free SDK does not come with any sort of editor, you'll need to use whatever editor you are comfortable with, and save the file as plain text. Then open a command prompt or terminal, navigate to the directory where you just saved your class file, and run the compiler, passing in the path to your class as a parameter on the command line, like so:

```
C:/flex_2_sdk/bin/mxmlc.exe Test.as
```

or like this on the Mac:

```
/Applications/flex_2_sdk/mxmlc Test.as
```

This should spit out a bunch of information about what the compiler is doing, and then end. If there are any errors in compiling, it will tell you about them, and where possible, it will point you to the exact line and character where it encountered the error.

You'll now have a SWF in the same directory, named Test.swf. Run that SWF and you should see your red circle. Congratulations, you are now an AS 3 power user!

Of course, that whole path to mxmlc is a lot to type each time you want to test your movie, and for this reason, some people avoid command-line tools. It's important to realize that you have numerous ways to automate this process. For example, almost every decent code editor lets you assign tools to shortcut keys or toolbar buttons, complete with parameters. You simply set up the editor with the path to the compiler as the tool, and the path of the current document as a parameter. This should give you one-click compiling.

Another way to automate the compile process is with a batch file or AppleScript file that replicates what you would type in by hand. You just run that batch or script file and it does all the work for you. If you are really industrious, you can look into Apache Ant, which is a program designed for exactly this purpose. You create an XML file that describes the path to your compiler and the various arguments to pass to it, and Ant parses that and runs the program. It can actually do a whole lot more than that, so if you get into some serious development with the AS 3 compiler, Ant is well worth learning about.

Many different editors are available these days, and everyone has his or her own development environment setup preferences, so I won't go into detail about how to set up any one particular editor. But, if you check my personal blog, located at www.bit-101.com/blog, you will find a lot of information relating to integrating the FlashDevelop editor with AS 3 using Ant and some other tools.

It may have come to your attention that in the setup just described, there is no way to set basic document properties such as the size of the SWF, frame rate, or background color. This can be accomplished a couple ways. The first way is through additional command-line parameters, with the important ones being the following:

```
-default-background-color=color
-default-frame-rate=fps
-default-size=width,height
```

You simply add these to the end of the command line after the class name, like so:

PC:

```
(path)mxmlc.exe Test.as -default-background-color=0xff0000
```

Mac:

```
(path)mxmlc Test.as -default-size=800,600
```

Note that you can add as many parameters as you need, just separate each one with a space on the command line. Here is where some automation really comes in handy!

The other way to set basic document properties is through metadata right in your class file. *Metadata* consists of any statements that are not actually ActionScript statements that get compiled, but rather are used by the compiler during the compile process. The SWF metadata tag allows you to set the previous four properties right in your class file, like so:

```
[SWF(backgroundColor="0xffffff", width="800",
    height="600", frameRate="31")]
```

This line will be placed within the package, immediately before the class declaration.

A note on tracing

In many examples, particularly early in the book, I will direct you to trace out values or messages, such as in the MyBaseClass and MySubClasses examples presented earlier. If you are using the Flash CS3 IDE, these examples will work without you having to do anything other than write the trace statement, and the messages you trace will appear in the Output panel in Flash.

If you are using Flex Builder 2, you can also use trace exactly as written. The one thing you will need to do differently is to *debug* your movie, rather than *run* it. This is as simple as clicking the Debug button on the toolbar instead of the Run button. Your movie will launch in an external browser, but if you switch back to Flex Builder, your traced messages will appear in the console.

Finally, if you are using the free Flex 2 SDK, you will need to do a little more work in order to trace. Probably the easiest thing to do is use a third-party trace panel. These usually consist of two pieces: an executable program or SWF that contains a text area for showing traced messages, and a custom tracing class. You have to put the tracing class in your class path. Use the -source-path command-line parameter to add a class path when compiling. For example, say you put the tracing class in C:/AS3Classes/. You could add the following command-line parameter when compiling:

```
-source-path="C:/AS3Classes/"
```

This will allow the compiler to compile the tracing class into your project.

Then, when you want to trace, you generally need to call the method specified for the particular trace panel you are using. For example, instead of typing this:

```
trace("Hello world");
```

You might write something like the following:

```
Logger.debug("Hello world");
```

You might also need to import the tracing class if it is within a nested package. Of course, you'll need to consult the documentation for exactly how to use the trace panel of your choice. One that I have found particularly nice and quite easy to use is called XPanel, which is available from www.ajaxmaker. com/xpanel/xpanel.htm.

If you are using the free SDK and one of these trace panels, remember to substitute whatever method it uses for trace in any examples that use trace.

Scaling the movie

One final note on setup before we begin coding for real: If you are testing your movie in the Flash IDE or the stand-alone Flash Player, it should scale to 100% and size itself appropriately. But if you are testing in a browser or some other program that is set up to display SWFs, it may attempt to scale to fill the available space, distorting the intended size of your movie. If this is the case, you can add the following two lines to the init() method of your class:

```
stage.scaleMode = StageScaleMode.NO_SCALE;
stage.align = StageAlign.TOP_LEFT;
```

This will prevent the movie from scaling at all and place it at the top-left corner of the window playing it. If you use these lines, make sure you import the flash.display.StageScaleMode and flash. display.StageAlign classes. The examples in this book won't use these lines, as they are not appropriate in all cases, but know that they are there if you need them, and they shouldn't adversely affect anything else.

Animating with code

OK, you should now understand enough of the basics to get started coding in AS 3. Assuming you have chosen a development environment, you are ready to get going. Let's dive in to some ActionScripted animation.

Looping

Almost all coded animation contains some kind of loop. If you think about a frame-by-frame animation, you might come up with a flowchart that would be something like a series of bitmaps, where each frame is already an image and just needs to be shown, as shown in Figure 2-3.

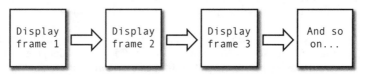

Figure 2-3. Frame-by-frame animation

When you get into shapes or symbols in Flash, though, things are a bit different. Flash doesn't create and store a new bitmap image for each frame, even in a frame-by-frame movie. For each frame, Flash stores the position, size, color, and so on of each object on the stage. So, if you had a ball moving across the screen, each frame would store the position of the ball on that frame. Maybe frame 1 would say the ball is 10 pixels from the left side, frame 2 would say it's 15 pixels, and so on. Flash Player reads in this data, sets up the stage according to the description given, and displays that frame. From that, you get a bit of an expanded flowchart, as shown in Figure 2-4.

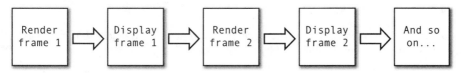

Figure 2-4. Rendering and then displaying frames

But when you consider how I described a dynamic, coded animation, the flowchart looks more like Figure 2-5.

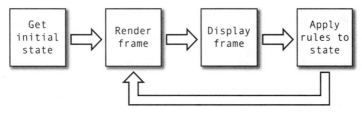

Figure 2-5. Scripted animation

As you see in Figure 2-5, there is no concept of frame 1, frame 2, and so on. ActionScripted animation generally can, and usually does, occur all in just one frame. And here you can start to see what I mean by a loop.

First, you set up an initial state. You can do this by dragging movie clips onto the stage, just as if you were creating a tweened animation. Or you can describe the entire scene in code alone. Either way, you then render and display the frame.

Next, you apply your rules. The rules can be as simple as, "The ball will move 5 pixels to the right," or they can be made up of dozens of lines of complex trigonometry. The examples in the book will cover most of that spectrum.

Applying the rules will result in a new state—a new description that is then rendered and displayed. Then you apply the same rules all over again.

Note that it is the same set of rules being applied over and over. You don't have one set of rules for the first frame, and then another set for the next, and so on. So, your challenge is to come up with a set of rules that will handle every possible situation that can arise in your scene. What happens when your ball moves so far to the right that it's off the stage? Your set of rules needs to account for this. Do you want to allow the user to interact with the ball with his mouse? Your rules will need to take that into account as well.

It sounds daunting, but it's really not that complex. Basically, you start off with some very simple behavior by creating a rule or two, and when that works, add another rule.

These "rules," as I keep calling them, are actually ActionScript statements. Each rule can be a single statement or composed of several or even many statements. In the example of moving the ball 5 pixels to the right, the rule would look something like this:

```
ball.x = ball.x + 5;
```

You're just saying take whatever the ball's x position (horizontal axis) is, add 5 to it, and make that its new x position. You can even simplify that by saying this:

```
ball.x += 5;
```

The += operator just says add the value on the right to the variable on the left, and assign the result back to that variable.

Here's a more advanced set of rules that you'll see later in the book:

```
var dx:Number = mouseX - ball.x;
var dy:Number = mouseY - ball.y;
var ax:Number = dx * spring;
var ay:Number = dy * spring;
vx += ax;
vy += ay;
vy += gravity;
vx *= friction;
vy *= friction;
ball.x += vx;
```

```
ball.y += vy;
graphics.clear();
graphics.lineStyle(1);
graphics.moveTo(ball.x, ball.y);
graphics.lineTo(mouseX, mouseY);
```

Don't worry about what it all means just yet. Just know that Flash is going to need to run this code over and over to generate each new frame.

So, how do you get these loops to run? I'll show you my first attempt to do this, which reflects the error that many beginning ActionScripters make. It's based on the loop structures that exist in almost every programming language, such as for and while. You set up a loop with one of those structures, which will cause the code within it to execute repeatedly. Here's what I did:

```
for(i = 0; i < 500; i++){
    ball.x = i;
}
```

It seems pretty simple. The variable i starts out as 0, so the ball movie clip is placed at zero on the x axis—the far left of the stage. The i++ causes the value of i to be increased by 1 each time through the loop, from 0 to 1 to 2, 3, 4, and so on, and each time, that value is assigned to ball.x, moving it across the stage from left to right. When it hits the value of 500, the statement i < 500 will be false, and the loop will end.

If you've made the same mistake, you know that the ball doesn't move across the stage—it simply appears on the right side. Why doesn't it move to all the points in between? Well, actually it did! You just didn't see it, because you never let Flash update the screen. Figure 2-6 is another flowchart that shows essentially what happened.

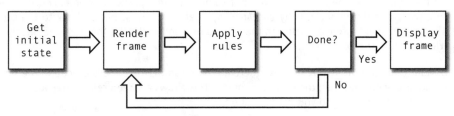

Figure 2-6. Why you can't animate with a for loop

You actually applied the rules and moved the ball into position, creating a new scene 500 times. But it didn't get displayed until after the loop was done. This is because Flash updates the screen only at the end of a frame. This is a very important point.

Here is the sequence of actions Flash takes on each frame:

1. Position all objects that are currently on the stage, in any level, layer, loaded movie clip, and so on.

2. Execute all ActionScript that needs to be called on that frame, on any layer or level on any movie clip or button, or nested within any movie clip, no matter how deep.

3. Check if it is time to display the frame yet. If you set your frame rate to 20 frames per second, Flash will check if at least 50 milliseconds have gone by since the last time it displayed a frame. If so, it will display the frame it just rendered and move to the next frame. If not, it will wait until the right amount of time has passed.

You should note a couple of things about this timing factor. First, frame rates are notoriously inaccurate (yes, even in Flash 9 movies). Never rely on them for strict timing. Second, it is possible that the amount of rendering and ActionScript execution will take longer than the allotted time for a frame. You don't have to worry about your script getting chopped off, though. Flash will finish executing the script (step 2) before it moves on to step 3, even if it slows down the frame rate. Flash will actually wait up to 15 seconds for your script to finish on any particular frame. It will then display the infamous "A script is causing the player to run slowly . . ." message.

In the preceding example, Flash waited for the for loop to finish before going to the next frame, and it updated the screen only just before it went to the next frame. That's why you saw the jump rather than the movement.

So, what you need to do is break up the loop across frames, so that you get back to the sequence of events shown in Figure 2-5.

Frame loops

Because this book doesn't really deal with the timeline and putting content on individual frames, I'm not going to give an actual sample of frame loops here; rather, I'll just describe the concept. If you are working with the Flash CS3 IDE, though, it might be a nice educational step to actually go ahead and try to create this example on your own.

The idea of *frame loops* goes back to the earliest versions of Flash, when ActionScript was not nearly as powerful as it is today. The idea is that you put some code in a particular frame, and then on the next frame you put a statement, usually gotoAndPlay, that sends the playhead back to the previous frame. This sets up an infinite loop between the two frames, and each time the playhead hits the code frame, it will execute the code there.

The important thing to note is that because there are two frames, the code is executed, the screen is updated and displayed, and then the playhead moves. This allows a screen refresh between each iteration of the code execution, and you get animation.

For example, you could have a movie clip on stage named ball. The code on frame 1 would be something like the following:

```
ball.x ++;
```

Frame 2 would just have this:

```
gotoAndPlay(1);
```

Actually, frame 2 wouldn't need anything in this case, as the timeline would automatically loop back to frame 1 by default.

As a variation of this example, you can have a three-frame setup, with frame 1 being an initialization frame, where you can put any code that you want to run only a single time, rather than loop. Frame 2 will now have the main actions, and frame 3 will just say

```
gotoAndPlay(2);
```

So frame 1 might specify the initial position of the ball, change the ball's color or size, or do anything else that should happen only once. The timeline then loops back and forth between frames 2 and 3 infinitely, running the animation and updating the screen.

This is the exact setup used extensively in Flash 5 and earlier, and it is still perfectly workable, if a bit outdated. Even though you will very shortly discover much more flexible and powerful setups, it is very educational to be able to see the different phases of the movie—initialization, action, and loop-ing—as these concepts will continue to be implemented in each animation setup you will investigate hereafter.

Clip events

Clip events have thankfully been completely removed from AS 3, but are worth mentioning as a foot-note. Back in the Flash 5 days, clip events were the main alternative to frame loops.

Clip events refer to code that was placed, not on the timeline, but directly on a movie clip itself. This was done by selecting a movie clip on the stage and then opening the Actions panel. When you did this and then typed some code in the Actions panel, that code was assigned directly to that clip.

I said that the code was placed "on" the movie clip. Any and all code on a clip had to appear within a clip event block, which looked something like this:

```
onClipEvent(eventName){
    // code goes here
}
```

In addition to onClipEvent(eventName), there was on(eventName). The "on" events have to do with mouse and keyboard actions, such as press and release.

The event name refers to one of the many events that may occur in a Flash movie. An event is simply that: something happening in the movie. Events fall into two main categories: system events and user events. A *system event* is when something happens within the computer, Flash, or your movie, such as data loading, content loading, or a new frame starting. *User events* refer to something the user has done, and generally have to do with keyboard or mouse activity.

The two most used clip events were load and enterFrame. The load event occurred when the movie clip instance first appeared on stage and occurred only once for any particular instance. Thus, it was a good place to put initialization code. You simply placed your code between the two curly brackets:

```
onClipEvent(load){
    // initialization code
}
```

The enterFrame event occurred each time Flash was ready to start rendering the next frame, even on a single-frame movie. For example, if the frame rate was set to 20 frames per second, enterFrame would fire approximately every 50 milliseconds. The enterFrame clip event was where you usually put your "rules," or action code, as you have your two requirements: repeating code and a redisplay after each execution. It looked like this:

```
onClipEvent(enterFrame){
    // action code
}
```

Thus, you could put a movie clip on the timeline, and put the following code "on" it (note the earlier AS 1 syntax here):

```
onClipEvent(load){
    this._x = 100;
    this._y = 100;
}
onClipEvent(enterFrame){
    this._x += 5;
}
```

Again, the examples in this book don't use this setup (because it is no longer a part of the language), but it's important to note the three points, initialization, repeating actions, and a screen refresh, which will be part of any animation you do in any system.

Events and event handlers

Flash MX introduced many important changes in ActionScript—changes and improvements that were largely responsible for catapulting Flash into the serious Rich Internet Application forefront. One of the biggest changes was the new event architecture that made programming very complex behaviors far easier than was possible in earlier versions.

I've already talked a little about events, which occur when something happens in the system or the user does something with the keyboard or mouse. Prior to Flash MX, the only real way to capture these events was with an onClipEvent(*eventName*) or on(*eventName*) block on a movie clip or button. This meant that you had to place a movie clip on stage at author time and write the code on it. Although various workarounds were discovered, none was really optimal. The MX event architecture wasn't perfect, but it was a vast improvement on previous versions and allowed you to access events from anywhere in your application, stop handling any particular event at any time, or change an event's behavior dynamically. You can imagine how much more power and flexibility that functionality provided.

With Flash MX 2004, even more enhancements were made to the event architecture within the included component framework. However, these enhancements were actually just built on top of the existing event architecture via additional AS 2 classes. These classes provided a lot of additional event handling power, but the underlying architecture still suffered from certain inadequacies that the classes attempted to provide workarounds for.

In AS 3, the event architecture has been rewritten from the ground up. It is fast, powerful, and fully integrated into Flash Player.

To understand events, you should understand a couple of additional concepts: listeners and handlers. Listeners and handlers are actually well-named entities, because that's exactly what they do. A *listener* is an object that listens for events. A *handler* is a function that handles the event when it occurs. Listeners and handlers have been implemented quite differently throughout the history of ActionScript, and they've even had different implementations within AS 2. To avoid confusion, I'm going to stick with AS 3, which has simplified the whole system, and made it nice and consistent.

Listeners and handlers

As just stated, a listener is an object that listens for events. You can specify your class as a listener for a particular event by calling a function named addEventListener. You pass in the name of the event you want to listen for and the name of a function in your class that will be the handler. Here's an example:

```
addEventListener("enterFrame", onEnterFrame);
```

Additional optional parameters can be used when adding event listeners, but we won't do so in this book; the preceding syntax is all you'll need for most applications of events.

Notice that the event name, "enterFrame", is a string. This is what is known, with a bit of contempt, as a *magic string*. Why magic? Because if you accidentally mistype it as, say, "entorFrame", the compiler will magically accept it without a complaint, even though there is no such event name, after which you will see hours of your time magically disappear while you try to figure out why your event handler is not being called.

But AS 3 has even this handled. Instead of using magic strings such as "enterFrame", you can use properties of the Event class instead. For example, in the preceding case, you would write the following:

```
addEventListener(Event.ENTER_FRAME, onEnterFrame);
```

If you went and looked at the value of Event.ENTER_FRAME, you would find that it is simply the string "enterFrame". Now, you might be thinking that it is just as easy to mistype the property as Event.ENTOR_FRAME. But the improvement here is that if you do, your program will refuse to compile and will tell you right away that there is no such property on the Event class. It will point you not only to the exact line where you made this error, but also to the exact character in that line where it first encountered a problem. It can't get much better than that, unless the compiler starts correcting your mistakes and writing code for you.

In addition to the event types on the Event class, there are other event types set up in the same way on other classes, such as MouseEvent.MOUSE_DOWN, KeyboardEvent.KEY_DOWN, TimerEvent.TIMER, and so on. While these all stand for simple strings, such as "mouseDown", "keyDown", and "timer", it is best if you just forget about the strings altogether and use the properties only.

The next important thing to know is that sometimes, such as in the previous example, you can call the addEventListener function directly in a class. In this case, you are actually telling the class to listen for its own enterFrame event. In some cases, though, you want to listen for an event generated by another object. An example is if you have a sprite named mySpriteButton that is acting as a button. When the user clicks that sprite, it will generate a mouseDown event. To listen for the mouseDown event coming from that sprite, you call the addEventListener method of that sprite, like so:

```
mySpriteButton.addEventListener(MouseEvent.MOUSE_DOWN, onSpritePress);
```

33

The final thing to take note of is that unlike earlier versions of ActionScript, which had to have specifically named event handler functions such as onEnterFrame, in AS 3 you can name your handler functions whatever you want when you add listeners. In the enterFrame example, I used onEnterFrame as a handler, but only because it's a fitting name and one I've gotten used to. In AS 3, onEnterFrame has no inherent meaning at all. I could have just as easily named my enterFrame handler move, run, or doSomethingCool. By convention, however, event handlers often start with on, followed by something that describes the event and perhaps where it came from, such as onStartButtonClick, onConfigXMLLoad, or even onRocketCrash. Alternatively, some people like to add the Handler suffix to the event name to create the handler's name—for example, enterFrameHandler. Again, it's a matter of preference. The most important thing is to be consistent, so that you know an event handler is an event handler just by looking at it.

Now, I've been saying that a listener listens for events, but perhaps a more accurate description is that the listener is *notified* of events. Internally, the object that is generating events keeps a list of every object that has added itself as a listener. If an object is capable of generating different types of events, such as mouseDown, mouseUp, and mouseMove, it will keep a list of listeners for each event type it can generate. Whenever one of these events occurs, the object runs through the corresponding list and lets each object in that list know what event has occurred.

Yet another way of describing events is to say that the object that becomes a listener is subscribing to a particular event. And the object that generates the event is broadcasting the event to all its subscribers.

Additionally, if you no longer want an object to listen to events, you can tell it to stop listening, or unsubscribe, by calling the removeEventListener method:

```
removeEventListener(Event.ENTER_FRAME, onEnterFrame);
```

This tells the object to remove the listener from its list of listeners for that particular event, so it will not receive further notifications.

Let's go ahead and see some of this in action. The following code creates a new sprite, puts it on stage, draws some graphics in it, and adds an event listener to it. Start out with the skeleton application presented earlier, and add the code to that:

```
package {
    import flash.display.Sprite;
    import flash.events.MouseEvent;

    public class EventDemo extends Sprite {
        private var eventSprite:Sprite;
        public function EventDemo() {
            init();
        }
        private function init():void {
            eventSprite = new Sprite();
            addChild(eventSprite);
            eventSprite.graphics.beginFill(0xff0000);
            eventSprite.graphics.drawCircle(0, 0, 100);
            eventSprite.graphics.endFill();
```

```
            eventSprite.x = stage.stageWidth / 2;
            eventSprite.y = stage.stageHeight / 2;
            eventSprite.addEventListener(MouseEvent.MOUSE_DOWN,
                                         onMouseDown);
            eventSprite.addEventListener(MouseEvent.MOUSE_UP,
                                         onMouseUp);
        }
        private function onMouseDown(event:MouseEvent):void {
            trace("mouse down");
        }
        private function onMouseUp(event:MouseEvent):void {
            trace("mouse up");
        }
    }
}
```

What is going on here? Most of the init function is simply there to create a sprite, draw a circle in it, and center it on the stage. It's the final two lines that are important. Here the class adds itself as a listener for two events, MOUSE_DOWN and MOUSE_UP. Note that these are properties of the MouseEvent class, and that class must be imported. As handlers, you pass in the functions onMouseDown and onMouseUp, which are defined right after that. Handlers generally get passed an event object that contains some information about the event. Minimally, it would contain information about what object triggered the event. In the case of mouse events, it contains information about the mouse location at the time of the event, which mouse button was pressed (if any), and so forth. For keyboard events, it would contain information about which keys were pressed at the time of the event; the state of other keys, such as the Ctrl, Alt, and Shift keys. Consult the help files to see what information is included with what types of events.

Save the preceding example as EventDemo.as and compile it using the method of your choice, as described earlier. When you run the SWF itself, you'll see that it traces a message each time the mouse is pressed or released on the new sprite. If you are using Flex Builder 2, don't forget to debug—not run—your application, and if you are using the free SDK, use the correct method for whatever solution you are using to trace. Make sure you get this sample working. It's a pretty simple example, but it's a good test to ensure your development environment is set up correctly.

If you are new to ActionScript, and you get this working and actually understand it, congratulations! You have just moved from "beginner" up to "intermediate" status.

OK, now that you know a little bit more about handlers, you can get a better understanding of listeners. Earlier, I said that an object that generates an event broadcasts that event, or notifies its listeners of the event. How does it do that exactly? Well, all it really does is call the function on that object that has the correct handler name. In the previous example, the class EventDemo added itself as a listener to a couple of the sprite's events. Internally, the sprite keeps a list for each event. So it has a list for the mouseDown event, and another list for the mouseUp event. These are probably just simple arrays. Each list now contains a reference to the main movie, which is an instance of the EventDemo class.

When the user presses the mouse button on the sprite, the sprite responds, "Whoa! Mouse down! Must notify listeners!" (or something like that). It then goes through its mouseDown list and sees what's in there. The sprite finds a reference to the main movie and a reference to the function that was specified as a handler, which in the example is a function named onMouseDown. It then simply calls that function on that listener. If other objects had registered as listeners to the mouseDown event, they would be on the list, too, and whatever handlers they had defined would also be called.

The same thing happens when the mouse is released, except it looks at its mouseUp list.

One important technical note on handlers in AS 3 is that most scope issues are totally handled. This issue is a bit complex, but an easy way to understand it has to do with where the handler function thinks it is when it is called. Although the AS 2 event architecture seems similar to that of AS 3 on the surface, a class method being called as an event handler in AS 2 is executed as if it were a method of the calling object, not the class in which it is defined. If this sounds confusing, that's because it really was, and there was a whole other class—the Delegate class—that was created just to try and handle this issue. And if this paragraph makes no sense to you at all, relax and be thankful that it is something you generally won't have to think about in AS 3!

Those are the basics of events and handlers through the ages. I'll introduce many other events as we move along, but for now, let's get back to animation.

Events for animation

So where does all this talk about events bring us? We were looking for a way to apply code to animate an object and allow for a screen refresh after each iteration. Earlier, you saw an example of using the enterFrame clip event for animation. Let's come up to the present time with this technique.

In AS 3, you can add a listener to the enterFrame event like so:

```
addEventListener(Event.ENTER_FRAME, onEnterFrame);
```

Remember that you have to import the Event class and actually create a method named onEnterFrame.

One point that is sometimes confusing to people is that you are getting an enterFrame event, even though the movie has only one frame. (And if you are using Flex Builder 2 or the SDK, you don't see any frames, but rest assured, there is one there!) The playhead is not actually entering a new frame; it's just stuck on frame 1. Realize that it isn't the act of the playhead moving to a new frame that generates the enterFrame event, but more the other way around—the event tells Flash when to move the playhead. Think of enterFrame more as a timer, albeit a pretty inaccurate one. Flash takes the frame rate set for the movie and determines how often it should enter a new frame. It then fires the event repeatedly at that interval. If there is another frame to go to, it goes there. But, regardless, you can count on the event firing.

> If you are really interested in some of the inner workings of Flash, check out Tinic Uro's blog at www.kaourantin.net. Tinic is an engineer at Adobe working on Flash Player and often posts very deep explanations of how things work behind the scenes.

The earlier examples had initialization code, either on an initialization frame or in an onClipEvent(load) block. As you might have guessed, that will all now happen in the init method. That method is called only once, by the constructor. You should make it a habit to never call init again in your movie. If you might need to reinitialize any other variables or call any other functions, break them out into other functions and call those functions as needed.

Here comes our first example of AS 3–based animation!

```
package {
    import flash.display.Sprite;
    import flash.events.Event;

    public class FirstAnimation extends Sprite {
        private var ball:Sprite;

        public function FirstAnimation() {
            init();
        }
        private function init():void {
            ball = new Sprite();
            addChild(ball);
            ball.graphics.beginFill(0xff0000);
            ball.graphics.drawCircle(0, 0, 40);
            ball.graphics.endFill();
            ball.x = 20;
            ball.y = stage.stageHeight / 2;
            ball.addEventListener(Event.ENTER_FRAME, onEnterFrame);
        }
        private function onEnterFrame(event:Event):void {
            ball.x++;
        }
    }
}
```

The init function creates a sprite named ball and sets up the event listener. The onEnterFrame function takes care of the animation, moving the ball, after which the screen will be refreshed. It's not much, but that's the foundation of just about everything else in the book, so know it well.

Well, that covers most of the basics of how to structure animation with ActionScript. I've explained how to get rules to run over and over, and how to update the screen after each application of those rules, causing the illusion of motion. But what do you move? So far, you have been moving around a sprite, but all of the code so far could have just as easily used a movie clip. Next, we'll look at how sprites and movie clips are created and made visible using the display list.

The display list

Prior to AS 3, you could create a number of different types of visual objects in a Flash movie, including movie clips, graphics, buttons, text fields, bitmaps, components, and basic shapes. These objects weren't really organized in a hierarchical structure, and they all had very different ways of being created, destroyed, and manipulated. For instance, movie clips could be attached, duplicated, put on stage in the IDE, or created from scratch. Text fields could be created from scratch or created in the

IDE. When you get into bitmaps, videos, components, and the rest, it seems like each type was created on a different planet and was shoved in to Flash and forced to work with the others.

The differences among these objects has been totally addressed in AS 3. Just about any type of object that you can see on stage is created from a class that extends the DisplayObject class. In other words, all of these objects are part of the same big family now, and they all behave the same basic way, in terms of how you create them, put them on stage, destroy them, and manipulate them on stage.

The code for creating a sprite, a movie clip, or a text field is now very similar. In fact, all display objects are now created the same way you would create any other type of object, with the new operator. To prove the point, here is how you create these three items:

```
var myTextfield:TextField = new TextField();
var myMovieClip:MovieClip = new MovieClip();
var mySprite:Sprite = new Sprite();
```

It doesn't get much simpler than that, does it?

As you saw in previous examples, if you've created a movie clip or sprite, you can now draw some content into that object, like so:

```
mySprite.graphics.beginFill(0xff0000);
mySprite.graphics.drawCircle(0, 0, 40);
mySprite.graphics.endFill();
```

But if you try it just like that, you won't see much. This is where our discussion of the display list comes in.

The term "display list" is new, but if you've worked with Flash for a while, it shouldn't be a foreign concept. Think of it as a tree of all the visual objects in your movie. At the base of the tree is the stage, which is visible by default. On the stage, you might have several movie clips or other types of visual objects (text fields, shapes, etc.). When you add them to the stage, they become visible too. Within those movie clips might be other movie clips or other visual objects, and within those, others. That is basically your display list.

The biggest difference between how the display list works in AS 2 and AS 3 is that in AS 2, when you created a movie clip by attaching it or using createEmptyMovieClip, you had to specify where it would go on the tree at the time of creation. At that point, the movie clip would be created and put on the list at the specified location, and that's where it would stay. Short of removing the clip, there was no way to change its location on the list or take it off the list without destroying it completely.

In AS 3, when you create a new movie clip, sprite, or any other display object, it is *not* automatically added to the display list. Note that in the sprite example just given, there is no parent or depth mentioned when the sprite is created. It is able to exist and be manipulated without being on the display list.

If you take the term "stage" literally, you can imagine these objects as actors behind the curtains, off in the wings, suspended above the stage, or even crawling around underneath it. You can't see them, but they are all there, busy getting ready for their big entrance, when they will jump on stage and steal the show.

So far, we have a tree metaphor and a theater metaphor—how about one more? We can also think of the display list in terms of a family, as a series of parent/child/sibling relationships. When you add something to the display list, the object you add it to is the parent, and that new object is the parent's child. Thus, it makes sense that when you add an object to the list, you do so with the addChild method.

Your document class represents the base of the tree (or the great-granddaddy of all other display objects, if you wish). It is automatically visible, and you start off by adding children to it. So, as you saw in earlier examples, to make a sprite or any other display object visible, you call the addChild method, passing it the newly created sprite:

```
var mySprite:Sprite = new Sprite();
mySprite.graphics.beginFill(0xff0000);
mySprite.graphics.drawCircle(0, 0, 40);
mySprite.graphics.endFill();
addChild(mySprite);
```

If you want to try this, put the code in the init function of the skeleton class presented earlier. Note that it will be placed at point 0, 0 initially; you can change it by adjusting its x and y properties.

Also note that there is no mention of depth here, as there was when creating new movie clips or attaching them in AS 2. Depth management is largely automatic, although there are methods to add a child at a particular depth or change its depth, which we will get into as they become necessary.

To remove an object from the display list, call removeChild, passing in a reference to the actual child object. The first key thing to realize is that removing a child does not destroy it! It continues to exist in the exact same state it was in prior to being removed, and it will be in that same state when you add it back on the display list. In other words, if you have drawn some shapes into the child, or loaded some external content into it, you won't have to redraw or reload that stuff when you put it back on the list, as you had to in AS 2.

The second key thing to realize is that when you put the child back on the list, you have the freedom to put it back on the list wherever you want. This is known as reparenting and is very exciting (at least to me). You can now remove an object from one movie clip and attach it to another one, in the exact same state it was in when you removed it, which was not possible before. In fact, you don't even need to remove it. Because a child can have only one parent, adding it to another parent automatically removes it from the first.

The following class demonstrates reparenting:

```
package {
    import flash.display.Sprite;
    import flash.events.MouseEvent;

    public class Reparenting extends Sprite {
        private var parent1:Sprite;
        private var parent2:Sprite;
        private var ball:Sprite;
```

```
        public function Reparenting() {
            init();
        }
        private function init():void {
            parent1 = new Sprite();
            addChild(parent1);
            parent1.graphics.lineStyle(1, 0);
            parent1.graphics.drawRect(-50, -50, 100, 100);
            parent1.x = 60;
            parent1.y = 60;

            parent2 = new Sprite();
            addChild(parent2);
            parent2.graphics.lineStyle(1, 0);
            parent2.graphics.drawRect(-50, -50, 100, 100);
            parent2.x = 170;
            parent2.y = 60;

            ball = new Sprite();
            parent1.addChild(ball);
            ball.graphics.beginFill(0xff0000);
            ball.graphics.drawCircle(0, 0, 40);
            ball.graphics.endFill();
            ball.addEventListener(MouseEvent.CLICK, onBallClick);
        }

        public function onBallClick(event:MouseEvent):void
        {
            parent2.addChild(ball);
        }
    }
}
```

The class creates three sprites: parent1, parent2, and ball. The parent sprites are added to the display list directly, and squares are drawn in them. The ball sprite is added to parent1, so it is now on the display list and visible.

When the ball is clicked, it is added to parent2. Note that there is no code to change its x, y position. It moves because now it is within a different sprite, which is at a different position. Also note that the dynamically drawn circle remains, even though the sprite was removed and added back.

Subclassing display objects

Earlier, you learned about subclassing the Sprite or MovieClip class in order to create a document class. There are plenty of other uses for subclassing one of these classes as well.

First off, you might be wondering, since attachMovieClip is no more in AS 3, how do you get a movie clip symbol from the Flash CS3 IDE library into your movie at runtime? The answer is with a class that extends either the Sprite or MovieClip class. Although I'm striving not to put too much emphasis on any one of the tools used to create SWFs, I'll take a short detour into the IDE to explain this one.

This concept is best shown through an example:

1. Create a new FLA, and draw some content on the stage.
2. Select the content and press F8 to convert it to a symbol.
3. In the Convert to Symbol dialog that appears, give the symbol a name, and choose Movie clip as the type.
4. Select Export for ActionScript.

At this point, in previous versions of Flash, you would get an automatically generated linkage identifier, and you could optionally enter a class.

In Flash CS3, the Identifier field is disabled, and the Class field is mandatory and filled in with a default value. There's also a new field, Base class, which is prefilled with flash.display.MovieClip. You can change this to some other custom class that extends MovieClip or Sprite if you want.

Enter any class name you want. Don't worry that you haven't created a class yet. Then click OK. Here's where things get interesting. Because Flash cannot find a class with the name you specified, it will automatically generate one at compile time. This doesn't mean that Flash will actually create an ActionScript class file that you can look at, but it will create the bytecode in your SWF that represents a new class based on Sprite or MovieClip. The class doesn't actually do anything other than extend the base class, but it will now be linked to that symbol in your library.

Now, say the class name you entered was Ball. In your document class, or right on the timeline, you can write the following:

```
var ball:Ball = new Ball();
addChild(ball);
```

This causes the library symbol to be created on stage, just like the old attachMovie method worked in AS 2.

That's fine if all you want to do is "attach" a movie clip with some content from the library. But rather than simply accepting the automatically generated class, you can give it the name and path of a real class that you have created, to give the symbol some additional functionality. Now let's jump back out of the Flash IDE and back to the world of classes for the next example.

Actually, we'll take another look at the reparenting example just given, as that has some duplication that could be cleaned up with another class. In that example, we created a sprite called parent1 and drew a box in it with the following code:

```
parent1.graphics.lineStyle(1, 0);
parent1.graphics.drawRect(-50, -50, 100, 100);
```

We then created another sprite, parent2, which had the same box drawn with the same lines of code. Although this is a trivial example, it clearly shows how subclassing the Sprite class can be useful. First, we'll make a class called ParentBox that extends Sprite. In that class, we'll have the code that draws the box.

```
package {
    import flash.display.Sprite;

    public class ParentBox extends Sprite {
        public function ParentBox()
        {
            init();
        }
        private function init():void
        {
            graphics.lineStyle(1, 0);
            graphics.drawRect(-50, -50, 100, 100);
        }
    }
}
```

Then we'll alter the class to create two ParentBoxes, rather than two Sprites.

```
package {
    import flash.display.Sprite;
    import flash.events.MouseEvent;

    public class Reparenting2 extends Sprite {
        private var parent1:ParentBox;
        private var parent2:ParentBox;
        private var ball:Sprite;

        public function Reparenting2() {
            init();
        }
        private function init():void {
            parent1 = new ParentBox();
            addChild(parent1);
            parent1.x = 60;
            parent1.y = 60;

            parent2 = new ParentBox();
            addChild(parent2);
            parent2.x = 170;
            parent2.y = 60;

            ball = new Sprite();
            parent1.addChild(ball);
            ball.graphics.beginFill(0xff0000);
            ball.graphics.drawCircle(0, 0, 40);
            ball.graphics.endFill();
            ball.addEventListener(MouseEvent.CLICK, onBallClick);
        }
```

```
            public function onBallClick(event:MouseEvent):void
            {
                parent2.addChild(ball);
            }
        }
    }
```

As instances of ParentBox, they are still Sprites, and thus can have children added to them. They also get the new init method, which automatically draws their graphics. Again, this is a trivial example, but hopefully you get the idea, as you'll be seeing a lot more complex examples as you move through the book.

You might want to try adding a Ball class to this example, to draw the ball's graphics. Doing so doesn't reduce any duplication, but as your classes get more complex, it is a good idea to separate functionality into different classes, rather than having everything piled into a single class. This approach also promotes reusability. In fact, you will soon create just such a Ball class that you will use throughout the rest of the book.

User interaction

Finally, we come to *user interaction*, probably one of the main reasons you're reading this book. After all, if it weren't for interaction or some sort of dynamic input going into the movie, you might as well just use tweens.

Actually, there is not a whole lot left to discuss here that I haven't already touched on earlier in the chapter. User interaction is based on user events, and these generally come down to mouse events and keyboard events. Let's quickly go through the various user events and their handlers.

Mouse events

Mouse events have changed dramatically in AS 3. In AS 2, movie clips were automatically listeners for all mouse events. Now any object has to specifically add itself as a listener for them. Also, for mouse events to fire in AS 3, it is required that the mouse cursor is over some visible content of the display object. This is different than in AS 2, where mouseUp, mouseDown, and mouseMove would fire for every movie clip no matter where the mouse cursor was located. The mouseUp and mouseDown events are now equivalent to onPress and onRelease from AS 2.

Mouse event names are defined by strings, but as mentioned earlier, it is better to use properties of the MouseEvent class to guard against errors. Here are the available mouse event properties of the MouseEvent class:

- CLICK
- DOUBLE_CLICK
- MOUSE_DOWN
- MOUSE_MOVE
- MOUSE_OUT
- MOUSE_OVER

- MOUSE_UP
- MOUSE_WHEEL
- ROLL_OUT
- ROLL_OVER

These properties are pretty self-explanatory. To get a feel for them, you can create and compile the following class, which will trace each mouse event as it occurs on the sprite it creates:

```
package {
    import flash.display.Sprite;
    import flash.events.MouseEvent;

    public class MouseEvents extends Sprite {
        public function MouseEvents() {
            init();
        }
        private function init():void
        {
            var sprite:Sprite = new Sprite();
            addChild(sprite);
            sprite.graphics.beginFill(0xff0000);
            sprite.graphics.drawCircle(0, 0, 50);
            sprite.graphics.endFill();
            sprite.x = stage.stageWidth / 2;
            sprite.y = stage.stageHeight / 2;

            sprite.addEventListener(MouseEvent.CLICK, onMouseEvent);
            sprite.addEventListener(MouseEvent.DOUBLE_CLICK,
                                    onMouseEvent);
            sprite.addEventListener(MouseEvent.MOUSE_DOWN,
                                    onMouseEvent);
            sprite.addEventListener(MouseEvent.MOUSE_MOVE,
                                    onMouseEvent);
            sprite.addEventListener(MouseEvent.MOUSE_OUT,
                                    onMouseEvent);
            sprite.addEventListener(MouseEvent.MOUSE_OVER,
                                    onMouseEvent);
            sprite.addEventListener(MouseEvent.MOUSE_UP,
                                    onMouseEvent);
            sprite.addEventListener(MouseEvent.MOUSE_WHEEL,
                                    onMouseEvent);
            sprite.addEventListener(MouseEvent.ROLL_OUT,
                                    onMouseEvent);
            sprite.addEventListener(MouseEvent.ROLL_OVER,
                                    onMouseEvent);
        }
        public function onMouseEvent(event:MouseEvent):void
```

```
        {
            trace(event.type);
        }
    }
}
```

Note that the class uses the same handler for every event type, and simply traces the type of the event that has been dispatched.

Mouse position

In addition to mouse events, two very important properties are available from your document class or any display object to determine the current location of the mouse pointer: mouseX and mouseY. Note that these are properties of a movie clip, and the values returned are the mouse's position in relation to the registration point of that clip. For example, if you have a sprite named sprite sitting at 100, 100 on the stage, and the mouse pointer is at 150, 250, you get the following results:

- mouseX is 150.
- mouseY is 250.
- sprite.mouseX is 50.
- sprite.mouseY is 150.

Notice how the movie clip is taking the mouse position in relation to its own position.

Keyboard events

Keyboard events is another area that has really been cleaned up in AS 3. For example, in AS 2, movie clips were automatic listeners for keyboard events, but they would only get those events under certain circumstances. So it was best to explicitly add a movie clip as a listener, but this sometimes ended up in the movie clip receiving multiple events for a single keyboard event. I could go on and on. A huge portion of the AS 2 component framework was dedicated to trying to deal with keyboard interaction–related problems in the underlying Flash Player architecture: tab management, focus management, handling of Enter keys and Tab keys in text fields, and so on.

Let's just say things are much better now.

Keyboard event names, like mouse events, are defined as strings, but they are also properties of the KeyboardEvent class. There are only two:

- KEY_DOWN
- KEY_UP

You can listen to keyboard events on a particular object, in the way we just listened for mouse events in the previous example. In order to do that, however, you need to set focus on that object so that it will capture those events. You can do so with a line like this:

```
stage.focus = sprite;
```

In many cases, though, it makes more sense to listen for keyboard events regardless of what has focus. To do that, you would listen to keyboard events on the stage directly. The following shows an example:

```
package {
    import flash.display.Sprite;
    import flash.events.KeyboardEvent;

    public class KeyboardEvents extends Sprite {
        public function KeyboardEvents() {
            init();
        }
        private function init():void {
            stage.addEventListener(KeyboardEvent.KEY_DOWN,
                                    onKeyboardEvent);
            stage.addEventListener(KeyboardEvent.KEY_UP,
                                    onKeyboardEvent);
        }
        public function onKeyboardEvent(event:KeyboardEvent):void {
            trace(event.type);
        }
    }
}
```

Key codes

Often, you want to know not just that a key has been pressed or released, but also which key it was. There are a couple ways to read this information within a keyboard event handler.

Earlier when discussing events, I said that an event handler gets passed an event object, which contains data about the event that just occurred. In a keyboard event, two properties relate to what key was involved with the event: charCode and keyCode.

The charCode property gives you the actual character that represents the key that was just pressed. For example, if the user pressed the "a" key on the keyboard, charCode would contain the string "a". If the user was also holding down the Shift key at the time, charCode would then contain "A".

The keyCode character contains a number that represents the physical key that was pressed. If the user pressed the "a" key, keyCode would contain the number 65, regardless of what other keys were being pressed. If the user pressed Shift first and then "a", you would get two keyboard events: one for Shift (keyCode 16) and then one for "a" (65).

The flash.ui.Keyboard class also has some properties to stand in for some of the nonalphanumeric keys, so you don't have to memorize them. For example, Keyboard.SHIFT is equal to the number 16, so you could test if the keyCode was equal to Keyboard.SHIFT to find out if the Shift key had been pressed. The final example of this chapter does something very similar:

```
package {
    import flash.display.Sprite;
    import flash.events.KeyboardEvent;
    import flash.ui.Keyboard;

    public class KeyCodes extends Sprite {
        private var ball:Sprite;

        public function KeyCodes() {
            init();
        }
        private function init():void {
            ball = new Sprite();
            addChild(ball);
            ball.graphics.beginFill(0xff0000);
            ball.graphics.drawCircle(0, 0, 40);
            ball.graphics.endFill();
            ball.x = stage.stageWidth / 2;
            ball.y = stage.stageHeight / 2;
            stage.addEventListener(KeyboardEvent.KEY_DOWN,
                                 onKeyboardEvent);
        }
        public function onKeyboardEvent(event:KeyboardEvent):void {
            switch(event.keyCode) {
                case Keyboard.UP :
                ball.y -= 10;
                break;

                case Keyboard.DOWN :
                ball.y += 10;
                break;

                case Keyboard.LEFT :
                ball.x -= 10;
                break;

                case Keyboard.RIGHT :
                ball.x += 10;
                break;

                default:
                break;
            }
        }
    }
}
```

One thing you should know about key handling is that when you are testing a movie in the Flash authoring environment, the IDE intercepts some keys to control the IDE itself. The Tab key, all function keys, and any keys assigned as shortcuts to menu items will not be received by your movie while testing. You can disable this by choosing Control ➤ Disable Keyboard Shortcuts from the menu while the movie is running. This allows you to test your movie as it will actually work in a browser.

Summary

This chapter covered just about all the basics of ActionScript needed for animation. You now know about frame loops, events, listeners, handlers, and the display list. I've touched on classes, objects, and basic user interaction. That's a lot of material! Don't worry if some of these areas are still a little vague. I cover most of them in much more detail as I get into specific techniques, and you can always come back here to brush up on any concepts. At the very least, now you are familiar with the terms and concepts, and you're ready to move forward.

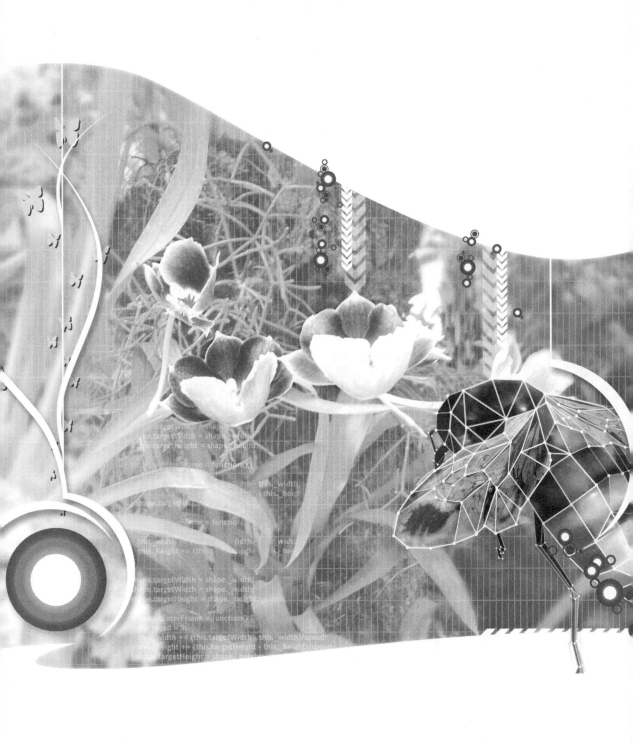

Chapter 3

TRIGONOMETRY FOR ANIMATION

What we'll cover in this chapter:

- What is trigonometry?
- Angles
- Trig functions
- Rotation
- Waves
- Circles and ellipses
- Pythagorean Theorem
- Distance between two points
- Important formulas in this chapter

I wanted to put this chapter near the beginning of the book, as you'll be using trigonometry extensively for animation techniques, starting with the examples in Chapter 5. In fact, I'll even touch on it in the next chapter on rendering techniques. However, feel free to jump ahead if you already know basic trig or are just anxious to get into animating things. You can always come back here when you come across something you don't understand.

A lot of people shy away from math and trigonometry, saying things like, "I'm not good with numbers. I can barely add two plus two." The funny thing is that in programming with trigonometry, you are hardly dealing with numbers at all. It's far more in the realm of visualizing shapes and relationships. For the most part, you are dealing with variables containing positions, distances, and angles. You never see the actual numbers. It's mostly a matter of memorizing various relationships. In fact, 90% of the trig you will need for basic animation will come down to two functions: Math.sin and Math.cos.

When I wrote the first edition of this book, I made a point of saying that I had no formal math training beyond high school algebra and geometry (most of which I had long forgotten), and that all of what I originally wrote in this chapter was stuff I had learned from various books, websites, and other online resources. The point was that it is not that hard to learn, and if I could get a grasp of this stuff, so can you. Since that time, I have actually completed college courses in algebra and precalculus, and learned a whole lot more about trigonometry than I knew existed. I'm happy to say, though, that the material in this chapter has held up pretty well. Few corrections were needed, and if anything, with a deeper understanding of the subject, I think I was able to make a few points a little more clear.

What is trigonometry?

Trigonometry is basically the study of triangles and the relationship of their sides and angles. If you look at any triangle, you'll see that it has three sides and three angles (hence the name *tri-angle*). It happens that these sides and angles have very specific relationships. For example, if you take any triangle and make one of the angles larger, the side opposite of that angle will get longer (assuming the other two sides stay the same length). Also, the other two angles will get smaller. Exactly how much each of these things changes takes a bit of calculation, but the ratios have all been figured out and codified.

A specific type of triangle has one of its angles equal to exactly 90 degrees. This is called a *right triangle* and is indicated by a little square in the corner of that angle. It happens that in a right triangle, the various relationships are far simpler and quite easy to figure out with some basic formulas. This makes a right triangle a very useful construct. All of the trig you will see in this chapter and most of what you will see in the rest of the book deals with right triangles.

Angles

As trigonometry is mostly about angles, let's tackle that subject first. An *angle* is simply the shape formed by two intersecting lines, or the space in between those lines. The more space, the higher the measurement of the angle. Actually, two intersecting lines will form four angles, as you can see in Figure 3-1.

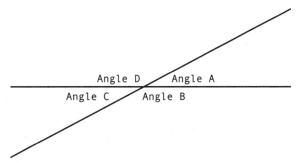

Figure 3-1. Two lines form four angles

Radians and degrees

The two major systems for measuring angles are *degrees* and *radians*. You are probably familiar with degrees, and no doubt you could draw a 45- or 90-degree angle in your sleep. The system of 360 degrees in a circle has become a part of our culture. We talk about "doing a 180," meaning "going in the opposite direction," even when we are not talking about physical direction, but referring to taking an opposite viewpoint. But it turns out that computers have a lot more affinity for radians when it comes to talking about angles. So, like it or not, you need to know about radians.

A *radian* is equal to approximately 57.2958 degrees. Now, you're probably rolling your eyes and saying, "Well, isn't that logical?" But there is some actual logic to it. A full circle, or 360 degrees, works out to 6.2832 radians. Still not making any sense? Well, remember pi—that symbol, π? That is equal to about 3.1416, meaning that a circle (6.2832 radians) measures exactly 2 pi. It still may not seem too logical now, but work with it enough, and you'll get used to thinking of 360 degrees as 2 pi, 180 degrees as pi, 90 degrees as pi/2, and so on. Figure 3-2 illustrates some common radian measurements.

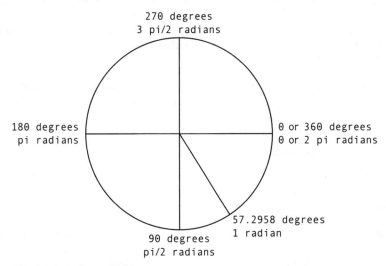

Figure 3-2. Radians and degrees

Now, I could pretty much leave the discussion there and just tell you that you'll be using radians from here on out. You might sigh a bit, and then get used to it and live happily ever after. But you're going to encounter many situations where you'll need to use degrees *with* radians. For example, it just so happens that the rotation property of a sprite or movie clip is measured in degrees, and you'll often need to use that property.

For example, say you have a vehicle that needs to turn in the direction of its motion. If you figure out the motion using trig, the angle you get will be in radians, but to rotate the vehicle, you need degrees. Or, conversely, suppose you want to move something in the direction it happens to be pointing. You can check its rotation to get the angle, but that's going to be in degrees, and to use it in any trig formula, you need radians.

Another place where degrees are used is in filters. If you want to use the drop shadow filter to make a shadow that extends 45 degrees from your object, you need to specify that angle in degrees, not radians, whether you are creating the filter in the Flash IDE or programming the DropShadowFilter class with ActionScript.

Why the heck are two completely different systems used in the same program? Well, it's kind of indicative of Flash's dual nature. On one hand, it's a designer tool. You have all your drawing and transformation tools in the Flash IDE to make pretty graphics. I'm sure most designers would look at you cross-eyed if you told them to enter a radian value to rotate the text for the logo they are creating. On the other hand, Flash is a developer tool, and like most programming languages, ActionScript uses radians. So, like it or not, you'll be working with both, and you'll need to know how to convert degrees to radians and vice versa. Here are the formulas:

```
radians = degrees * Math.PI / 180
degrees = radians * 180 / Math.PI
```

As you go through this book, you'll be running into a lot of formulas. Here and there, I will point out a formula as one that you should memorize—burn into the backs of your eyelids. These are the first ones. If you need to look up these formulas every time you want to use them, you'll never get any code written. They should just roll off your fingers onto the keyboard whenever you need them. I even wrote them in ActionScript for you, with Math.PI rather than just pi or its funny symbol, because that's how you'll be typing them over and over.

From this, you can easily see that 180 degrees is about 3.14 . . . radians. In other words, half a circle is pi radians, which makes sense, since a full circle is 2 pi. Going the other way, you can see that one radian is indeed roughly 57.29 . . . degrees.

Flash's coordinate system

While I'm on the subject of angles, this would be a good time to say a word about how space is laid out in Flash, numerically speaking. If you've dealt with any coordinate systems prior to Flash, you're probably going to get a little dizzy here, as everything is pretty much upside down and backward.

The most common two-dimensional coordinate systems signify horizontal measurements with x and vertical measurements with y. Flash does this, too. However, the zero x, zero y position (0, 0) is usually shown in the center, with positive x going off to the right, negative x to the left, positive y going up, and negative y going down, as shown in Figure 3-3.

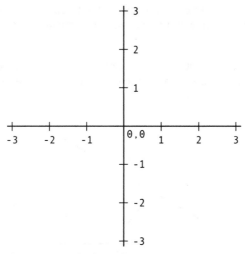

Figure 3-3. Standard coordinate system

Flash, however, is based on a video screen coordinate system, where 0, 0 is at the top left, as shown in Figure 3-4. The x values still increase from left to right, but the y axis is reversed, with positive values going down and negative values going up. I believe this system has its historical roots in the way the electron gun scans the screen to build the picture—left to right, top to bottom—but it doesn't really matter. That's the way it works, and it's probably not going to change very soon.

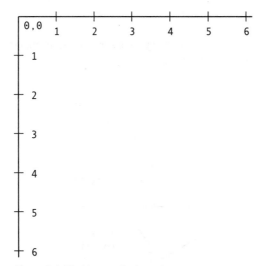

Figure 3-4. Flash's coordinate system

It's possible to build a system in which you can work with numbers in a standard coordinate system and convert them to Flash's coordinates just before rendering. Basically, you would flip the y values and offset everything half a screen to move the center to the top-left corner. However, the problem is that all those calculations take time. Although it's gotten a lot faster over the years, Flash still suffers a bit in the performance department compared with other languages; so personally, I trade my brain-power for CPU cycles. Learn to live with the backward coordinates, and reserve the calculations for the cool effects.

But wait, there's more! Let's talk about measuring angles. In most systems, angles are measured counterclockwise, with 0 degrees being shown as a line extending into the positive x axis, as shown in Figure 3-5.

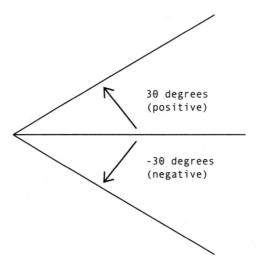

Figure 3-5. Usual angle measurements

Again, Flash has it backward, as illustrated in Figure 3-6. It rotates its angles clockwise as they go positive. Counterclockwise means a negative angle.

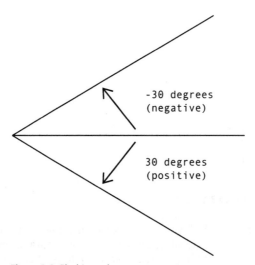

Figure 3-6. Flash's angle measurements

And again, you can work out a system to reverse the angles before rendering, or conserve the computation and learn to live with it. I suggest the latter, and this is the tactic I will use for all the code in this book.

Triangle sides

There's not too much to say about the sides of a triangle by themselves, but there are some specific terms to cover. Until further notice, I will be talking about right triangles, where one of the angles is 90 degrees. In this case, the sides have special names, as shown in Figure 3-7. The two sides that touch the 90-degree angle are called *legs*, and the opposite side is called the *hypotenuse*. The hypotenuse is always the longest side.

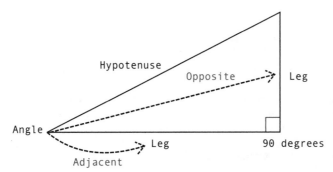

Figure 3-7. The parts of a right triangle

When we refer to the side *opposite* an angle, we are talking about the side that does not touch that angle. When we refer to an *adjacent* side, we mean one of the sides that does touch the angle. Mostly, examples will deal with one of the two non-90-degree angles. In this case, when we say *adjacent*, we mean the adjacent leg, not the hypotenuse.

The interesting thing about triangles is the relationships between the measurements of the sides and the measurements of the angles. These relationships become useful for animation, so let's take a look at them next.

Trig functions

ActionScript has trig functions for calculating the various triangle relationships: sine, cosine, tangent, arcsine, arccosine, and arctangent. Here, I'll define these and the ActionScript functions for accessing them. Then I'll get to some real-life uses for these functions.

Sine

Here is your first bit of real-life trigonometry. The *sine* of an angle is the ratio of the angle's opposite leg to the hypotenuse. (When referring to sine, we are always referring to the sine of an angle.) In ActionScript, you can use the function Math.sin(angle).

Figure 3-8 shows the sine of an angle that is 30 degrees. The opposite leg has a measurement of 1, and the hypotenuse has a measurement of 2. The ratio is thus one to two, or mathematically speaking, 1/2 or 0.5. Thus, you can say that the sine of a 30-degree angle is 0.5. You can test this in Flash like so:

```
trace(Math.sin(30));
```

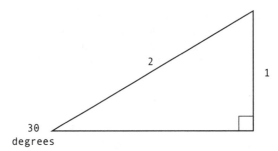

Figure 3-8. The sine of an angle is the opposite leg/hypotenuse.

Now, hold on, that traces out –0.988031624092862, which is not even close. Can you spot the error? We forgot to convert to radians. I guarantee you will make this mistake on occasion (I still do), so get used to looking out for it. Here's the corrected code, with the conversion:

```
trace(Math.sin(30 * Math.PI / 180));
```

Success! That traces 0.5.

Actually, you might get something like 0.4999 . . . something, which is not an error in your program, but the way binary computers sometimes end up representing floating-point numbers. It's close enough, though, that you can consider it 0.5.

Now, it's fine for an abstract triangle like that to say that the angle is 30 degrees, and the measurements of the sides are 1 and 2. But let's move it into the real world, or at least the world of the Flash coordinate system. Remember that in Flash, positive vertical measurements go down, and positive angle measurements go clockwise. So, in this case, the opposite side and the angle are both negative, as you can see in Figure 3-9.

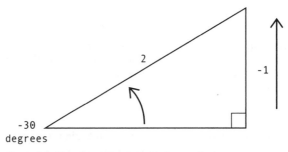

Figure 3-9. The same triangle in Flash coordinate space

So, the ratio becomes –1/2, and we are talking about the sine of –30. So, we say that the sine of –30 degrees is –0.5. Go ahead and alter the Flash trace statement to verify that.

```
trace(Math.sin(-30 * Math.PI / 180));
```

OK, that wasn't too painful, was it? Let's take a look at another trig function: cosine.

Cosine

You can access cosine in Flash with Math.cos(angle). Cosine is defined as the ratio of the adjacent leg of an angle to the hypotenuse. Figure 3-10 shows that relationship.

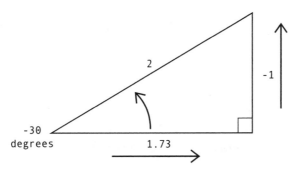

Figure 3-10. The cosine of an angle is the adjacent leg/hypotenuse.

Figure 3-10 shows the same angle as Figure 3-9, but now I've added the approximate measurement of the adjacent leg: 1.73. Notice that it goes to the right, so as an x measurement, it's positive. The cosine of the angle is thus 1.73/2, or 0.865. So we can say that the cosine of –30 degrees is 0.865. Test it as follows:

```
trace(Math.cos(-30 * Math.PI / 180));
```

This is the same as the last trace, but with the call to Math.cos, rather than to Math.sin. This traces to 0.866025403784439, which is pretty close to 0.865. The difference is due to the fact that I rounded off the length of the adjacent leg. For the triangle shown, the actual length would be closer to 1.73205080756888. You'll find that if you divide that by 2, you'll get pretty darned close to the actual cosine of –30 degrees.

So far, everything has been taken from the lower-left angle. What if you looked at things from the viewpoint of the top-right angle? Well, first you'd need to reorient the triangle so that the angle in question aligns with the coordinate system, as you can see in Figure 3-11. This is known as *putting the angle in standard position* (even though "standard" in Flash is upside down and backward from the usual "standard"). That angle is equal to 60 degrees, and as it's going clockwise, it's positive. The vertical measurement now goes down from that angle, so it's positive, and the horizontal measurement goes to the right, so it's positive too. (I added plus signs in the figure to point out the difference, but in general, this is not necessary; values will be positive unless specifically indicated as being negative.)

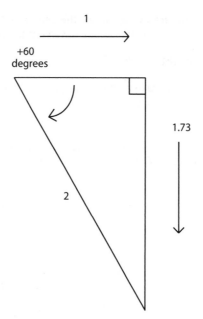

Figure 3-11. Looking at the opposite angle

Now, the sine of that angle is its opposite leg over the hypotenuse, or 1.73/2 (0.865). And the cosine is the adjacent over the hypotenuse, 1/2, or 0.5. So, basically, the cosine of one angle is the same as the sine of the other angle, and the sine of one is the cosine of the other. I'm not sure how useful that will ever be in Flash, but it's important to note that these are just relationships and ratios, and everything is connected.

Tangent

Another major trig function is tangent, retrieved in Flash with `Math.tan(angle)`. This is the relationship of the opposite leg to the adjacent leg, as shown in Figure 3-12.

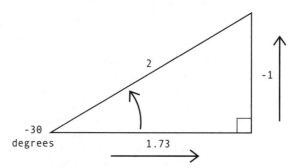

Figure 3-12. The tangent of an angle is the opposite leg/adjacent leg.

Here, the ratio works out to –1/1.73, or –0.578. For more accuracy, check it directly in Flash:

```
trace(Math.tan(-30 * Math.PI / 180));
```

You'll get –0.577350269189626.

Truth be told, you won't use tangent too much by itself in your day-to-day ActionScript animation code. You'll find yourself using sine and cosine a *lot* more, though tangent can be used to create some interesting effects now and then.

On the other hand, arctangent can be extremely useful, as you'll see shortly, so keep that tangent ratio in your head.

Arcsine and arccosine

Similar to tangent, arcsine and arccosine are not that useful in your normal Flash animation endeavors. However, it's important to know that they are there and how to use them. Basically, all these do is the reverse of sine and cosine. In other words, you feed in a ratio, and you get back an angle (in radians). The ActionScript functions are Math.asin(ratio) and Math.acos(ratio). Let's just give them a quick test to make sure they work.

OK, you learned that the sine of 30 degrees is 0.5. Thus, it follows that the arcsine of 0.5 should be 30 degrees. Check it out:

```
trace(Math.asin(0.5) * 180 / Math.PI);
```

Remember to convert back to degrees in order to see 30, not 0.523, which is the equivalent value in radians.

And you know that the cosine of 30 degrees is roughly 0.865. Remember that if you test this value, which is rounded off, you aren't going to get exactly 30, but it will be close enough to prove the point. Here's the test:

```
trace(Math.acos(0.865) * 180 / Math.PI);
```

You should get 30.1172947473221 as the result. If you want to go back and plug in the actual cosine of 30 degrees, you should get a more accurate result.

See, this stuff isn't so hard, is it? And you're almost finished learning the basic functions. You just have one more to go, and then you'll start looking at what you can actually do with trig.

Arctangent

As you no doubt have already guessed, arctangent is simply the opposite of tangent. You feed it the ratio of the opposite and adjacent sides, and it gives you back the angle. In Flash, you actually have two functions to check arctangent. The first is named and works just as you'd expect from the previous examples. It's Math.atan(ratio), and you supply it the fraction you got by dividing the opposite and adjacent sides.

For example, you know from the earlier discussion that the tangent of 30 degrees is 0.577 (rounded off). You can try this:

```
trace(Math.atan(0.577) * 180 / Math.PI);
```

You'll get back something pretty close to 30. Now, that seems so basic and straightforward, why would you ever need another function to do the same thing? Well, to answer that, look at the diagram shown in Figure 3-13.

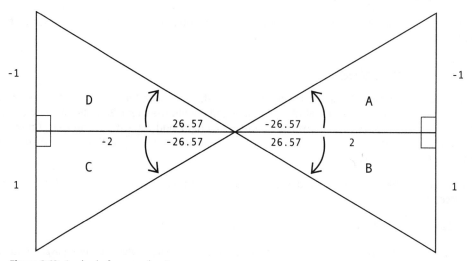

Figure 3-13. Angles in four quadrants

Figure 3-13 shows four different triangles: A, B, C, and D. Triangles A and B have a positive x value, and triangles C and D extend into negative x dimensions. Likewise, triangles A and D are in the negative y space, while triangles B and C have positive y measurements. So, for the ratios of the four inner angles, you get this:

- A: –1/2 or –0.5
- B: 1/2 or 0.5
- C: 1/ –2 or –0.5
- D: –1/ –2 or 0.5

So, say you divide your opposite leg by your adjacent leg and come up with a ratio of 0.5. You feed that in with Math.atan(0.5), convert it to degrees, and you get approximately 26.57. But which triangle are you talking about now: B or D? There is really no way of knowing, since they both have a ratio of 0.5. This may seem like a minor point, but as you will see in some real-life examples coming up shortly, it becomes quite important.

Welcome Math.atan2(y, x). This is the other arctangent function in Flash, and it is quite a bit more useful than Math.atan(ratio). In fact, I would go so far as to say you will probably wind up using this one exclusively. This function takes two values: the measurement of the opposite side and the measurement of the adjacent side. For most purposes in Flash, this means the y measurement and the x measurement. A common mistake is to enter them as x, y, rather than y, x, as specified. For the example given, you'd enter Math.atan2(1, 2). Go ahead and try it out, remembering to convert to degrees:

```
trace(Math.atan2(1, 2) * 180 / Math.PI);
```

This should give you the angle, 26.565051177078, which is correct for triangle B as shown earlier. Now, knowing that –1/ –2 (triangle D) gave us some confusion, let's try that out.

```
trace(Math.atan2(-1, -2) * 180 / Math.PI);
```

This gives you the possibly unexpected result of –153.434948822922. What is that all about? Perhaps the diagram in Figure 3-14 will explain.

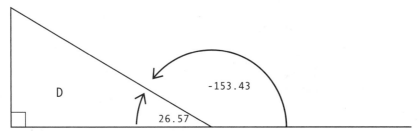

Figure 3-14. Two ways of measuring an angle

While the inner angle of triangle D is indeed +26.57, as taken from its own bottom leg, remember that in Flash, angles are measured clockwise from the positive x axis. Thus, from Flash's viewpoint of screen measurements, the angle you are looking at is –153.43.

How is this useful? Well, let's get to your first practical application of trigonometry in Flash.

Rotation

Here is the challenge: You want to rotate a sprite or movie clip so that it always points to the mouse. Rotation is a very useful tool to add to your toolbox. It can be used in games, mouse trailers, those eyes that follow the mouse around the screen, interface elements, and so on. In fact, rotation is not just limited to the mouse. Since the mouse coordinates are just x and y values, you can extend this technique to force a movie clip to aim itself at any particular point, such as another movie clip or the center or corner of the screen.

Let's work through an example. You can follow along with the steps or just open the document class RotateToMouse.as and Arrow.as (which you can download from www.friendsofed.com, along with all of the other code for this book) to have all the work done for you.

First, you need a something to rotate. This will be a sprite with an arrow drawn in it. In fact, since you might use this arrow sprite again, you'll make it in a class that extends the Sprite class:

```
package {
    import flash.display.Sprite;

    public class Arrow extends Sprite {
        public function Arrow() {
            init();
        }
        public function init():void {
            graphics.lineStyle(1, 0, 1);
            graphics.beginFill(0xffff00);
            graphics.moveTo(-50, -25);
            graphics.lineTo(0, -25);
            graphics.lineTo(0, -50);
            graphics.lineTo(50, 0);
            graphics.lineTo(0, 50);
            graphics.lineTo(0, 25);
            graphics.lineTo(-50, 25);
            graphics.lineTo(-50, -25);
            graphics.endFill();
        }
    }
}
```

This just uses the drawing API (which I'll cover in the next chapter) to draw an arrow as soon as the sprite is created. Now, whenever you need an arrow sprite, you just say new Arrow()! You can see the result of this in Figure 3-15. The most important thing to remember when drawing any content made to rotate like this is to make sure that it is "pointing" to the right, or positive x axis, because this is how it will look when rotated to 0 degrees.

Figure 3-15.
The arrow drawn with
the drawing API

You'll be creating an instance of the Arrow class, placing it in the center of the stage and having it point at the mouse. Figure 3-16 shows what you will be doing.

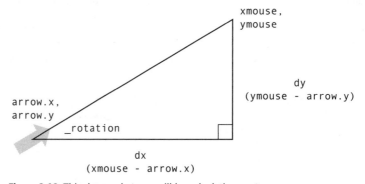

Figure 3-16. This shows what you will be calculating next.

Look familiar? It's the same triangle you've been dealing with for a while now, just mapped to the mouse and arrow coordinates. The mouse position can always be read with the mouseX and mouseY properties. You can get the location of the arrow with its x and y properties. Subtracting these, you get the length of the two triangle legs. Now, you simply need to use Math.atan2(dy, dx) to find the angle. Then convert it to degrees and set the arrow's rotation property to the result. It will look like this:

```
var dx:Number = mouseX - arrow.x;
var dy:Number = mouseY - arrow.y;
var radians:Number = Math.atan2(dy, dx);
arrow.rotation = radians * 180 / Math.PI;
```

Of course, to get animation, you need to set up a loop. As discussed in detail in the previous chapter, event handlers are your best bet. Let's go with the enterFrame event. Here's the document class in full:

```
package {
    import flash.display.Sprite;
    import flash.events.Event;

    public class RotateToMouse extends Sprite {
        private var arrow:Arrow;

        public function RotateToMouse()    {
            init();
        }
        private function init():void {
            arrow = new Arrow();
            addChild(arrow);
            arrow.x = stage.stageWidth / 2;
            arrow.y = stage.stageHeight / 2;
            addEventListener(Event.ENTER_FRAME, onEnterFrame);
        }
        public function onEnterFrame(event:Event):void {
            var dx:Number = mouseX - arrow.x;
            var dy:Number = mouseY - arrow.y;
            var radians:Number = Math.atan2(dy, dx);
            arrow.rotation = radians * 180 / Math.PI;
        }
    }
}
```

Make sure that you have the Arrow.as file in the same directory as the RotateToMouse.as file and build the SWF with RotateToMouse as the document class. What do you know? It works like a charm!

Now, suppose that you didn't have Math.atan2. You could get the ratio of opposite to adjacent angle by dividing dy by dx and pass that in to Math.atan. All you need to do is change the Math.atan2 line in the preceding code to use Math.atan instead, as follows:

```
var radians = Math.atan(dy / dx);
```

Try that one, and you'll see the problem pretty quickly. If the mouse is to the left of the arrow, the arrow will not point to it, but directly away from it. Can you figure out what is going on? Going back to the diagram showing triangles A, B, C, and D (Figure 3-13), remember that triangles A and C share the same ratio, as do triangles B and D. There is no way for Flash to know which angle you are referring to, so it simply gives you A or B. So, if your mouse is in the D quadrant, Flash is going to return the angle for the B quadrant and rotate the mouse into that area.

You can no doubt see the benefits of Math.atan2 now. You'll be using it many times throughout the book.

Waves

Let's get into some more concrete uses of trig in Flash. Surely you've heard the term *sine wave* before, and surely you've seen the shape shown in Figure 3-17, which is a graphical representation of a sine wave.

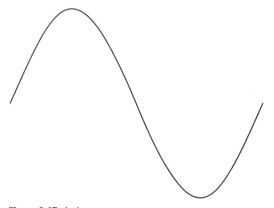

Figure 3-17. A sine wave

But what exactly does that shape have to do with the sine function? It is the graph of the results of the sine function, when fed in all the angles from 0 to 360 (or 0 to 2 pi in radians). From left to right is the value of the angle used, and the y value of the graph is the sine of that particular angle. In Figure 3-18, I've indicated some specific values.

Now you can see that the sine of 0 is 0. The sine of 90 degrees, or pi/2 radians, is 1. The sine of 180 degrees, or pi radians, is 0 again. The sine of 270 degrees, or 3/2 pi, is –1. The sine of 360 degrees, or 2 pi, is back to 0 once again. Let's play with this sine wave a bit in Flash. Put the following code into a skeleton document class and test it:

```
for(var angle:Number = 0;angle < Math.PI * 2; angle += .1){
    trace(Math.sin(angle));
}
```

From here on out, you should start getting used to radians alone. You'll be leaving degrees behind, except when you actually need them for rotation or some other purpose.

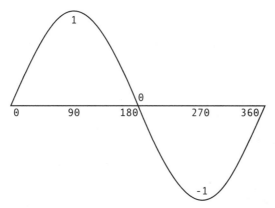

Figure 3-18. Values of sine

In this example, the variable angle starts out as 0 and increments by 0.1 until it's greater than Math.PI * 2. It then traces the sine of that angle. If you look at the long list of results, you'll see it starts out at 0, goes up to almost 1, then down to almost –1, and back to around 0. You'll never hit exactly 1 or 0 because, using an increment of 0.1, you'll never get an exact multiple of pi or pi/2.

Smooth up and down motion

So what can you use Math.sin(angle) for? Have you ever needed to move something up and down or back and forth smoothly? This is your function. Consider this: Instead of just going from 0 to 1 and –1 and back to 0, and stopping there, keep adding on to the angle. You'll keep getting the wave over and over again. And instead of just taking the 1 and –1, multiply those values by some higher value, say 100, and you have a stream of values that goes from 100 to –100, back and forth, continuously.

The next document class, Bobbing.as, uses a new custom sprite, defined by the Ball class. You can see that here:

```
package {
    import flash.display.Sprite;

    public class Ball extends Sprite {
        private var radius:Number;
        private var color:uint;

        public function Ball(radius:Number=40, color:uint=0xff0000) {
            this.radius = radius;
            this.color = color;
            init();
        }
        public function init():void {
            graphics.beginFill(color);
            graphics.drawCircle(0, 0, radius);
            graphics.endFill();
        }
    }
}
```

67

This just draws a circle when it is created. You can pass in a radius and a color if you want. If not, it will use the default arguments of 40 for the radius and red for the color (another neat AS 3 addition). This class is very simple, but so useful that you will use it many times throughout the rest of the book. So keep it handy.

The document creates an instance of the Ball class, adds it to the stage, and sets up an enterFrame listener that causes the ball to bob up and down:

```
package {
    import flash.display.Sprite;
    import flash.events.Event;

    public class Bobbing extends Sprite {
        private var ball:Ball;
        private var angle:Number = 0;
        public function Bobbing()    {
            init();
        }
        private function init():void {
            ball = new Ball();
            addChild(ball);
            ball.x = stage.stageWidth / 2;
            addEventListener(Event.ENTER_FRAME, onEnterFrame);
        }
        public function onEnterFrame(event:Event):void {
            ball.y = stage.stageHeight / 2 + Math.sin(angle) * 50;
            angle += .1;
        }
    }
}
```

First, you need to create an angle property and initialize it to 0.

In the onEnterFrame method, you take the sine of that angle and multiply it by 50. This will give you a range of values from 50 to –50. If you add that to the height of the stage divided by 2, your values will be from 250 to 150 (based on a 400-pixel-high stage). Make that the y position of the ball. Then add 0.1 to the angle for the next time around. You get a nice smooth up and down motion.

Play around with the various values. You'll notice that changing the 0.1 to another value changes the speed of the motion. This makes sense, because the faster or slower the angle is increasing, the faster or slower the return values from Math.sin will go from 1 to –1. Obviously, changing the 50 changes how far the ball moves, and changing the stage.stageHeight / 2 to some other value changes the point that it oscillates around. From this, you could abstract the values into variables like so (just showing the additional or changed parts of the class):

```
// at the top of the class:
private var angle:Number = 0;
private var centerY:Number = 200;
private var range:Number = 50;
private var speed:Number = 0.1;
```

```
// and the handler function:
public function onEnterFrame(event:Event):void {
    ball.y = centerY + Math.sin(angle) * range;
    angle += speed;
}
```

Keeping actual numbers out of your motion code is a very good practice, and you should strive to do it as much as possible. In this case, it's all pretty much in the same place anyway. But what happens when you get a couple pages' worth of code, and those values are used in several places throughout? Every time you want to change the speed, you need to hunt down every instance of that 0.1 value and change it. You could do a search and replace, but if something else in the file has 0.1 in it, that would get replaced as well. By keeping the numbers out of the code, preferably up at the top of the listing, you know exactly where all your variables are.

Linear vertical motion

In the Wave1.as file, I added linear vertical motion, just to give you some inspiration for your own animation. Here's the code for that file:

```
package
{
    import flash.display.Sprite;
    import flash.events.Event;

    public class Wave1 extends Sprite {
        private var ball:Ball;
        private var angle:Number = 0;
        private var centerY:Number = 200;
        private var range:Number = 50;
        private var xspeed:Number = 1;
        private var yspeed:Number = .05;

        public function Wave1()    {
            init();
        }
        private function init():void {
            ball = new Ball();
            addChild(ball);
            ball.x = 0;
            addEventListener(Event.ENTER_FRAME, onEnterFrame);
        }
        public function onEnterFrame(event:Event):void {
            ball.x += xspeed;
            ball.y = centerY + Math.sin(angle) * range;
            angle += yspeed;
        }
    }
}
```

Pulsing motion

One important thing to keep in mind is that you can apply sine values to items other than physical locations. In the Pulse.as file, I used the values to affect the scale of the ball instead. This gives it a pulsating appearance. Here's the code:

```
package {
    import flash.display.Sprite;
    import flash.events.Event;

    public class Pulse extends Sprite {
        private var ball:Ball;
        private var angle:Number = 0;
        private var centerScale:Number = 1;
        private var range:Number = .5;
        private var speed:Number = .1;

        public function Pulse()   {
            init();
        }
        private function init():void {
            ball = new Ball();
            addChild(ball);
            ball.x = stage.stageWidth / 2;
            ball.y = stage.stageHeight / 2;
            addEventListener(Event.ENTER_FRAME, onEnterFrame);
        }
        public function onEnterFrame(event:Event):void {
            ball.scaleX = ball.scaleY = centerScale +
                                    Math.sin(angle) * range;
            angle += speed;
        }
    }
}
```

The principles are the same. You have a center point (which is 100% scale in this case), a range, and a speed. Don't stop there. Apply some sine waves to alpha, rotation, or any other interesting property.

Waves with two angles

Here's another idea to get you started: Rather than just a single angle, set up two sets of values, angle1 and angle2, along with separate centers and speeds for both. Apply one sine wave to one property and the other sine wave to another property, such as position and scale. I can't guarantee you'll come up with anything useful, but playing around like this, you will really get a feel for how these functions work.

I've included one example in the Random.as document class to get you started. This takes two angles, speeds, and centers, and applies one of the angles to the ball's x position and the other angle to the y position. The result is something like a bug flying around a room. Although it is all very mathematically predetermined, it looks pretty random. Here's the code:

```
package
{
    import flash.display.Sprite;
    import flash.events.Event;

    public class Random extends Sprite {
        private var ball:Ball;
        private var angleX:Number = 0;
        private var angleY:Number = 0;
        private var centerX:Number = 200;
        private var centerY:Number = 200;
        private var range:Number = 50;
        private var xspeed:Number = .07;
        private var yspeed:Number = .11;

        public function Random()    {
            init();
        }
        private function init():void {
            ball = new Ball();
            addChild(ball);
            ball.x = 0;
            addEventListener(Event.ENTER_FRAME, onEnterFrame);
        }
        public function onEnterFrame(event:Event):void {
            ball.x = centerX + Math.sin(angleX) * range;
            ball.y = centerY + Math.sin(angleY) * range;
            angleX += xspeed;
            angleY += yspeed;
        }
    }
}
```

Waves with the drawing API

Finally, in Wave2.as, I took out the ball and used the drawing API to draw the sine wave. Here is the code for that file:

```
package
{
    import flash.display.Sprite;
    import flash.events.Event;

    public class Wave2 extends Sprite {
        private var angle:Number = 0;
        private var centerY:Number = 200;
        private var range:Number = 50;
        private var xspeed:Number = 1;
        private var yspeed:Number = .05;
```

```
        private var xpos:Number;
        private var ypos:Number;

        public function Wave2()    {
            init();
        }
        private function init():void {
            xpos = 0;
            graphics.lineStyle(1, 0, 1);
            graphics.moveTo(0, centerY);
            addEventListener(Event.ENTER_FRAME, onEnterFrame);
        }
        public function onEnterFrame(event:Event):void {
            xpos += xspeed;
            angle += yspeed;
            ypos = centerY + Math.sin(angle) * range;
            graphics.lineTo(xpos, ypos);
        }
    }
}
```

I'll cover the drawing API in detail in the next chapter, but you should have fun playing with this file and seeing the various waves you can draw with it. Note that the sine wave comes out upside down, again due to the y axis being reversed in Flash.

Circles and ellipses

Now that you've mastered sine waves, let's move on to their lesser-known cousins, cosine waves. These are formed in the same way as sine waves, but use the cosine function instead of sine. If you recall from the earlier discussion about how sine and cosine basically end up being the inverse of each other, you won't be surprised to learn that the two waves form the same shape, but in a different position. Figure 3-19 shows a cosine wave.

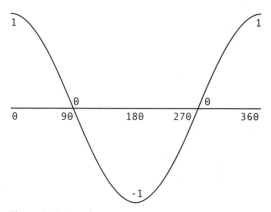

Figure 3-19. A cosine wave

This shows that the cosine of 0 is 1, and as it moves through to 2 pi radians, or 360 degrees, it goes to 0, −1, 0, and then back to 1. So, it's essentially the same curve as produced by the sine wave, just shifted over a bit.

Circular movement

It goes without saying that you can use cosine in place of sine in just about any situation where all you need is an oscillating motion. But cosine actually has a much more common and useful function in coordination with sine: moving an object in a circle. Figure 3-20 shows an object at several points as it moves around a circle.

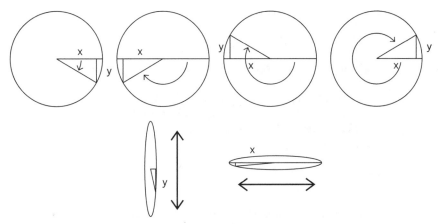

Figure 3-20. Positions of an object as it moves around a circle

If you were to take the circle in Figure 3-20 and turn it so you were looking straight at its edge from the right, you would just see the object going up and down. Its center would be the center of the circle, and its range would be the radius of the circle. You would calculate its position just as you did in the first sine experiment: by taking the sine of the angle times the range. In this case, sine would be the appropriate function to use, because if you look at the triangle formed, you are calculating the length of y—the leg opposite the angle.

Now, imagine that you are looking at the circle from its bottom edge instead. In this view, you see the object moving back and forth, left to right. This time, you are calculating the length of x—the leg adjacent to the angle—so you should be using cosine.

The important thing to realize is that these calculations are operating off the same angle, unlike the Random.as example you saw earlier, which used two different angles to compute the x and y positions. You just use sine to calculate y and cosine to calculate x. Here's how it looks in ActionScript:

```
package
{
    import flash.display.Sprite;
    import flash.events.Event;
```

```
public class Circle extends Sprite {
    private var ball:Ball;
    private var angle:Number = 0;
    private var centerX:Number = 200;
    private var centerY:Number = 200;
    private var radius:Number = 50;
    private var speed:Number = .1;

    public function Circle()    {
        init();
    }
    private function init():void {
        ball = new Ball();
        addChild(ball);
        ball.x = 0;
        addEventListener(Event.ENTER_FRAME, onEnterFrame);
    }
    public function onEnterFrame(event:Event):void {
        ball.x = centerX + Math.sin(angle) * radius;
        ball.y = centerY + Math.cos(angle) * radius;
        angle += speed;
    }
}
```

You can create this example yourself, or open and use Circle.as as your document class, which has all the work done for you. Test it and verify that you do indeed have a perfect circle.

Notice that the range in both cases is the hypotenuse of the triangle, and it's equal to the radius of the circle. Thus, I changed range to radius, to reflect that fact.

All the code is doing is using cosine to get the x position and sine to get the y position. You should get very used to those relationships. In Flash, almost any time you are talking about x, you should immediately think cosine, and you should almost always connect y with sine. In fact, spend as much time as you need to fully understand that last bit of code. It is going to be one of the most useful tools in your ActionScript animation toolbox.

Elliptical movement

While circles are lovely, sometimes a perfect circle isn't exactly what you need. What you might be looking for is more of an oval or ellipse. The problem is with the radius. It makes the ranges of the x motion and y motion the same, which is why you get a circle.

To make a more oval shape, all you need to do is use different values for the radius when you calculate the x and y positions. I call them radiusX and radiusY. This is probably a horrendous choice of terminology from a strict geometric viewpoint, but it is simple, straightforward, and easy to remember and visualize. So I stick by my variable names. And here's how they fit in, as I've included in Oval.as:

```
package
{
    import flash.display.Sprite;
    import flash.events.Event;

    public class Oval extends Sprite {
        private var ball:Ball;
        private var angle:Number = 0;
        private var centerX:Number = 200;
        private var centerY:Number = 200;
        private var radiusX:Number = 200;
        private var radiusY:Number = 100;
        private var speed:Number = .1;

        public function Oval()    {
            init();
        }
        private function init():void {
            ball = new Ball();
            addChild(ball);
            ball.x = 0;
            addEventListener(Event.ENTER_FRAME, onEnterFrame);
        }
        public function onEnterFrame(event:Event):void {
            ball.x = centerX + Math.sin(angle) * radiusX;
            ball.y = centerY + Math.cos(angle) * radiusY;
            angle += speed;
        }
    }
}
```

Here, radiusX is 200, which means that the ball is going to go back and forth 200 pixels from centerX as it circles around. radiusY is 100, which means it will go up and down only 100 pixels each way. So, now you have an uneven circle, which is not a circle at all anymore, but an ellipse.

Pythagorean Theorem

Finally, we come to the Pythagorean Theorem. I'm not sure how officially this is a part of trigonometry, but it's pretty interwoven with the subject and is another formula that you will use a lot. So, this is the best place to put it.

Pythagorus was a Greek guy who lived a long time ago. That's your history lesson. Simply stated, his theorem says A squared + B squared = C squared. Now, if you know what the theorem is all about beforehand, that communicates it perfectly. Otherwise, it sounds like some kind of bizarre nursery rhyme. So let's explore it in more depth.

A more descriptive statement of the theorem is the sum of the squares of the two legs of a right triangle is equal to the square of the hypotenuse. That's a mouthful. Say you have the triangle shown in Figure 3-21.

The two legs, A and B, have measurements of 3 and 4. The hypotenuse, C, measures 5. Mr. Pythagorus tells us that $A^2 + B^2 = C^2$. Let's test it. Plug in the numbers, and you have $3^2 + 4^2 = 5^2$, which works out to 9 + 16 = 25. Yup, that works out pretty well.

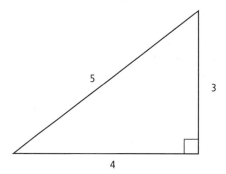

Figure 3-21. A right triangle

Now, if you happen to know all three measurements like that, the Pythagorean Theorem is nothing more than an interesting relationship. But, if you know only two of the measurements, it becomes a powerful tool to quickly find the third. In Flash, the most common situation is where you know the lengths of the two legs and you want to know the hypotenuse. Specifically, you want to find the distance between two points.

Distance between two points

Say you have two sprites on stage and you want to find out how far apart they are. This is the most common use of the Pythagorean Theorem in Flash.

What do you have to work with? You have the x and y positions of each of sprite. Let's call the position of one x1, y1, and the other x2, y2. So, you have a situation like the one illustrated in Figure 3-22.

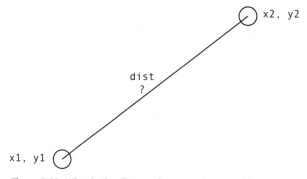

Figure 3-22. What is the distance between the two objects?

If you have been particularly brainwashed during the reading of this chapter, you will already see a right triangle forming in the diagram in Figure 3-22, with the distance line as the hypotenuse. In Figure 3-23, I finish it off for you and add some actual numbers.

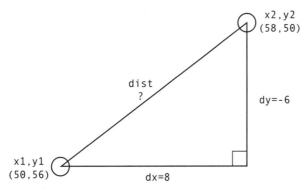

Figure 3-23. Turn it into a right triangle.

Here, dx is the distance between the two sprites on the x axis, and dy is the distance on the y axis. You can now easily find dx by subtracting x1 from x2: 58 – 50 = 8. Similarly, you subtract y1 from y2 to get dy, which is 6. Now, per Pythagorus, if you square both of these and add them together, you'll get the square of the distance. In other words $-6^2 + 8^2 = dist^2$. Breaking that down, you get 36 + 64, or 100 = $dist^2$. Basic algebra says that you can reduce that to $\sqrt{100}$ = dist. And from that, you can easily figure out that the distance between the two clips is 10.

Now, let's abstract that a bit so you have a formula that you can use in any situation. Given two points, x1, y1 and x2, y2, you figure the x distance and y distance, square them, sum them, and take the square root. Here it is in ActionScript:

```
dx = x2 - x1;
dy = y2 - y1;
dist = Math.sqrt(dx*dx + dy*dy);
```

Pay particular attention to these lines. They make up the next big tool in your toolbox. The first two lines just get the distances on each axis. Note that if you are just interested in the distance, and won't be using dx and dy to calculate any angles, it doesn't really matter whether you subtract x1 from x2 or vice versa. The final result for dist will always be positive. The last line performs three steps in one shot: It squares each of the values, adds them, and finds the square root. For clarity, you could break down those steps into separate statements. But once you are familiar with that single line, it will be crystal clear to you. You'll see it and think "Pythagorean Theorem." And then, you'll really know you are brainwashed.

Now, let's try it in the real world. The next document class, Distance.as, creates a couple of sprites, randomly positions them, and then calculates and traces out the distance between them.

```
package
{
    import flash.display.Sprite;

    public class Distance extends Sprite {

        public function Distance()    {
            init();
        }
        private function init():void {
            var sprite1:Sprite = new Sprite();
            addChild(sprite1);
            sprite1.graphics.beginFill(0x000000);
            sprite1.graphics.drawRect(-2, -2, 4, 4);
            sprite1.graphics.endFill();
            sprite1.x = Math.random() * stage.stageWidth;
            sprite1.y = Math.random() * stage.stageHeight;

            var sprite2:Sprite = new Sprite();
            addChild(sprite2);
            sprite2.graphics.beginFill(0xff0000);
            sprite2.graphics.drawRect(-2, -2, 4, 4);
            sprite2.graphics.endFill();
            sprite2.x = Math.random() * stage.stageWidth;
            sprite2.y = Math.random() * stage.stageHeight;

            var dx:Number = sprite1.x - sprite2.x;
            var dy:Number = sprite1.y - sprite2.y;
            var dist:Number = Math.sqrt(dx * dx + dy * dy);
            trace(dist);
        }
    }
}
```

Compile the movie, and you'll get the distance between the two sprites. Each time you run it, the two sprites will be in different positions. It shouldn't matter if one is to the right, left, top, or bottom of the other. You'll always get a positive value for the distance.

OK, that's interesting, but not very dynamic. Just to show you that you can do this in real time, and that it isn't limited to sprites or movie clips, try the next document class, MouseDistance.as:

```
package
{
    import flash.display.Sprite;
    import flash.events.MouseEvent;
    import flash.text.TextField;

    public class MouseDistance extends Sprite {
        private var sprite1:Sprite;
        private var textField:TextField;
```

```
    public function MouseDistance()    {
        init();
    }
    private function init():void {
        sprite1 = new Sprite();
        addChild(sprite1);
        sprite1.graphics.beginFill(0x000000);
        sprite1.graphics.drawRect(-2, -2, 4, 4);
        sprite1.graphics.endFill();
        sprite1.x = stage.stageWidth / 2;
        sprite1.y = stage.stageHeight / 2;

        textField = new TextField();
        addChild(textField);
        stage.addEventListener(MouseEvent.MOUSE_MOVE, onMouseMove);
    }
    public function onMouseMove(event:MouseEvent):void {
        graphics.clear();
        graphics.lineStyle(1, 0, 1);
        graphics.moveTo(sprite1.x, sprite1.y);
        graphics.lineTo(mouseX, mouseY);
        var dx:Number = sprite1.x - mouseX;
        var dy:Number = sprite1.y - mouseY;
        var dist:Number = Math.sqrt(dx * dx + dy * dy);
        textField.text = dist.toString();
    }
  }
}
```

Here, dx and dy are calculated by subtracting the current mouse position from sprite1's position. The dist value is thrown into a text field, and a line is drawn from the movie clip to the mouse location (you'll find more on the drawing API in the next chapter). Finally, the whole thing is put in an onMouseMove handler, to update it each time the mouse moves.

Test the file and move your mouse around. A line will connect it to the movie clip, and you'll get a constant readout of the length of that line.

In later chapters, when I talk about collision detection, you'll find out about some weaknesses with the built-in hit testing methods, and see how you can use the Pythagorean Theorem formula to create a distance-based method of collision detection. It is also very useful in calculating forces like gravity or springs, where the force between two objects is proportional to the distance between them.

Important formulas in this chapter

Look at this. You have a brand-new shiny toolbox, and already you have more than a half-dozen tools to put in it. The full set of tools will also appear Chapter 19, but let's look at what you've added so far. Note that I've kept these formulas as simple and abstract as possible, not including data types or variable declarations. It's up to you to work the formulas into your own classes using all the proper syntax required for the situation.

Calculate basic trigonometric functions:

```
sine of angle = opposite / hypotenuse
cosine of angle = adjacent / hypotenuse
tangent of angle = opposite / adjacent
```

Convert radians to degrees and degrees to radians:

```
radians = degrees * Math.PI / 180
degrees = radians * 180 / Math.PI
```

Rotate to the mouse (or any point):

```
// substitute mouseX, mouseY with the x, y point to rotate to
dx = mouseX - sprite.x;
dy = mouseY - sprite.y;
sprite.rotation = Math.atan2(dy, dx) * 180 / Math.PI;
```

Create waves:

```
// assign value to x, y or other property of sprite or movie clip,
// use as drawing coordinates, etc.
public function onEnterFrame(event:Event){
   value = center + Math.sin(angle) * range;
   angle += speed;
}
```

Create circles:

```
// assign position to x and y of sprite or movie clip,
// use as drawing coordinates, etc.
public function onEnterFrame(event:Event){
   xposition = centerX + Math.cos(angle) * radius;
   yposition = centerY + Math.sin(angle) * radius;
   angle += speed;
}
```

Create ovals:

```
// assign position to x and y of sprite or movie clip,
// use as drawing coordinates, etc.
public function onEnterFrame(event:Event){
   xposition = centerX + Math.cos(angle) * radiusX;
   yposition = centerY + Math.sin(angle) * radiusY;
   angle += speed;
}
```

Get the distance between two points:

```
// points are x1, y1 and x2, y2
// can be sprite / movie clip positions, mouse coordinates, etc.
dx = x2 - x1;
dy = y2 - y1;
dist = Math.sqrt(dx*dx + dy*dy);
```

Of course, if I just wanted to publish a list of formulas, I could have saved myself a lot of time and done just that. So look these over and make sure you fully understand how each one works. If you have any questions, go back to the point in the chapter where it was introduced, experiment with it, and research it more if you need to, until you can really think with the concept.

Summary

This chapter covered nearly all the trigonometry you will need for animating in ActionScript. There is one principle, called The Law of Cosines, that I left out for now, as it is a lot more complex and deals with triangles that are not right triangles (they have no angle measuring 90 degrees). If you are now addicted to trig and just can't get enough, you can jump ahead to Chapter 14, which covers inverse kinematics, where trig really comes in handy.

But, for now, you know about sine, cosine, and tangent and their opposites: arcsine, arccosine, and arctangent, as well as the ActionScript methods to calculate each one.

Best of all, you got some hands-on experience using most of them in ActionScript, with some of the most common real-life uses of them. As you move through the book, you'll see many more ways in which these techniques become useful. But you now have a solid footing with the concepts, and when you come across those examples, you should have no problem understanding them or how they work.

The next chapter covers some of the more common rendering techniques for getting graphics on the screen, including the all-important drawing API. As you go through that chapter, see if you can find ways to use the rendering methods to visualize some of the trig functions you've learned here. I'm sure you'll have no trouble creating some beautiful pictures or animations with trigonometry.

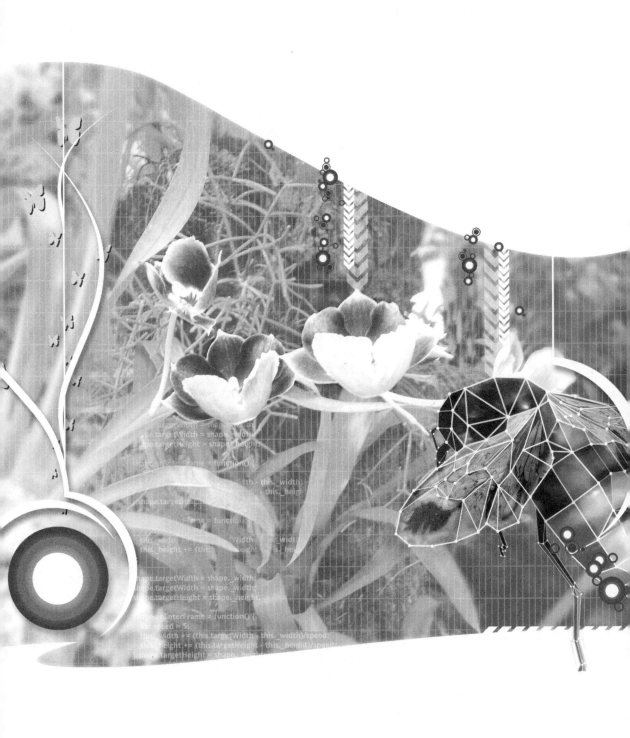

Chapter 4

RENDERING TECHNIQUES

What we'll cover in this chapter:

- Colors in Flash
- The drawing API
- Color transforms
- Filters
- Bitmap control
- Important formulas in this chapter

The graphics in the sample programs in the book so far have been drawn using a few simple drawing commands, and I've alluded to this mythical "drawing API" a few times. But for the most part I've just thrown the code at you without much explanation.

In this chapter, I'm going to dive into visual content creation in ActionScript. Specifically, I'm going to go over color in ActionScript and the drawing API, the ColorTransform class, filters, and the BitmapData class.

You'll be working with a lot of colors in this chapter, so let's cover that subject first.

Colors in Flash

In Flash, colors are specified as numbers. A color number can be anything from 0 to 16,777,215 for what is called 24-bit color. In case you are wondering about the significance of that number, it comes from the fact that there are 16,777,216 possible color values, which is $256 \times 256 \times 256$. Flash uses RGB color, meaning that every color is made up of a red, a green, and a blue component. Each of these component colors can have a value from 0 to 255. So, there are 256 possible shades each of red, green, and blue, resulting in the nearly 16.8 million colors.

This system is called 24-bit color because it takes eight bits—ones or zeros—to represent the number 256. Eight bits times three (red, green, blue) means it takes 24 bits to represent the 16.8 million possible colors. Additionally, there is a 32-bit color system, which I will cover shortly. This has an extra 8-bit number set aside for alpha, or transparency.

Now, since it's pretty tough to visualize what color 11,273,634 might look like, developers often tend to resort to another system of representing such numbers: hexadecimal. If you've used color values in HTML, this is nothing new to you, but let's cover the basics anyway.

Using hexadecimal color values

Hexadecimal, or hex for short, is a base 16 system. In other words, each digit can be from 0 to 15, rather than 0 to 9 as in the usual base 10 system. We don't have any single digits to represent the numbers 10 to 15, so we borrow the first six letters of the alphabet, A to F. So, each digit in a hex number can be from 0 to F. (In Flash, hex values are not case-sensitive, so you can use A through F or a through f.) To signal that we are using a hex number in HTML, we prefix it with #. In ActionScript, as with many other languages, we use the prefix 0x. For example, the number 0xA is equal to decimal 10, 0xF is equal to 15, and 0x10 is equal to 16.

In decimal, each digit is worth ten times the digit to its right. In other words, the number 243 means two times 100, four times 10, and three times 1. In hex, each digit is worth 16 times its right-hand neighbor. For example, 0x2B3 means two times 256, B (or eleven) times 16, and three times 1.

For 24-bit colors, this goes all the way up to 0xFFFFFF, which, if you do the math, is magically equal to 16,777,215. Furthermore, those six hex digits can be broken down into three pairs. The first pair represents the red component, the second pair represents the green, and the last two digits represent blue. This is often symbolized as 0xRRGGBB. (You would never put R, G, or B into an actual hex number; this is merely a symbolic way of telling you what color channel each digit controls.)

Remember that each component color can have a value anywhere from 0 to 255, or in hex, 0x00 to 0xFF. Thus, the color red can be represented as 0xFF0000, which denotes full red, zero green, and zero blue. Likewise, 0x0000FF is completely blue.

If you took the earlier mentioned value of 11,273,634, and converted it to hex (I'll show you an easy way to do that in a minute), you'd get 0xAC05A2. You can easily break this down into red = AC, green = 05, blue = A2. Seeing that red and blue are rather high, and green is almost nothing, you can guess that this color is rather purplish, something you'd never be able to tell from the decimal value.

Note that it doesn't matter which number format you use in ActionScript. For any function that takes a color value, you can use either decimal or hex. The numbers 11273634 and 0xAC05A2 are exactly the same thing to Flash. It's just that one is more readable to us poor humans.

You might be wondering how to convert between the two formats. Well, converting from hex to decimal is pretty easy. Just trace the value. The trace function will convert to decimal for you.

```
trace(0xAC05A2);
```

One way to get hex is to use the toString(16) method, like so:

```
trace((11273634).toString(16));
```

This will trace ac05a2. If you are going to use that value somewhere, don't forget to add the 0x.

Transparency and 32-bit color

As mentioned earlier, in addition to 24-bit color, there is 32-bit color, which contains an extra 8 bits for specifying transparency. Like degrees and radians (covered in Chapter 3), AS 3 uses a bit of a mish mash of 24- and 32-bit colors. The drawing API in AS 3 is largely built on the drawing API that was introduced in Flash MX (Flash 6). Generally the drawing API functions take an extra parameter to specify transparency, so they continue to use 24-bit colors. The BitmapData class, on the other hand, was introduced in Flash 8 and ushered in 32-bit colors. If there is any doubt about which color system a particular function uses, just check the ActionScript language reference.

I covered the fact that you could create 24-bit colors as hexadecimal numbers in the format 0xRRGGBB. Likewise, 32-bit colors are expressed as hexadecimal numbers in the format 0xAARRGGBB, where AA stands for alpha or transparency. Thus, 0xFFFFFFFF creates an opaque white color, 0x00FFFFFF creates a completely transparent white color, and 0x80FFFFFF creates an approximately 50% transparent white color.

New number types: int and uint

In prior versions of ActionScript, there was only one type of number. It was represented by the type Number, which could be a positive or negative integer or floating-point value (or zero). The Number type is still with us, and you are free to use it just like you always have. But there are now a couple of additional types that you can use to make your code clearer.

The first new type is int. This type can hold a positive or negative integer or zero. If you try to assign a floating-point number to a variable declared as an int, the decimal part will be truncated. For example, if you assign an int variable the value 1.9, it will wind up holding the value 1. Thus, an int should only be used when you are sure a variable is only ever going to be used for integers. One area ints are often used is as counting variables in for loops. In the following snippet, the variable i will never be a floating-point number, so it makes sense to type it as an int.

```
for(var i:int = 0; i < 100; i++) {
    // do something in here!
}
```

The next new type is uint. This stands for *unsigned integer*. "Unsigned" means that it does not have a plus or minus sign, and therefore is always positive. Colors are almost always stored as uints in AS 3, and this is due to the introduction of 32-bit colors. This is because an unsigned integer can hold a much larger positive value than a regular (signed) integer. Both ints and uints are stored internally as 32-bit numbers, which can hold just over four billion values. But an int uses one of those bits to specify the sign (plus or minus) of the number. So what you really get is a 31-bit number (just over two billion values) that can be marked positive or negative.

So a positive 32-bit color value is just plain too big to fit in an int! What happens if you try? Test the following code and see:

```
var color1:int = 0xffffffff;
trace(color1);
var color2:uint = 0xffffffff;
trace(color2);
```

The value 0xFFFFFFFF is equal to 4,294,967,295 in decimal. Since this is too big to fit in an int, it "rolls over" and becomes −1! Certainly not the result you'd expect. If you use a uint, though, it comes out just fine.

Therefore, because color values will always be positive, and may need to go beyond what an int can hold, we use uints to store them.

Combining colors

A common question is how to combine three red, green, and blue values to form a valid overall color value. Say you have three variables, red, green, and blue. Each of them holds a value from 0 to 255, and you want to create a valid color value. Here's the formula to do just that:

```
color24 = red << 16 | green << 8 | blue;
```

If you also have an alpha value, you can create a 32-bit number with this formula:

```
color32 = alpha << 24 | red << 16 | green << 8 | blue;
```

This makes use of two bitwise operators you may not have seen before. *Bitwise operators* work on numbers on a binary level—on ones and zeros.

Sticking with 24-bit colors for a moment, if you were to list the bits of a color value, you would have a string of 24 ones and zeros. Breaking up the hex 0xRRGGBB into binary, you have this:

RRRRRRRRGGGGGGGGBBBBBBBB

You see eight bits for red, eight for green, and eight for blue. This makes sense, because eight bits are equal to 256.

In the color combination formula, the first bitwise operator is <<, which is the bitwise left shift operator. This shifts the binary representation of the value a number of places to the left. Say you have a red value of 0xFF or 255. This can be represented in binary as follows:

11111111

Shifting it 16 places to the left gives you this:

111111110000000000000000

As a 24-bit color number, this is red. Seen in hex, this is 0xFF0000—again, full red.

Now, say you have a green value of 0x55 (85 decimal). In binary, it looks like this:

01010101

Shift this eight places, and you get this:

00000000**01010101**00000000

So, the original eight bits now fall completely in the green range.

Finally, you have a blue value of 0xF3 (243 decimal), which is this in binary:

11110011

Since this already all falls into the blue range, you don't need to touch it.

Now, you have three values for red, green, and blue:

111111110000000000000000
00000000**01010101**00000000
0000000000000000**11110011**

You could simply add them together to get a single 24-bit number, but there's a quicker and cooler way: Use bitwise OR, the | symbol. This compares the digits of two numbers on a binary level and says if either digit is equal to one, the result will be one. If both digits are zero, the result is zero. You can OR the red, green, and blue values together to say, "If this OR this OR this is one, the result is one." And you get this result:

111111110101010111110011

If you convert that to hex, you get 0xFF55F3. Of course, you never see the bits or deal with the ones or zeros at all. You'd just type this:

```
var color24:Number = 0xFF << 16 | 0x55 << 8 | 0xF3;
```

Or, if you are working with decimal values, you could use this form:

```
var color24:Number = 255 << 16 | 85 << 8 | 243;
```

Again, Flash doesn't care whether you use hex or decimal.

You could do something similar by converting each of the red, green, and blue values to a hex string, concatenating them into one long string, and converting that back to a number. But if you've ever tried it, you'll know that you get into some complicated and slow string logic. Conversely, bitwise operators are probably the fastest operators in ActionScript, since they work on such a low level.

Jumping back to 32-bit numbers, it's exactly the same concept. You just take your 8-bit alpha channel and shift it left, 24 bits. For example, if we were to take the 32-bit color number, 0xFFFF55F3, and shift the alpha value to the left 24 places, we'd have this:

1111111111111110101010111110011

The first eight digits represent the transparency level. The rest are the red, green, and blue values, just like before.

Extracting component colors

Finally, you might also need to take a color value and extract the various component values from it. Let's go the opposite way and take the value 0xFFFF55F3 and try to get the red, green, and blue values from it. Here's the next formula for your toolbox, again, first for 24-bit colors:

```
red = color24 >> 16;
green = color24 >> 8 & 0xFF;
blue = color24 & 0xFF;
```

Let's take the lines one at a time. First, you've probably guessed that >> is the bitwise right shift operator, which shifts the bits so many places to the right. You can't have fractional bits, so any bits that are shifted too far right are just discarded. So, begin with red:

111111110101010111110011

When you shift the color value 16 places to the right, it becomes this:

11111111

Or it's simply 0xFF, or 255.

For green, shift it eight places, and you get this:

1111111101010101

Here, you've knocked the blue values out, but you still have the red ones hanging around. This is where you use another bitwise operator, &, also called AND. Like OR, this compares two values, but says, "If this digit AND this digit are both one, then the result is one. If either one is zero, the result is zero." You compare it to 0xFF, so you are comparing these two numbers:

1111111101010101
0000000011111111

Since all the red digits are being compared with zero, they will all result in zero. Only the digits that are both one will fall through, so you get this:

```
0000000001010101
```

With blue, you don't need to shift anything, just AND it with 0xFF, which will preserve the blue and knock out the red and green.

For 32-bit colors, you can use the same technique, but you need a slight change:

```
alpha = color32 >> 24;
red = color32 >> 16 & 0xFF;
green = color32 >> 8 & 0xFF;
blue = color32 & 0xFF;
```

Here, when getting the alpha value, shift it 24 places to the right. You still shift it 16 places for red, but you then need to AND it with 0xFF in order to knock out the alpha value. The green and blue lines are the same.

Now that you know more than you ever hoped to know about colors in Flash, let's start using them.

The Drawing API

Just so I don't lose you, let me tell you right off the bat what an API is. It stands for application programming interface. Generally, API refers to a set of methods and properties that you can use in your program to access a certain set of related behaviors and properties. The drawing API refers to the properties and methods that allow you to draw lines, curves, fills, gradient fills, and so on with ActionScript. This API has surprisingly few methods, but there is a lot to know about them and a lot of neat tricks you can do with them.

The drawing API was introduced in Flash MX. Prior to that, all graphical content had to be drawn in the authoring environment. With the drawing API, a lot more became possible.

Because of the drawing limitations in earlier versions of Flash, people thought up ingenious ways to do dynamic drawing. One of the best examples was the 45-degree line movie clip. This consisted of a single movie clip in the library, set to export so that it could be attached at runtime or placed on stage somewhere so it could be duplicated. It contained a simple line drawn from 0, 0 to 100, 100. At runtime, to draw a line between any two points, you would create a new instance of this line clip, position it on the first point, and scale it so that it fit between the first and second points. While this technique had some drawbacks, such as not allowing for fills or different widths of lines, it was surprisingly efficient, and was the way that almost all dynamic drawing was done prior to Flash MX.

Beginning with Flash MX, you got the following methods:

- `clear()`
- `lineStyle(width, color, alpha)`
- `moveTo(x, y)`
- `lineTo(x, y)`
- `curveTo(x1, y1, x2, y2)`
- `beginFill(color, alpha)`
- `endFill()`
- `beginGradientFill(fillType, colors, alphas, ratios, matrix)`

In Flash 8, several enhancements were added to the `lineStyle` and `beginGradientFill` methods. This version also introduced the `beginBitmapFill` and `lineGradientStyle` methods. AS 3 added several very useful methods:

- `drawCircle(x, y, radius)`
- `drawEllipse(x, y, width, height)`
- `drawRect(x, y, width, height)`
- `drawRoundRect(x, y, width, height, ellipseWidth, ellipseHeight)`

As this is just a quick overview, I'm not going to go into every method in detail, but I'll cover the basics and you can check the documentation for any additional details you might need.

The graphics object

In earlier versions of Flash, the drawing API methods were methods of the `MovieClip` class, and could be called directly from a movie clip instance, like this:

```
myMovieClip.lineTo(100, 100);
```

Now, both sprites and movie clips can access the drawing API. But it is done a bit differently. Now, sprites and movie clips have a property called `graphics`, which is used to access all the drawing API methods. So instead of accessing the drawing functions directly like the example just shown, you would do it like this:

```
mySprite.graphics.lineTo(100, 100);
```

Now let's look at some of these methods and see some examples of their basic use.

Removing drawing with clear

`clear` is the simplest method of them all. It simply removes any previously drawn lines, curves, or fills from the sprite or movie clip. Note that it will affect *only* graphics that were created using other drawing API methods. In other words, if you drew a shape on stage in the authoring environment, calling `clear()` at runtime would not affect that shape.

Use of the clear method has an important and somewhat unexpected effect on drawing efficiency. In the drawing API, it happens that the more you draw in a particular movie clip, the slower it goes. For a few dozen shapes, the slowdown is not noticeable, but little by little, each new shape takes longer and longer to draw. Even if the new shape completely covers and obliterates everything else, the vector information for those older shapes is still there and will be completely redrawn each time. This can be important in animation, where you are redrawing almost the same thing over and over. Using clear handles this by completely removing all prior vector information from the clip.

Setting line appearance with lineStyle

With the lineStyle(width, color, alpha) method, you set up the appearance of all subsequently drawn lines. This command has no effect on previously drawn lines. In fact, other than clearing them, or drawing something else on top of them, there is no way of affecting or changing lines or fills that have been drawn. Once they are there, that's that.

The parameters I've listed are the ones you will use most often. There are additional optional parameters for pixel hinting, scale mode, caps, joints, and mitres. If you need to tweak those things, they are available for you, but most of the time, you'll probably just need the things I've shown. These parameters are pretty self-explanatory, but let's review them quickly:

- width: The width of the line in pixels. The only valid values are zero or positive integers. Although you can pass in decimal values, they will be rounded off to the nearest positive integer. If you pass in zero or a negative value, Flash will draw a 1-pixel thick line that will not scale. This is synonymous to choosing "hairline" in the line properties of the Properties panel in the Flash IDE.
- color: The color you want the line to be. This is in a 24-bit number in decimal or hex format, as described earlier in this chapter.
- alpha: The transparency of the lines. This can be from 0.0 to 1.0, representing a percent of opacity. A setting of 1.0 is obviously fully opaque, and 0.0 is fully transparent or invisible. Note that this is different from the AS 2 version, which used values from 0 to 100.

Even these parameters are optional. You can say lineStyle(1) and get a 1-pixel thick, black line, with all the other default parameters. Actually, even the first parameter is optional. If you leave off the width, just calling lineStyle(), the line style will be cleared, and you'll get an invisible line. This is the same as if you had started issuing drawing commands without setting the line style: You won't see any lines.

Another little fact that often trips people up is that the clear method clears not only the current drawing, but the current line style settings as well. If you set up a custom style, draw some lines into a movie clip, and then clear them, you'll need to reset your line style before drawing anything else. Otherwise, you'll be back to drawing invisible lines again. Calling clear will also move the drawing cursor back to 0, 0. You'll understand this a bit more after reading the following entry.

Drawing lines with lineTo and moveTo

There are a couple of different ways to implement line drawing in a graphics language. One is to have a line command that takes a starting point and an ending point, and draws a line between them. The other way is to have a lineTo command that takes a single point: the ending point of the line. This is how ActionScript works. So, if you're drawing a line *to* some point, where are you drawing it *from*?

Well, if you haven't drawn anything yet, you'll be drawing from the point 0, 0 of whatever graphics object you are drawing into. Say you just type this line in a movie:

```
lineTo(100, 100);
```

You'll see a line going from the top-left corner (0, 0), to 100, 100 (assuming you've set a line style). After you've drawn at least one line, the ending point for that line will be the starting point for the next line. Finally, you can use the moveTo method to specify a new starting point for the next line.

Think of the drawing API as a robot holding a pen on a piece of paper. When you start, the pen is at 0, 0. When you tell it to draw a line to a point, it just moves the pen across the paper to that new point. For each new line, it just moves from wherever it left off, to the next new point. The moveTo method is like saying, "OK, now lift up the pen and move it to this next point." Although issuing a moveTo command does not result in any new graphic content, it will affect how the next graphics command is carried out. Unless you specifically want to draw your first line from 0, 0, you will generally call moveTo as your first drawing command to place the drawing API "pen" where you want to begin.

You now have enough commands under your belt to do something serious. Let's create a simple drawing application. This program will rely completely on the drawing API for its content. Here's the document class:

```
package
{
    import flash.display.Sprite;
    import flash.events.MouseEvent;

    public class DrawingApp extends Sprite
    {
        public function DrawingApp()
        {
            init();
        }

        private function init():void
        {
            graphics.lineStyle(1);
            stage.addEventListener(MouseEvent.MOUSE_DOWN, onMouseDown);
            stage.addEventListener(MouseEvent.MOUSE_UP, onMouseUp);
        }

        private function onMouseDown(event:MouseEvent):void
        {
            graphics.moveTo(mouseX, mouseY);
            stage.addEventListener(MouseEvent.MOUSE_MOVE, onMouseMove);
        }

        private function onMouseUp(event:MouseEvent):void
        {
            stage.removeEventListener(MouseEvent.MOUSE_MOVE,
```

```
                                    onMouseMove);
        }

        private function onMouseMove(event:MouseEvent):void
        {
            graphics.lineTo(mouseX, mouseY);
        }
    }
}
```

You can find this file among the book's downloadable files (available from www.friendsofed.com) as DrawingApp.as. I'll go through it piece by piece. In addition to the drawing functions, this program makes pretty good use of event handlers (discussed in Chapter 2).

The class is based on the skeleton class found in Chapter 2, which you should be getting pretty used to by now. It first imports the MouseEvent class, as it will be using mouse events for everything. In the init method, the line style is set to a 1-pixel black line and event listeners are added for mouseDown and mouseUp.

Then there's the onMouseDown method. This gets called whenever the user presses a mouse button. Generally, this means the user wants to start drawing a line at the current mouse cursor position. Well, that's exactly what this function does. It puts the virtual pen down at the mouse location by calling moveTo and passing in the mouse coordinates. It then adds a listener for the mouseMove event.

At this point, every time the user moves the mouse, the onMouseMove method is called. And what does that do? Not too much, although it's the meat of the program. It just draws a line to the current mouse location.

Finally, there's the onMouseUp method. This removes the mouseMove handler so that no more drawing will happen.

OK, you have a neat little drawing program there. You could probably set up some simple controls to make it a full-featured drawing application without too much effort. Just create some variables for color and width, and create some buttons or other controls to change them, and call the lineStyle method again with the new values. Oh, and throw in a button that calls the clear method. I'm going to leave that as an exercise for you to do on your own, if you are interested. Meanwhile, I'm going to dive back into the rest of the drawing API.

Drawing curves with curveTo

The next drawing function, curveTo(x1, y1, x2, y2), starts off the same as lineTo, in that it begins its drawing at the point where the last drawing ended, at the point where the last moveTo command moved the pen to, or at 0, 0 if no drawing has been done yet. It also makes use of lineStyle in exactly the same way as moveTo. The only difference is the shape of the line drawn.

As you can see, curveTo takes two points. The first is a control point that affects the shape of the curve. The second is the ending point of the curve. The formula used is a standard formula for what is called a quadratic Bezier curve. This formula calculates a curve from one point to another, which curves toward the control point. Note that the curve will not *touch* the control point. It's more like the curve is attracted to it.

Let's see it in action, in the following document class, DrawingCurves.as:

```
package
{
    import flash.display.Sprite;
    import flash.events.MouseEvent;

    public class DrawingCurves extends Sprite
    {
        private var x0:Number = 100;
        private var y0:Number = 200;
        private var x1:Number;
        private var y1:Number;
        private var x2:Number = 300;
        private var y2:Number = 200;

        public function DrawingCurves()
        {
            init();
        }

        private function init():void
        {
            stage.addEventListener(MouseEvent.MOUSE_MOVE, onMouseMove);
        }

        private function onMouseMove(event:MouseEvent):void
        {
            x1 = mouseX;
            y1 = mouseY;
            graphics.clear();
            graphics.lineStyle(1);
            graphics.moveTo(x0, y0);
            graphics.curveTo(x1, y1, x2, y2);
        }
    }
}
```

Test the file and move your mouse around. The file uses two preset points for the beginning and ending points, and uses the mouse position for the control point. Notice that the curve never actually reaches the control point, but gets about halfway there.

Curving through the control point

Now, say you actually wanted to have the curve hit the control point. Well, here's another toolbox tip. You can use the following formula to calculate the actual control point so that the curve will go through the point you specify. Again, you'll be starting out with x0, y0 and x2, y2 as the end points, and x1, y1 as the control point. I'll call the point you want the curve to go through xt, yt (t for target). In other words, if you want the curve to be drawn through xt, yt, what x1, y1 do you need to use? Here's the formula:

```
x1 = xt * 2 - (x0 + x2) / 2;
y1 = yt * 2 - (y0 + y2) / 2;
```

Basically, you just multiply the target by two, and subtract the average of the starting and ending point. If you want, you can graph it all out and see exactly how it works. Or, you can just test it, see that it works, and have faith that it always will.

To see it in action, using the mouse coordinates as xt, yt, you just need to change two lines from the last document class. Change the lines

```
x1 = mouseX;
y1 = mouseY;
```

to the following:

```
x1 = mouseX * 2 - (x0 + x2) / 2;
y1 = mouseY * 2 - (y0 + y2) / 2;
```

Or you can just check out CurveThroughPoint.as, where I've done it for you.

Creating multiple curves

The next direction you're probably looking at going is creating multiple curves, where instead of a single curve, you have a long line that curves smoothly in several directions. First, I'll show you the wrong way of going about it, which is the way I originally tried it. Basically, you start out with a number of points, draw a curve from the first through the second to the third, then through the fourth to the fifth, then through the sixth to the seventh, and so on. Here it is in code (in document class MultiCurve1.as):

```
package
{
    import flash.display.Sprite;

    public class MultiCurves1 extends Sprite
    {
        private var numPoints:uint = 9;

        public function MultiCurves1()
        {
            init();
        }

        private function init():void
        {
            // first set up an array of random points
            var points:Array = new Array();
            for (var i:int = 0; i < numPoints; i++)
            {
                points[i] = new Object();
                points[i].x = Math.random() * stage.stageHeight;
                points[i].y = Math.random() * stage.stageHeight;
```

```
        }
graphics.lineStyle(1);

// now move to the first point
graphics.moveTo(points[0].x, points[0].y);

// and loop through each next successive pair
for (i = 1; i < numPoints; i += 2)
{
    graphics.curveTo(points[i].x, points[i].y,
                        points[i + 1].x, points[i + 1].y);
}
        }
    }
}
```

The first for loop in the init method just sets up an array of nine points. Each point is an object with an x and y property, and they are randomly thrown around the stage. Of course, in a real program, your points might not be random. I just used that method for quick setup.

Then the line style is set, and the pen is moved to the first point. The next for loop starts at one and increments by two each time, so it draws a curve through point one to point two, then through three to four, then through five to six, and then through seven to eight. The loop will stop there, which is perfect because point eight is the last one. You also might notice that there must be a minimum of three points, and the number of points must be odd.

It all seems fine until you test it. As shown in Figure 4-1, it doesn't look very curvy at all. In fact, it often looks a bit spiky. The problem is that there is no coordination between one curve and the next, except that they share a point.

Figure 4-1. Multiple curves, the wrong way. You can plainly see where one curve ends and the next begins.

You're going to have to plug in a few more points to make it work right. Here's the strategy: Between each set of two points, you need a new point that sits exactly in the middle. You then use these as the starting and ending points for each curve, and use the original points as the control points.

Figure 4-2 illustrates the solution. In the figure, the white dots are the original points, and the black dots are the in-between points. There are three curveTo methods here, which I've given different colors so you can see where they start and end. (Figure 4-2 is actually a screenshot from a file called multicurvedemo.fla, which you can download from this book's page on www.friendsofed.com.)

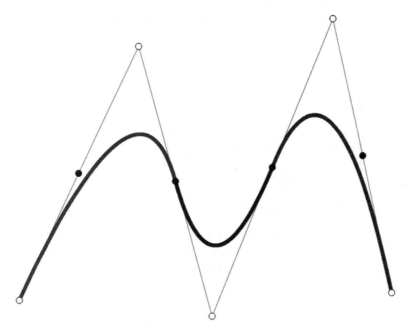

Figure 4-2. Multiple curves with midpoints

Notice in Figure 4-2 that the first and last midpoints are not used, and the first and last original points remain terminal points for the curves. You really need to make in-between points only for the second point up to the second-to-last point. Here's an updated version of the previous example for the random curves, document class MultiCurve2.as:

```
package
{
    import flash.display.Sprite;

    public class MultiCurves2 extends Sprite
    {
        private var numPoints:uint = 9;

        public function MultiCurves2()
        {
            init();
        }

        private function init():void
        {
```

```
// first set up an array of random points
var points:Array = new Array();
for (var i:int = 0; i < numPoints; i++)
{
    points[i] = new Object();
    points[i].x = Math.random() * stage.stageHeight;
    points[i].y = Math.random() * stage.stageHeight;
}
graphics.lineStyle(1);

// now move to the first point
graphics.moveTo(points[0].x, points[0].y);

// curve through the rest, stopping at each midpoint
for (i = 1; i < numPoints - 2; i ++)
{
    var xc:Number = (points[i].x + points[i + 1].x) / 2;
    var yc:Number = (points[i].y + points[i + 1].y) / 2;
    graphics.curveTo(points[i].x, points[i].y, xc, yc);
}
// curve through the last two points
graphics.curveTo(points[i].x, points[i].y, points[i+1].x,
                 points[i+1].y);
        }
    }
}
```

Note that in the new code, the for loop starts at 1 and ends at points.length - 2. This prevents it from processing the first and last pairs of points. What it does is create a new x, y point, which is the average of the next two points in the array. Then it draws a curve through the next array point, to the new average point. When the loop ends, the index, i, will still be pointing to the second-to-last element. Thus, you can draw a curve through that to the last point.

This time, you will come up with a nice smooth shape, rather than those spikes, as shown in Figure 4-3. Also note that you are not limited to an odd number of original points anymore. As long as you start with at least three points, you'll be fine.

As a bit of a variation on a theme, the following code, document class MultiCurve3.as, creates a closed curve using the same technique. Basically, it computes an initial midpoint, which is the average of the first and last points, and moves to that. Then it loops through all the rest, figuring midpoints for each one, finally drawing its last curve back to the initial midpoint.

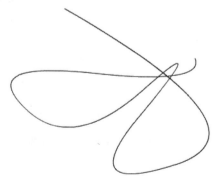

Figure 4-3. Smooth multiple curves

```
package
{
    import flash.display.Sprite;

    public class MultiCurves3 extends Sprite
    {
      private var numPoints:uint = 9;

      public function MultiCurves3()
      {
          init();
      }

      private function init():void
      {
          var points:Array = new Array();
          for (var i:int = 0; i < numPoints; i++)
          {
              points[i] = new Object();
              points[i].x = Math.random() * stage.stageHeight;
              points[i].y = Math.random() * stage.stageHeight;
          }

          // find the first midpoint and move to it
          var xc1:Number = (points[0].x + points[numPoints - 1].x) / 2;
          var yc1:Number = (points[0].y + points[numPoints - 1].y) / 2;
          graphics.lineStyle(1);
          graphics.moveTo(xc1, yc1);

          // curve through the rest, stopping at midpoints
          for (i = 0; i < numPoints - 1; i ++)
          {
              var xc:Number = (points[i].x + points[i + 1].x) / 2;
              var yc:Number = (points[i].y + points[i + 1].y) / 2;
              graphics.curveTo(points[i].x, points[i].y, xc, yc);
          }

          // curve through the last point, back to the first midpoint
          graphics.curveTo(points[i].x, points[i].y, xc1, yc1);
      }
    }
}
```

Figure 4-4 shows the result.

Figure 4-4. Multiple closed curves

Creating shapes with beginFill and endFill

The beginFill(color, alpha) method is so simple that there's not really too much to say about it. One thing worth noting, though, is that like lineStyle, the alpha value is now specified in values from 0.0 to 1.0, rather than 0 to 100. It is also optional, and will default to 1.0. You can issue a beginFill command almost any time during the process of drawing. Flash will compute a shape beginning with wherever the drawing location happens to be and ending wherever the drawing location is when the endFill command is issued or, if it never is, wherever the location is when the code completes for that frame and the frame is rendered. Generally, though, the sequence is as follows:

- moveTo
- lineStyle (if any)
- beginFill
- A series of lineTo and curveTo methods, ending at the original point moved to
- endFill

Actually, you can use the first three methods in just about any order without affecting what is drawn. You don't need to specify a line style. Remember that if you do not specify a line style, you get an invisible line, which is perfectly valid for drawing fills. It's also fine to draw both at the same time.

If you do not draw a line back to the original point from which you started, Flash will draw it for you in order to close the shape as soon as you call endFill. This final line will be drawn with whatever line style is present at the time you call endFill. However, it is definitely a good practice to get into the habit of finishing your own shapes. Not only are you guaranteed that the last line will be drawn even if Adobe decides to change that particular behavior, but another person who looks at your code later will know that you actually did intend to draw the shape.

Go ahead and play around with drawing fills. You can even use the closed curve example from the previous section (MultiCurve3.as), as that is already generating a closed shape. Just throw in a beginFill statement anywhere before the first curveTo—say, beginFill(0xff00ff);, which will create a bright purple fill—and finish off the code with endFill();.

If you did this, I'm sure you noticed that where sections of the curve cross over itself, the fill kind of disappears. There's not much you can do about that, but for the most part, you'll probably be drawing shapes that don't intersect like that anyway. On the other hand, once you get used to how it works, you can use that behavior to create some interesting shapes.

Creating gradient fills with beginGradientFill

Now we come to the monster function of the drawing API: beginGradientFill(fillType, colors, alphas, ratios, matrix). Like lineStyle, this method has a few additional optional parameters—spreadMethod, interpolationMethod, and focalPointRatio. These can be used to fine-tune the properties of the gradient, but in most simple cases they aren't really necessary and won't be discussed here. In many senses, this works in the same way as beginFill; it has the same quirks and behaviors, and you always end it with the same old endFill. The big difference is in how the fill looks. I feel like I shouldn't have to say that beginGradientFill creates a gradient fill, but then again, I feel like I'd be leaving something out if I *didn't* say it. So there you go.

A gradient fill is basically a fill of at least two colors. One part of the shape starts out with one color, and it slowly blends into another color, perhaps moving through one or several other predefined colors on its way.

Specifying the fill type

You can create two kinds of gradient fills: linear and radial. In a linear fill, the gradient of colors lies along a line from one point to another. By default, that line goes left to right, but you can make it go up and down or at any other angle. Figure 4-5 shows a few examples of linear fills.

Figure 4-5. Linear fills

In order to see a linear fill, you need at least two different colors. If that's all you specify, the fill will blend from the first to the second. If you specify more colors, the fill will blend smoothly from the first, to the second, to the third, and so on until it hits the last one.

Figure 4-6.
A radial fill

A radial fill works with pretty much all the same parameters that a linear fill uses, but interprets them a bit differently, creating a gradient that starts in the center of the space you define and radiates outward in all directions, creating a circle or oval. The first color you specify will be used as the center of the circle, and the final color will be the outline of the circle. The only item that is not needed is the angle. Figure 4-6 shows an example of a radial fill.

So, for the beginGradientFill(fillType, colors, alphas, ratios, matrix) method, the first parameter is fillType. That's pretty simple. It's a string that can contain one of two values: "linear" or "radial". You get what you ask for. Similar to the event types you saw in Chapter 3, fill types are now frozen into static properties of the flash.display.GradientType class, to avoid any misspellings. So, rather than typing the strings, you can (and should) import the GradientType class and type GradientType.LINEAR or GradientType.RADIAL.

Setting the colors, alphas, and ratios

Along with the colors parameter—to specify the colors, of course—you must also specify the position of each color in the fill by assigning it a number from 0 to 255, where 0 is the start of the fill and 255 is the end. These numbers, one for each color, are known as the ratios of the fill. Thus, if you wanted to make a two-color fill, you'd probably specify 0 and 255 as the ratios. To make an even blend of three colors, you could say 0, 128, 255. This would put the second color exactly in the middle of the other two. If you did something like 0, 20, 255, the first color would almost immediately blend into the second, and then very slowly blend into the third. Remember that these are not pixel values, but fractions of 255.

You must also specify the transparency of each color in the blend. This is known as alpha and can be from 0.0 to 1.0. Again, note the change from AS 2, where it was 0 to 100. If you don't want any transparency, you can make each alpha 1.0. If you set the first alpha to 1.0 and the last to 0.0, the gradient will not only blend the colors, but also smoothly fade out. This can be useful for creating soft shadows (though you'd probably have better luck with a drop shadow filter).

Each one of these arguments is an array. This makes sense, because you are probably going to be passing in at least two colors, alphas, and ratios, and possibly many more. You could create a new array and populate it with your values for each parameter, like so:

```
var colors:Array = new Array();
colors[0] = 0xffffff;
colors[1] = 0x000000;
```

But there's a much easier way to do it. You can create and populate an array on the fly by listing the elements you want in it between square brackets, separated by commas:

```
var colors:Array = [0xffffff, 0x000000];
```

In fact, you don't even need to make a colors variable. You can plug that array right into the beginGradientFill statement as an argument. Thus, you can get something like this:

```
graphics.beginGradientFill(GradientType.LINEAR,
                          [0xffffff, 0x000000],
                          [1, 1],
                          [0, 255],
                          matrix);
```

This defines two colors, two alpha values (both 100%), and start and end ratio values, so the gradient will start as white and blend into black at the end. Of course, you can create variables for each parameter if you want, and if you are defining a lot of colors, it will be clearer that way. The one caveat here is that these three arrays *must* all contain the same number of elements. If you define three colors, you *must* have three alphas and three ratios. If any one contains more or fewer than the others, it's going to fail silently—no gradient, no fill, no error message.

All you need now is the start and end position and the angle of the fill. As you might have guessed, that's what the mysterious matrix parameter is for.

Creating the matrix

A *matrix* is a two-dimensional grid containing rows and columns of values used for calculating various values. Matrices are used extensively in graphics for rotating, scaling, and moving things. That's exactly what you're doing here with the gradient. You need to position it, size it, and possibly rotate it. To use the matrix, you need to create a matrix object. This is an instance of the flash.geom.Matrix class, which essentially holds a grid of values that Flash can use to position, size, and rotate your gradient. (Actually, the Matrix class is used to manipulate more than just gradient fills, but that's all we are using it for here. See Chapter 18 for more uses of matrices.)

While use of the Matrix class can get pretty complex, there is a special method in there specifically for use in creating the type of matrix you need for a gradient fill. It's called createGradientBox. It takes minimally the width and height, and optionally the rotation and starting x, y position of the gradient you want to create. First you create an instance of the Matrix class, and then you call its createGradientBox method to automatically set its internal values. Here's how it looks:

```
var matrix:Matrix = new Matrix();
matrix.createGradientBox(width, height, rotation, x, y);
```

Don't forget to import the flash.geom.Matrix class at the top of your class if you are using this class.

If you only specify a width and height, the last three values will default to 0.

Let's see it in action. Here's document class, GradientFill.as:

```
package
{
    import flash.display.GradientType;
    import flash.display.Sprite;
    import flash.events.MouseEvent;
    import flash.geom.Matrix;

    public class GradientFill extends Sprite
    {
        public function GradientFill()
        {
            init();
        }

        private function init():void
        {
            graphics.lineStyle(1);
            var colors:Array = [0xffffff, 0xff0000];
            var alphas:Array = [1, 1];
            var ratios:Array = [0, 255];
            var matrix:Matrix = new Matrix();
            matrix.createGradientBox(100, 100, 0, 0, 0);
            graphics.beginGradientFill(GradientType.LINEAR, colors,
                                       alphas, ratios, matrix);
```

103

```
                graphics.drawRect(0, 0, 100, 100);
                graphics.endFill();
            }
        }
    }
```

When you test this, you'll see a nice white-to-red gradient square. Now let's draw the square in a different location, by changing the drawing code so you have the following code (in GradientFill2.as):

```
graphics.drawRect(100, 100, 100, 100);
```

Now your square is all red. What happened? Well, the gradient starts at 0 on the x axis, and it's only 100 pixels wide, so at the point your square begins, the gradient has already reached full red, and it's red from there on out. So again, you are going to want the x, y of the matrix to be at the top-left point of your shape, like so:

```
matrix.createGradientBox(100, 100, 0, 100, 100);
```

Here, the x, y is the same as the start of the square. Using the same square, you can now play around with the matrix and gradient fill settings to see what kind of effects you can create. First, try three colors:

```
var colors:Array = [0xffffff, 0x0000ff, 0xff0000];
var alphas:Array = [1, 1, 1];
var ratios:Array = [0, 128, 255];
```

Don't forget the alphas and ratios. Move the middle ratio around to see how that affects the gradient. Instead of 128, try 64 or 220.

The next example is a straight alpha blend. The colors are the same; only the alpha changes:

```
var colors:Array = [0x000000, 0x000000];
var alphas:Array = [1, 0];
var ratios:Array = [0, 255];
```

Try changing the angle now. Here's a 45-degree angle:

```
matrix.createGradientBox(100, 100, Math.PI / 4, 100, 100);
```

Using Math.PI/2 will make a vertical gradient by rotating it 90 degrees. –Math.PI/2 will make it go up, and Math.PI will make it go from right to left, rather than from left to right.

Finally, switch over to a radial gradient type:

```
beginGradientFill(GradientType.RADIAL, colors, alphas, ratios, matrix);
```

And now try all the same tricks that you used on the linear gradient fill on the radial version.

Color transforms

Next up in your rendering arsenal is the flash.geom.ColorTransform class and its methods. Unlike the drawing API, these don't allow you to create graphics, but merely change the color of an existing graphic contained in a sprite or other display object instance. Let's dive in and see how it all works.

Changing colors with the ColorTransform class

In ActionScript 2, the most common way to manipulate colors of movie clips was the Color class, which had methods like setRGB and setTransform. The ColorTransform class was introduced in Flash 8 and deprecated the Color class, but I think most people continued to use Color since they were used to it. Well, the Color class is not a part of AS 3, so it's time to buckle up and learn the new way of doing things. The methods of ColorTransform work in essentially the same way as Color, and do pretty much the same things, but the syntax is a little different.

First, you should know that a sprite, movie clip, or any other display object has a property called transform. This is an instance of the flash.geom.Transform class, and contains various properties that you can use to scale, rotate, position, and colorize the movie clip. The property of interest here is colorTransform. Realize that this is a property of a property of a display object, so it's accessed like this:

```
mySprite.transform.colorTransform
```

Or, within a class that extends Sprite, you can simply refer to that class's own transform property:

```
transform.colorTransform
```

To change an object's coloring, you assign a new ColorTransform object to this property. And just what, you might ask, is a ColorTransform object? Well, if you've used the AS 2 Color method, setTransform, you know you pass it in an object with various properties that tell it how to alter the color. Well, ColorTransform is pretty much the same thing, but rather than a generic object, it now has its own official class. In AS 2, you'd do something like this:

```
myTransform = new Object();
myTransform.ra = 50;
myTransform.ga = 40;
myTransform.ba = 12;
myTransform.aa = 40;
myTransform.rb = 244;
myTransform.gb = 112;
myTransform.bb = 90;
myTransform.ab = 70;
```

In AS 3, you would create the same ColorTransform object like this:

```
myTransform = new ColorTransform(0.5, 0.4, 0.12, 0.4, 244, 112, 90, 70);
```

The first four values are multipliers, and the last four are offsets. I'll show you the formula that is used in a moment, and you'll see why they have those names. Also, you might notice that the percent values of the multipliers are now decimals in the range of −1.0 to 1.0, rather than −100 to 100. Actually, the documentation says 0.0 to 1.0, but you can still use negative multipliers for interesting effects (as you'll see shortly). The offsets still go from −255 to 255. The actual constructor for the ColorTransform object looks like this:

```
ColorTransform(redMultiplier,
               greenMultiplier,
               blueMultiplier,
               alphaMultiplier,
               redOffset,
               greenOffset,
               blueOffset,
               alphaOffset)
```

The formula for transforming a particular color channel is like so, using the red channel as an example:

```
newRed = oldRed * redMultiplier + redOffset;
```

When using ColorTransform, remember that it is part of the flash.geom package, so you'll need to import the class from there.

Just to give you an example of how this all works, the following document class, TransformColor.as, embeds a picture in the SWF as a bitmap (an instance of the Bitmap class). Since the Bitmap class is a display object, it has a transform property. The code sets the colorTranform property of the bitmap's transform, using settings designed to produce a negative image. Feel free to play around with the multipliers and offsets and get a feel for what they do.

```
package
{
    import flash.display.Bitmap;
    import flash.display.Sprite;
    import flash.geom.ColorTransform;

    public class TransformColor extends Sprite
    {
        [Embed(source="picture.jpg")]
        public var Picture:Class;

        public function TransformColor()
        {
            init();
        }

        private function init():void
        {
            var pic:Bitmap = new Picture();
            addChild(pic);
```

```
pic.transform.colorTransform = new ColorTransform(-1, -1,
                                                  -1, 1,
                                                  255, 255,
                                                  255, 0);
        }
    }
}
```

If you try this yourself, just change the line

```
[Embed(source="picture.jpg")]
```

to match the path of whatever picture you are using. And if you are using the Flash IDE, just import your picture into the library, export it for ActionScript, and enter the class name Picture. Either way, don't worry too much about embedding stuff just yet. We'll cover that in the "Bitmaps" section later in the chapter. The important line is where the colorTransform is set.

Filters

Filters are bitmapped effects that can be applied to any display object. They can be applied in the Flash IDE via the Filters panel or at runtime via ActionScript. Since this book is about ActionScript, I'll limit the discussion to the scripted methods of applying filters. The following filters are included in AS 3:

- Drop shadow
- Blur
- Glow
- Bevel
- Gradient bevel
- Gradient glow
- Color matrix
- Convolution
- Displacement map

I'm not going to go into the details of each and every filter. They are documented in the help files, and an entire chapter (if not a whole book) could be devoted to them. But since I have enough material to cover in this book as it is, I'm just going to give you an overview of their use and a couple of examples.

Creating a filter

Filters are created by using the new operator and the name of the filter, passing in the required parameters. For example, to make a blur filter, one of the simplest, you would say this:

```
var blur:BlurFilter = new BlurFilter(5, 5, 3);
```

In this case, the parameters are blurX, blurY, and quality. This example will blur an object 5 pixels on both axes, with a medium-quality blur.

Another thing to realize is that filters are in their own package, called flash.filters. So, you can put this at the beginning of the file:

```
import flash.filters.BlurFilter;
```

If you want to import *all* the filters in the package, you can use this shortcut:

```
import flash.filters.*;
```

Now, you can create any type of filter directly. But generally, unless you will be using all or most of the classes in a package, it is best to avoid the wildcard and explicitly list the classes you will be importing. This is mostly just for clarity, so you know exactly what you intended to import and what not.

So now you have a blur filter, but how do you make it blur a particular object?

Any display object has a property called filters. This is an array containing all the filters that have been applied to that object, since any object can have multiple filters applied. You just need to get your blur filter into that array. Ideally, this would be as simple as applying a basic array operation, push, and saying mySprite.filters.push(blur);. But alas, it's not that easy. Flash does not listen for changes to the filters array and won't take note of the change until a whole new array is assigned to filters.

If you know that the object doesn't have any filters applied, or you are willing to overwrite them, you can just make a brand-new array, stick your blur filter in it, and assign that new array to the filters property. Let's try that. The following document class, Filters.as, creates a new sprite and draws a yellow square in it. It then creates a filter, adds it to an array, and assigns that array to the sprite's filters property:

```
package
{
    import flash.display.Sprite;
    import flash.filters.BlurFilter;

    public class Filters extends Sprite
    {
        public function Filters()
        {
            init();
        }

        private function init():void
        {
            var sprite:Sprite = new Sprite();
            sprite.graphics.lineStyle(2);
            sprite.graphics.beginFill(0xffff00);
            sprite.graphics.drawRect(100, 100, 100, 100);
            sprite.graphics.endFill()
            addChild(sprite);
```

```
                    var blur:BlurFilter = new BlurFilter(5, 5, 3);
                    var filters:Array = new Array();
                    filters.push(blur);
                    sprite.filters = filters;
                }
            }
        }
```

Voila! You have a blurry yellow box. The important part is in bold. You can shortcut this section a little:

```
var blur:BlurFilter = new BlurFilter(5, 5, 3);
var filters:Array = [blur];
sprite.filters = filters;
```

Or shortcut it a lot:

```
sprite.filters = [new BlurFilter(5, 5, 3)];
```

As long as you are creating a new array, putting your filter in it, and applying it to the filters property, Flash will be happy.

But what if you already have a filter applied and want to keep it, or worse yet, you aren't sure if there are any filters? In Flash 8 this was complicated because a display object's filters property would be undefined if it had no filters applied. But in AS 3, the filters array is always created as an empty array. All you have to do is get a reference to the array, push your filter onto it, and assign it back to the object's filters property. Here's how that looks:

```
var filters:Array = sprite.filters;
filters.push(new BlurFilter(5, 5, 3));
sprite.filters = filters;
```

With this method, it doesn't matter whether there are already filters applied or not, your filter will just be added to the list. Since the filters property is a full-fledged array, there are probably dozens of ways to accomplish the same thing using the various array methods. For example, here's one that uses the concat method:

```
sprite.filters = sprite.filters.concat(new BlurFilter(5, 5, 3));
```

I don't think there's really a "right" way to do it. As long as you get an array containing filters assigned to your filters property, you are golden.

Animating filters

Now that you know the basics of how to use filters with ActionScript, let's apply what you've already learned to make an animated drop shadow. For this effect, use the document class AnimatedFilters.as:

```
package
{
    import flash.display.Sprite;
    import flash.events.Event;
    import flash.filters.DropShadowFilter;

    public class AnimatedFilters extends Sprite
    {
        private var filter:DropShadowFilter;
        private var sprite:Sprite;

        public function AnimatedFilters()
        {
            init();
        }

        private function init():void
        {
            sprite = new Sprite();
            sprite.graphics.lineStyle(2);
            sprite.graphics.beginFill(0xffff00);
            sprite.graphics.drawRect(-50, -50, 100, 100);
            sprite.graphics.endFill();
            sprite.x = 200;
            sprite.y = 200;
            addChild(sprite);

            filter = new DropShadowFilter(0, 0, 0, 1, 20, 20, .3);

            addEventListener(Event.ENTER_FRAME, onEnterFrame);
        }

        private function onEnterFrame(event:Event):void
        {
            var dx:Number = mouseX - sprite.x;
            var dy:Number = mouseY - sprite.y;

            filter.distance = -Math.sqrt(dx * dx + dy * dy) / 10;
            filter.angle = Math.atan2(dy, dx) * 180 / Math.PI;
            sprite.filters = [filter];
        }
    }
}
```

The class first draws the square in a sprite so that the square graphic is centered on the sprite, and then moves the sprite itself out onto the stage. The drop shadow filter is created with some default properties.

A listener is added for the enterFrame event and the handler; the onEnterFrame method calculates the angle and distance from the mouse to the sprite using trig, which was covered in Chapter 3. It uses these to set the angle and distance properties of the drop shadow filter, and applies that filter back to the sprite. Note that you don't need to make a brand new filter each time. You can continue using the same one, just changing its properties. However, simply changing those properties will not update the visual display of the sprite. Again, you need to reassign the filter to the filters property for any change to take effect.

Bitmaps

As with filters, I could fill an entire book telling you everything about the Bitmap and BitmapData classes. That would be fun, but it's not the purpose of *this* book. I'll run through some of the basics with a couple of examples, and will point out some of the changes from handling bitmaps from AS 2 to AS 3.

As in AS 2, you first create a new BitmapData object by calling new BitmapData () with the following parameters:

```
new BitmapData (width:Number,
                height:Number,
                transparent:Boolean,
                fillColor:Number)
```

As you might have guessed by now, BitmapData is also within a nested package. It's fully qualified name is flash.display.BitmapData. So, you'll need to import that package. As for the parameters, width and height are pretty obvious. Transparent means that the image you create can contain an alpha channel for transparency, so choose true or false for this. fillColor is the initial color with which the image will be created. Bitmaps will be created using 32-bit color if transparency is true, so you would specify the color using 0xAARRGGBB. If transparency is false, you are safe using 24-bit colors.

When you create a BitmapData object, you probably want some way to make it visible. In AS 2, you would use attachBitmap to add the bitmap to a movie clip. You might be thinking that you can now substitute addChild to add the bitmap to a display object. Well, yes and no.

The problem is that addChild only works for objects that extend the DisplayObject class, such as sprites, movie clips, and text fields. However, if you dig into the class structures, you'll find that BitmapData does not extend DisplayObject, so it can't be directly added. That's where the Bitmap class comes in. The Bitmap class pretty much has a single function in life—to serve as a container for a BitmapData instance. You create one like so:

```
var myBitmapData:BitmapData = new BitmapData(100, 100, false, 0xff0000);
var myBitmap:Bitmap = new Bitmap(myBitmapData);
```

The important thing is that Bitmap does inherit from DisplayObject, so now you can add this object to the display list:

```
addChild(myBitmap);
```

and make it visible. The Bitmap instance is also what you can use to position the bitmap, scale it, add filters to it, etc.

To test this out, just add those three lines to the init method of the skeleton class I gave you in Chapter 2. Don't forget to import flash.display.Bitmap and flash.display.BitmapData. When you run it, you should see a red square. At first glance, this doesn't seem any more interesting than if you had just done the same thing with the drawing API. But realize that this is not a vector drawing of a square with a red fill. This is a bitmap image, in which each pixel is separately defined and alterable.

In fact, the value of each and every pixel can be read or changed with getPixel, getPixel32, setPixel, and setPixel32. The difference between the two versions is that getPixel and setPixel use 24-bit numbers and ignore the alpha channel, and the "32" versions use 32-bit numbers to include transparency information. Let's play with that a bit and make a rudimentary spray paint tool like one you'd find in any bitmap paint program.

Here is the document class, SprayPaint.as:

```
package
{
    import flash.display.Sprite;
    import flash.display.Bitmap;
    import flash.display.BitmapData;
    import flash.events.MouseEvent;
    import flash.events.Event;
    import flash.filters.BlurFilter;

    public class SprayPaint extends Sprite
    {
        private var canvas:BitmapData;
        private var color:uint;
        private var size:Number = 50;
        private var density:Number = 50;

        public function SprayPaint()
        {
            init();
        }

        private function init():void
        {
            canvas = new BitmapData(stage.stageWidth,
                                    stage.stageHeight,
                                    true, 0x00000000);
            var bmp:Bitmap = new Bitmap(canvas);
            addChild(bmp);

            stage.addEventListener(MouseEvent.MOUSE_DOWN, onMouseDown);
            stage.addEventListener(MouseEvent.MOUSE_UP, onMouseUp);
        }
```

```
        private function onMouseDown(event:MouseEvent):void
        {
            color = Math.random() * 0xffffff + 0xff000000;
            addEventListener(Event.ENTER_FRAME, onEnterFrame);
        }

        private function onMouseUp(event:MouseEvent):void
        {
            removeEventListener(Event.ENTER_FRAME, onEnterFrame);
        }

        private function onEnterFrame(event:Event):void
        {
            for(var i:int = 0; i < density; i++)
            {
                var angle:Number = Math.random() * Math.PI * 2;
                var radius:Number = Math.random() * size;
                var xpos:Number = mouseX + Math.cos(angle) * radius;
                var ypos:Number = mouseY + Math.sin(angle) * radius;
                canvas.setPixel32(xpos, ypos, color);
            }
        }
    }
}
```

This is probably the most complex code I've given you so far, but other than the BitmapData stuff, it's all stuff that I've already covered. I'm just using more of it all at once. Let's step through it though.

First, it creates some class variables, including a canvas variable to hold the BitmapData instance. The instance itself is created, sized to the dimensions of the stage, with a transparent background. Then, a bitmap is created using canvas, and this is added to the display list.

The mouse event handlers just choose a random color and add and remove a handler for the enterFrame event, which is where all the action takes place. Here, we get back into a bit of trigonometry. First, you calculate a random angle from 0 to Math.PI * 2, which you'll remember is in radians and is equal to 360 degrees. Next, you calculate a random radius and use a bit of trig to convert the radius and angle into x, y values. Then use setPixel32 to set the pixel at the mouse location plus the random x, y value to the spray color, which is randomly determined each time you start to draw.

Actually, you'll see there's a for loop in this example, so this happens a whole bunch of times on each frame. How many times is determined by the density value.

It's also worth noting that the color is calculated as a random 24-bit color, and then 0xFF000000 is added to that to make the alpha channel fully opaque. If you didn't add the extra value, the colors would all be completely transparent. If you multiplied Math.random() by 0xFFFFFFFF, you would get randomly transparent colors as well, which might be what you want, but wasn't what I wanted.

Go ahead and test it, and play with the density and size values to see the different effects they create. You're probably already thinking how you could throw in some controls to let the user change these parameters.

At first glance, you might think, "Big deal. I could do the same thing with the drawing API or by attaching small movie clips and coloring them." True, you could do just that, but if you've tried drawing hundreds and hundreds of individual shapes with the drawing API, you'll notice that the more you draw, the slower it goes. After several hundred shapes are drawn, the lag becomes very noticeable and the program becomes unusable. The same goes for attaching movie clips. A bitmap is quite different, though. You could spray new layers of paint on with this program all day, with no change in its speed or efficiency.

If you want to begin to see some even cooler effects, throw the following line into the file, right after creating the Bitmap object, bmp:

```
bmp.filters = [new BlurFilter(2, 2, 3)];
```

This adds a blur to the content and really makes it obvious that you are dealing with bitmaps, not vectors.

Of course, setting pixels is one of the simplest operations you can do to a BitmapData object. In addition to getting and setting pixels, you can apply about another two dozen methods to a BitmapData object. Using these, you can copy pixels, set thresholds, dissolve, merge, scroll, and more. One of my personal favorites is the Perlin noise function, which allows you to create random, organic patterns. These are useful for anything from smoke and clouds to landscapes and water ripples. Experiment with the methods that interest you.

Loading and embedding assets

One final important topic in rendering graphics is the concept of getting external assets, such as bitmaps or external SWFs, into your movie. There are two ways of doing this. One is to pull the asset in while the movie is running. This is known as *loading*. The other way is to *embed* the asset right in the SWF during compilation.

Loading assets

To load an asset, you create a Loader object. This is an instance of the flash.display.Loader class. A loader is a display object, meaning that you can add it to the display list using the addChild method, just like a sprite or bitmap. You then tell the loader to load either an external SWF or a bitmap, such as a JPEG, PNG, etc.

Here's where things get a little tricky. In AS 2, when you were dealing with paths to external files or URLs, you just used a simple string as the path. In AS 3, you need to create an instance of flash.net. URLLoader, passing in the path as a string. It's one extra step, and a bit of a pain in the neck, but you'll get used to it.

Here's an example of loading an external asset at runtime (document class LoadAsset.as):

```
package
{
    import flash.display.Sprite;
    import flash.display.Loader;
    import flash.net.URLRequest;
```

```
    public class LoadAsset extends Sprite
    {
        public function LoadAsset()
        {
            init();
        }

        private function init():void
        {
            var loader:Loader = new Loader();
            addChild(loader);
            loader.load(new URLRequest("picture.jpg"));
        }
    }
}
```

Embedding assets

Although loading assets at runtime is fine in some cases, there are many times when you have some external graphic that you just want to include in the SWF itself. If you are using the Flash IDE, you can simply import the item into the library and export it for ActionScript. But if you are using Flex Builder 2 or the Flex 2 SDK and command-line compiler, there is no library. So how do you include external assets in the SWF?

The answer is to embed them using the [Embed] metadata tag. *Metadata* refers to statements that you include in an ActionScript file that aren't actually ActionScript. Instead, they instruct the compiler to do certain things during the compilation process. In the case of the [Embed] tag, it tells the compiler to include a particular external asset into the final SWF file. The asset can be a bitmap or an external SWF. You tell the compiler which asset to embed by passing it in via the source property, like so:

```
[Embed(source="picture.jpg")]
```

Directly after the metadata line, you declare a variable of type Class, like so:

```
[Embed(source="picture.jpg")]
private var Image:Class;
```

You can now use that variable to create a new instance of that asset, like so:

```
var img:Bitmap = new Image();
```

Note that the object created is of type Bitmap. Had you embedded an external SWF, the object created would be of type Sprite, like so:

```
[Embed(source="animation.swf")]
private var Anim:Class;
var anim:Sprite = new Anim();
```

Here's an example of embedding an external JPEG in a SWF:

```
package
{
    import flash.display.Sprite;
    import flash.display.Bitmap;

    public class EmbedAsset extends Sprite
    {
        [Embed(source="picture.jpg")]
        private var Image:Class;

        public function EmbedAsset()
        {
            init();
        }

        private function init():void
        {
            var img:Bitmap = new Image();
            addChild(img);
        }
    }
}
```

Again, if you are using the Flash IDE, you should just import the item into the library, export it for ActionScript, and give it a class name. You won't need the [Embed] metadata tag and Class variable. In fact, the [Embed] metadata tag is not even supported by the compiler that is used by the Flash IDE.

I've given this rather brief coverage here, as we won't be using this technique further in the book. However, it is obviously useful enough to mention here.

Important formulas in this chapter

You've added a few more valuable tools to your collection in this chapter, mostly relating to handling color.

Convert hex to decimal:

```
trace(hexValue);
```

Convert decimal to hex:

```
trace(decimalValue.toString(16));
```

Combine component colors:

```
color24 = red << 16 | green << 8 | blue;
color32 = alpha << 24 | red << 16 | green << 8 | blue;
```

Extract component colors:

```
red = color24 >> 16;
green = color24 >> 8 & 0xFF;
blue = color24 & 0xFF;

alpha = color32 >> 24;
red = color32 >> 16 & 0xFF;
green = color32 >> 8 & 0xFF;
blue = color232 & 0xFF;
```

Draw a curve through a point:

```
// xt, yt is the point you want to draw through
// x0, y0 and x2, y2 are the end points of the curve
x1 = xt * 2 - (x0 + x2) / 2;
y1 = yt * 2 - (y0 + y2) / 2;
moveTo(x0, y0);
curveTo(x1, y1, x2, y2);
```

Summary

This chapter didn't cover too much about making anything move, but it did show you a number of ways to create visual content, which you'll learn how to animate in future chapters. Specifically, the chapter covered the following topics:

- Color, 24-bit and 32-bit
- The drawing API
- Filters
- The Bitmap and BitmapData classes

These subjects will give you the tools you need to make dynamic, expressive content for your animation, and since everything covered here is based on ActionScript, you can animate directly using all of these methods. Just use some code to create content, change the variables used in the code, and render it again.

You'll be using many of the techniques introduced in this chapter throughout the book, so it will be useful for you to know and understand them well now. In fact, you'll get your first hands-on experience using several of these techniques in the next chapter, which covers velocity and acceleration.

Part Two

BASIC MOTION

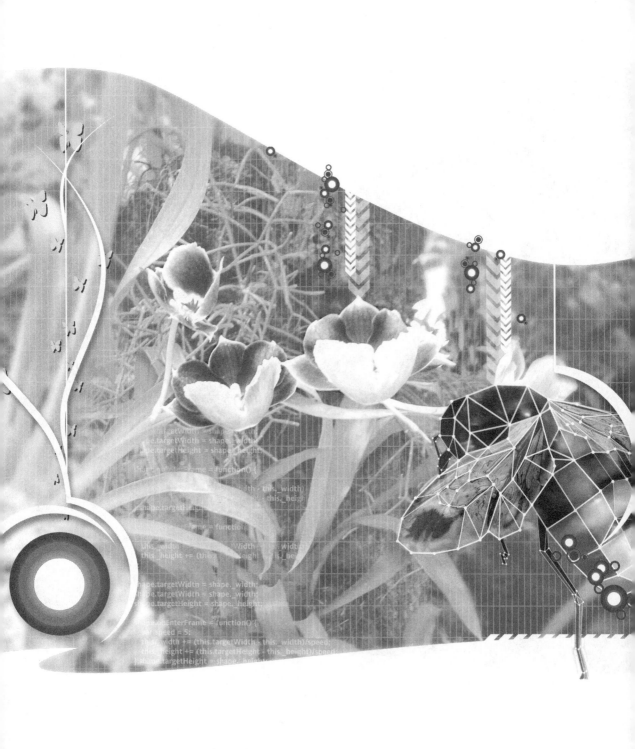

Chapter 5

VELOCITY AND ACCELERATION

What we'll cover in this chapter:

- Velocity
- Acceleration
- Important formulas in this chapter

Well, congratulations! You've made it to the point in the book where the action really starts. This means that (a) you've persevered through all the chapters so far, (b) you skimmed over the previous chapters and felt like you knew enough of it to get by, or (c) you got bored and jumped ahead. However it happened, here you are. Just remember, if you start having trouble, you can probably find help in an earlier chapter.

This chapter gets you started with basic motion: velocity, vectors, and acceleration. These concepts will be used for almost every bit of ActionScripted animation you do from here on out.

Velocity

The most basic property of something that is moving is velocity. Many people equate the term *velocity* with speed. That's part of it, but only part. The concept of velocity contains a very important second factor: *direction*. And that is pretty much our layman's definition for velocity: *speed in a particular direction*. Let's take a look at exactly how this definition differs from simple speed.

If I tell you that I got in my car at point X and drove 30 miles per hour for one hour, you'd have a pretty hard time finding me. On the other hand, if I said I drove due north for one hour at the same speed, you'd know precisely where I was. This is pretty important in animation, because you need to know where to put your sprite. It's fine to say a sprite is moving at a certain speed, but you're going to need some specific x, y coordinates to assign to it on each frame to give it the illusion of motion. This is where velocity comes in. If you know where something is at the start of a particular frame, how fast it is moving, and in what direction, you know where to put it at the start of the next frame.

The speed part of it is usually defined in terms of pixels per frame. In other words, if a movie clip is at a certain point as it enters a frame, it's going to be so many pixels away from that point at the end of the frame.

In most cases, using pixels per frame works fine, and it is definitely the simplest to program. However, due to the unstable nature of frame rates in Flash, using pixels per frame may make your animation slow down at certain points when too much is happening, there is too much to compute, or the CPU is busy doing something else. If you are programming some kind of game or simulation in which it is crucial that the animation proceeds at a very uniform rate, you might want to use an interval-based animation instead. I've included an example of that approach in Chapter 19.

Before getting into coding velocity, I want to talk a little bit about vectors, as that's how velocity is generally depicted.

Vectors and velocity

A *vector* is something that has magnitude and direction. In the case of velocity, the magnitude is the speed. Vectors are drawn as arrows. The length of the arrow is its magnitude, and the direction the arrow is pointing in is, naturally, the direction of the vector. Figure 5-1 shows some vectors.

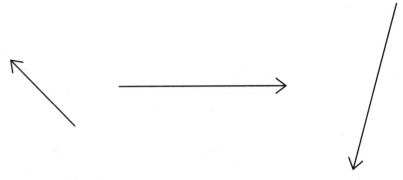

Figure 5-1. A few vectors

One thing to note is that the magnitude is always positive. A vector with a negative magnitude would simply be a vector going in the opposite direction, as illustrated in Figure 5-2.

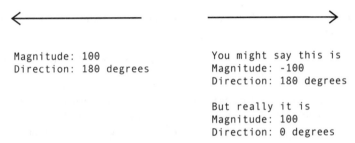

```
Magnitude: 100              You might say this is
Direction: 180 degrees      Magnitude: -100
                            Direction: 180 degrees

                            But really it is
                            Magnitude: 100
                            Direction: 0 degrees
```

Figure 5-2. Negative velocity is really velocity in the opposite direction.

Another thing to note is that vectors don't really have any set position. Even in the case of velocity, the vector doesn't state where something is starting or where it ends up; it just indicates how fast and in which direction the object is moving. Thus, two vectors can be equal if they have the same direction and magnitude, even if they are describing two different objects in two different locations, as shown in Figure 5-3.

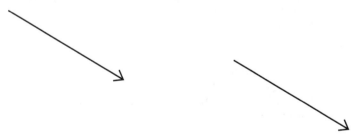

Figure 5-3. If vectors have the same magnitude and direction, they are the same. Position doesn't matter.

Velocity on one axis

I'm going to simplify things at first, by limiting velocity to a single axis: the x axis, or horizontal motion. This is basically saying that the direction is zero degrees, due east, or from the left side of the screen to the right side of the screen—however you want to look at it. The speed is just how many pixels it moves in that direction each frame. Thus, if I say that the velocity on the x axis is 5, I mean that the object will move 5 pixels each frame from left to right. This also means that if I say the velocity is –5 on the x axis, it will move from right to left, 5 pixels each frame.

Now, you caught me there, didn't you? Already I'm talking about a negative magnitude when I just told you there's no such thing. Technically speaking, the velocity would actually be 5 and the direction 180 degrees. Similarly, a positive y velocity would be that speed at 90 degrees (straight down), and a negative y velocity would be 270, or –90 degrees (straight up). In practice, though, when you are calculating component x, y velocities, they always come through as positive and negative numbers, and you are often going to see me writing things like, "The x velocity is –5." So, if it helps you, think of the minus sign as indicating "to the left" for x velocity or "up" for y velocity, rather than meaning negative.

Throughout the book, I will use vx to stand for velocity on the x axis, and vy to mean velocity on the y axis. Positive vx means to the right, and negative vx means to the left. Positive vy means down, and negative vy means up.

For velocity on one axis, you simply add the velocity to the object's position on that axis. Whatever your vx is, you add it to the object's x property on each frame.

Let's see it in action. Many of the examples in this chapter (and later) will need some kind of object to move around. Rather than using up valuable space drawing such an object in every class and example, we're going to make a Ball class that we can and will reuse quite often. Here it is:

```
package {
    import flash.display.Sprite;

    public class Ball extends Sprite {
        public var radius:Number;
        private var color:uint;

        public function Ball(radius:Number=40, color:uint=0xff0000) {
            this.radius = radius;
            this.color = color;
            init();
        }
        public function init():void {
            graphics.beginFill(color);
            graphics.drawCircle(0, 0, radius);
            graphics.endFill();
        }
    }
}
```

Now, any time I refer to this class, you should put this class in with your project, and you can create a new ball just by including new Ball(size, color). Alternatively, you can put a class in a fixed location, and add that directory to your class path, as described in Chapter 2.

Now that you have something to move, here's the first velocity example, document class Velocity1.as:

```
package
{
    import flash.display.Sprite;
    import flash.events.Event;

    public class Velocity1 extends Sprite
    {
        private var ball:Ball;
        private var vx:Number = 5;

        public function Velocity1()
        {
            init();
        }

        private function init():void
        {
            ball = new Ball();
            addChild(ball);
            ball.x = 50;
            ball.y = 100;
            addEventListener(Event.ENTER_FRAME, onEnterFrame);
        }
        private function onEnterFrame(event:Event):void
        {
            ball.x += vx;
        }
    }
}
```

In this example, first you set an x velocity (vx) of 5. Remember that is 5 pixels per frame, so on each frame, the vx is added to the ball's x property. The init method goes through the business of getting the ball onto the stage and setting up the event handler for the enterFrame event. On each frame, the ball will be placed 5 pixels to the right of where it was on the last frame. Try it out. Pretty good illusion of motion, eh?

Play around with it. Give it higher values or lower values for vx. Try some negative values and watch the object move in the other direction. See if you can make the object move on the y axis instead.

Velocity on two axes

Moving along two axes is pretty simple. You just define a vx and a vy, and then add the vx to the x property and the vy to the y property on each frame. So, what you are saying is that for each frame, the object is going to move so many pixels on the x axis and so many pixels on the y axis.

The next example (Velocity2.as) demonstrates this, and here it is:

```
package
{
    import flash.display.Sprite;
    import flash.events.Event;

    public class Velocity2 extends Sprite
    {
        private var ball:Ball;
        private var vx:Number = 5;
        private var vy:Number = 5;

        public function Velocity2()
        {
            init();
        }

        private function init():void
        {
            ball = new Ball();
            addChild(ball);
            ball.x = 50;
            ball.y = 100;
            addEventListener(Event.ENTER_FRAME, onEnterFrame);
        }
        private function onEnterFrame(event:Event):void
        {
            ball.x += vx;
            ball.y += vy;
        }
    }
}
```

Again, play around with the velocity variables until you get a good feel for them. Don't forget to try out some negative values.

Angular velocity

OK, so far, so good. You have some real animation going on, using velocity on two axes. But in many cases—maybe most cases—x and y velocity won't be the initial data you have.

The fact is I'm kind of cheating with the definition of velocity here. I said it's speed in a direction, but now I've given you two different speeds in two different directions. The reason I did that is because, in Flash, you position objects by placing them on x, y coordinates. So you need to end up with a velocity and position on both axes, but that's not necessarily what you start out with.

What if you just have a value for speed and an angle for direction, per the definition. Say you want something to move at an angle of 45 degrees and a speed of 3 pixels per frame. I don't see any vx or vy, or anything even similar in that description.

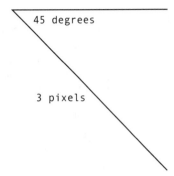

Figure 5-4. A magnitude and a direction

Fortunately, you've already been introduced to the tools you need to derive vx and vy from that description. Think back to the discussion of trigonometry in Chapter 3. Now, look at Figure 5-4, which shows what you want the ball to do on each frame: Move 3 pixels at an angle of 45 degrees.

Does this diagram look familiar? How about if I add another line, as shown in Figure 5-5? What do you know? You have a right triangle, with one angle and the hypotenuse defined!

Notice that the two legs of that triangle lie on the x and y axes. In fact, the leg that lies on the x axis is equal to the distance the ball is going to move on the x axis. The same goes for the leg on the y axis. Remember that in a right triangle, if you have one side and one angle, you can find all the rest. So, given the 45 degrees and the hypotenuse of 3 pixels, you should be able to use Math.cos and Math.sin to find the lengths of vx and vy.

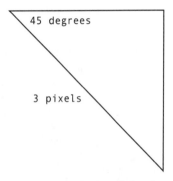

Figure 5-5. Magnitude and direction mapping becomes a right triangle.

The side adjacent to the angle is vx. The cosine of an angle is the adjacent/hypotenuse. Or, stated another way, the adjacent side is the cosine of the angle times the hypotenuse. Similarly, the opposite side is vy. Sine is opposite/hypotenuse, or the opposite is the sine times hypotenuse.

Here's the exact code you would use:

```
vx = Math.cos(angle) * speed;
vy = Math.sin(angle) * speed;
```

Now don't you dare forget to convert the 45 degrees to radians before passing it into the Math functions! Once you have the vx and the vy, you can easily add these to the x, y position of the object you are animating.

The next example (VelocityAngle.as) has the following code:

```
package
{
    import flash.display.Sprite;
    import flash.events.Event;
```

127

```
public class VelocityAngle extends Sprite
{
    private var ball:Ball;
    private var angle:Number = 45;
    private var speed:Number = 3;

    public function VelocityAngle()
    {
        init();
    }

    private function init():void
    {
        ball = new Ball();
        addChild(ball);
        ball.x = 50;
        ball.y = 100;
        addEventListener(Event.ENTER_FRAME, onEnterFrame);
    }
    private function onEnterFrame(event:Event):void
    {
        var radians:Number = angle * Math.PI / 2;
        var vx:Number = Math.cos(angle) * speed;
        var vy:Number = Math.sin(angle) * speed;
        ball.x += vx;
        ball.y += vy;
    }
}
}
```

The main difference here is that you're starting off with angle and speed rather than vx and vy. The velocities are calculated as local variables, used, and discarded. Of course, in a simple case like this, where the angle and speed are never changing, it would make more sense to calculate the velocities once and save them as class variables. But in most advanced motion, both the direction and speed of motion will be constantly changing, so the vx and vy will not remain the same.

To experiment with this example, change the angle around. See for yourself that you can make the ball travel at any speed and any angle by simply changing those two numbers.

Now, let's take another look at this example in terms of vectors.

Vector addition

Vector addition is when you have two vectors working in a system and you want to find the resultant overall vector. Here, you have a vector on the x axis, another vector on the y axis, and an overall velocity vector. You add vectors by simply placing them together head to tail. The resultant vector is the line you can draw from the starting point of the first vector on the chain to the ending point of the last one. In Figure 5-6, you can see three vectors being added together and their resultant vector.

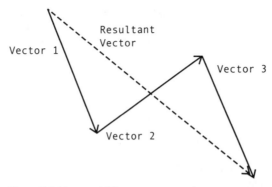

Figure 5-6. Vector addition

It doesn't matter in what order you place the vectors; the result will always be the same. And time has no part in it. You could say an object moved this way, then it moved that way, and then it moved the other way, in any order. Or you could say that it moved in all three ways at once. The result is that it wound up moving at a certain speed in a certain direction when all was said and done.

Let's go back to our example. If you lay down the x-axis velocity vector, and then put the y-axis velocity vector on the end of that, the resulting line is the overall velocity. Figure 5-7 illustrates the velocities as vectors.

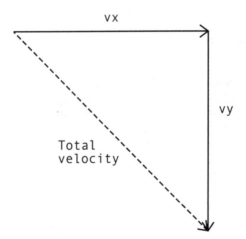

Figure 5-7. Velocities as vectors

What do you know? It's the same picture! Take that as a sign that you are doing something right.

A mouse follower

Let's use the velocity concepts to expand on an earlier concept. Back in Chapter 3, you built an example with an arrow that always pointed to the mouse. That example used Math.atan2 to compute the angle between the mouse and the arrow, and then rotated the arrow so it lined up with that angle.

With what you just learned, you can now throw some speed into the mix and get a velocity based on the current angle. This example uses the same Arrow class, rather than the ball, so dig up, download, or rewrite that class and put it in the same directory as the next document class, FollowMouse.as:

```
package
{
    import flash.display.Sprite;
    import flash.events.Event;

    public class FollowMouse extends Sprite
    {
        private var arrow:Arrow;
        private var speed:Number = 5;

        public function FollowMouse()
        {
            init();
        }

        private function init():void
        {
            arrow = new Arrow();
            addChild(arrow);
            addEventListener(Event.ENTER_FRAME, onEnterFrame);
        }
        private function onEnterFrame(event:Event):void
        {
            var dx:Number = mouseX - arrow.x;
            var dy:Number = mouseY - arrow.y;
            var angle:Number = Math.atan2(dy, dx);
            arrow.rotation = angle * 180 / Math.PI;
            var vx:Number = Math.cos(angle) * speed;
            var vy:Number = Math.sin(angle) * speed;
            arrow.x += vx;
            arrow.y += vy;
        }
    }
}
```

While this is a pretty complex effect, there shouldn't be anything in here that you don't fully understand by now. You're getting the x distance and y distance to the mouse, and from that using Math.atan2 to get the angle that forms. You're then using that angle to rotate the arrow, and using Math.cos and Math.sin along with the speed to find the x and y velocities. Finally, you're adding the velocities to the position.

Velocity extended

I'm entering into dangerous territory here, but I'm going to start taking the definition of velocity into places it was never meant to go. While in a strict sense velocity refers to change of position and physical motion through space, there's no need to limit the concepts you've just learned to only the x and y properties of display objects.

A sprite, movie clip, or other display object has a lot of properties you can tinker with, and almost all of them can accept a wide range of values that you can change over time to produce animation. Perhaps *velocity* isn't the correct word for it, but the concept is similar, so I often continue to use the word *velocity* in my variable names when describing something that changes a property over time.

An example would be having a sprite spin around. In this case, you are changing the object's rotation property on each frame by adding a value to it. You can make the object spin quickly by adding a high value to the rotation property on each frame, or have it spin more slowly by adding a smaller value. Correct or not, I usually refer to the variable that holds the spinning speed as vr, for rotational velocity.

Using the familiar arrow movie clip, you can come up with something like this (RotationalVelocity.as):

```
package
{
    import flash.display.Sprite;
    import flash.events.Event;

    public class RotationalVelocity extends Sprite
    {
        private var arrow:Arrow;
        private var vr:Number = 5;

        public function RotationalVelocity()
        {
            init();
        }

        private function init():void
        {
            arrow = new Arrow();
            addChild(arrow);
            arrow.x = stage.stageWidth / 2;
            arrow.y = stage.stageHeight / 2;
            addEventListener(Event.ENTER_FRAME, onEnterFrame);
        }
        private function onEnterFrame(event:Event):void
        {
            arrow.rotation += vr;
        }
    }
}
```

In terms of velocity here, the speed is 5 and the direction is clockwise. I might even get away with that one, as there's still some motion going on, but when I start using terms like "alpha velocity" (how fast something is fading in or out), I'm sure I'll ruffle some feathers. Still, I find it useful to think of such properties in these same terms. I want to change the alpha at a certain rate by adding or subtracting to its value on each frame. As I often find myself changing several properties over time, each at certain rates, it's nice to relate them all by calling them velocities. Thus, I might wind up with something like this:

```
arrow.x += vx;
arrow.y += vy;
arrow.alpha += vAlpha;
arrow.rotation += vr;
arrow.scaleX = arrow.scaleY += vScale;
// etc.
```

You'll see a lot of examples like this later in the book, so I hope you'll forgive my occasional v.

That about does it for velocity and its "cousins." Now, let's move on to acceleration.

Acceleration

It's common to think of acceleration as speeding up and deceleration as slowing down. And while this is not incorrect, for this book, I use a slightly more technical definition for acceleration.

Many similarities exist between velocity and acceleration in terms of how they are described. They are both vectors. Like velocity, acceleration is described as a value and a direction. However, whereas velocity changes the position of an object, acceleration changes its velocity.

Think of it this way. You get in your car, start it up, and put it in gear. What is your velocity? It's zero. By stepping on the gas pedal (also known as the *accelerator*, hmmm . . .), your velocity begins to change (at least the speed portion of it; the direction is changed with the steering wheel). After a second or two, you're going 4 or 5 miles per hour (mph). Then your speed increases to 10 mph, 20 mph, 30 mph, and so on. The engine is applying force to the car to change its velocity.

Thus, you have the layman's definition for acceleration: *a force that changes the velocity of an object*.

In purely ActionScript terms, you can say that acceleration is a value that you add to a velocity property.

Here's another example. Say you have a spaceship that needs to go from planet A to planet B. Its direction will be whatever direction planet B happens to be in relation to planet A. It points in that direction and fires its rockets. As long as those rockets are firing, force is being applied to the ship, and its velocity is going to change. In other words, the spaceship will continue to go faster and faster.

At some point, the captain decides the ship is going fast enough, and he might as well conserve fuel, so he shuts down the rockets. Assuming there is no friction in space, the ship is going to continue along at the same velocity. As the rockets are no longer firing, no more force is being applied to the ship. Since there is no more acceleration, the velocity does not change.

Then the ship approaches its goal. It needs to slow down or it's going to fly right past planet B (or if the navigator was accurate enough, the ship is going to become a *part* of planet B). So what does the captain do? You don't have brakes in space—there's nothing for them to grab a hold of. Instead, the captain turns the ship around so it faces the opposite direction, and fires up the rockets again. This applies negative acceleration, or acceleration in the opposite direction. Really, this is the same thing I covered while discussing vectors. The force is again changing the velocity, but this time it is reducing the velocity. The velocity will get less and less, and eventually arrive at zero. Ideally, that will coincide with the point when the ship is a couple of inches above the surface of the planet. At that point, the captain can kill the rockets and let gravity finish the job. (I'll talk about gravity in the "Gravity as acceleration" section, coming up soon.)

Acceleration on one axis

Let's put what you've just learned into practice in Flash. Like the first velocity example, this first acceleration example stays on one axis. We'll jump back to the Ball class for the next few examples.

Here's the code for the first example (Acceleration1.as):

```
package
{
    import flash.display.Sprite;
    import flash.events.Event;

    public class Acceleration1 extends Sprite
    {
        private var ball:Ball;
        private var vx:Number = 0;
        private var ax:Number = .2;

        public function Acceleration1()
        {
            init();
        }

        private function init():void
        {
            ball = new Ball();
            addChild(ball);
            ball.x = 50;
            ball.y = 100;
            addEventListener(Event.ENTER_FRAME, onEnterFrame);
        }
        private function onEnterFrame(event:Event):void
        {
            vx += ax;
            ball.x += vx;
        }
    }
}
```

Here, you start out with velocity (vx) being zero. The acceleration (ax) is 0.2. This is added to the velocity on each frame, and then the velocity is added to the ball's position.

Test this example. You'll see that the ball starts out moving very slowly, but by the time it leaves the stage, it's zipping right along.

Now, let's get closer to the spaceship example, and allow the ball to turn the acceleration off and on, and even reverse it. You can use the cursor keys for this. You know how to listen for keyboard events, and you can find the key that caused that event by checking the keyCode property of the event object that gets passed to the event handler. You can then compare that to constants found in the flash.ui.Keyboard class, which contains human-readable properties for key codes, such as Keyboard.LEFT, Keyboard.SPACE, Keyboard.SHIFT, etc. For now, we just care about the left and right cursor keys, which are Keyboard.LEFT and Keyboard.RIGHT. We can use these to change the acceleration. Here's the code (Acceleration2.as):

```
package
{
    import flash.display.Sprite;
    import flash.events.Event;
    import flash.events.KeyboardEvent;
    import flash.ui.Keyboard;

    public class Acceleration2 extends Sprite
    {
        private var ball:Ball;
        private var vx:Number = 0;
        private var ax:Number = 0

        public function Acceleration2()
        {
            init();
        }

        private function init():void
        {
            ball = new Ball();
            addChild(ball);
            ball.x = stage.stageWidth / 2;
            ball.y = stage.stageHeight / 2;
            addEventListener(Event.ENTER_FRAME, onEnterFrame);
            stage.addEventListener(KeyboardEvent.KEY_DOWN, onKeyDown);
            stage.addEventListener(KeyboardEvent.KEY_UP, onKeyUp);
        }

        private function onKeyDown(event:KeyboardEvent):void
        {
            if(event.keyCode == Keyboard.LEFT)
            {
                ax = -0.2;
            }
```

```
            else if(event.keyCode == Keyboard.RIGHT)
            {
                ax = 0.2;
            }
        }

        private function onKeyUp(event:KeyboardEvent):void
        {
            ax = 0;
        }

        private function onEnterFrame(event:Event):void
        {
            vx += ax;
            ball.x += vx;
        }
    }
}
```

In this example, you're simply checking whether either the left or right cursor key is down. If the left cursor key is down, you set ax to a negative value. If the right cursor key is down, make it positive. If neither is down, set it to zero. In the onEnterFrame method, the velocity is added to the position just like before.

Test the example. You'll see that you don't have complete control over the speed of the object. You can't stop it on a dime, so to speak. You can only slow it down to the point it stops. And if you slow it down too much, it starts going in the opposite direction. See whether you can stop it just before it hits the edge of the stage.

I'm sure some game ideas are already popping into your head. Hold onto them, you're about to expand your mastery of this technique many times over.

Acceleration on two axes

As with velocity, you can have acceleration on the x axis and y axis at the same time. You just set up an acceleration value for each axis (I usually use the variable names ax and ay), add those to vx and vy, and finally add vx and vy to the x and y properties.

It's pretty easy to adapt the previous example to work with the y axis as well. You just need to add the following:

- The ay and vy variables
- Checks for the up and down cursor keys
- The right acceleration to the right velocity
- Velocity to the corresponding axis position

Here's the code (Acceleration3.as):

```
package
{
    import flash.display.Sprite;
    import flash.events.Event;
    import flash.events.KeyboardEvent;
    import flash.ui.Keyboard;

    public class Acceleration3 extends Sprite
    {
        private var ball:Ball;
        private var vx:Number = 0;
        private var vy:Number = 0;
        private var ax:Number = 0
        private var ay:Number = 0

        public function Acceleration3()
        {
            init();
        }

        private function init():void
        {
            ball = new Ball();
            addChild(ball);
            ball.x = stage.stageWidth / 2;
            ball.y = stage.stageHeight / 2;
            addEventListener(Event.ENTER_FRAME, onEnterFrame);
            stage.addEventListener(KeyboardEvent.KEY_DOWN, onKeyDown);
            stage.addEventListener(KeyboardEvent.KEY_UP, onKeyUp);
        }

        private function onKeyDown(event:KeyboardEvent):void
        {
            switch(event.keyCode)
            {
                case Keyboard.LEFT :
                ax = -0.2;
                break;

                case Keyboard.RIGHT :
                ax = 0.2;
                break;

                case Keyboard.UP :
                ay = -0.2;
                break;
```

```
                case Keyboard.DOWN :
                ay = 0.2;
                break;

                default :
                break;
            }
        }

    private function onKeyUp(event:KeyboardEvent):void
    {
        ax = 0;
        ay = 0;
    }

    private function onEnterFrame(event:Event):void
    {
        vx += ax;
        vy += ay;
        ball.x += vx;
        ball.y += vy;
    }
    }
}
```

Notice that I moved the left/right/up/down checks into a switch statement, as all of those if statements were getting to be too much.

Play around with this one for a while. You'll see that you can now navigate all over the screen. Try to get the object moving, say, left to right, and then press the up key. Note that the x velocity is not affected at all. The object keeps moving on the x axis at the same rate. You've just added some y velocity into the picture. This is equivalent to the spaceship turning 90 degrees and firing the rockets.

Gravity as acceleration

So far, I've been talking about acceleration in terms of a force being applied to an object by the object itself, such as a car engine or a rocket. That's certainly valid, but there's another aspect to acceleration. It happens that any force that acts to change the velocity of an object uses the principle of acceleration. This includes such things as gravity, magnetism, springs, rubber bands, and so on.

You can look at gravity in a couple of ways. From the wide-angle perspective of the solar system, gravity is an attraction between two bodies. The distance and angle between those two bodies must be taken into account to figure the actual acceleration on each body.

The other way to look at gravity is from a close-up viewpoint, here on earth, or very near it. In our everyday existence, gravity does not noticeably change depending on our distance from the earth. Although technically speaking, the force of gravity is slightly less when you are flying in a plane or up on a mountain, it's nothing you would notice. So, when simulating gravity on this level, you can pretty much define it as a set value, as you saw in the earlier examples with the acceleration variables.

Also, because the earth is so large and we are so small, it's easy to ignore any actual direction of acceleration and just say that the direction is "down." In other words, no matter where your object is, you can safely define gravity as acceleration on the y axis alone.

To put it into ActionScript, all you need to do is define a value for the force of gravity and add it to the vy on each frame. Generally speaking, a fraction works well, something like 0.5 or below. Much more than that, and things will "feel" too heavy. With smaller values, things seem to float like feathers. Of course, you can always use these effects to your advantage; for example, to create simulations of different planets with varying gravities.

This next example adds gravity. The full code for this is in Gravity.as, but I'm not going to list it all out. It has only a few differences from Acceleration3.as. In addition to the class and constructor name being changed, I added one variable to the list of variables described at the beginning of the class:

```
private var gravity:Number = 0.1;
```

and added one line to the onEnterFrame method:

```
private function onEnterFrame(event:Event):void
{
    vx += ax;
    vy += ay;
    vy += gravity;
    ball.x += vx;
    ball.y += vy;
}
```

I made the gravity value pretty low so the ball doesn't go off the screen too quickly, and you can still control it with the keys. What you've just created are all the physics of the old *Lunar Lander* game. Add in some better graphics and some collision detection, and you've got yourself a hit! (I'll help you with the latter point; graphics are up to you.)

Notice that first you add the acceleration from the key presses to the vx and vy, then you add the gravity to the vy. Dealing with complex systems of multiple forces winds up not being that complex. You just calculate the acceleration of each force and tack it onto the velocity. No complex averaging or factoring is going on. Each force just gets added on. When you've gone through and handled all the forces, you add the velocity to the position. Here, you are using only a couple of forces, but later in the book, you will be calculating many different forces acting on a single object.

This goes right back to vector addition. If you start off with the original velocity as a vector, each acceleration, gravity, or force is an additional vector tacked on to that velocity. When you've added all of them on, you just draw a line from the beginning to the end, and you have your resulting velocity. You'll find it's the same as if you had added on the x and y components of each force.

Now imagine that your sprite is a hot air balloon. You probably want to add a force called *lift*. This is another acceleration on the y axis. This time, however, it's negative, or in the "up" direction. Now, you have three forces acting on the object: the key force, gravity, and lift. If you think about it, or try it out, you'll see that the lift force needs to be slightly stronger than the gravity force in order for the balloon to rise. This is pretty logical—if they were exactly equal, they would cancel each other out, and you'd be back to square one, with only the key force having any effect.

Another one to try is creating some wind. Obviously, this is a force on the x axis. Depending on which direction the wind is blowing, it could be a positive or negative force, or as you now know, a 0- or 180-degree direction.

Angular acceleration

As I mentioned, acceleration has a value—the force—and a direction, just like velocity. And like velocity, if you are starting with those two factors, you need to break them down into the component x and y forces. Now, if you've been paying attention, you know that the way to do that is by using Math.cos and Math.sin. Here's how that looks:

```
var force:Number = 10;
var angle:Number = 45; // degrees. Need to convert!
var ax:Number = Math.cos(angle * Math.PI / 180) * force;
var ay:Number = Math.sin(angle * Math.PI / 180) * force;
```

Now that you have acceleration for each axis, you can update the velocity on each axis, and from that, update the object's position.

Let's resurrect the mouse follower from earlier in the chapter and make it work with acceleration instead of just plain velocity. Remember that in the earlier incarnation, you took the angle from the arrow to the mouse and used that to determine vx and vy. This time, you'll use the same calculations, but employ them to determine ax and ay instead. Then you'll add the acceleration values to the velocity values and the velocity values to the x and y properties. Here's the code (FollowMouse2.as):

```
package
{
    import flash.display.Sprite;
    import flash.events.Event;

    public class FollowMouse2 extends Sprite
    {
        private var arrow:Arrow;
        private var vx:Number = 0;
        private var vy:Number = 0;
        private var force:Number = 0.5;

        public function FollowMouse2()
        {
            init();
        }

        private function init():void
        {
            arrow = new Arrow();
            addChild(arrow);
            addEventListener(Event.ENTER_FRAME, onEnterFrame);
        }
        private function onEnterFrame(event:Event):void
        {
```

```
            var dx:Number = mouseX - arrow.x;
            var dy:Number = mouseY - arrow.y;
            var angle:Number = Math.atan2(dy, dx);
            arrow.rotation = angle * 180 / Math.PI;
            var ax:Number = Math.cos(angle) * force;
            var ay:Number = Math.sin(angle) * force;
            vx += ax;
            vy += ay;
            arrow.x += vx;
            arrow.y += vy;
        }
    }
}
```

Notice that we also turn speed into force and make it much smaller. Since acceleration is additive, you want to start with small amounts. It builds up quickly. Also note that now vx and vy are declared as class variables, which will be accessible from any method in the class. Earlier, they were calculated newly on each frame, but now you need to keep track of them and add or subtract from their value each time. Of course, you could do away with the ax and ay variables here altogether and just add the result of the sine and cosine lines directly to the velocities. I kept them separated for clarity.

Now, that code isn't *too* complex is it? But look back to the first motion example you did at the beginning of the chapter, and see just how far you've come. The first one was so flat, it might as well have been a tween. By learning just a couple of basic principles, you've now created something a million times more fluid and dynamic—something that almost feels alive. And you're not even at the end of the chapter yet!

OK, let's pull everything together and see how much farther you can go with it.

A spaceship

I've been talking a lot about spaceships traveling from here to there. Well, with the ground you've covered so far, you should be able to put together a reasonable spaceship simulation.

Here's the plan. The spaceship will be a class of its own that just takes care of drawing itself, much like the Arrow or Ball classes you've already been using. You can use the left and right keys to rotate it left and right. The up key will act to fire the rocket. Of course, the rocket is in the back of the ship and fires straight back. Thus, the force that the rocket applies will cause acceleration in the direction the ship is facing at that time. Actually, what you're going to make is a lot like the ship in the old game *Asteroids*, minus the actual asteroids.

First, you need a ship. Mine uses a class with a few lines of drawing API code to draw four short, white lines, as a homage to the original that I'm copying. If you have more artistic talent than I seem to have, go right ahead and whip something up in PhotoShop or Swift 3D, save it as a bitmap, and embed it using the technique for embedding external bitmaps discussed in Chapter 4. It will work the same when you get to the code. At any rate, the following class is what I created, and is found in Ship.as.

```
package
{
    import flash.display.Sprite;

    public class Ship extends Sprite
    {
        public function Ship()
        {
            draw(false);
        }

        public function draw(showFlame:Boolean):void
        {
            graphics.clear();
            graphics.lineStyle(1, 0xffffff);
            graphics.moveTo(10, 0);
            graphics.lineTo(-10, 10);
            graphics.lineTo(-5, 0);
            graphics.lineTo(-10, -10);
            graphics.lineTo(10, 0);

            if(showFlame)
            {
                graphics.moveTo(-7.5, -5)
                graphics.lineTo(-15, 0);
                graphics.lineTo(-7.5, 5);
            }
        }
    }
}
```

Note that there is a public draw method, which takes a true/false value. This way, you can draw it with or without a flame showing. This will be useful to show that the ship's engines are firing. You can see how it looks with and without the flame in Figures 5-8 and 5-9.

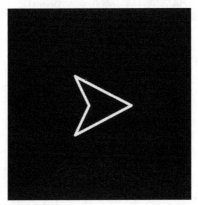

Figure 5-8. Behold the future of space travel.

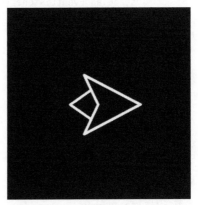

Figure 5-9. Beware of the flame.

Ship controls

OK, now that you have built your ship, let's get its controls working. As I just mentioned, it has three controls: turn left, turn right, and fire rocket, mapped to the left, right, and up keys, respectively. The basic structure of this example is going to be very similar to Acceleration3.as, listed earlier in the chapter, with handlers for the keyDown and keyUp events and a switch statement to handle the keys that were pressed. I'll just dump the whole thing on you and then go through it (you can find this in ShipSim.as):

```
package
{
    import flash.display.Sprite;
    import flash.events.Event;
    import flash.events.KeyboardEvent;
    import flash.ui.Keyboard;

    public class ShipSim extends Sprite
    {
        private var ship:Ship;
        private var vr:Number = 0;
        private var thrust:Number = 0;
        private var vx:Number = 0;
        private var vy:Number = 0;
        public function ShipSim()
        {
            init();
        }

        private function init():void
        {
            ship = new Ship();
            addChild(ship);
            ship.x = stage.stageWidth / 2;
            ship.y = stage.stageHeight / 2;
            addEventListener(Event.ENTER_FRAME, onEnterFrame);
            stage.addEventListener(KeyboardEvent.KEY_DOWN, onKeyDown);
            stage.addEventListener(KeyboardEvent.KEY_UP, onKeyUp);
        }

        private function onKeyDown(event:KeyboardEvent):void
        {
            switch(event.keyCode)
            {
                case Keyboard.LEFT :
                vr = -5;
                break;

                case Keyboard.RIGHT :
                vr = 5;
                break;
```

```
            case Keyboard.UP :
            thrust = 0.2;
            ship.draw(true);
            break;

            default :
            break;
        }
    }

    private function onKeyUp(event:KeyboardEvent):void
    {
        vr = 0;
        thrust = 0;
        ship.draw(false);
    }

    private function onEnterFrame(event:Event):void
    {
        ship.rotation += vr;
        var angle:Number = ship.rotation * Math.PI / 180;
        var ax:Number = Math.cos(angle) * thrust;
        var ay:Number = Math.sin(angle) * thrust;
        vx += ax;
        vy += ay;
        ship.x += vx;
        ship.y += vy;
    }
  }
}
```

First you define vr, rotational velocity, or how fast the ship is going to turn when you tell it to turn. It's set to zero to start, which means the ship won't turn at all:

```
private var vr:Number = 0;
```

But in the onMouseDown method, if the switch statement finds that the left or right cursor keys are pressed, it sets vr to –5 or 5, respectively:

```
case Keyboard.LEFT :
vr = -5;
break;

case Keyboard.RIGHT :
vr = 5;
break;
```

Then, in the onEnterFrame handler function, you add vr to the ship's current rotation, turning the ship one way or the other. When a key is released, reset vr to zero. OK, that takes care of rotation. Now let's look at thrust.

You've got your spaceship there, you've aimed it where you want it to go—3, 2, 1, blastoff! So, how do you get this thing to go somewhere? Well, it's pretty much just the opposite of what you just did in the revised mouse follower example. In that example, you calculated an angle and then figured out rotation and acceleration based on that. Here, you'll start with the rotation and work backward to find the angle and then the force on x and y.

Declare a thrust variable to keep track of how much force is being applied at any given time. Obviously, acceleration is going to happen only if the rocket is being fired, so this will start out as zero:

```
private var thrust:Number = 0;
```

Then the switch statement comes back into play. If the up cursor key is being held down, set thrust to a small value, say 0.2. This is also where you want to visually indicate that some thrust is being applied, by drawing the flame on the ship:

```
case Keyboard.UP :
thrust = 0.2;
ship.draw(true);
break;
```

Again, when a key is released, set thrust back to zero, and kill the flame.

```
private function onKeyUp(event:KeyboardEvent):void
{
    vr = 0;
    thrust = 0;
    ship.draw(false);
}
```

Now, when you get down to the onEnterFrame function, you'll know the rotation, which is in degrees, and you'll know the force being applied, if any. Convert rotation to radians and use sine and cosine, along with the thrust variable, to find out the acceleration on each axis:

```
private function onEnterFrame(event:Event):void
{
    ship.rotation += vr;
    var angle:Number = ship.rotation * Math.PI / 180;
    var ax:Number = Math.cos(angle) * thrust;
    var ay:Number = Math.sin(angle) * thrust;
    vx += ax;
    vy += ay;
    ship.x += vx;
    ship.y += vy;
}
```

Test it and fly your ship around. It's pretty amazing just how easily you can make some complex motion like that. If you've used my ship-drawing code, you'll want to make sure you set the background to black, or some other dark color, so the white lines will show up.

Important formulas in this chapter

So, now you have a few more tools for your toolbox. Here they are.

Convert angular velocity to x, y velocity:

```
vx = speed * Math.cos(angle);
vy = speed * Math.sin(angle);
```

Convert angular acceleration (any force acting on an object) to x, y acceleration:

```
ax = force * Math.cos(angle);
ay = force * Math.sin(angle);
```

Add acceleration to velocity:

```
vx += ax;
vy += ay;
```

Add velocity to position:

```
movieclip._x += vx;
sprite.y += vy;
```

Summary

This chapter covered basic velocity and acceleration, the two factors that will make up the vast majority of your scripted animations. You've learned about vectors and vector addition. You've seen how to accomplish velocity on a single axis, on two axes, and on an angle by converting it to its x and y components. And you've learned about acceleration—how it relates to velocity and how to apply it to a single axis, two axes, or an angle.

The biggest thing to take from this chapter is a basic understanding of the application of acceleration and velocity, as described in the following steps:

- Convert existing angular velocity to component x, y velocities.
- Convert angular acceleration to component x, y acceleration.
- Add the acceleration on each axis to the velocity on that axis.
- Add the velocity on each axis to the position on that axis.

In the next chapter, you'll build on these concepts, adding some environmental interaction with bouncing and friction.

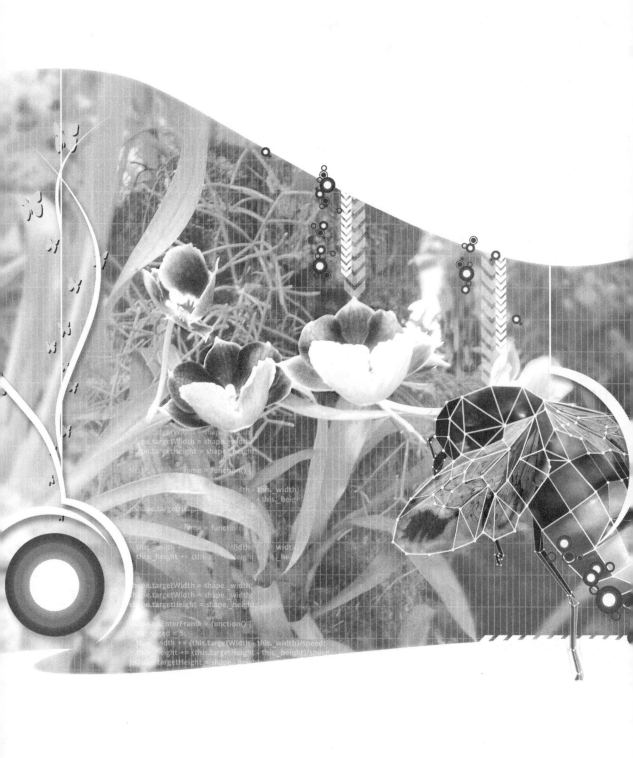

Chapter 6

BOUNDARIES AND FRICTION

What we'll cover in this chapter:

- Environmental boundaries
- Friction
- Important formulas in this chapter

You've covered a lot of ground in the preceding chapters; you can now get some kind of graphic into a sprite and use all kinds of forces to move it around the screen. However, you've probably already run into a small annoyance with many of the examples you've created so far: When you move the object off the screen, bang—it's gone. Sometimes, if it's moving fast at some angle, you have no way of knowing how to get it back. Your only option is to restart the movie.

In most real-world scenarios, some *boundaries* exist—sometimes walls and a ceiling, but at the very least, almost always the ground. Unless you're making a space simulator, you want to have some kind of environmental barriers to keep your objects in view. If you are doing the space thing, you need at least some way to keep your main objects in view.

Another thing you may or may not have noticed is how this environment, or lack thereof, fails to have any effect on the object as it moves. You start an object moving, and it just keeps on going in the direction it's headed at the same speed, until you apply some other force. Actually, this isn't a bug at all, but the way the universe works. The term *inertia* is used to describe the fact that an object traveling through space will continue to travel at the direction and speed at which it is moving until some other force is applied. Or, to state it differently, its velocity won't change unless something changes it. In common experience, one of the things that changes an object's velocity is some sort of *friction*— even if only the friction of air. So, while you've successfully simulated an object moving in a vacuum, you're probably itching to make it a little more like something in your everyday environment.

This chapter will cover both of these issues. First you'll learn how to work with boundaries, and then how to mimic friction. Let's go.

Environmental boundaries

We'll start by setting some boundaries, literally. With any activity you're involved in—whether it's playing a sport, working at your job, building a house, and so on—there's usually some concept of the space for that activity. You're saying, "I'm only interested in things that happen in this area. If something is happening somewhere outside this area, I don't really care about it at this moment. If something is happening inside this space though, I need to pay attention to it."

If one of the objects in your zone of interest moves outside that space, you have a choice to make. You can move it back into the zone somehow, or you can cross it off the list of things that you're paying attention to. Another option is to follow it. In other words, you move the space so that it continues to enclose the object, even though the object is moving. It's not so much different in Flash.

In your movie, you set up a space for your objects. Generally, this is the whole stage, but the area can be some portion of the stage, or even a space that is larger than the stage. Since the objects are moving, there's a good chance that they will eventually leave that space. When they leave, you can forget about them, move them back into the area, or follow them. I'll cover strategies for the first two of these approaches. First, though, let's just figure out where the boundaries are and how to specify them.

Setting boundaries

In most cases, a simple rectangle works as a boundary. Let's start with the simplest example, with the boundaries based on the size of the stage. In AS 3, the stage is represented by a property called stage, which is part of every display object. So, in your document class (which extends MovieClip or Sprite), you can access the stage and its properties directly with this property. If you want the stage size to change to match the size of the player when the player window resizes, you should set these two properties:

```
stage.stageAlign = StageAlign.TOP_LEFT;
stage.scaleMode = StageScaleMode.NO_SCALE;
```

Note that you will need to import the classes flash.display.StageAlign and flash.display.StageScaleMode at the top of your class.

Now the top and left boundaries of the movie will be zero, and the right and bottom boundaries will be stage.stageWidth and stage.stageHeight. You can store these in variables if you want, like so:

```
private var left:Number = 0;
private var top:Number = 0;
private var right:Number = stage.stageWidth;
private var bottom:Number = stage.stageHeight;
```

If you do store them in variables like this, realize that they will not change when the stage size changes. This is good if you want to have a fixed area for your boundaries.

If, however, you always want to use the full stage area's boundaries, even when the stage size changes, just refer directly to stage.stageWidth and stage.stageHeight in your code. Most of the examples in this chapter will use this tactic.

Also note that just because I'll be using the full stage in these examples doesn't mean that you have to. You could, for example, make a "room" that an object needed to stay within. In this case, the boundaries might be something like top = 100, bottom = 300, left = 50, right = 400.

OK, now that you have your boundaries in place, what do you do with them? Well, you check all the movable objects you're paying attention to at the moment and see whether they are still within this space. You can do this with a couple of if statements. Here is a simplified version of what they look like:

```
if(ball.x > stage.stageWidth) {
    // do something
} else if(ball.x < 0) {
    // do something
}

if(ball.y > stage.stageHeight) {
    // do something
} else if(ball.y < 0) {
    // do something
}
```

Here I've used if and else statements for efficiency. If the ball's x position is greater than the right edge, it is way over there on the right. There's no way it could also be way over by the left edge, so you don't need to check that in a separate if statement. You need to check the left variable only in the case that the first if fails. Do the same for the top and bottom. However, it is possible for the object to be out of bounds on the x and y axis at the same time, so keep those two checks separate.

But what is this "something" you're supposed to do when the object goes out of bounds? You'll learn about these four options:

- Remove it.
- Bring it back into play as if it were a brand-new object (regeneration).
- Wrap it back onto the screen, as if it were the same object reappearing at a different location.
- Have it bounce back into the area.

Let's start with simple removal.

Removing objects

Simply removing the object once it goes out of bounds is especially useful if you have objects being continually generated. The ones you remove will be replaced by new ones coming in, so you won't end up with an empty stage. Also, you won't wind up with too many objects being moved around, which would eventually slow down Flash Player.

To remove a sprite or any other display object, simply call removeChild(*objectName*). This will remove the instance from the stage. Note that removing a display object no longer destroys it. If you are actually done with the object, you should then call delete *objectName* to get rid of it.

You'll also want to make sure that the code doesn't continue to try to move the sprite from an external enterFrame handler. If the instance is the only thing being moved, and that motion is the only thing being done by the enterFrame handler, you can simply stop executing that handler by including removeEventListener(Event.ENTER_FRAME, onEnterFrame);. On the other hand, if you have a number of objects that you are moving around, you want to keep running the code to continue moving most of the objects, but take the removed sprite off the list of things to move. In this case, you should store references to the moving objects in an array and loop through the array to move each object. Then, when you remove one of these objects, use the Array.splice method to remove it from the array as well. You'll see this in action shortly.

So, if you want to remove a sprite, knowing what the boundaries are, you can come up with something like this for your if statement:

```
if(ball.x > stage.stageWidth ||
    ball.x < 0 ||
    ball.y > stage.stageHeight ||
    ball.y < 0)
{
    removeChild(ball);
}
```

The || symbol means "OR." So, you're essentially saying, "If the object is off to the right, OR the object is off to the left, OR it is off to the top OR the bottom, remove it." This technique is probably fine for most cases of removal, as it doesn't really matter *where* the object went out of bounds, just that it did. In other cases, though, you might want to respond differently if the object hit a particular boundary, such as the left wall as opposed to the right wall. In those instances, you will need to use separate if statements. You'll see that in the example of screen wrapping, coming up shortly.

A note on the garbage collector: Garbage collection is the term given to the process of cleaning up stuff in your program that is no longer needed or used, or has been deleted. In AS 3, when you delete an object, it is not immediately destroyed as in earlier versions of ActionScript. Instead, it is just marked for deletion. The garbage collector makes periodic sweeps through memory, deleting things it finds should be deleted. Thus, if you delete an object and then trace it, you may find that it still exists for some time. In these examples, you are just moving a sprite with code external to the sprite, so the sprite itself is really nothing more than a holder for a graphic. The new deletion behavior becomes really important, however, if you have an object that has its own internal `enterFrame` code or some kind of timer or interval. This code may continue to run even after you "delete" the object that's running it. So it's up to you to stop the `enterFrame`, interval, or timer code and not just rely on deletion to stop it. I'll be sure to point out examples of this kind of thing as we run into them later in the book.

All seems well and good. But there is one small problem. Now, you might not even notice this problem in many cases, but sometimes it could wind up making things look wrong. To see what I mean, take a look at Figure 6-1.

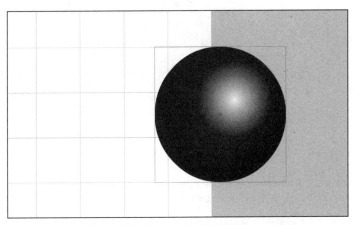

Figure 6-1. This ball isn't fully off stage, but it will be removed.

In Figure 6-1, you can see that the ball's position, as determined by its registration point in the center, is indeed past the right edge of the screen. It will be removed. If the ball is moving fast enough, that will probably look OK. But what if it's moving very slowly, just a pixel per frame or less? You're watching it ease off the edge of the screen, it gets halfway, and POP! It's gone. It's kind of like an actor removing his costume when he is only halfway off stage. It kind of ruins the illusion.

So, instead, you want to let the ball get all the way out of the picture. Then, when it's out of sight and out of mind, you can quietly execute it.

To do this, you need to take into account the object's width. Actually, since the registration point is in the center, you just need to worry about half of its width, which just happens to be stored in its radius property. To do this, your if statement needs to become a bit more complex. It will look something like this:

```
if(ball.x - ball.radius > stage.stageWidth ||
    ball.x + ball.radius < 0 ||
    ball.y - ball.radius > stage.stageHeight ||
    ball.y + ball.radius < 0)
{
    removeChild(ball);
}
```

This gives you the picture shown in Figure 6-2.

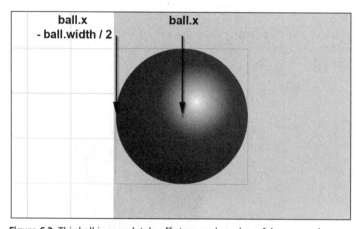

Figure 6-2. This ball is completely off stage and can be safely removed.

Note that although this particular example uses a ball, or round object, the same code should work for an object of any shape, as long as the registration point of the object is in the center.

Let's try it out. In the next example, we'll use the Ball class we used in the last chapter, with a small addition. We add public vx and vy properties to it, so that each ball could have its own velocity. Here it is in its entirety:

```
package {
    import flash.display.Sprite;

    public class Ball extends Sprite {
        public var radius:Number;
        private var color:uint;
        public var vx:Number = 0;
        public var vy:Number = 0;
```

```
        public function Ball(radius:Number=40, color:uint=0xff0000) {
            this.radius = radius;
            this.color = color;
            init();
        }
        public function init():void {
            graphics.beginFill(color);
            graphics.drawCircle(0, 0, radius);
            graphics.endFill();
        }
    }
}
```

In pure object-oriented programming, you probably wouldn't make public properties like this, but instead keep them private and use public getter/setter methods to change them. But to keep things simple, we're going to break the rule here and just make them public.

The following document class, Removal.as, sets up a number of these balls and removes them when they go off stage:

```
package
{
    import flash.display.Sprite;
    import flash.display.StageAlign;
    import flash.display.StageScaleMode;
    import flash.events.Event;

    public class Removal extends Sprite
    {
        private var count:int = 20;
        private var balls:Array;

        public function Removal()
        {
            init();
        }

        private function init():void
        {
            stage.scaleMode = StageScaleMode.NO_SCALE;
            stage.align=StageAlign.TOP_LEFT;
            balls = new Array();
            for(var i:int = 0; i < count; i++)
            {
                var ball:Ball = new Ball(10);
                ball.x = Math.random() * stage.stageWidth;
                ball.y = Math.random() * stage.stageHeight;
                ball.vx = Math.random() * 2 - 1;
                ball.vy = Math.random() * 2 - 1;
                addChild(ball);
```

```
            balls.push(ball);
        }
        addEventListener(Event.ENTER_FRAME, onEnterFrame);
    }

    private function onEnterFrame(event:Event):void
    {
        for(var i:Number = balls.length - 1; i > 0; i--)
        {
            var ball:Ball = Ball(balls[i]);
            ball.x += ball.vx;
            ball.y += ball.vy;
            if(ball.x - ball.radius > stage.stageWidth ||
                ball.x + ball.radius < 0 ||
                ball.y - ball.radius > stage.stageHeight ||
                ball.y + ball.radius < 0)
            {
                removeChild(ball);
                balls.splice(i, 1);
                if(balls.length <= 0)
                {
                    removeEventListener(Event.ENTER_FRAME,
                                        onEnterFrame);
                }
            }
        }
    }
}
```

This should be pretty simple for you to follow. First, you create 20 instances of Ball, randomly placing them on the stage, giving them random x and y velocities, adding them to the display list, and pushing them into the array.

The onEnterFrame method simply uses a flat velocity to move the balls around, checks the boundaries, and removes any balls that are out of bounds. Note that it not only removes the ball from the display list, but also uses the Array.splice function to remove the reference from the array. Array.splice takes the index at which you want to start removing elements and how many elements you want to remove. In this case, you are removing only one element: the one at the current index. When you test this, you won't even be aware of them being removed, which is a good thing, but you can rest assured that they are not hanging around off stage, consuming valuable memory and CPU cycles.

You might notice that the for statement in this example is a little different from those in other examples:

```
for(var i:Number = balls.length - 1; i > 0; i--)
```

This causes the for statement to go backward through the array instead of forward. This is necessary because, if you use splice on the array, the indexing for the array will change, and when you increment i, you will wind up skipping over one of the elements. Going backward handles this.

Finally, note that after splicing an element out of the array, it checks to see whether the array length is down to zero. In this case, there is nothing left to move around, so the `enterFrame` listener is removed.

Regenerating objects

The next strategy is to regenerate the object that has gone off stage. Actually, it's not really so much regeneration as repositioning and revelocitizing (yeah, I just made up that word). The idea is that when an object has gone off stage and is no longer necessary, you can bring it back into play as if it were a brand-new object. This gives you a steady stream of objects without ever having to worry about having too many objects on stage, as there will always be a set number.

This technique is very useful for things like fountain effects, where you have a stream of particles spraying constantly. The particles go off stage and are reintroduced at the source point of the stream.

The mechanics of regeneration are pretty similar to removal. You need to wait until the object is out of bounds, but instead of removing it, you just move it.

Let's dive right in by making a fountain. For the fountain particles, we use the same Ball class, but set it to be just 2 pixels across and give it a random color. The source of the fountain will be the bottom center of the stage. All particles will originate there, and when they go off stage, they will be replaced there. Also, all particles will start out with a random negative y velocity and a smaller random x velocity. This means they will shoot upward and also move slightly to the left or the right. When particles regenerate, their velocities will be reset the same way. Particles will also react to gravity. Here's the document class Fountain.as:

```
package
{
    import flash.display.Sprite;
    import flash.display.StageAlign;
    import flash.display.StageScaleMode;
    import flash.events.Event;

    public class Fountain extends Sprite
    {
        private var count:int = 100;
        private var gravity:Number = 0.5;
        private var balls:Array;

        public function Fountain()
        {
            init();
        }

        private function init():void
        {
            stage.scaleMode = StageScaleMode.NO_SCALE;
            stage.align=StageAlign.TOP_LEFT;
            balls = new Array();
            for(var i:int = 0; i < count; i++)
```

155

```
        {
            var ball:Ball = new Ball(2, Math.random() * 0xffffff);
            ball.x = stage.stageWidth / 2;
            ball.y = stage.stageHeight;
            ball.vx = Math.random() * 2 - 1;
            ball.vy = Math.random() * -10 - 10;
            addChild(ball);
            balls.push(ball);
        }
        addEventListener(Event.ENTER_FRAME, onEnterFrame);
    }

    private function onEnterFrame(event:Event):void
    {
        for(var i:Number = 0; i < balls.length; i++)
        {
            var ball:Ball = Ball(balls[i]);
            ball.vy += gravity;
            ball.x += ball.vx;
            ball.y += ball.vy;
            if(ball.x - ball.radius > stage.stageWidth ||
               ball.x + ball.radius < 0 ||
               ball.y - ball.radius > stage.stageHeight ||
               ball.y + ball.radius < 0)
            {
                ball.x = stage.stageWidth / 2;
                ball.y = stage.stageHeight;
                ball.vx = Math.random() * 2 - 1;
                ball.vy = Math.random() * -10 - 10;
            }

        }
    }
}
```

You start off in the init function by setting all the particles at the starting point and giving them an initial random upward velocity.

The onEnterFrame method loops through all the elements of the balls array. For each one, it adds gravity to its vy value, adds the velocity to the position, and then checks to see whether it has crossed any boundaries. If it has, it gets sent back to the starting position and is "reborn" with a new velocity. It will act the same as a newly created particle. Thus, your fountain will flow forever.

You should definitely play around with this one. Have the fountain shoot off in different directions. Make it shoot out of a wall, or even the ceiling. Change the random factors to make a wider or narrower fountain, or one that shoots higher or lower. Try adding some wind into the mix (hint: make a wind variable and add it to vx).

Screen wrapping

The next common way to handle objects going out of bounds is what I call *screen wrapping*. The concept is simple: If an object goes off the left side of the screen, it reappears on the right. If it goes off the right, it comes back on the left. If it goes off the top, it comes back on the bottom. You get the idea.

Screen wrapping is pretty similar to regeneration, in that you put the object back on the screen at a different location. But in regeneration, you generally return all objects to the same location, making them look like brand-new objects. In wrapping, you are usually trying to maintain the idea that this is the same object; that it has just gone out the back door and in the front, so to speak. Thus, you generally don't change velocity during a screen wrap.

This again hearkens back to one of my old favorite games, *Asteroids*. As you remember from Chapter 5, this was one of the problems with the spaceship movie: The ship would fly off stage, and it was sometimes impossible to figure out where it was and how to get it back. With screen wrapping, your sprite is never more than a pixel from the edge of the screen.

Let's rebuild that spaceship example and add this behavior. Here's the document class you'll want to use (ShipSim2.as), with the new stuff in bold:

```
package
{
    import flash.display.Sprite;
    import flash.events.Event;
    import flash.events.KeyboardEvent;
    import flash.ui.Keyboard;
    import flash.display.StageAlign;
    import flash.display.StageScaleMode;

    public class ShipSim2 extends Sprite
    {
        private var ship:Ship;
        private var vr:Number = 0;
        private var thrust:Number = 0;
        private var vx:Number = 0;
        private var vy:Number = 0;
        public function ShipSim2()
        {
            init();
        }

        private function init():void
        {
            stage.scaleMode = StageScaleMode.NO_SCALE;
            stage.align=StageAlign.TOP_LEFT;
            ship = new Ship();
            addChild(ship);
            ship.x = stage.stageWidth / 2;
            ship.y = stage.stageHeight / 2;
            addEventListener(Event.ENTER_FRAME, onEnterFrame);
```

```
        stage.addEventListener(KeyboardEvent.KEY_DOWN, onKeyDown);
        stage.addEventListener(KeyboardEvent.KEY_UP, onKeyUp);
    }

    private function onKeyDown(event:KeyboardEvent):void
    {
        switch(event.keyCode)
        {
            case Keyboard.LEFT :
            vr = -5;
            break;

            case Keyboard.RIGHT :
            vr = 5;
            break;

            case Keyboard.UP :
            thrust = 0.2;
            ship.draw(true);
            break;

            default :
            break;
        }
    }

    private function onKeyUp(event:KeyboardEvent):void
    {
        vr = 0;
        thrust = 0;
        ship.draw(false);
    }

    private function onEnterFrame(event:Event):void
    {
        ship.rotation += vr;
        var angle:Number = ship.rotation * Math.PI / 180;
        var ax:Number = Math.cos(angle) * thrust;
        var ay:Number = Math.sin(angle) * thrust;
        vx += ax;
        vy += ay;
        ship.x += vx;
        ship.y += vy;
        var left:Number = 0;
        var right:Number = stage.stageWidth;
        var top:Number = 0;
        var bottom:Number = stage.stageHeight;
        if (ship.x - ship.width / 2 > right)
        {
```

```
            ship.x = left - ship.width / 2;
        }
        else if (ship.x + ship.width / 2 < left)
        {
            ship.x = right + ship.width / 2;
        }
        if (ship.y - ship.height / 2 > bottom)
        {
            ship.y = top - ship.height / 2;
        }
        else if (ship.y < top - ship.height / 2)
        {
            ship.y = bottom + ship.height / 2;
        }
    }
  }
}
```

This uses the Ship class from Chapter 5 as well, so make sure that's in your class path. And, as the ship is drawn in white lines, don't forget to change your background color to black (see Chapter 4 for info on how to do that). As you can see, this new class just adds boundary definitions and the checks for them. Note that you are back to separate if and else statements, as the actions are different for each circumstance.

Bouncing

And now we arrive at probably the most common and possibly the most complex of bounds handling methods. But it's really not much more complicated than wrapping, so don't get scared.

The strategy with bouncing is to detect when the object has gone off screen, only this time, you leave it pretty much where it is and just change its velocity. The rules are simple: If it went off the left or right edge, you reverse its x velocity. If it went off the top or bottom, you reverse its y velocity. Reversing an axis velocity is pretty simple. Just multiply the value by –1. If the velocity is 5, it becomes –5. If it's –13, it becomes 13. The code is even simpler: vx *= -1 or vy *= -1.

There are a couple more changes from wrapping. First, in wrapping, you let the object go completely off stage before you reposition it. You do that by taking its position and adding or subtracting half its width. For bouncing, you want to do almost exactly the opposite. You don't want to wait until the object is totally off stage before you make it bounce. In fact, you don't want it to be even partway out of the picture. If you were to throw a real ball against a real wall, you wouldn't expect to see it go part-way into the wall before bouncing back. It would hit the wall, stop right there, and then bounce back. So, the first thing you want to know is the instant that *any part* of the object has gone over the edge. All you need to do is reverse the way you are adding the half width/height. So, for example, instead of saying this:

```
if(ball.x - ball.radius > right) . . .
```

you say this:

```
if(ball.x + ball.radius > right) . . .
```

The difference between these two can be seen in Figure 6-3.

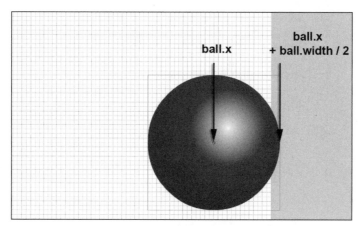

Figure 6-3. This ball is just slightly off stage, but it needs to bounce.

So, you've now determined that the object has crossed at least a bit of one of the boundaries. I said before that you now reverse the velocity on that axis. But there's a little more to it than that. You also need to reposition the object so that it is sitting right on the edge of the boundary. This has the obvious cosmetic effect of making the object look more like it's hitting and bouncing, rather than sinking into the wall. But it is also a necessary step for other reasons. You'll find that if you don't adjust the object's position, then on the next frame, it may still be past that boundary, even after it moves. If this happens, the object will again reverse its velocity and head back *into* the wall! Then you get a situation where the object seems to be stuck halfway in and out of the wall, just sitting there and vibrating. It's not pretty.

The point where you need to place the object to have it sitting right on the boundary is actually the same point you are checking in the if statement. You just need to restate it a bit with a little basic algebra. Here's the full if statement for the x axis:

```
if(ball.x + ball.radius > right)
{
    ball.x = right - ball.radius;
    vx *= -1;
}
else if(ball.x - ball.radius < left)
{
    ball.x = left + ball.radius;
    vx *= -1;
}
```

Figure 6-4 shows what the ball would look like after being repositioned.

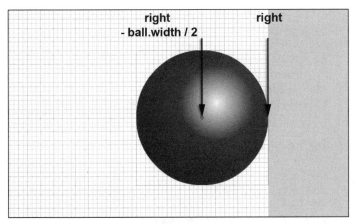

Figure 6-4. The ball has been repositioned to be exactly against the boundary.

So, the steps for bouncing are as follows:

- Check whether the object went past any boundary.
- If so, place it on the edge of that boundary.
- Then reverse the velocity.

That's all there is to it. I guess it's time to stop talking and show you some action. This next example uses the same Ball class once again, but scaled back up to a decent size. Here's the document class (Bouncing.as):

```
package
{
    import flash.display.Sprite;
    import flash.display.StageAlign;
    import flash.display.StageScaleMode;
    import flash.events.Event;

    public class Bouncing extends Sprite
    {
        private var ball:Ball;
        private var vx:Number;
        private var vy:Number;

        public function Bouncing()
        {
            init();
        }

        private function init():void
        {
            stage.scaleMode = StageScaleMode.NO_SCALE;
            stage.align=StageAlign.TOP_LEFT;
```

```
            ball = new Ball();
            ball.x = stage.stageWidth / 2;
            ball.y = stage.stageHeight / 2;
            vx = Math.random() * 10 - 5;
            vy = Math.random() * 10 - 5;
            addChild(ball);
            addEventListener(Event.ENTER_FRAME, onEnterFrame);
        }

        private function onEnterFrame(event:Event):void
        {
            ball.x += vx;
            ball.y += vy;
            var left:Number = 0;
            var right:Number = stage.stageWidth;
            var top:Number = 0;
            var bottom:Number = stage.stageHeight;

            if(ball.x + ball.radius > right)
            {
                ball.x = right - ball.radius;
                vx *= -1;
            }
            else if(ball.x - ball.radius < left)
            {
                ball.x = left + ball.radius;
                vx *= -1;
            }
            if(ball.y + ball.radius > bottom)
            {
                ball.y = bottom - ball.radius;
                vy *= -1;
            }
            else if(ball.y - ball.radius < top)
            {
                ball.y = top + ball.radius;
                vy *= -1;
            }
        }
    }
}
```

Test this a few times to see the ball moving at different angles. Try making the velocity higher or lower.

I have to admit that this is one of those many areas in the book where the math and calculations are not exactly in accordance with real-world physics. If you look at Figure 6-5, you'll see where the ball should actually hit the wall, and also where this simulation places it.

What we are doing:

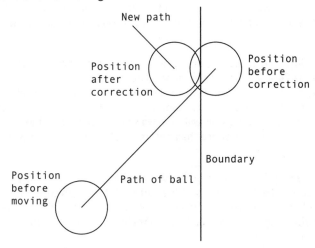

Real-world situation:

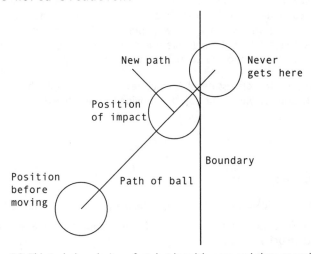

Figure 6-5. This technique isn't perfect, but is quick, easy, and close enough for most situations.

Determining the correct position takes more complex calculations. Although you are free to figure out how to do this (using the trigonometry covered in Chapter 3), I guarantee you wouldn't really notice much of a difference in most situations. Again, if you're doing some kind of simulation where exact calculations and positions are vital, you'll really need to find another book, and probably reconsider your choice of software. But for almost any game or visual effect you'll be creating with Flash, this method will serve you just fine. However, you can add one more thing to take the realism just one notch higher.

If you were to hold the most rubbery, bounciest rubber ball ever made out at arm's length and drop it, it would fall to the floor and bounce up *almost* back to where it started. The fact is that it will never make it all the way back to your hand. This is because it loses a little bit of energy in the bounce. It might lose some energy in the form of sound; maybe a little heat. The floor will absorb some of its energy, and maybe the surrounding air will, too. However it works out, the important point is that the ball is traveling slower after the bounce than before. In other words, it loses some velocity on the axis of the bounce.

You can easily re-create this with Flash. So far, you've been using –1 as your bounce factor. That means that the object bounces back with 100% of the force it hit with. To make it lose some energy, simply use a fraction of –1. As with other numeric values, it's best to define this as a variable up at the top of your file and use the variable in your code. Just create a variable named bounce and set it to something like –0.7 at the top of your file:

```
private var bounce:Number = -0.7;
```

Then replace each instance of -1 in the if statements with the variable bounce. Go ahead and try that, and you'll see how much more real the bounces look. Try different factors for the bounce variable until you get a feel for how it works.

One of the best ways to learn this stuff is to take each principle you learn and see how many other principles you can combine it with. You can check the book's files on line at www.friendsofed.com for document class Bouncing2.as, which has an example of bouncing and gravity. But I'm sure you have enough knowledge to start adding things like this on your own. Perhaps you want to try to use the keyboard to add some acceleration to the ball, or apply something else you've already learned.

Now, let's leave behind the discussion of boundaries and talk about what happens in between the boundaries—what happens while your object is moving through space.

Friction

So far, you've seen two scenarios:

- The object is simply moving with whatever velocity it has until it hits a boundary.
- Either the object itself or some external force is applying some acceleration to the object, changing its velocity.

With either setup, unless the object is being pushed or pulled, or it hits something, it will keep going in the same direction at the exact same speed. But in the real world, it doesn't happen just like that.

Here's an example. Grab a piece of paper, crumple it up very loosely, and throw it as hard as you can. There's a good chance it didn't even make it across the room. Sure, gravity was pulling it down (y axis), but when it left your hand, it was moving pretty fast on the x axis. Yet, very quickly, it had almost zero x velocity.

Obviously, no "negative acceleration" was pulling the paper back toward your hand, yet its velocity was changed. This is known as *friction*, *drag*, *resistance*, or *damping*. Although it's not technically a force, it does kind of act that way, in that it changes an object's velocity. The rule is that friction reduces only the magnitude of the velocity. Whichever direction the object is headed in, this will not be changed by friction. In other words, friction can reduce velocity to zero, but it will never make an object turn around and go in the other direction.

So, how do you implement friction in code? It turns out there are two ways. Like most things in life, you have the right way and the easy way. But unlike your parents, I'm going to recommend the easy way. Even so, I'm going to show you both ways, starting with the "right" one, and let you make up your own mind.

Friction, the right way

Friction is actually subtractive of velocity, which is to say you have a certain value for friction, and you subtract that from your velocity. Actually, you need to subtract it from the magnitude, or speed, of the velocity. You can't just subtract the friction from the x axis and y axis separately. If you do that for an object traveling at an angle, one of the component velocities will reach zero before the other, and the object will continue on for a while either vertically or horizontally, which will look pretty strange.

So, what you need to do is find the angular velocity in terms of speed and direction (if you don't have it already). To find the speed, you take the square root of vx squared plus vy squared (yes, that's the Pythagorean Theorem, which you should recognize from Chapter 3). To find the angle, you calculate `Math.atan2(vy, vx)`, which looks like this in code:

```
var speed:Number = Math.sqrt(vx * vx + vy * vy);
var angle:Number = Math.atan2(vy, vx);
```

Then you can subtract the friction from the speed. But you want to make sure you don't send the speed into negative values, which would reverse the velocity. So, if your friction is greater than your speed, the speed just becomes zero. Here is the code for that calculation:

```
if(speed > friction)
{
    speed -= friction;
}
else
{
    speed = 0;
}
```

At that point, you need to convert the angular velocity back into vx and vy, using sine and cosine, like so:

```
vx = Math.cos(angle) * speed;
vy = Math.sin(angle) * speed;
```

Quite a bit of work, eh? Here's how it looks all together in document class Friction1.as:

```
package
{
    import flash.display.Sprite;
    import flash.display.StageAlign;
    import flash.display.StageScaleMode;
    import flash.events.Event;

    public class Friction1 extends Sprite
    {
        private var ball:Ball;
        private var vx:Number = 0;
        private var vy:Number = 0;
        private var friction:Number = 0.1;

        public function Friction1()
        {
            init();
        }

        private function init():void
        {
            stage.scaleMode = StageScaleMode.NO_SCALE;
            stage.align=StageAlign.TOP_LEFT;

            ball = new Ball();
            ball.x = stage.stageWidth / 2;
            ball.y = stage.stageHeight / 2;
            vx = Math.random() * 10 - 5;
            vy = Math.random() * 10 - 5;
            addChild(ball);
            addEventListener(Event.ENTER_FRAME, onEnterFrame);
        }

        private function onEnterFrame(event:Event):void
        {
          var speed:Number = Math.sqrt(vx * vx + vy * vy);
          var angle:Number = Math.atan2(vy, vx);
          if (speed > friction)
          {
              speed -= friction;
          }
          else
          {
              speed = 0;
          }
```

```
            vx = Math.cos(angle) * speed;
            vy = Math.sin(angle) * speed;
            ball.x += vx;
            ball.y += vy;
        }
    }
}
```

Here, I've given you a scaled-back velocity code. The friction is set to 0.1, and the ball is given a random velocity on the x and y axes. In the onEnterFrame method, speed and angle are calculated as I just described. If speed is less than friction, subtract; otherwise, speed equals zero. Finally, vx and vy are recalculated and added to the position.

Go ahead and test this example several times to see it at different speeds and angles. That's how friction looks. It took a dozen lines of code and four trig functions to accomplish. You could probably come up with a more optimized version, but all those calculations will be in there, one way or the other. I think you'll agree that it's time to look at the easy way.

Friction, the easy way

As you would expect, the easy way to do friction is not as accurate as the technique I just described, but I bet nobody will ever notice. It consists of two lines of simple multiplication. All you need to do is multiply the x and y velocities by some fraction of 1. A number like 0.9 or 0.8 usually works quite well. So, on each frame, the vx and vy become 80% or 90% of what they were last time. In theory, the velocity will approach zero, but never actually reach it. In practice, the computer can calculate such minute numbers only so far, and eventually it's going to round down to zero velocity. But long before that, the motion will be so small it will be indiscernible.

The good news is that the velocity is never going to go negative with this method, so you don't have to worry about checking for that. Also, the x and y velocities will approach zero at the same rate, so there's no need to convert axis velocities to angular and back.

The only alterations to the code (which can be found in document class Friction2.as) is changing the friction variable to 0.9 and the following changes to the onEnterFrame method:

```
private function onEnterFrame(event:Event):void
{
    vx *= friction;
    vy *= friction;
    ball.x += vx;
    ball.y += vy;
}
```

Now, that's certainly easier! Test this version a number of times and get a feel for it. Can you see the difference in motion between this and the correct method? Probably you can, because you've just seen them side by side. To the average viewer though, this one will look pretty realistic.

167

Friction applied

Now, let's return to our familiar spaceship and apply some friction to that universe. For document class ShipSimFriction.as, we just take ShipSim2.as and add a friction variable:

```
private var friction:Number = 0.97;
```

along with the other class variables and change the onEnterFrame method to the following:

```
private function onEnterFrame(event:Event):void
{
    ship.rotation += vr;
    var angle:Number = ship.rotation * Math.PI / 180;
    var ax:Number = Math.cos(angle) * thrust;
    var ay:Number = Math.sin(angle) * thrust;
    vx += ax;
    vy += ay;
    vx *= friction;
    vy *= friction;
    ship.x += vx;
    ship.y += vy;
    var left:Number = 0;
    var right:Number = stage.stageWidth;
    var top:Number = 0;
    var bottom:Number = stage.stageHeight;
    if (ship.x - ship.width / 2 > right)
    {
        ship.x = left - ship.width / 2;
    }
    else if (ship.x + ship.width / 2 < left)
    {
        ship.x = right + ship.width / 2;
    }
    if (ship.y - ship.height / 2 > bottom)
    {
        ship.y = top - ship.height / 2;
    }
    else if (ship.y < top - ship.height / 2)
    {
        ship.y = bottom + ship.height / 2;
    }
}
```

That's quite a different feel for just three new lines of code.

Don't forget to think outside the x, y box. Friction can be applied anywhere you have any type of velocity. Say you have something rotating (with a vr). Applying friction to that will eventually cause it to slow down and stop spinning. You can try that with the spinning arrow from Chapter 5.

You can see how you could use this approach for all types of objects, such as a roulette wheel, an electric fan, or a propeller.

Important formulas in this chapter

Let's review the important formulas introduced in this chapter.

Remove an out-of-bounds object:

```
if(sprite.x - sprite.width / 2 > right ||
   sprite.x + sprite.width / 2 < left ||
   sprite.y - sprite.height / 2 > bottom ||
   sprite.y + sprite.height / 2 < top)
{
     // code to remove sprite
}
```

Regenerate an out-of-bounds object:

```
if(sprite.x - sprite.width / 2 > right ||
   sprite.x + sprite.width / 2 < left ||
   sprite.y - sprite.height / 2 > bottom ||
   sprite.y + sprite.height / 2 < top)
{
     // reset sprite position and velocity.
}
```

Screen wrapping for an out-of-bounds object:

```
if(sprite.x - sprite.width / 2 > right)
{
   sprite.x = left - sprite.width / 2;
}
else if(sprite.x + sprite.width / 2 < left)
{
   sprite.x = right + sprite.width / 2;
}
if(sprite.y - sprite.height / 2 > bottom)
{
   sprite.y = top - sprite.height / 2;
}
else if(sprite.y + sprite.height / 2 < top)
{
   sprite.y = bottom + sprite.height / 2;
}
```

Apply friction (the correct way):

```
speed = Math.sqrt(vx * vx + vy * vy);
angle = Math.atan2(vy, vx);
if(speed > friction)
{
    speed -= friction;
}
else
{
    speed = 0;
}
vx = Math.cos(angle) * speed;
vy = Math.sin(angle) * speed;
```

Apply friction (the easy way):

```
vx *= friction;
vy *= friction;
```

Summary

This chapter covered an object's interaction with its own environment—specifically, an object's interaction with the edges of its universe and the universe itself. You learned the possible ways to deal with an object that has gone off the edge of the world, including removing, regenerating, wrapping, and bouncing. And, you now know more about friction than you probably ever wanted to know. But with these simple techniques, you can make the objects in your movies move with a great deal of realism. In the next chapter, you'll delve into allowing the user to interact with the objects.

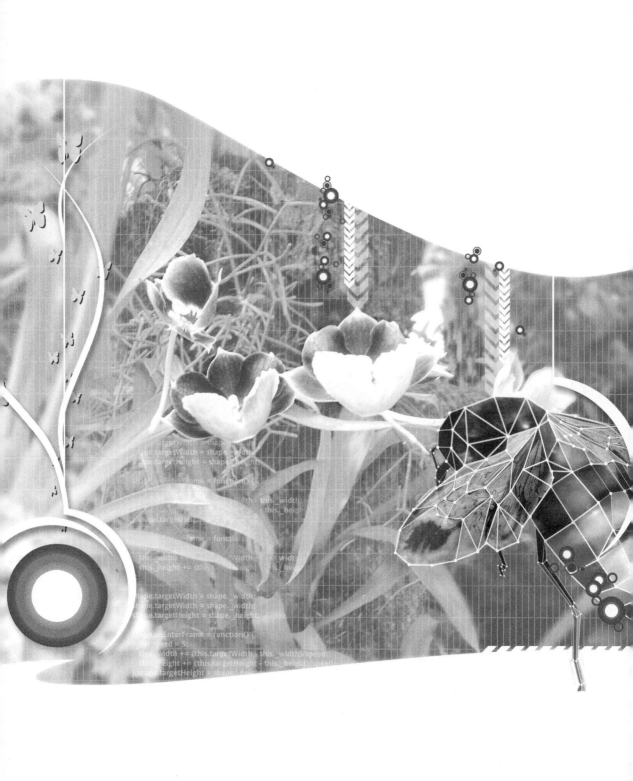

Chapter 7

USER INTERACTION: MOVING OBJECTS AROUND

What we'll cover in this chapter:

- Pressing and releasing a sprite
- Dragging a sprite
- Throwing

It's likely that a primary goal of your animation is to allow smooth user interaction, and a lot of this interaction will be through the mouse. I talked about mouse events back in Chapter 2, but you haven't really done much with them yet. Now, you'll get some hands-on practice with them.

In this chapter, you're going to take your first steps into the field of user interaction. You'll learn how to handle dragging, dropping, and throwing. But first, let's get started with the basics of press and release.

Pressing and releasing a sprite

The mouse is a pretty cool invention, but in essence, it's a simple device. It really does only two things: It detects motion and button clicks. The computer then uses that information to do a lot more: keeping track of the position of a mouse cursor, determining where the cursor is when the click occurs, determining how fast the mouse is moving, and figuring out when a double-click occurs. But really, when you look at it in terms of events, it all comes down to clicks and movement. (Of course, some mice today have scroll wheels and track balls and more buttons than a cheap cell phone, but we'll stick to the basic garden variety mouse here.)

You can also break clicks down into two parts: the event that occurs when the mouse button goes down and the next event when it comes up. Sometimes, those events occur almost instantaneously. Other times, the events are separated by time and motion, which is usually interpreted as a *drag*—click, move, and then release. In this chapter, you'll concentrate on those three things: the mouse going down, the mouse going up, and any motion that occurs in between the two.

Mouse handling in AS 3 has changed quite a bit, and while it will take some time to relearn the basics, overall, it is all for the better. The whole architecture of events in AS 3 is well thought out and logical, unlike the black magic it sometimes seemed to be in earlier versions of the language.

Basically, mouse events will only be received by a sprite, movie clip, or other interactive object if the mouse is over some visible graphic portion of that object. In AS 2, this was true for some mouse events, but not for others. This led to quite a bit of confusion. It also led to the necessity of multiple events such as onRelease and onReleaseOutside, which usually you wanted to do the same thing, but had to be handled separately.

Another thing that has radically changed relates to nested objects and mouse events. In AS 2, if you listened for mouse events on a movie clip, there was no way to listen for them on any movie clips within that clip. The outer movie clip would catch all mouse events and not let them pass through. In AS 3, there is no such limitation. You can listen for mouse events on a movie clip or sprite, as well as its nested objects.

The main mouse events you need to know about are mouseDown, mouseUp, and mouseMove. These have been made static properties of the MouseEvent class:

- MouseEvent.MOUSE_DOWN
- MouseEvent.MOUSE_UP
- MouseEvent.MOUSE_MOVE

The mouseDown event occurs when you press a mouse button while the mouse pointer is over the visible graphic portion of a sprite, movie clip, or other interactive object. It is essentially the same as onPress in AS 2.

The mouseUp event occurs when you release the mouse button while over the graphic of a sprite, etc., and is equivalent to onRelease.

The mouseMove event occurs when you move the mouse—but only when you move it over the sprite or other object. This is quite different than in AS 2, where onMouseMove would fire for every movie clip whenever the mouse moved, no matter where the pointer was.

Sometimes, however, you just want to register the fact of the mouse moving or going up or down, regardless of where the pointer is. This was done with onMouseMove, onMouseUp, and onMouseDown in AS 2, which paid no attention to the mouse location. In AS 3, there are no equivalent methods, but you can listen for the mouseDown, mouseUp, and mouseMove events on the stage, in which case, they will fire regardless of any graphical content.

OK, enough talk, let's put it into action. The first example of this chapter, document class MouseEvents.as, uses the Ball class from the earlier chapters. Here it is:

```
package
{
    import flash.display.Sprite;
    import flash.events.MouseEvent;

    public class MouseEvents extends Sprite
    {
        public function MouseEvents()
        {
            init();
        }

        private function init():void
        {
            var ball:Ball = new Ball();
            ball.x = 100;
            ball.y = 100;
            addChild(ball);

            ball.addEventListener(MouseEvent.MOUSE_DOWN,
                              onMouseDownBall);
            ball.addEventListener(MouseEvent.MOUSE_UP,
                              onMouseUpBall);
            ball.addEventListener(MouseEvent.MOUSE_MOVE,
                              onMouseMoveBall);

            stage.addEventListener(MouseEvent.MOUSE_DOWN,
                              onMouseDownStage);
            stage.addEventListener(MouseEvent.MOUSE_UP,
                              onMouseUpStage);
```

```
                    stage.addEventListener(MouseEvent.MOUSE_MOVE,
                                           onMouseMoveStage);
            }

            private function onMouseDownBall(event:MouseEvent):void
            {
                trace("mouse down - ball");
            }

            private function onMouseUpBall(event:MouseEvent):void
            {
                trace("mouse up - ball");
            }

            private function onMouseMoveBall(event:MouseEvent):void
            {
                trace("mouse move - ball");
            }

            private function onMouseDownStage(event:MouseEvent):void
            {
                trace("mouse down - stage");
            }

            private function onMouseUpStage(event:MouseEvent):void
            {
                trace("mouse up - stage");
            }

            private function onMouseMoveStage(event:MouseEvent):void
            {
                trace("mouse move - stage");
            }

        }
    }
```

This just sets up handlers for the three mouse events I've been talking about, first on the ball, then on the stage. Then it lets you know when they occur. You can build this file and play around with it to see exactly when and where particular mouse events occur, until it is all clear. Here are some things to notice:

- The ball events happen only when the mouse pointer is over the ball.
- Particularly important to note is that the ball's mouseMove event only occurs when the mouse is over the ball.
- You get the stage events no matter where the mouse is—even if it is over the ball. In such a case, you will get two events—one for the ball and one for the stage.
- It's impossible to get a mouseUp event without first getting a mouseDown event.

176

Now that you know the basics of the important events, we'll move on to dragging.

Dragging a sprite

You can handle dragging a sprite using two different techniques: with the mouseMove event or with the startDrag/stopDrag methods. Although you'll be using the latter for the examples in this chapter, let's look at how to use the mouseMove event for dragging first. It will give you some experience in handling the mouseMove event and a deeper understanding of how events work.

Dragging with mouseMove

By manually handling the mouseMove event, you can update the sprite's position to match the mouse cursor's each time the mouse moves. It's worth noting that this is the only way to drag more than one object at a time. You sometimes run into this when making a custom cursor out of a sprite. The cursor needs to follow the mouse position around, but what if you want to drag something, too? One solution is to use mouseMove for the cursor, and leave the usual drag methods (startDrag/stopDrag) free for normal dragging. So it's a nice little technique to have under your belt, even if you don't use it on a regular basis.

The strategy is this: On the mouseDown event, you want to set up a mouseMove handler. This handler will just set the ball's x and y positions to equal the current mouse position. On the mouseUp event, you remove that handler.

Now here's the tricky part. You want to set the mouseDown listener on the sprite you are going to drag, but for the other two events, you want to listen to them on the stage. The reason for this is that you might get into a situation where you are dragging faster than Flash can update the sprite to keep it under the mouse. At that point, if you were listening for the mouseUp and mouseMove events on the sprite, they would never fire, as the mouse pointer is no longer over the sprite. Remember, though, that the stage will fire these events no matter where the mouse is.

The next document class, MouseMoveDrag.as, should make this more clear:

```
package
{
    import flash.display.Sprite;
    import flash.events.MouseEvent;

    public class MouseMoveDrag extends Sprite
    {
        private var ball:Ball;

        public function MouseMoveDrag()
        {
            init();
        }

        private function init():void
        {
```

```
        ball = new Ball();
        ball.x = 100;
        ball.y = 100;
        addChild(ball);
        ball.addEventListener(MouseEvent.MOUSE_DOWN, onMouseDown);
    }

    private function onMouseDown(event:MouseEvent):void
    {
        stage.addEventListener(MouseEvent.MOUSE_UP, onMouseUp);
        stage.addEventListener(MouseEvent.MOUSE_MOVE, onMouseMove);
    }

    private function onMouseUp(event:MouseEvent):void
    {
        stage.removeEventListener(MouseEvent.MOUSE_UP, onMouseUp);
        stage.removeEventListener(MouseEvent.MOUSE_MOVE,
                                    onMouseMove);
    }

    private function onMouseMove(event:MouseEvent):void
    {
        ball.x = mouseX;
        ball.y = mouseY;
    }
    }
}
```

Initially, you just want to listen for the mouseDown event, and only on the ball. The onMouseDown method adds listeners to the stage for the mouseUp and mouseMove events. The onMouseMove method updates the ball's position to match the mouse's. The onMouseUp method removes the mouseUp and mouseMove listeners from the stage, as you aren't interested in them except during the dragging phase.

You might have noticed one problem with this setup. If you click the edge of the ball and start dragging it, you'll see that it suddenly jumps and centers itself on the mouse cursor. This is because you're setting the ball's x and y positions to exactly equal to the mouse position. You could do some fancy footwork to get around that, finding the offset of the mouse to the ball when the mouse is pressed, and adding that to the ball's position as you drag. I'll leave that as a project for you, if you're interested in pursuing it. But I'm going to move on to the usual method of dragging a sprite.

Dragging with startDrag/stopDrag

All sprites and movie clips have built-in methods called startDrag and stopDrag, which handle all of the functionality of the method I just described (in what was an educational detour, I hope), and then some. About the only drawback is that it allows for dragging only a single object at a time.

The concept is pretty simple. In your mouseDown handler, you call startDrag. In the mouseUp handler, you call stopDrag.

startDrag can be called without any parameters. You can take the last document class and change the onMouseDown and onMouseUp methods to the following (as seen in document class Drag.as):

```
private function onMouseDown(event:MouseEvent):void
{
    stage.addEventListener(MouseEvent.MOUSE_UP, onMouseUp);
    ball.startDrag();
}

private function onMouseUp(event:MouseEvent):void
{
    stage.removeEventListener(MouseEvent.MOUSE_UP, onMouseUp);
    ball.stopDrag();
}
```

You can also get rid of the onMouseMove method, as it won't be needed here.

Pretty simple, eh? Test this, and you'll also notice that the "snapping" problem is gone. The ball will drag from whatever position you clicked on it. If you actually *want* it to snap to the center, though, you can do so by passing true to the first parameter of startDrag:

```
ball.startDrag(true);
```

You can also limit the dragging to a rectangular area by passing in coordinates for the left, top, right, and bottom of the area you want to be able to drag in. A change in AS 3 is that these are now passed in as a single Rectangle object (an instance of the flash.geom.Rectangle class—don't forget to import it). You can pass these four values right into the Rectangle constructor, like so:

```
var rect:Rectangle = new Rectangle(10, 10, 200, 200);
```

Here is the full syntax for startDrag:

```
startDrag(lockCenter, boundsRectangle)
```

Try changing the last example by using the following line for starting the drag:

```
ball.startDrag(false, new Rectangle(100, 100, 300, 300));
```

And I'll say it again: Don't forget to import the Rectangle class!

Combining dragging with motion code

At this point you know pretty much everything about simple dragging and dropping in Flash. Unfortunately, in the process, you've reverted back to a static object that just kind of sits there unless you're dragging it. Let's add some velocity and maybe even some acceleration and bouncing.

You already have a nice setup for velocity, gravity, and bouncing in the Bouncing2.as document class from the previous chapter. That's a good starting point. It would seem logical to simply add your drag-and-drop code to that code. Let's try it. You should end up with something like this (DragAndMove1.as):

```
package
{
    import flash.display.Sprite;
    import flash.display.StageAlign;
    import flash.display.StageScaleMode;
    import flash.events.Event;
    import flash.events.MouseEvent;

    public class DragAndMove1 extends Sprite
    {
        private var ball:Ball;
        private var vx:Number;
        private var vy:Number;
        private var bounce:Number = -0.7;
        private var gravity:Number = .5;

        public function DragAndMove1()
        {
            init();
        }

        private function init():void
        {
            stage.scaleMode = StageScaleMode.NO_SCALE;
            stage.align=StageAlign.TOP_LEFT;

            ball = new Ball();
            ball.x = stage.stageWidth / 2;
            ball.y = stage.stageHeight / 2;
            vx = Math.random() * 10 - 5;
            vy = -10;
            addChild(ball);
            ball.addEventListener(MouseEvent.MOUSE_DOWN, onMouseDown);
            addEventListener(Event.ENTER_FRAME, onEnterFrame);
        }

        private function onEnterFrame(event:Event):void
        {
            vy += gravity;
            ball.x += vx;
            ball.y += vy;
            var left:Number = 0;
            var right:Number = stage.stageWidth;
            var top:Number = 0;
            var bottom:Number = stage.stageHeight;
```

```
            if(ball.x + ball.radius > right)
            {
                ball.x = right - ball.radius;
                vx *= bounce;
            }
            else if(ball.x - ball.radius < left)
            {
                ball.x = left + ball.radius;
                vx *= bounce;
            }
            if(ball.y + ball.radius > bottom)
            {
                ball.y = bottom - ball.radius;
                vy *= bounce;
            }
            else if(ball.y - ball.radius < top)
            {
                ball.y = top + ball.radius;
                vy *= bounce;
            }
        }

        private function onMouseDown(event:MouseEvent):void
        {
            stage.addEventListener(MouseEvent.MOUSE_UP, onMouseUp);
            ball.startDrag();
        }

        private function onMouseUp(event:MouseEvent):void
        {
            stage.removeEventListener(MouseEvent.MOUSE_UP, onMouseUp);
            ball.stopDrag();
        }
    }
}
```

As you can see, all that you've added to the original code is the handlers for onMouseDown and onMouseUp.

If you test this now, you'll see the problem immediately when you start to drag. Yes, the dragging works, but the motion code is working at the same time. The result is the feeling that the ball is slipping out of your hand. You need some way of switching on or off the motion code, so that it doesn't happen while you're dragging. The simplest way to do this is to just remove the enterFrame handler when you start dragging, and reset it when you stop.

This just takes a couple extra lines in the onMouseDown and onMouseUp methods.

```
private function onMouseDown(event:MouseEvent):void
{
    stage.addEventListener(MouseEvent.MOUSE_UP, onMouseUp);
    ball.startDrag();
    removeEventListener(Event.ENTER_FRAME, onEnterFrame);
}

private function onMouseUp(event:MouseEvent):void
{
    stage.removeEventListener(MouseEvent.MOUSE_UP, onMouseUp);
    ball.stopDrag();
    addEventListener(Event.ENTER_FRAME, onEnterFrame);
}
```

When you test this, you'll see that you're getting closer, but you're not quite there yet.

When you start dragging, all you're doing is dragging. When you drop the ball, the motion code resumes where it left off. The main problem now is that the velocity also resumes where it left off. This sometimes results in the ball flying off in some direction when you release it, which is pretty unnatural. You can easily fix that by just setting vx and vy to zero, either when you start dragging or when you stop. Either one works, as long as it is done before the motion code resumes. Let's put it in the start drag section:

```
private function onMouseDown(event:MouseEvent):void
{
    vx = 0;
    vy = 0;
    stage.addEventListener(MouseEvent.MOUSE_UP, onMouseUp);
    ball.startDrag();
    removeEventListener(Event.ENTER_FRAME, onEnterFrame);
}
```

That takes care of the problem and leaves you with a fully functional drag-and-drop feature, with integrated velocity, acceleration, and bouncing. You can see the full code listing in document class DragAndMove2.as.

Just one issue remains: When you drop the ball, it falls straight down—no more x-axis motion. Although this is the correct behavior it's a bit boring. If you could actually throw the ball and have it fly off in whatever direction you threw it, that would be some heavy-duty interactivity. Well, that's exactly what you're going to do next.

Throwing

What does *throwing* mean when it comes to a Flash movie? It means you click an object to start dragging it, move it in a particular direction, and when you release it, it keeps moving in the direction you were dragging it.

For the velocity, you need to determine what velocity the object has while it is being dragged, and then set the object's velocity to that value when it is dropped. In other words, if you were dragging a sprite 10 pixels per frame to the left, then when you release it, its velocity should be vx = -10.

Setting the new velocity should be no problem for you; just assign new values to vx and vy, as shown in Figure 7-1. But determining what those values are might be a little tricky. Actually, calculating dragging velocity turns out to be almost exactly the opposite of applying velocity in your motion code. In applying velocity, you add velocity to the object's old position to come up with the object's new position. So, the formula would be old + velocity = new. To determine the velocity of an object while it's being dragged, you simply rearrange the equation to get velocity = new - old.

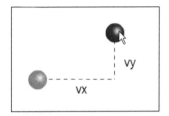

Figure 7-1. The ball has been dragged to a new position. The velocity is the distance from its last position to this new position.

As you are dragging the sprite, it's going to have a new position on each frame. If you take that and subtract the position it was in on the previous frame, you'll know how far it moved in one frame. That's your pixels-per-frame velocity!

Let's take an example, simplifying it to a single axis. A sprite is being dragged. On a particular frame, you note that its x position is 150. On the next frame, you see that its x position is 170. Thus, in one frame, it was dragged 20 pixels on the x axis, and its x velocity at that point is +20. If you were to release it just then, you would expect it to continue moving at an x velocity of 20. So, of course, you would set vx = 20.

This requires a couple of changes to your existing class. First, since you will need to keep track of velocity on each frame, you are going to need a handler for the enterFrame event. But since what you are doing on each frame is quite different than what the current onEnterFrame method does, let's just create a whole new method to track the dragging velocity. In fact, let's call it trackVelocity. You'll also need a couple of variables to hold the old x and y position values. You can call those oldX and oldY, and declare them as class variables. Now, as soon as you start dragging, you want to note the ball's position and store it in oldX and oldY. Then, after you remove onEnterFrame as a handler for the enterFrame event, you add trackVelocity as a listener. This is all done in the onMouseDown method, as follows:

```
private function onMouseDown(event:MouseEvent):void
{
    oldX = ball.x;
    oldY = ball.y;
    stage.addEventListener(MouseEvent.MOUSE_UP, onMouseUp);
    ball.startDrag();
    removeEventListener(Event.ENTER_FRAME, onEnterFrame);
    addEventListener(Event.ENTER_FRAME, trackVelocity);
}
```

Then, in the trackVelocity method, you just subtract oldX from the current x position, and oldY from the current y. This gives you the current velocity, so you can store these values directly in vx and vy. Then you can reset oldX and oldY to the current position of the ball again.

```
    private function trackVelocity(event:Event):void
    {
        vx = ball.x - oldX;
        vy = ball.y - oldY;
        oldX = ball.x;
        oldY = ball.y;
    }
```

Finally, when you release the ball, you swap the enterFrame handlers again, this time removing trackVelocity and adding back onEnterFrame:

```
    private function onMouseUp(event:MouseEvent):void
    {
        stage.removeEventListener(MouseEvent.MOUSE_UP, onMouseUp);
        ball.stopDrag();
        removeEventListener(Event.ENTER_FRAME, trackVelocity);
        addEventListener(Event.ENTER_FRAME, onEnterFrame);
    }
```

At this point you don't need to do anything at all about the velocity. It has been kept track of all through the drag, and the latest velocity is already stored in vx and vy. As soon as you reenable the motion code, the ball will move at whatever velocity it was just being dragged with. The result: You threw the ball!

In case you got lost along the way, here is the final document class (Throwing.as):

```
    package
    {
        import flash.display.Sprite;
        import flash.display.StageAlign;
        import flash.display.StageScaleMode;
        import flash.events.Event;
        import flash.events.MouseEvent;

        public class Throwing extends Sprite
        {
            private var ball:Ball;
            private var vx:Number;
            private var vy:Number;
            private var bounce:Number = -0.7;
            private var gravity:Number = .5;
            private var oldX:Number;
            private var oldY:Number;

            public function Throwing()
            {
                init();
            }
```

```
private function init():void
{
    stage.scaleMode = StageScaleMode.NO_SCALE;
    stage.align=StageAlign.TOP_LEFT;

    ball = new Ball();
    ball.x = stage.stageWidth / 2;
    ball.y = stage.stageHeight / 2;
    vx = Math.random() * 10 - 5;
    vy = -10;
    addChild(ball);
    ball.addEventListener(MouseEvent.MOUSE_DOWN, onMouseDown);
    addEventListener(Event.ENTER_FRAME, onEnterFrame);
}

private function onEnterFrame(event:Event):void
{
    vy += gravity;
    ball.x += vx;
    ball.y += vy;
    var left:Number = 0;
    var right:Number = stage.stageWidth;
    var top:Number = 0;
    var bottom:Number = stage.stageHeight;

    if(ball.x + ball.radius > right)
    {
        ball.x = right - ball.radius;
        vx *= bounce;
    }
    else if(ball.x - ball.radius < left)
    {
        ball.x = left + ball.radius;
        vx *= bounce;
    }
    if(ball.y + ball.radius > bottom)
    {
        ball.y = bottom - ball.radius;
        vy *= bounce;
    }
    else if(ball.y - ball.radius < top)
    {
        ball.y = top + ball.radius;
        vy *= bounce;
    }
}
```

```
        private function onMouseDown(event:MouseEvent):void
        {
            oldX = ball.x;
            oldY = ball.y;
            stage.addEventListener(MouseEvent.MOUSE_UP, onMouseUp);
            ball.startDrag();
            removeEventListener(Event.ENTER_FRAME, onEnterFrame);
            addEventListener(Event.ENTER_FRAME, trackVelocity);
        }

        private function onMouseUp(event:MouseEvent):void
        {
            stage.removeEventListener(MouseEvent.MOUSE_UP, onMouseUp);
            ball.stopDrag();
            removeEventListener(Event.ENTER_FRAME, trackVelocity);
            addEventListener(Event.ENTER_FRAME, onEnterFrame);
        }

        private function trackVelocity(event:Event):void
        {
            vx = ball.x - oldX;
            vy = ball.y - oldY;
            oldX = ball.x;
            oldY = ball.y;
        }
    }
}
```

Now that's pretty darned interactive, and a good representation of real-world physics re-created in Flash. It really feels like you're throwing something around. You can even play catch with yourself. Play around with all the variables for gravity, bounce, and so on. If you want, you can add in a bit of friction to simulate some atmosphere. This is a great sample file to get a feel for how all of these things work, because you can experiment in real time and see how all the parameters affect the motion.

Summary

While this was not a long chapter, it covered some extremely valuable ground, and made some great headway in interactivity. By now, you should be able to drag any object, drop it, and throw it.

Most important, you've worked with a lot of the small details that go into doing a really professional job with interactivity. In future chapters, you'll be looking at many other ways of allowing the user to interact with objects in your movies. The complexity is going to start building up fast, but if you have these basics down, you'll do great.

Part Three

ADVANCED MOTION

Chapter 8

EASING AND SPRINGING

What we'll cover in this chapter:

- Proportional motion
- Easing
- Springing
- Important formulas in this chapter

It's hard to believe that it took seven chapters to get through "the basics," but here you are at Chapter 8, the beginning of the advanced stuff. Or, as I prefer to think of it, the point where things start to get *really* interesting. Up to now, each chapter covered more general techniques and concepts. Beginning with this chapter, I'll be concentrating on one or two specialized types of motion per chapter.

In this chapter, I'll cover easing (proportional velocity) and springing (proportional acceleration). But don't think that because there are only two items, this is a chapter you can skim through quickly. I've gotten more mileage from these two techniques than just about any others. And I'm going to run you through plenty of examples, so you can get an idea of just how powerful these techniques are.

Proportional Motion

Easing and springing are closely related. Even though I had planned from the beginning to put these two subjects in the same chapter, it wasn't until I sat down to plan this chapter in more detail that I realized just *how* similar they are to each other.

Both techniques involve moving an object (usually a sprite or movie clip) from an existing position to a target position. In easing, the sprite kind of slides into the target and stops. In springing, it bounces around back and forth for a bit, and then finally settles down at the target. The two techniques have the following in common:

- You set a target.
- You determine the distance to that target.
- Your motion is proportional to that distance—the bigger the distance, the more the motion.

The difference between easing and springing is in what aspect of the motion is proportional. In easing, *velocity* is proportional to the distance; the further away from the target, the faster the object moves. As it gets very, very close to the object, it's hardly moving at all.

In springing, *acceleration* is proportional to the distance. If the object is far away from the target, a whole lot of acceleration is applied, increasing the velocity quickly. As the object gets closer to its target, less acceleration is applied, but it's still accelerating! It flies right past the target, and then acceleration pulls it back. Eventually, friction causes it to settle down.

Let's dive in to each technique separately, starting with easing.

Easing

One thing I want to clear up right off the bat is that there is more than one type of easing. Even in the Flash IDE, while you're making a motion tween, you have the ability to "ease in" or "ease out." The type of easing I will be discussing here is the same as the "ease out" of a motion tween. A bit later in this chapter, in the "Advanced easing" section, I'll provide you with a link where you can find out how to do all kinds of easing.

Simple easing

Simple easing is a very basic concept. You have something over here and you want to move it over there. Since you're creating the "illusion of motion," you want to move it there gradually, over several frames. You could simply find the angle between the two, set a speed, use some trigonometry to work out the vx and vy, and set it in motion. Then you could check the distance to the target on each frame (using the Pythagorean Theorem, as described in Chapter 3), and when it was there, stop it. That approach might actually be adequate in some situations, but if you're trying to make something look like it's moving naturally, it won't do.

The problem is that your object would move along at a fixed velocity, reach its target, and stop dead. If you're talking about some object moving along and hitting a brick wall, yes, it might be sort of like that. But when you're moving an object to a *target*, this generally implies that someone or something knows where this target is, and is moving something into place there deliberately. In such a case, the motion will start out fairly fast, and then slow down as it gets closer to the target. In other words, its velocity is going to be proportional to the distance to the target.

Let's take an example. You're driving home. When you are a few miles away, you're going to be traveling as fast as the speed limit allows you (OK, maybe even faster—maybe even fast enough to earn yourself a ticket). When you pull off the highway and into your neighborhood, you'll be going a bit slower. Once you're on your own street, a block or two away, you'll be going far slower. As you approach your driveway, you're down to a few miles per hour. When you reach the last few feet of the driveway, you're moving a lot slower than when you pulled into the driveway. And inches before you stop, you're moving at a fraction of that speed.

If you take the time to look, you'll see this behavior manifests itself even in small things like closing a drawer or door. You start out fast and gradually slow down. The next time you go to close a door, make an effort to follow through with the same speed you started with. Just be prepared to explain to anyone nearby why you're slamming doors.

So, when you use easing to move an object into position, it automatically takes on a very natural appearance. One of the coolest things is that simple easing is actually very easy to do. In fact, it's probably easier than figuring out the angle, the vx, and the vy, and moving at a fixed speed.

Here is the strategy for easing:

1. Decide on a number for your proportional motion. This will be a fraction of 1.
2. Determine your target.
3. Calculate the distance from the object to the target.
4. Multiply the distance by the fraction. This is your velocity.
5. Add the velocity value to the current position.
6. Repeat steps 3 through 5 until the object is at the target.

Figure 8-1 illustrates the concept.

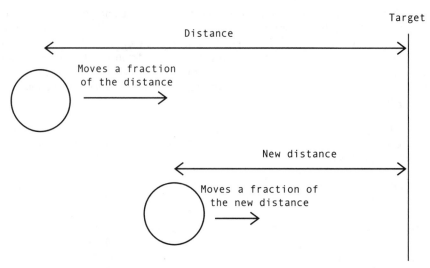

Figure 8-1. Basic easing

Let's go through these steps one at a time, and see how each looks in ActionScript. Don't worry about where to put the code yet. I'm just showing you what the code looks like and what it means.

First, decide on a fraction to represent the proportion. As I said, the velocity will be proportional to the motion. Specifically, this means that the velocity will be a fraction of the distance, something between 0 and 1. The closer it is to 1, the quicker the object will move. The closer it is to 0, the slower it will move, but be careful, because too low a value will prevent the object from reaching the target at all. For starters, choose something like 0.2. I'm going to call this variable easing. So you can start off with the following code:

```
var easing:Number = 0.2;
```

Next, determine your target. This is a simple x, y position. You can make it center stage for lack of anything better.

```
var targetX:Number = stage.stageWidth / 2;
var targetY:Number = stage.stageHeight / 2;
```

Then calculate the distance to the target. Assuming you have a sprite named ball, you just subtract the ball's x and y from the target x and y.

```
var dx:Number = targetX - ball.x;
var dy:Number = targetY - ball.y;
```

Your velocity is then the distance times the fraction:

```
vx = dx * easing;
vy = dy * easing;
```

And you know what to do from there:

```
ball.x += vx;
ball.y += vy;
```

Steps 3 to 5 need to be repeated, so those will go in your enterFrame handler. Let's take a closer look at those three steps, as they can be largely simplified:

```
var dx:Number = targetX - ball.x;
var dy:Number = targetY - ball.y;
vx = dx * easing;
vy = dy * easing;
ball.x += vx;
ball.y += vy;
```

You can condense the first two lines into the second two pretty easily:

```
vx = (targetX - ball.x) * easing;
vy = (targetY - ball.y) * easing;
ball.x += vx;
ball.y += vy;
```

Or, if you're into the whole brevity thing, you can shrink it even further:

```
ball.x += (targetX - ball.x) * easing;
ball.y += (targetY - ball.y) * easing;
```

The first few times you do easing, you might want to go with one of the more verbose syntaxes to make it clearer. But once you've done it a few hundred times, the third version communicates perfectly. I'll stick with the second version here, just to reinforce the idea that you're dealing with velocity.

Now, let's see it in action. You'll need the Ball class you've been using all along. Here's the document class, Easing1.as:

```
package
{
    import flash.display.Sprite;
    import flash.events.Event;

    public class Easing1 extends Sprite
    {
        private var ball:Ball;
        private var easing:Number = 0.2;
        private var targetX:Number = stage.stageWidth / 2;
        private var targetY:Number = stage.stageHeight / 2;

        public function Easing1()
        {
            init();
        }
```

```
                private function init():void
                {
                    ball = new Ball();
                    addChild(ball);
                    addEventListener(Event.ENTER_FRAME, onEnterFrame);
                }

                private function onEnterFrame(event:Event):void
                {
                    var vx:Number = (targetX - ball.x) * easing;
                    var vy:Number = (targetY - ball.y) * easing;
                    ball.x += vx;
                    ball.y += vy;
                }
            }
        }
```

Play around with the easing variable to see how it affects the resulting motion.

The next thing you might want to do is make the ball draggable so you can move it around and see how it always goes back to its target. This is pretty similar to the drag-and-drop technique you set up in Chapter 7. Here, you start dragging the ball when it is pressed with the mouse. At the same time, you remove the enterFrame event handler and listen for mouseUp on the stage. On the mouseUp handler, you stop dragging, remove the mouseUp handler, and reenable the enterFrame. Here's the document class, Easing2.as:

```
package
{
    import flash.display.Sprite;
    import flash.events.Event;
    import flash.events.MouseEvent;

    public class Easing2 extends Sprite
    {
        private var ball:Ball;
        private var easing:Number = 0.2;
        private var targetX:Number = stage.stageWidth / 2;
        private var targetY:Number = stage.stageHeight / 2;

        public function Easing2()
        {
            init();
        }

        private function init():void
        {
            ball = new Ball();
            addChild(ball);
            ball.addEventListener(MouseEvent.MOUSE_DOWN, onMouseDown);
            addEventListener(Event.ENTER_FRAME, onEnterFrame);
        }
```

```
    private function onMouseDown(event:MouseEvent):void
    {
        ball.startDrag();
        removeEventListener(Event.ENTER_FRAME, onEnterFrame);
        stage.addEventListener(MouseEvent.MOUSE_UP, onMouseUp);
    }

    private function onMouseUp(event:MouseEvent):void
    {
        ball.stopDrag();
        addEventListener(Event.ENTER_FRAME, onEnterFrame);
        stage.removeEventListener(MouseEvent.MOUSE_UP, onMouseUp);
    }

    private function onEnterFrame(event:Event):void
    {
        var vx:Number = (targetX - ball.x) * easing;
        var vy:Number = (targetY - ball.y) * easing;
        ball.x += vx;
        ball.y += vy;
    }
  }
}
```

When to stop easing

If you are doing simple easing to a single target, eventually you'll get to the point where the object is at the target and the purpose of the easing has been achieved. But, in the examples so far, the easing code continues to execute, even though the object isn't visibly moving anymore. If you are just easing to that point and leaving the object there, continuing to run the easing code is a waste of CPU resources. If you've reached your goal, you might as well stop trying. At first glance, this would be as simple as checking whether the object is at its target and turning off the enterFrame code, like so:

```
if(ball.x == targetX && ball.y == targetY)
{
    // code to stop the easing
}
```

But it winds up being a little more tricky.

The type of easing we are discussing involves something known as *Xeno's Paradox*. Xeno was yet another Greek guy who liked to measure things. Xeno tried to break down motion as follows: In order for something to move from point A to point B, it first must move to a point halfway between the two. Then it needs to travel from that point to a point halfway between there and point B. And then halfway again. Since you always need to move halfway to the target, you can never actually reach the target.

The paradox is that this sounds logical, but obviously we do move from one point to another every day, so there's something wrong there. Let's take a look at it in Flash. On the x axis, a sprite is at position 0. Say you want to move it to 100 on the x axis. To fit into the paradox, make the easing variable 0.5, so it always moves half the distance to the target. It progresses like this:

- Starting at 0, after frame 1, it will be at 50.
- Frame 2 will bring it to 75.
- Now the distance is 25. Half of that is 12.5, so the new position will be 87.5.
- Following the sequence, the position will be 93.75, 96.875, 98.4375, and so on. After 20 frames, it will be 99.999809265.

As you can see, it gets closer and closer but never actually reaches the target—theoretically. However, things are a bit different when you examine what the code does. It comes down to the question, "How small can you slice a pixel?" The answer is 20. In fact, there's a name for a twentieth of a pixel: a *twip*. Internally, Flash calculates anything that uses pixels with twips. This includes positions of sprites, movie clips, and any other object on the stage. Thus, if you trace the position of a sprite, you might notice that it is always in multiples of 0.05.

In the example here, the closest a sprite can get to 100 without actually getting there is 99.95. When you try to split the difference at that point, you're trying to add on (100 – 99.95) / 2. This comes out to 0.025, or a fortieth of a pixel. But a twip is as low as you can go. You can't add "half a twip," so you wind up adding 0. If you don't believe me, try the following code (hint: put it in the init method of the skeleton class I gave you in Chapter 2):

```
var sprite:Sprite;
sprite = new Sprite();
addChild(sprite);
sprite.x = 0;
var targ:Number = 100;
for(var i:Number=0;i<20;i++)
{
    trace(i + ": " + sprite.x);
    sprite.x += (targ - sprite.x) * .5;
}
```

This just loops through 20 times, moving the sprite half the distance to the target. It's basic easing code. I threw it in a for loop because I was only interested in tracing the positions, not actually seeing the motion. What you'll find is that by the eleventh iteration, the ball has reached 99.95, and that's as far as it gets.

> In tracing positions, you might also notice that occasionally you get a number like 96.85000000000001. This has to do with the way fractions are stored in a binary format, and has nothing to do with pixels, twips, or Flash itself. For more information, do a web search for "binary round-off errors."

To make a long story short, no, your sprite object is not going to get closer and closer, but yes, your sprite might never reach its target. So, if you're doing a simple comparison, as in the previous example, your easing code will never get shut off. What you need to do is answer the question, "When is it close enough?" This comes down to determining whether the distance to the target is less than a certain amount. For many applications, I've found that if an object is within a pixel of its target, it's safe to say it has arrived, and I can shut off easing.

If you are dealing with two dimensions, you can calculate the distance using the formula I introduced in Chapter 3:

```
distance = Math.sqrt(dx * dx + dy * dy)
```

If you are dealing with a single value for distance, as when you are moving an object on a single axis, you need to use the absolute value of that distance, as it may be negative. You can do this by using the `Math.abs` method.

OK, I've done way too much talking, or writing anyway. Let's see it in some code. Here's a simple document class to demonstrate turning off easing (EasingOff.as):

```
package
{
    import flash.display.Sprite;
    import flash.events.Event;

    public class EasingOff extends Sprite
    {
        private var ball:Ball;
        private var easing:Number = 0.2;
        private var targetX:Number = stage.stageWidth / 2;

        public function EasingOff()
        {
            init();
        }

        private function init():void
        {
            ball = new Ball();
            addChild(ball);
            ball.y = stage.stageHeight / 2;
            addEventListener(Event.ENTER_FRAME, onEnterFrame);
        }


        private function onEnterFrame(event:Event):void
        {
            var dx:Number = targetX - ball.x;
            if(Math.abs(dx) < 1)
            {
                ball.x = targetX;
                removeEventListener(Event.ENTER_FRAME, onEnterFrame);
                trace("done");
            }
            else
```

```
            {
                var vx:Number = dx * easing;
                ball.x += vx;
            }
        }
    }
}
```

As you can see, this example expands the easing formula a bit to first calculate the distance, since you'll need this to see whether easing should be stopped. Perhaps now you can see why you need to use the absolute value of dx. If the ball were to the right of the target, dx would wind up as a negative number, the statement if(dx < 1) would evaluate as true, and that would be the end of things. By using Math.abs, you make sure that the actual distance is less than 1. You then place the ball where it is trying to go and disable the motion code.

Remember that if you are doing something like a drag-and-drop with easing, you'll want to reenable the motion code when the ball is dropped. Why don't you go ahead and see whether you can figure that one out for yourself.

A moving target

In the examples so far, the target point has been a single, fixed location, but that's not a requirement. The distance is calculated on each frame, and the velocity is then calculated based on that. Flash doesn't care whether or not it reaches the target, or if the target keeps moving. It just happily goes on saying, "Where's my target? What's the distance? What's my velocity?" on each and every frame.

You can easily make the mouse an easing target. Just plug in the mouse coordinates (mouseX and mouseY) where you had targetX and targetY before. Here's a simpler version that does just that (EaseToMouse.as):

```
package
{
    import flash.display.Sprite;
    import flash.events.Event;

    public class EaseToMouse extends Sprite
    {
        private var ball:Ball;
        private var easing:Number = 0.2;

        public function EaseToMouse()
        {
            init();
        }

        private function init():void
        {
            ball = new Ball();
```

```
            addChild(ball);
            addEventListener(Event.ENTER_FRAME, onEnterFrame);
        }


        private function onEnterFrame(event:Event):void
        {
            var vx:Number = (mouseX - ball.x) * easing;
            var vy:Number = (mouseY - ball.y) * easing;
            ball.x += vx;
            ball.y += vy;
        }
    }
}
```

Move the mouse around and see how the ball follows, and how it goes faster when you get further away.

Think of what other moving targets you could have. Maybe a sprite could ease to another sprite. Back in the early days of Flash, mouse trailers—a trail of movie clips that followed the mouse around—were all the rage. Easing was one way of doing this. The first clip eased to the mouse, the second clip eased to the first, the third to the second, and so on. Go ahead and try it out (but if you put it on a live website, I'll deny any responsibility).

Easing isn't just for motion

If there is one point I want to get across in this book, it's that the examples I give are simply that: examples. In each case, I'm mainly just manipulating numbers that are used for various properties of a sprite or other object. For the most part, I'm using the x and y properties to control positions of sprites. Just remember that sprites, movie clips, and other display objects have many other properties that you can manipulate, and most of them are represented by numbers. So when you read a particular example, definitely try it out, but don't leave it at that. Try the same example on other properties. Here, I'll give you a few ideas to get you started.

Transparency

Apply easing to the alpha property of a clip. Start out by setting it to 0, and making the target 1 (realizing that in AS 3, alpha is a value from 0.0 to 1.0):

```
ball.alpha = 0;
var targetAlpha:Number = 1;
```

Then you can fade it in with easing in an enterFrame handler:

```
ball.alpha += (targetAlpha - ball.alpha) * easing;
```

Or reverse the 0 and 1 to make it fade out.

Rotation

Set the rotation property and a target rotation. Of course, you need something that can be visibly rotated, like an arrow:

```
arrow.rotation = 90;
var targetRotation:Number = 270;
```

And then ease it:

```
arrow.rotation += (targetRotation - arrow.rotation) * easing;
```

Colors

If you are up for a real challenge, try easing on 24-bit colors. You'll need to start with red, green, and blue initial values and target values, perform the easing on each separate component color, and then combine them into a 24-bit color. For instance, you could ease from red to blue. Start with the initial and target colors:

```
red = 255;
green = 0;
blue = 0;
redTarget = 0;
greenTarget = 0;
blueTarget = 255;
```

Then in your enterFrame handler, perform easing on each one. Here is just the red value:

```
red += (redTarget - red) * easing;
```

Then combine the three into a single value (as described in Chapter 4):

```
col = red << 16 | green << 8 | blue;
```

And use that in ColorTransform (see Chapter 4) or for a line color, a fill color, or anyplace else where color is used.

Advanced easing

Now that you've seen how simple easing works, you might consider using more complex easing formulas for additional effects. For instance, you might want something to start slowly, build up speed, and then slow down as it approaches its target. Or you might want to ease something into position over a certain time period or number of frames.

Robert Penner has become famous for collecting easing formulas, cataloging them, and implementing them in ActionScript. You can find his easing formulas at www.robertpenner.com. At the time of writing this, there were no AS 3 versions, but they would be easy enough to convert to AS 3, knowing just what you have learned so far in this book.

OK, let's move on to perhaps my most favorite subject in Flash: springing.

Springing

Maybe it's just me, but I've always found springing to be one of the most powerful and useful physics concepts in ActionScripted animation. It seems like you can do almost anything with a spring. Of course, it's just another technique that has its specific uses. I've gotten so much mileage out of this one, however, that I get a bit enthusiastic about it. So, let's look at what a spring is and how you can program it in Flash.

As I mentioned at the beginning of the chapter, a spring's acceleration is proportional to its distance from a target. Think about a real, physical spring, or better yet, a ball on the end of a rubber band. You attach the other end to something solid. As the ball is hanging there with no force applied, that's its target point. That's where it wants to be. Now pull it away a tiny bit and let it go. At that point, the ball's velocity is zero, but the rubber band applies force to it, pulling it back to the target. Now pull it away as far as you can and let it go. The rubber band applies a lot more force. The ball zooms right past its target and starts going the other way. Its velocity is very high. But when it gets a little bit past the target, the rubber band starts pulling it back a bit—changes its velocity. The ball keeps going, but the farther it goes, the more the band pulls back on it. Eventually, the velocity reaches zero, the direction reverses, and the whole thing starts over again. Finally, after bouncing back and forth a few times, it slows down and comes to a stop at—you guessed where—its target.

Now, let's start translating this into ActionScript so you can use it. To keep things simple, let's start off with one dimension.

Springing in one dimension

Let's drag our good friend, the red ball, back into active service. You'll leave it over at its default x position of zero and have it spring to the middle. As with easing, you'll need a variable to hold the proportionate value of the spring. You can think of this as the proportion of the distance that will be added to the velocity. A high spring value will make a very stiff spring. Something lower will look more like a loose rubber band. You'll start off with 0.1. Here's what you have so far:

```
private var spring:Number = 0.1;
private var targetX:Number = stage.stageWidth / 2;
private var vx:Number = 0;
```

Again, don't worry about where to put this just yet. Just make sure you know what these variables and statements are about.

Then move to the motion code and find the distance to the target:

```
var dx:Number = targetX - ball.x;
```

Now, compute some acceleration. The acceleration will be proportional to that distance. In fact, it will be the distance multiplied by the spring value:

```
var ax:Number = dx * spring;
```

Once you have a value for acceleration, you should be back on familiar ground. Add the acceleration to the velocity and add the velocity to the position, right?

```
vx += ax;
ball.x += vx;
```

Before you write any code, let's simulate it with some sample numbers. Let's say the x position is 0, vx is 0, the target x is 100, and the spring variable is 0.1. Here is how it might progress:

1. Multiply distance (100) by spring, and you get 10. Add that to vx, which then becomes 10. Add velocity to position, making the x position 10.

2. Next round, distance (100 – 10) is 90. Acceleration is 90 times 0.1, or 9 this time. This gets added to vx, which becomes 19. The x position becomes 29.

3. Next round, distance is 71, acceleration is 7.1, which added to vx makes it 26.1. The x position becomes 55.1.

4. Next round, distance is 44.9, acceleration is 4.49, and vx becomes 30.59. The x position is then 85.69.

The thing to note is that the acceleration on each frame becomes less and less as the object approaches its target, but the velocity continues to build. It's not building as rapidly as it was on previous frames, but it's still moving faster and faster.

After a couple more rounds, the object goes right past the target to an x position of around 117. The distance is now 100 – 117, which is –17. A fraction of this gets added to the velocity, slowing the object down a bit.

Now that you understand how springing works, let's make a real file. As usual, make sure the Ball class is available, and use the following document class (Spring1.as):

```
package
{
    import flash.display.Sprite;
    import flash.events.Event;

    public class Spring1 extends Sprite
    {
        private var ball:Ball;
        private var spring:Number = 0.1;
        private var targetX:Number = stage.stageWidth / 2;
        private var vx:Number = 0;

        public function Spring1()
        {
            init();
        }

        private function init():void
        {
            ball = new Ball();
            addChild(ball);
            ball.y = stage.stageHeight / 2;
            addEventListener(Event.ENTER_FRAME, onEnterFrame);
        }
```

```
        private function onEnterFrame(event:Event):void
        {
            var dx:Number = targetX - ball.x;
            var ax:Number = dx * spring;
            vx += ax;
            ball.x += vx;
        }
    }
}
```

Test this, and you'll see you definitely have something spring-like going on there. The only problem is that it kind of goes on forever. Earlier, when I described a spring, I said that "it slows down and comes to a stop." As is though, the ball builds up the same velocity on each leg of its swing, so it keeps bouncing back and forth at the same speed. You need something to reduce its velocity and slow it down. Hmmm . . . sound familiar? That's right, you need to apply some friction. Easy enough—just make a friction variable, with a value like 0.95 for starters. This goes up at the top of the class with the rest of the class variables:

```
private var friction:Number = 0.95;
```

Then multiply vx by friction somewhere in the enterFrame handler. Here's the corrected onEnterFrame method in document class Spring2.as:

```
private function onEnterFrame(event:Event):void
{
    var dx:Number = targetX - ball.x;
    var ax:Number = dx * spring;
    vx += ax;
    vx *= friction;
    ball.x += vx;
}
```

At this point, you have a full-fledged, albeit one-dimensional, spring. Definitely play with this one a lot. See what different values for spring and friction do and how they interact. Check out how a different starting position or target position affects the action of the system, the speed of the ball, and the rate at which it slows down and comes to a stop. Knowing this one file well will take you a long way. When you've got it down cold, you're ready to move on to a two-dimensional spring.

Springing in two dimensions

If you are thinking that a two-dimensional spring is as simple as adding a second target, velocity, and acceleration, I have news for you: You're right. So, without further ado, here is a two-dimensional spring (Spring3.as):

```
package
{
    import flash.display.Sprite;
    import flash.events.Event;
```

```
public class Spring3 extends Sprite
{
    private var ball:Ball;
    private var spring:Number = 0.1;
    private var targetX:Number = stage.stageWidth / 2;
    private var targetY:Number = stage.stageHeight / 2;
    private var vx:Number = 0;
    private var vy:Number = 0;
    private var friction:Number = 0.95;

    public function Spring3()
    {
        init();
    }

    private function init():void
    {
        ball = new Ball();
        addChild(ball);
        addEventListener(Event.ENTER_FRAME, onEnterFrame);
    }


    private function onEnterFrame(event:Event):void
    {
        var dx:Number = targetX - ball.x;
        var dy:Number = targetY - ball.y;
        var ax:Number = dx * spring;
        var ay:Number = dy * spring;
        vx += ax;
        vy += ay;
        vx *= friction;
        vy *= friction;
        ball.x += vx;
        ball.y += vy;
    }
}
}
```

As you can see, the only difference is adding in all the y-axis stuff. The problem is, it still seems rather one-dimensional. Yes, the ball is now moving on the x and y axes, but it's just going in a straight line. That's because its velocity starts out as zero, and the only force acting on it is the pull toward the target, so it goes in a straight line toward its target.

To make things a little more interesting, initialize vx to something other than 0. Try something nice and big like 50. Now, you have something that looks a little more loose and fluid. But you're only getting started. It gets a lot cooler.

Springing to a moving target

You probably won't be surprised to hear that springing doesn't require the target to be the same on each frame. When I covered easing, I gave you a quick and easy example of the ball following the mouse. It's pretty easy to adapt that example to make the ball spring to the mouse. Instead of the targetX and targetY you've been using, use the mouse coordinates. In springing, as with easing, the distance to the target is always calculated newly on each frame. Acceleration is based on that, and that acceleration is added to the velocity.

The effect is so cool, I feel like I should be writing on and on about it. But the fact is, there's really not much more to say on the subject, and the code isn't all that different. In the preceding example, simply change these lines:

```
var dx:Number = targetX - ball.x;
var dy:Number = targetY - ball.y;
```

to read like this:

```
var dx:Number = mouseX - ball.x;
var dy:Number = mouseY - ball.y;
```

You can also remove the lines that declare the targetX and targetY variables, though they are not going to hurt anything if you leave them in. The updated document class is available as Spring4.as.

This is another good point to stop and play. Get a really good feeling for how all these variables work, and try out many variations. Break it. Find out what breaks it. Have fun with it!

So where's the spring?

At this point, you have a very realistic-looking ball on the end of a rubber band. But it seems to be an invisible rubber band. Well, you can remedy that pretty easily with a few lines of drawing API code!

Since you have a fairly simple file without much else going on, you can safely apply your drawing code directly to the main class, which extends the Sprite class. In a more complex application, you might want to create an empty sprite and use that as a kind of drawing layer.

The strategy is simple. In each frame, after the ball is in position, you call clear() to erase any previous lines. Then you reset lineStyle and draw a line from the ball to the mouse. You just need the following code in the enterFrame handler, immediately after you set the ball's position (you'll see it in the full code shortly):

```
graphics.clear();
graphics.lineStyle(1);
graphics.moveTo(ball.x, ball.y);
graphics.lineTo(mouseX, mouseY);
```

Well, this is fun! What else can you do? How about adding some gravity so the ball looks like it's actually hanging off the end of the mouse? That's easy. Just add a gravity variable and add that to the vy for each frame. You know the drill by now. The following code (Spring5.as) incorporates the line drawing and gravity additions:

```
package
{
    import flash.display.Sprite;
    import flash.events.Event;

    public class Spring5 extends Sprite
    {
        private var ball:Ball;
        private var spring:Number = 0.1;
        private var vx:Number = 0;
        private var vy:Number = 0;
        private var friction:Number = 0.95;
        private var gravity:Number = 5;

        public function Spring5()
        {
            init();
        }

        private function init():void
        {
            ball = new Ball();
            addChild(ball);
            addEventListener(Event.ENTER_FRAME, onEnterFrame);
        }


        private function onEnterFrame(event:Event):void
        {
            var dx:Number = mouseX - ball.x;
            var dy:Number = mouseY - ball.y;
            var ax:Number = dx * spring;
            var ay:Number = dy * spring;
            vx += ax;
            vy += ay;
            vy += gravity;
            vx *= friction;
            vy *= friction;
            ball.x += vx;
            ball.y += vy;
            graphics.clear();
            graphics.lineStyle(1);
            graphics.moveTo(ball.x, ball.y);
            graphics.lineTo(mouseX, mouseY);
        }
    }
}
```

When you test this version, you should see something like Figure 8-2.

Notice how you need to increase the gravity variable to 5 in order to get the ball to actually hang down. Much less than that, and the force of the spring overcomes the force of gravity and you don't see the effect.

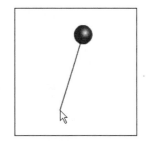

Figure 8-2.
Springing from the mouse,
with a visible spring

Now, here's another point where I've just butchered real-world physics. Of course, you can't go around "increasing gravity" on objects! Gravity is a constant, based on the size and mass of the planet you happen to be on. What you can do is increase the mass of the object, so that gravity has more of an effect on it. So, technically I should keep gravity at something like 0.5, and then create a mass property and make it something like 10. Then I could multiply mass by gravity and come up with 5 again. Or I could change the name of the gravity variable to something like forceThatGravityIsExertingOnThisObjectBasedOnItsMass. But as long as you know that's what I mean, I'll save the space and shorten it to gravity.

Again, experiment with this one. Try decreasing the gravity and spring values. Try changing the friction value. You'll see you can have a nearly endless number of combinations, allowing you to create all kinds of systems.

Chaining springs

Moving right along, let's chain a few springs together. In the easing section, I discussed mouse trailers briefly, where one object eases to the mouse, another object eases to that object, and so on. I didn't give you an example because it's an old, and somewhat cheesy, effect. But, when you apply the same concept using springing instead, well, that's just different.

Here's the plan: Start off by creating three balls, named ball0, ball1, and ball2. The first one, ball0, will behave pretty much like the single ball did in the previous example. Then ball1 will spring to ball0, and ball2 will spring to ball1. All will have gravity, so they should kind of hang down in a chain. The code isn't really anything you haven't seen before, just a little more complex. Here it is, in document class Chain.as:

```
package
{
    import flash.display.Sprite;
    import flash.events.Event;

    public class Chain extends Sprite
    {
        private var ball0:Ball;
        private var ball1:Ball;
        private var ball2:Ball;
        private var spring:Number = 0.1;
        private var friction:Number = 0.8;
        private var gravity:Number = 5;
```

```
    public function Chain()
    {
        init();
    }

    private function init():void
    {
        ball0 = new Ball(20);
        addChild(ball0);
        ball1 = new Ball(20);
        addChild(ball1);
        ball2 = new Ball(20);
        addChild(ball2);
        addEventListener(Event.ENTER_FRAME, onEnterFrame);
    }


    private function onEnterFrame(event:Event):void
    {
        moveBall(ball0, mouseX, mouseY);
        moveBall(ball1, ball0.x, ball0.y);
        moveBall(ball2, ball1.x, ball1.y);

        graphics.clear();
        graphics.lineStyle(1);
        graphics.moveTo(mouseX, mouseY);
        graphics.lineTo(ball0.x, ball0.y);
        graphics.lineTo(ball1.x, ball1.y);
        graphics.lineTo(ball2.x, ball2.y);
    }

    private function moveBall(ball:Ball,
                             targetX:Number,
                             targetY:Number):void
    {
        ball.vx += (targetX - ball.x) * spring;
        ball.vy += (targetY - ball.y) * spring;
        ball.vy += gravity;
        ball.vx *= friction;
        ball.vy *= friction;
        ball.x += ball.vx;
        ball.y += ball.vy;
    }
  }
}
```

If you take another look at the Ball class, you'll see that each instance of the class gets its own vx and vy properties, and these are initialized to 0. So, in the init method, you just need to create each ball and add it to the display list.

Then in the onEnterFrame function, you perform all the springing. Note that rather than duplicating the same code three times for each ball, we include a moveBall method, which takes care of all the motion code. This takes a reference to a ball and an x and y target. You call the function for each ball, passing in the x and y mouse position for the first ball, and the location of the first and second balls as targets for the second and third.

Finally, when all of the balls are in place, you set a line style, move the drawing cursor to the mouse position, and then draw a line to each successive ball, creating the rubber band holding them all together. Note that the friction here was pushed to 0.8 to force things to settle down a bit quicker.

You could make this class a bit more flexible, by creating an array to hold references to each object in the chain, and looping through that array to move each one, and then draw the lines. This would just take a few changes. First, you'd need a couple new variables for the array and the number of objects to create:

```
private var balls:Array;
private var numBalls:Number = 5;
```

The init function creates each object in a for loop, and adds it to the array:

```
private function init():void
{
    balls = new Array();
    for(var i:uint = 0; i < numBalls; i++)
    {
        var ball:Ball = new Ball(20);
        addChild(ball);
        balls.push(ball);
    }
    addEventListener(Event.ENTER_FRAME, onEnterFrame);
}
```

Finally, the onEnterFrame method has the biggest changes. It starts by setting the line style, moving the drawing position to the mouse position, moving the first ball, and drawing a line to it. Then it loops through all the rest of the balls in the array, moving and drawing a line to each one in turn. You can add as many objects as you want simply by changing the value of the one variable, numBalls.

```
private function onEnterFrame(event:Event):void
{
    graphics.clear();
    graphics.lineStyle(1);
    graphics.moveTo(mouseX, mouseY);
    moveBall(balls[0], mouseX, mouseY);
    graphics.lineTo(balls[0].x, balls[0].y);

    for(var i:uint = 1; i < numBalls; i++)
    {
        var ballA:Ball = balls[i-1];
        var ballB:Ball = balls[i];
        moveBall(ballB, ballA.x, ballA.y);
```

```
            graphics.lineTo(ballB.x, ballB.y);
        }
    }
```

You can see the result in Figure 8-3 and can find this class in ChainArray.as.

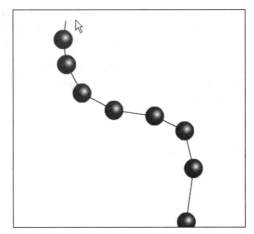

Figure 8-3. Chained springs

Springing to multiple targets

Back when I introduced the subjects of velocity and acceleration in Chapter 5, I talked about how you could have multiple forces acting on an object. Each force is an acceleration, and you just add them on to the velocity, one by one. Well, since a spring is nothing more than something exerting acceleration on an object, it's pretty simple to create multiple springs acting on a single object.

Here's the setup for demonstrating springing to multiple targets: You'll create three "handles," which will just be instances of the Ball class, and give them simple drag-and-drop functionality. These will also be targets for the ball to spring to. The ball will try to spring to all three of them at once and find its equilibrium somewhere between them. Or, to put it another way, each target will exert a certain amount of acceleration on the ball, and its motion will be the sum total of all of those forces.

This example gets pretty complex, with several methods in place to handle the various behaviors. I'll give you the code (document class MultiSpring.as) and then discuss it section by section.

```
    package
    {
        import flash.display.Sprite;
        import flash.events.Event;
        import flash.events.MouseEvent;

        public class MultiSpring extends Sprite
        {
            private var ball:Ball;
            private var handles:Array;
```

```
private var spring:Number = 0.1;
private var friction:Number = 0.8;
private var numHandles:Number = 3;

public function MultiSpring()
{
    init();
}

private function init():void
{
    ball = new Ball(20);
    addChild(ball);

    handles = new Array();
    for(var i:uint = 0; i < numHandles; i++)
    {
        var handle:Ball = new Ball(10, 0x0000ff);
        handle.x = Math.random() * stage.stageWidth;
        handle.y = Math.random() * stage.stageHeight;
        handle.addEventListener(MouseEvent.MOUSE_DOWN,
                                onPress);
        addChild(handle);
        handles.push(handle);
    }

    addEventListener(Event.ENTER_FRAME, onEnterFrame);
    addEventListener(MouseEvent.MOUSE_UP, onRelease);
}

private function onEnterFrame(event:Event):void
{
    for(var i:uint = 0; i < numHandles; i++)
    {
        var handle:Ball = handles[i] as Ball;
        var dx:Number = handle.x - ball.x;
        var dy:Number = handle.y - ball.y;
        ball.vx += dx * spring;
        ball.vy += dy * spring;
    }

    ball.vx *= friction;
    ball.vy *= friction;
    ball.x += ball.vx;
    ball.y += ball.vy;

    graphics.clear();
    graphics.lineStyle(1);
    for(i = 0; i < numHandles; i++)
```

```
                {
                    graphics.moveTo(ball.x, ball.y);
                    graphics.lineTo(handles[i].x, handles[i].y);
                }
            }

            private function onPress(event:MouseEvent):void
            {
                event.target.startDrag();
            }

            private function onRelease(event:MouseEvent):void
            {
                stopDrag();
            }
        }
    }
```

The init method creates a ball and three handles via a for loop, randomly positioning them, and setting them up for drag-and-drop behavior.

The onEnterFrame method loops through each handle, springing the ball toward it. It then applies the ball's new velocity to its position, and loops through again, drawing a line from the ball to each handle.

The onPress method is pretty straightforward, but note that in the onRelease function, you have no way of knowing which handle has been being dragged. Fortunately, calling stopDrag on any display object stops all dragging, so you can just call it in the main class.

Note that you can easily change the number of handles to use by simply changing the numHandles variable.

Figure 8-4 shows an example of the results of this code.

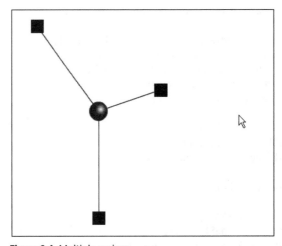

Figure 8-4. Multiple springs

By now, I'm sure you've already started taking many detours and creating a few things that I haven't even mentioned (or perhaps thought of). If so, that's excellent! That's exactly my goal in writing this book.

Offsetting the target

If you took a real spring—an actual coil of bouncy metal—and attached one end of it to something solid and the other end to a ball or some other object, what would be the target? Would the target be the point where the spring is attached? No, not really. The ball would never be able to reach that point, because the spring itself would be in the way. Furthermore, once the spring had contracted to its normal length, it wouldn't be applying any more force on the ball. So, the target would actually be the position of the loose end of the spring in its unstretched state. But that point could vary as the spring pivots around the fixed point.

To find the actual target, you need to first find the angle between the object and the fixed point, and then move out from the fixed point at that angle—the length of the spring. In other words, if the length of the spring were 50, and the angle between the ball and fixed point were 45, you would move out 50 pixels from the fixed point, at an angle of 45 degrees, and that would be the ball's target to spring to. Figure 8-5 illustrates how this works.

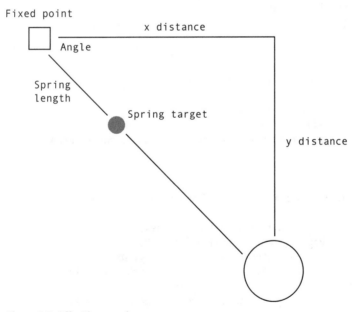

Figure 8-5. Offsetting a spring

The code to find the target in this case is roughly as follows:

```
var dx:Number = ball.x - fixedX;
var dy:Number = ball.y - fixedY;
var angle:Number = Math.atan2(dy, dx);
var targetX:Number = fixedX + Math.cos(angle) * springLength;
var targetY:Number = fixedY + Math.sin(angle) * springLength;
```

So, the result is that the object will spring *toward* the fixed point, but will come to rest some distance away from it. Also, note that although I'm calling it a "fixed point," this just means the point to which the spring is fixed. It doesn't mean that point cannot move. Perhaps it's better just to see it in action. You'll go back to using the mouse position, but this time, it will be the spring's fixed point. The spring's length will be 100 pixels. Here's the document class (OffsetSpring.as):

```
package
{
    import flash.display.Sprite;
    import flash.events.Event;

    public class OffsetSpring extends Sprite
    {
        private var ball:Ball;
        private var spring:Number = 0.1;
        private var vx:Number = 0;
        private var vy:Number = 0;
        private var friction:Number = 0.95;
        private var springLength:Number = 100;

        public function OffsetSpring()
        {
            init();
        }

        private function init():void
        {
            ball = new Ball(20);
            addChild(ball);
            addEventListener(Event.ENTER_FRAME, onEnterFrame);
        }


        private function onEnterFrame(event:Event):void
        {
            var dx:Number = ball.x - mouseX;
            var dy:Number = ball.y - mouseY;
            var angle:Number = Math.atan2(dy, dx);
            var targetX:Number = mouseX + Math.cos(angle) *
                                 springLength;
            var targetY:Number = mouseY + Math.sin(angle) *
                                 springLength;
            vx += (targetX - ball.x) * spring;
            vy += (targetY - ball.y) * spring;
            vx *= friction;
            vy *= friction;
            ball.x += vx;
            ball.y += vy;
            graphics.clear();
```

```
            graphics.lineStyle(1);
            graphics.moveTo(ball.x, ball.y);
            graphics.lineTo(mouseX, mouseY);
        }
    }
}
```

Even though you can see what is happening here, it might not be too obvious exactly where you would find this technique particularly useful. Well, the next section will give you a specific example.

Attaching multiple objects with springs

I remember the exact moment I realized I could do this. It was something like, "OK, I know how to spring an object to a point. And I know that point does not have to be fixed. I can even have one object spring to another object. Well, what if I have the other object spring back to the first object? So these two objects were linked to each other by a spring. Move either one, and the other one springs to it."

My initial impression was that it would probably cause some weird feedback loop that would crash Flash, or at least bring up some kind of warning message. But I bravely went ahead and tried it anyway. And to my complete amazement, it worked perfectly!

I've already pretty much described the strategy, but to recap: Object A has object B as its target. It springs toward it. Object B in turn has object A as its target. Actually, this is the point where the offset has a great role. If each object had the other as a direct target, they would collapse in on each other and occupy the same point. By applying an offset, you keep them apart a bit, as shown in Figure 8-6.

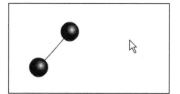

Figure 8-6. Two objects connected by a spring

For this next example, you'll need two instances of the Ball class. I'll call them ball0 and ball1. ball0 springs to ball1 with an offset. And ball1 springs to ball0 with an offset. Rather than writing out all the offset, spring, and motion code twice, I put it all into a function called springTo. So, you can spring ball0 to ball1 by saying springTo(ball0, ball1), and then spring ball1 to ball0 by saying springTo(ball1, ball0). I also put in a couple of variables, ball0Dragging and ball1Dragging, to disable the springing for each ball when it is being dragged. Here's the class (DoubleSpring.as):

```
package
{
    import flash.display.Sprite;
    import flash.events.Event;
    import flash.events.MouseEvent;

    public class DoubleSpring extends Sprite
    {
        private var ball0:Ball;
        private var ball1:Ball;
        private var ball0Dragging:Boolean = false;
        private var ball1Dragging:Boolean = false;
```

```
private var spring:Number = 0.1;
private var friction:Number = 0.95;
private var springLength:Number = 100;

public function DoubleSpring()
{
    init();
}

private function init():void
{
    ball0 = new Ball(20);
    ball0.x = Math.random() * stage.stageWidth;
    ball0.y = Math.random() * stage.stageHeight;
    ball0.addEventListener(MouseEvent.MOUSE_DOWN, onPress);
    addChild(ball0);

    ball1 = new Ball(20);
    ball1.x = Math.random() * stage.stageWidth;
    ball1.y = Math.random() * stage.stageHeight;
    ball1.addEventListener(MouseEvent.MOUSE_DOWN, onPress);
    addChild(ball1);

    addEventListener(Event.ENTER_FRAME, onEnterFrame);
    stage.addEventListener(MouseEvent.MOUSE_UP, onRelease);
}


private function onEnterFrame(event:Event):void
{
    if(!ball0Dragging)
    {
        springTo(ball0, ball1);
    }
    if(!ball1Dragging)
    {
        springTo(ball1, ball0);
    }
    graphics.clear();
    graphics.lineStyle(1);
    graphics.moveTo(ball0.x, ball0.y);
    graphics.lineTo(ball1.x, ball1.y);
}

private function springTo(ballA:Ball, ballB:Ball):void
{
    var dx:Number = ballB.x - ballA.x;
    var dy:Number = ballB.y - ballA.y;
```

```
            var angle:Number = Math.atan2(dy, dx);
            var targetX:Number = ballB.x - Math.cos(angle) *
                                 springLength;
            var targetY:Number = ballB.y - Math.sin(angle) *
                                 springLength;
            ballA.vx += (targetX - ballA.x) * spring;
            ballA.vy += (targetY - ballA.y) * spring;
            ballA.vx *= friction;
            ballA.vy *= friction;
            ballA.x += ballA.vx;
            ballA.y += ballA.vy;
        }

        private function onPress(event:MouseEvent):void
        {
            event.target.startDrag();
            if(event.target == ball0)
            {
                ball0Dragging = true;
            }
            if(event.target == ball1)
            {
                ball1Dragging = true;
            }
        }

        private function onRelease(event:MouseEvent):void
        {
            ball0.stopDrag();
            ball1.stopDrag();
            ball0Dragging = false;
            ball1Dragging = false;
        }
    }
}
```

For this file, the balls are placed on stage and are set up for drag-and-drop. The enterFrame handler function simply calls the springTo function on each ball. Note that in the program, each of these lines is surrounded by a check to make sure the ball isn't being dragged:

```
        springTo(ball0, ball1);
        springTo(ball1, ball0);
```

The springTo function is where all the action happens. Everything in this function should be familiar to you. First, it finds the distance and angle to the other ball, and calculates a target point based on that. It then performs basic spring mechanics on that target point. When the function is called again, with the parameters reversed, the balls swap roles, and the original target ball springs toward the other one. This may not be the most efficient code, but it demonstrates what is happening as clearly as possible.

You'll see that neither ball is attached to any fixed point or the mouse; they are both free-floating. Their only constraint is that they maintain a certain distance from each other. The great thing about this setup is that it is now very easy to incorporate additional objects. For example, if you create a third ball (ball2) and set it up like the others (along with a ball2Dragging variable), you can add that into the mix like so:

```
if(!ball0Dragging)
{
    springTo(ball0, ball1);
    springTo(ball0, ball2);
}
if(!ball1Dragging)
{
    springTo(ball1, ball0);
    springTo(ball1, ball2);
}
if(!ball2Dragging)
{
    springTo(ball2, ball0);
    springTo(ball2, ball1);
}
```

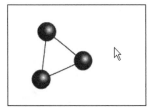

This will create a triangle formation, as shown in Figure 8-7, which to me is pretty cool. I'm sure once you get the hang of this, you'll quickly move on to a square, and from there, all kinds of complex springy structures.

Figure 8-7. Three objects connected by a spring

Important formulas in this chapter

Once again, it's time to review the important formulas presented in this chapter.

Simple easing, long form:

```
var dx:Number = targetX - sprite.x;
var dy:Number = targetY - sprite.y;
vx = dx * easing;
vy = dy * easing;
sprite.x += vx;
sprite.y += vy;
```

Simple easing, abbreviated form:

```
vx = (targetX - sprite.x) * easing;
vy = (targetY - sprite.y) * easing;
sprite.x += vx;
sprite.y += vy;
```

Simple easing, short form:

```
sprite.x += (targetX - sprite.x) * easing;
sprite.y += (targetY - sprite.y) * easing;
```

Simple spring, long form:

```
var ax:Number = (targetX - sprite.x) * spring;
var ay:Number = (targetY - sprite.y) * spring;
vx += ax;
vy += ay;
vx *= friction;
vy *= friction;
sprite.x += vx;
sprite.y += vy;
```

Simple spring, abbreviated form:

```
vx += (targetX - sprite.x) * spring;
vy += (targetY - sprite.y) * spring;
vx *= friction;
vy *= friction;
sprite.x += vx;
sprite.y += vy;
```

Simple spring, short form:

```
vx += (targetX - sprite.x) * spring;
vy += (targetY - sprite.y) * spring;
sprite.x += (vx *= friction);
sprite.y += (vy *= friction);
```

Offset spring:

```
var dx:Number = sprite.x - fixedX;
var dy:Number = sprite.y - fixedY;
var angle:Number = Math.atan2(dy, dx);
var targetX:Number = fixedX + Math.cos(angle) * springLength;
var targetY:Number = fixedX + Math.sin(angle) * springLength;
// spring to targetX, targetY as above
```

Summary

This chapter covered the two basic techniques of proportional motion: easing and springing. You've learned that easing is proportional motion and springing is proportional velocity, and you should have a very good understanding of how to apply both of these techniques.

I hope that you now understand why I get so excited about springs, and that you have begun to play with them and create some really fun and interesting effects yourself.

Now that you've learned all sorts of ways of moving things around, let's move on to the next chapter, where you'll find out what to do when they start hitting each other!

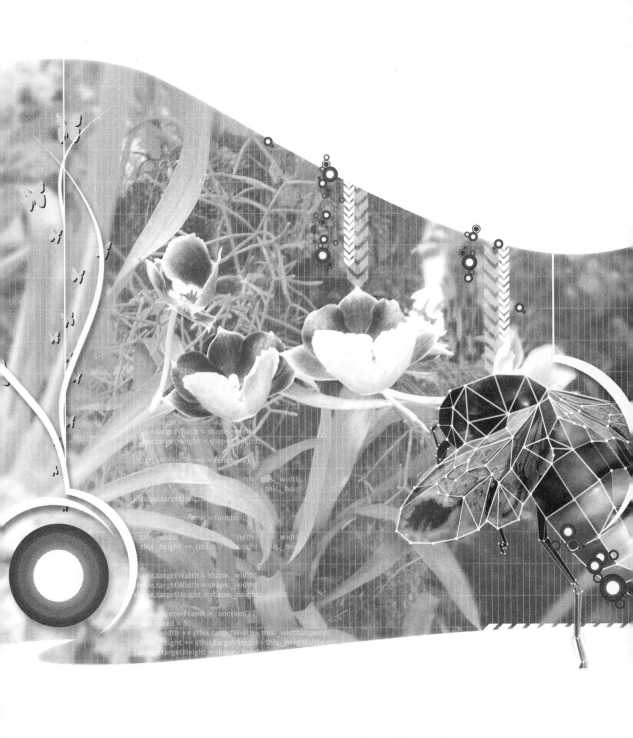

Chapter 9

COLLISION DETECTION

What we'll cover in this chapter:

- Collision detection methods
- Built-in hit testing methods
- Distance-based collision detection
- Multiple-object collision detection strategies
- Important formulas in this chapter

As you've progressed through the book to this point, you've seen how to make objects move and make them interact with the space they occupy. Now, you're going to delve into making these objects interact with each other. For the most part, this will involve determining when two objects have touched each other. This is a subject known as *collision detection* or *hit testing*.

In this chapter, I'll attempt to cover just about everything you need to know about detecting collisions. This includes hit testing between two sprites, hit testing between a sprite and a point, distance-based collision detection, and multiple-object collision testing strategies. First, let's see what options are available for collision detection.

Collision detection methods

Basically, collision detection, or hit testing, is a very simple concept. You want to know whether two objects are occupying any part of the same space at the same time. Of course, you may have a lot more than two objects, and you may want to know whether any of them are hitting any others. But when you break it down, you need to test each object one at a time against each other object. So, it always comes down to testing one object against another.

As the title of this section indicates, you have a couple of ways of doing collision detection:

- You can base the test on the actual pixels of each object (sprite or movie clip); that is, does the shape of this sprite overlap the shape of that sprite? And for that test, are you considering the actual visible pixels that make up the graphics of that sprite, or are you going to base it on the rectangular bounds of that sprite? So, there are two built-in hit testing methods with additional options to customize how you want to perform the test.

- You can base the test on distance. You get the distance between the two objects and you ask, "Is that close enough for them to be colliding?" This is more of a "roll your own" method of collision detection. You need to calculate the distance and decide when the objects are close enough.

Each method has its uses. I'll cover both in detail in this chapter, and you'll get a good chance to see how they are used.

One thing I won't go into in too much detail in this chapter is what to do when you *do* get a collision. How are two objects supposed to react when they bump into each other? I'll cover that subject in exhaustive detail in Chapter 11, when I talk about conservation of momentum.

hitTestObject and hitTestPoint

For quite a few versions of Flash now, movie clips have had a built-in method called hitTest, which you could use in a couple of different ways. This has been more logically broken into two separate methods. The hitTestObject method is used to test whether one display object (sprite, movie clip, and so on) is hitting another, and the hitTestPoint method checks whether a specific point is hitting a display object.

Hit testing two sprites

Using hitTestObject to see whether two sprites are hitting each other is probably the simplest method of collision detection. It is also the easiest to program and the quickest to execute. You call the function as a method of one sprite and pass it in a reference to another sprite. Note that although I'm specifically talking about sprites here, both of these hit test methods are members of the DisplayObject class, and apply to any class that extends that, such as MovieClip, Bitmap, Video, TextField, and so on. It looks like this:

```
sprite1.hitTestObject(sprite2)
```

This would normally go within an if statement, like so:

```
if(sprite1.hitTestObject(sprite2))
{
    // react to collision
}
```

The method will return true if there is a collision, and the statements within the if block will execute.

However, as with all things, there is a trade-off. As collision detection methods get easier, they get less accurate. As they get more accurate, they become more complex and time-consuming. So, while this is the easiest method, it is also the least accurate.

Now, what do we mean by accuracy in hit testing? Either something is hitting or it's not, right? I wish it were that easy. It goes back to this question: Based on the positions of two sprites, how do you determine if they are hitting?

Here's the simplest method of determining whether a collision has occurred: You take the first object and draw a rectangle around it. The top edge of the rectangle goes on the topmost visible pixel of the object's graphics, the bottom edge goes on the lowest visible pixel, and the left and right edges are on their furthest visible pixels. Then you do the same for the object you're testing against. Then you check whether these two rectangles are intersecting in any way. If so, you have a collision.

This rectangle around the object is known as a *bounding box*. Every display object has one. If you click a symbol on the stage in the Flash IDE, you'll see it as a blue outline, as shown in Figure 9-1.

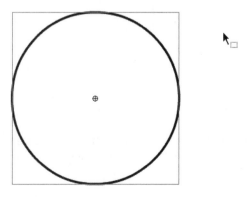

Figure 9-1. A bounding box

Of course, in the Flash player, nothing is actually drawing rectangles and checking them. It's all done mathematically, based on the sprites' positions and sizes.

Now, why would this be inaccurate? One would think that if the bounding boxes intersected, the objects must be touching. Well, take a look at the pictures in Figure 9-2. Which pairs would you say are touching each other?

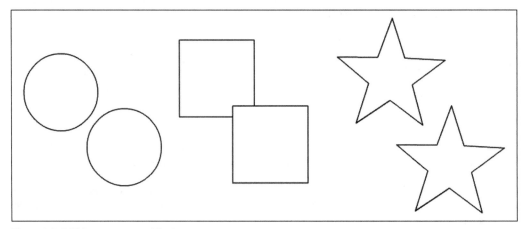

Figure 9-2. Which ones are touching?

Obviously, only the squares are actually hitting, right? Well, let's draw in the bounding boxes and see what Flash sees. Figure 9-3 shows the results.

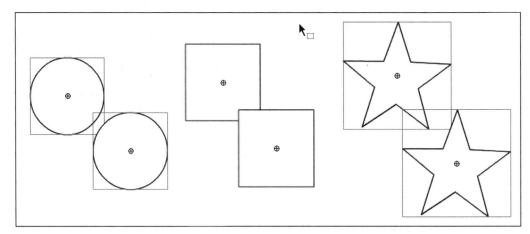

Figure 9-3. Not what you expected?

What do you know? All of these pairs are colliding as far as Flash is concerned. If you don't believe me, test the following document class, ObjectHitTest.as. It uses the Ball class we created earlier, so make sure that is in your class path.

```
package
{
    import flash.display.Sprite;
    import flash.events.Event;

    public class ObjectHitTest extends Sprite
    {
        private var ball1:Ball;
        private var ball2:Ball;

        public function ObjectHitTest()
        {
            init();
        }

        private function init():void
        {
            ball1 = new Ball();
            addChild(ball1);
            ball1.x = stage.stageWidth / 2;
            ball1.y = stage.stageHeight / 2;

            ball2 = new Ball();
            addChild(ball2);
            ball2.startDrag(true);

            addEventListener(Event.ENTER_FRAME, onEnterFrame);
        }

        private function onEnterFrame(event:Event):void
        {
            if(ball1.hitTestObject(ball2))
            {
                trace("hit");
            }
        }
    }
}
```

The class merely creates two instances of the Ball class and sets one to drag. It then uses the hitTestObject method on each frame to check whether the two are hitting. Note that if you approach the stationary ball from the top, bottom, or sides, it is accurate, but you always get a false positive if you come in diagonally. If you want, try drawing some other shapes in sprites and using them instead of Ball. You'll see that rectangular shapes work perfectly, but the more irregular the shape you use, the more inaccuracies you'll find. So, you should be very careful about using this method for anything other than rectangular shapes.

Let's try an example that demonstrates a simple hitTestObject with rectangles. This uses a new Box class that is very similar to Ball, and which I'm sure you'll have no trouble understanding. Here it is:

```
package {
    import flash.display.Sprite;

    public class Box extends Sprite {
        private var w:Number;
        private var h:Number;
        private var color:uint;
        public var vx:Number = 0;
        public var vy:Number = 0;

        public function Box(width:Number=50,
                            height:Number=50,
                            color:uint=0xff0000) {
            w = width;
            h = height;
            this.color = color;
            init();
        }
        public function init():void {
            graphics.beginFill(color);
            graphics.drawRect(-w / 2, -h / 2, w, h);
            graphics.endFill();
        }
    }
}
```

The idea is that a box is created at the top of the screen and falls to the bottom. When the box is placed, it falls down until it hits the bottom of the stage or collides with another box. If it hits another box, it positions itself so it is sitting right on top of it. Here's the code (document class Boxes.as):

```
package
{
    import flash.display.Sprite;
    import flash.events.Event;

    public class Boxes extends Sprite
    {
        private var box:Box;
        private var boxes:Array;
        private var gravity:Number = 0.2;

        public function Boxes()
        {
            init();
        }
```

```
private function init():void
{
    boxes = new Array();
    createBox();
    addEventListener(Event.ENTER_FRAME, onEnterFrame);
}

private function onEnterFrame(event:Event):void
{
    box.vy += gravity;
    box.y += box.vy
    if(box.y + box.height / 2 > stage.stageHeight)
    {
        box.y = stage.stageHeight - box.height / 2;
        createBox();
    }
    for(var i:uint = 0; i < boxes.length; i++)
    {
        if(box != boxes[i] && box.hitTestObject(boxes[i]))
        {
            box.y = boxes[i].y - boxes[i].height / 2 -
                    box.height / 2;
            createBox();
        }
    }
}

private function createBox():void
{
    box = new Box(Math.random() * 40 + 10,
                  Math.random() * 40 + 10);
    box.x = Math.random() * stage.stageWidth;
    addChild(box);
    boxes.push(box);
}
    }
}
```

In the onEnterFrame method, the code first checks whether the box has gone below the bottom of the stage. If so, it stops it and creates a new box. Then it runs a for loop, checking the current box against all the other boxes. First it makes sure it is not doing a hit test against itself, and then, in the heart of the whole program, is the hitTestObject line, where you determine whether the box has hit any other box. If it has, the code repositions the moving box to be on top of the one it just hit and again creates a new box. If you really want to see the inaccuracy of this method in action, switch from using the Box class back to the Ball class, or some other irregular shape, and see the objects hovering in mid air as they "hit" other objects.

Hit testing a sprite and a point

The hitTestPoint method works quite a bit differently, and even has a couple of options of its own. The truth be told, this method by itself is not usually very useful for testing for the collision between two sprites. This method takes two numbers as arguments and uses them to define a point. It then returns true or false, based on whether or not that point is hitting the sprite in question. In its most basic form, it might be used like this (where 100, 100 refers to the x and y locations of a point):

```
sprite.hitTestPoint(100, 100)
```

Again, you would use this within an if statement to designate some conditional code to run only if the hit test is true.

But once again, we come back to the question: What constitutes a hit? And, once again, we see our old friend the bounding box coming into play. Flash merely checks whether the point provided is within the sprite's bounding box.

Let's do a quick test to see that in action with document class PointHitTest.as:

```
package
{
    import flash.display.Sprite;
    import flash.events.Event;

    public class PointHitTest extends Sprite
    {
        private var ball:Ball;

        public function PointHitTest()
        {
            init();
        }

        private function init():void
        {
            ball = new Ball();
            addChild(ball);
            ball.x = stage.stageWidth / 2;
            ball.y = stage.stageHeight / 2;

            addEventListener(Event.ENTER_FRAME, onEnterFrame);
        }

        private function onEnterFrame(event:Event):void
        {
            if(ball.hitTestPoint(mouseX, mouseY))
            {
                trace("hit");
            }
        }
    }
}
```

This uses the x, y coordinates of the mouse position as the point the ball will test against. As you move the mouse close to the ball, you will see that it probably starts registering a hit before you actually hit the graphics, especially if you come at it from a corner. Try it again with a square and it should be perfectly accurate.

So again, this method seems to be useful only for rectangle-shaped objects. But there is another option here called shapeFlag.

Hit testing with shapeFlag

shapeFlag is the third and optional parameter to the hitTestPoint method. It is a Boolean value, so it's true or false. Setting shapeFlag to true means that now your hit test will check against the visible graphics of sprite, rather than just the bounding box. Note that shapeFlag is applicable only for testing a sprite against a point. If you are testing two sprites, you cannot use shapeFlag as an option.

Let's play with this one for a bit. It's as simple as adding in that one value. Just take the preceding example and add to it. Change your code so that the hitTestPoint line reads like this:

```
if(ball.hitTestPoint(mouseX, mouseY, true))
```

(If you want to explicitly say that you don't want to use shapeFlag, you could set the parameter to false, but this would be the same as if you left it off entirely.) Test this version with a ball, or draw some other irregular shape. You'll see that now you must actually touch the shape itself with the mouse in order to trigger a hit.

So, here you have a perfectly accurate hit test. Accurate, but perhaps not entirely useful for collision detection. The problem is that it tests only a single point, which makes it rather difficult to see whether any part of a sprite is touching any part of another. Your first impulse might be to do something like this:

```
sprite1.hitTestPoint(sprite2.x, sprite2.y, true)
```

But in that case, all you're checking is whether or not the registration point of sprite2 is within sprite1. That's pretty limited. Any other part of the sprite could be touching sprite1. In fact, half of sprite2 could be overlapping sprite1. But as long as that registration point were outside, Flash would consider it as not colliding. In practice, hit testing against a point is best used for mouse interaction or for very small sprites, where there might be only a pixel or two between the registration point and outer edges.

One way people have attempted to use this method for collision detection is to test several points along the perimeter of the object. For example, say you had a star-shaped sprite. You could calculate where the five points of the star were, and do a hit test from another sprite to each of those five points. But then if you had two stars, you would need to test each one against the other's five points. For a star, this would probably work pretty well. A more complex shape would obviously need a few more points. You can see this gets very complex and CPU-intensive pretty quickly. Just two stars, and you're up to ten times the number of hit tests you would use for the more simple method. Accuracy costs you.

Summary of hitTest

So, how do you do collision detection between two irregularly shaped sprites, so that if any part of one touches the other, you get a hit? Sadly, the answer is that this is not supported in sprites with the hitTest methods.

To summarize, your basic options are as follows:

- For roughly rectangular clips, use hitTestObject(displayObject).
- For very small sprites, you can get away with hitTestPoint(x, y, true) (note that shapeFlag is set to true).
- For very irregularly shaped sprites, you either live with the inaccuracy or custom program some sort of solution, probably using hitTestPoint(x, y, true).

Of course, the chapter is far from done yet, and there are solutions beyond the built-in methods. If you have circular or roughly circular objects, distance-based collision detection will probably be your best bet. Actually, you'd be surprised at how many shapes fall into the "roughly rectangular" or "roughly circular" categories.

Distance-based collision detection

In this section, you'll abandon the built-in hitTest family of methods and take collision detection into your own hands. This involves using the distance between two objects to determine whether they have collided.

Taking it to the real world, if the center of your car is 100 feet from the center of my car, you know that the two cars are far enough apart that they couldn't possibly be touching. However, if both of our cars are 6 feet wide and 12 feet long, and the center of my car is 5 feet from the center of your car, you can be pretty certain there is some twisted metal involved, and some insurance papers to fill out. In other words, there is no way for the centers to be that close together without some parts of the cars touching. That's the whole concept behind distance-based testing. You determine the minimum distance required to separate the two objects, calculate the current distance, and compare the two. If the current distance is less than the minimum, you know they are hitting.

Naturally, there is a catch. Where the simplest hitTestObject method worked perfectly with rectangles, but degraded with any departure from that shape, this method favors perfect circles. In fact, it works perfectly for perfect circles. So, if that's what you're dealing with, this is the way to go.

As you depart from a circular shape, you are going to see less accuracy. But rather than the problem of reporting things that aren't hitting as collisions, as you saw earlier with hitTest and the bounding box, you may have the opposite problem: Things that appear to be touching don't register a collision because their centers are still not close enough.

Simple distance-based collision detection

Let's start out with the ideal situation: a couple of perfectly round circles. We can use the Ball class yet again. (Maybe now you can see why the word "reusable" is used so often with object-oriented programming.) When doing this type of collision detection, the registration point should be in the exact center of the circle. The Ball class fits this bill. As before, you'll create two balls and set up one of them to drag. You'll also perform your collision detection in an enterFrame handler. So, up to this point, it is pretty much identical to the first example in this chapter. But instead of using if(ball1.hitTestObject(ball2)) to check for a collision, you'll be using distance in the if statement. You should already know how to compute the distance between two objects. Remember the good old Pythagorean Theorem from back in Chapter 3. So, you start off with something like this:

```
var dx:Number = sprite2.x - sprite1.x;
var dy:Number = sprite2.y - sprite1.y;
var dist:Number = Math.sqrt(dx * dx + dy * dy);
```

OK, now you have the distance, but how do you know whether that distance is small enough to consider that a collision has occurred? Well, take a look at the picture in Figure 9-4.

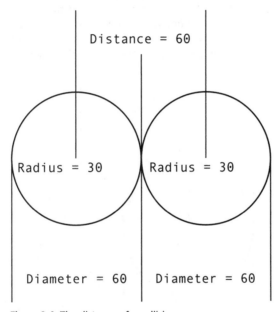

Figure 9-4. The distance of a collision

Here, you see the two circular sprites in a position where they are just touching. Consider that each sprite is 60 pixels across. This would give it a radius of 30. Thus, at the exact moment they touch, they are exactly 60 pixels apart. Aha! There's the answer. For two circular sprites of the same size, if the distance is less than their diameter, they are colliding. The code for this example (Distance.as) is exactly the same as ObjectHitTest.as, save the onEnterFrame method, which is here:

```
private function onEnterFrame(event:Event):void
{
    var dx:Number = ball2.x - ball1.x;
    var dy:Number = ball2.y - ball1.y;
    var dist:Number = Math.sqrt(dx * dx + dy * dy);
    // default ball diameter is 80 (radius is 40)
    if(dist < 80)
```

```
    {
        trace("hit");
    }
}
```

When you run this, you'll notice that it doesn't matter from which angle you approach the target ball. It doesn't register a hit until that exact point when the graphics actually overlap.

Now, I've already covered the fact that hard-coding numbers into code like that is generally a bad idea. You would need to change the code every time you had different-sized objects. Furthermore, what about the case where the two sprites are not the same size? You need to abstract this concept into some kind of formula that will fit any situation.

Consider Figure 9-5. It shows two sprites of different sizes, again, just touching. The one on the left is 60 pixels across, and the one on the right is 40 pixels. You can get this programmatically by inspecting their width properties. Thus, the radius of one is 30, and the radius of the other is 20. So, the distance between them at the moment they touch is exactly 50. Of course, in the case of the Ball class, we've already programmed in this radius property, so we can check it directly.

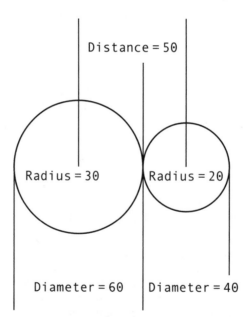

Figure 9-5. The distance of a collision between two different-sized objects

A pattern begins to emerge. The magic distance is the radius of one ball, plus the radius of the other. You can now remove all hard-coded numbers from the code and get something like this (which can be found in document class Distance2.as):

```
private function onEnterFrame(event:Event):void
{
    var dx:Number = ball2.x - ball1.x;
    var dy:Number = ball2.y - ball1.y;
    var dist:Number = Math.sqrt(dx * dx + dy * dy);
    if(dist < ball1.radius + ball2.radius)
    {
        trace("hit");
    }
}
```

Go ahead and change the size of one or both of the balls (remember, you can pass in a radius as the first parameter) and see that this code works, even if one circle is huge and one circle is tiny. In fact, in the full class mentioned earlier, I declared both of the objects like this:

```
ball1 = new Ball(Math.random() * 100);
```

This way, they will be different sized each time the file is run, and yet the collision detection always works perfectly.

Collision-based springing

The problem with giving you a good working example of distance-based hit testing is that a complete program would involve a lot of issues related to things I haven't covered yet, such as the reaction of two objects when they hit and how to efficiently handle interactions between many objects. But I did manage to create something that demonstrates hit testing without too much stuff that you haven't already seen.

Here is the idea: Place one large ball, called centerBall, in the center of the stage. Then add in a bunch of smaller ones, giving them random sizes and velocities. These will move with basic motion code and bounce off the walls. On each frame, do a distance-based collision check between each moving ball and the center ball. If you get a collision, calculate an offset spring target based on the angle between the two balls and the minimum distance to avoid collision. OK, that might not be crystal clear. All it really means is that if a moving ball collides with the center ball, you make it spring back out again. You do this by setting a target just outside the center ball. The moving ball springs to that target. Then, once it reaches the target, it is no longer colliding, so the spring action ends, and it just moves with its regular motion code.

The result is kind of like bubbles bouncing off a large bubble, as shown in Figure 9-6. The little bubbles enter into the big one a bit, depending on how fast they are going, but then spring back out. (Ah, you see my obsession with springs has resurfaced.)

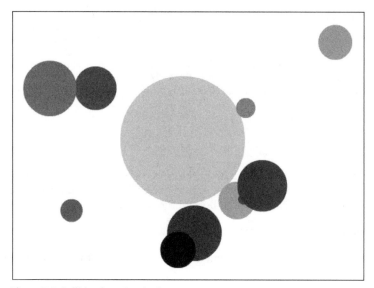

Figure 9-6. Collision-based springing

Here is the code (which you can also find in Bubbles.as):

```
package
{
    import flash.display.Sprite;
    import flash.events.Event;

    public class Bubbles extends Sprite
    {
        private var balls:Array;
        private var numBalls:Number = 10;
        private var centerBall:Ball;
        private var bounce:Number = -1;
        private var spring:Number = 0.2;

        public function Bubbles()
        {
            init();
        }

        private function init():void
        {
            balls = new Array();
            centerBall = new Ball(100, 0xcccccc);
            addChild(centerBall);
            centerBall.x = stage.stageWidth / 2;
            centerBall.y = stage.stageHeight / 2;
```

```
    for(var i:uint = 0; i < numBalls; i++)
    {
        var ball:Ball = new Ball(Math.random() *
                        40 + 5,
                        Math.random() * 0xffffff);
        ball.x = Math.random() * stage.stageWidth;
        ball.y = Math.random() * stage.stageHeight;
        ball.vx = Math.random() * 6 - 3;
        ball.vy = Math.random() * 6 - 3;
        addChild(ball);
        balls.push(ball);
    }

    addEventListener(Event.ENTER_FRAME, onEnterFrame);
}

private function onEnterFrame(event:Event):void
{
    for(var i:uint = 0; i < numBalls; i++)
    {
        var ball:Ball = balls[i];
        move(ball);
        var dx:Number = ball.x - centerBall.x;
        var dy:Number = ball.y - centerBall.y;
        var dist:Number = Math.sqrt(dx * dx + dy * dy);
        var minDist:Number = ball.radius + centerBall.radius;
        if(dist < minDist)
        {
            var angle:Number = Math.atan2(dy, dx);
            var tx:Number = centerBall.x +
                        Math.cos(angle) * minDist;
            var ty:Number = centerBall.y +
                        Math.sin(angle) * minDist;
            ball.vx += (tx - ball.x) * spring;
            ball.vy += (ty - ball.y) * spring;
        }
    }
}

private function move(ball:Ball):void
{
    ball.x += ball.vx;
    ball.y += ball.vy;
    if(ball.x + ball.radius > stage.stageWidth)
    {
        ball.x = stage.stageWidth - ball.radius;
        ball.vx *= bounce;
    }
    else if(ball.x - ball.radius < 0)
```

```
            {
                ball.x = ball.radius;
                ball.vx *= bounce;
            }
            if(ball.y + ball.radius > stage.stageHeight)
            {
                ball.y = stage.stageHeight - ball.radius;
                ball.vy *= bounce;
            }
            else if(ball.y - ball.radius < 0)
            {
                ball.y = ball.radius;
                ball.vy *= bounce;
            }
        }
    }
}
```

Yes, this is a whole lot of code, but you've already seen most of these techniques in earlier chapters. Let's walk through it quickly.

Starting with the init function, you create the centerBall and then loop through and create the smaller, moving balls. They are given a random size, position, color, and velocity.

The enterFrame handler just loops through and gets a reference to each ball. To separate functionality, I've moved the motion code to a function called move. This takes a reference to one of the balls and applies all the basic motion code to it. This function should be old hat to you. It's basic velocity code with bouncing. Then you find the distance from this ball to the centerBall, and compute the minimum distance to determine a collision. If there is a collision, you find the angle between the two, and use that plus the minimum distance to calculate a target x and y. This target will be right on the outer edge of the centerBall.

From there, you just apply basic spring code to spring to that point (as described in Chapter 8). Of course, once it reaches that point, it's no longer colliding and will fly off in whatever direction it's heading.

See how you can build up and layer simple techniques to wind up with some very complex motion?

Multiple-object collision detection strategies

When you have just a couple of objects moving around the screen, it's pretty simple to test them against each other. But when you get several objects, or even dozens, you need some kind of strategy for how to test them so that you don't miss any possible collisions. Furthermore, as you have more and more objects being tested, it becomes very important to perform your tests with some kind of efficiency in mind.

Basic multiple-object collision detection

With just two objects, only one collision is possible—A versus B. With three objects, you have three possibilities: A-B, B-C, and C-A. Four objects give you six collisions, and five objects give you ten collisions. When you get up to 20 objects, you need to take into account 190 separate collisions! That means that in your enterFrame handler, you need to run an if statement with a hitTest call or a distance calculation 190 times.

That's enough as it is. You certainly don't need to be adding any unnecessary hit testing to the game plan. But many people who dive into this type of calculation for the first time wind up doing not just a few extra hit tests, but exactly *twice* as many as necessary! For 20 objects, they do 380 if statements (20 clips each testing 19 others, or 20 × 19 = 380). So, you can see why you should have a solid understanding of this subject.

To see the problem, let's take a look at what needs to be done, and how it is often approached. Say you have six sprites, named sprite0, sprite1, sprite2, sprite3, sprite4, and sprite5. You have them moving around nicely, bouncing or whatever, and you want to know when any one of the clips hits any other one. The normal thing to do, when you've thought it through a bit, is to make two nested for loops. The outer one loops through each of the six sprites, gets a reference to each one in turn, and then loops through again, comparing it to each of the others. Here it is in a sort of pseudocode:

```
numSprites = 6;
for(i = 0; i < numSprites; i++)
{
    spriteA = sprites[i];
    for(j = 0; j < numSprites; j++)
    {
        spriteB = sprites[j];
        if(spriteA.hitTestObject(spriteB))
        {
            // do whatever
        }
    }
}
```

That's 36 hit tests for six sprites. Seems reasonable, right? Well, this code has two huge problems.

First, take a look what happens the first time through it. The variables i and j will both equal 0. So spriteA will hold a reference to sprite0, as will spriteB. Hey, you're testing a sprite against itself! That's kind of dumb. Well, you could make sure that spriteA != spriteB before performing the hitTest, or you could even go simpler and just make sure i != j. Then you get something like this:

```
numSprites = 6;
for(i = 0; i < numSprites; i++)
{
    spriteA = sprites[i];
    for(j = 0; j < numSprites; j++)
    {
        spriteB = sprites[j];
        if(i != j && spriteA.hitTestObject(spriteB))
```

```
                    {
                        // do whatever
                    }
                }
            }
```

OK, so you've eliminated six hit tests with that. Now you're down to 30. But this is still way too many. Let's chart out the exact tests you're doing. You are comparing the following:

```
sprite0    with    sprite1, sprite2, sprite3, sprite4, sprite5
sprite1    with    sprite0, sprite2, sprite3, sprite4, sprite5
sprite2    with    sprite0, sprite1, sprite3, sprite4, sprite5
sprite3    with    sprite0, sprite1, sprite2, sprite4, sprite5
sprite4    with    sprite0, sprite1, sprite2, sprite3, sprite5
sprite5    with    sprite0, sprite1, sprite2, sprite3, sprite4
```

Look at the very first test: sprite0 with sprite1. Now look at the first test on the second row: sprite1 with sprite0. Well, that's the same thing, isn't it? If sprite0 is not hitting sprite1, sprite1 is surely not hitting sprite0. Or if one is hitting the other, you can be sure the other is hitting the first. It turns out that you have a whole lot of these double checks in there. If you remove all the duplicate checks, you get a table like this:

```
sprite0    with    sprite1, sprite2, sprite3, sprite4, sprite5
sprite1    with    sprite2, sprite3, sprite4, sprite5
sprite2    with    sprite3, sprite4, sprite5
sprite3    with    sprite4, sprite5
sprite4    with    sprite5
sprite5    with    nothing!
```

You see that in the first round of tests, you're testing sprite0 with every other sprite. So no other sprite needs to test against that one again. You drop sprite0 off the list. Then sprite1 tests against the remaining sprites, and you drop it off the list. By the time you get to the last one, sprite5, every other sprite has already tested itself for a collision with it. There's no need to test it against anything. The result is that you're down to 15 tests. So, you see why I said the initial solution usually ends up being double what is needed.

Now, how do you code this thing? Well, you still have two nested for loops. But now it looks like this:

```
numSprites = 6;
for(i = 0; i < numSprites - 1; i++)
{
    spriteA = sprites[i];
    for(j = i + 1; j < numSprites; j++)
    {
        spriteB = sprites[j];
        if(spriteA.hitTestObject(spriteB))
        {
            // do whatever
        }
    }
}
```

Notice that the first outer `for` loop now goes to one less than the total number of clips. As you just saw in the final comparison chart, you don't need to test the last clip against anything, as it's already been thoroughly tested.

In the inner loop, you always start with one higher than the index of the outer loop. This is because you've already tested everything lower, and you don't want to test the same index, which, as you saw, would be testing a clip against itself. So, this even lets you get rid of that check. The result is just a few characters different from the original code, but gives you a 100% performance increase!

Also, even beyond its performance impact, in many cases, doing double hit testing might have unwanted results. If you're changing the velocity or some other value when you detect a collision, you may wind up changing it twice, resulting in who knows what kind of effect. Of course, the specifics would vary according to the actions you're taking, but in general, you want one collision to result in one action.

Multiple-object springing

Let's make another quick application to see this in action. Again, you'll go with the bubble-type reaction, but this time, all bubbles can bounce off of each other. Figure 9-7 illustrates the effect.

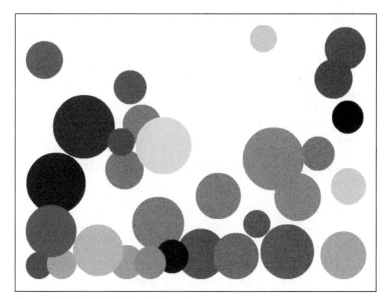

Figure 9-7. Multiple-object collision

Here's the code in document class Bubbles2.as:

```
package
{
    import flash.display.Sprite;
    import flash.events.Event;
```

```
public class Bubbles2 extends Sprite
{
    private var balls:Array;
    private var numBalls:Number = 30;
    private var bounce:Number = -0.5;
    private var spring:Number = 0.05;
    private var gravity:Number = 0.1;


    public function Bubbles2()
    {
        init();
    }

    private function init():void
    {
        balls = new Array();

        for(var i:uint = 0; i < numBalls; i++)
        {
            var ball:Ball = new Ball(Math.random() * 30 + 20,
                                     Math.random() * 0xffffff);
            ball.x = Math.random() * stage.stageWidth;
            ball.y = Math.random() * stage.stageHeight;
            ball.vx = Math.random() * 6 - 3;
            ball.vy = Math.random() * 6 - 3;
            addChild(ball);
            balls.push(ball);
        }

        addEventListener(Event.ENTER_FRAME, onEnterFrame);
    }

    private function onEnterFrame(event:Event):void
    {
        for(var i:uint = 0; i < numBalls - 1; i++)
        {
            var ball0:Ball = balls[i];
            for(var j:uint = i + 1; j < numBalls; j++)
            {
                var ball1:Ball = balls[j];
                var dx:Number = ball1.x - ball0.x;
                var dy:Number = ball1.y - ball0.y;
                var dist:Number = Math.sqrt(dx * dx + dy * dy);
                var minDist:Number = ball0.radius + ball1.radius;
                if(dist < minDist)
                {
                    var angle:Number = Math.atan2(dy, dx);
                    var tx:Number = ball0.x + Math.cos(angle) *
                                    minDist;
```

```
                    var ty:Number = ball0.y +
                                    Math.sin(angle) *
                                    minDist;
                    var ax:Number = (tx - ball1.x) *
                                    spring;
                    var ay:Number = (ty - ball1.y) *
                                    spring;
                    ball0.vx -= ax;
                    ball0.vy -= ay;
                    ball1.vx += ax;
                    ball1.vy += ay;
                }
            }
        }

        for(i = 0; i < numBalls; i++)
        {
            var ball:Ball = balls[i];
            move(ball);
        }
    }

    private function move(ball:Ball):void
    {
        ball.vy += gravity;
        ball.x += ball.vx;
        ball.y += ball.vy;
        if(ball.x + ball.radius > stage.stageWidth)
        {
            ball.x = stage.stageWidth - ball.radius;
            ball.vx *= bounce;
        }
        else if(ball.x - ball.radius < 0)
        {
            ball.x = ball.radius;
            ball.vx *= bounce;
        }
        if(ball.y + ball.radius > stage.stageHeight)
        {
            ball.y = stage.stageHeight - ball.radius;
            ball.vy *= bounce;
        }
        else if(ball.y - ball.radius < 0)
        {
            ball.y = ball.radius;
            ball.vy *= bounce;
        }
    }
  }
}
```

Here, you are simply using the double-nested for loop to perform collision detection. In this case, the reaction might need some additional explanation. Here's the collision reaction code:

```
if(dist < minDist)
{
    var angle:Number = Math.atan2(dy, dx);
    var tx:Number = ball0.x + Math.cos(angle) * minDist;
    var ty:Number = ball0.y + Math.sin(angle) * minDist;
    var ax:Number = (tx - ball1.x) * spring;
    var ay:Number = (ty - ball1.y) * spring;
    ball0.vx -= ax;
    ball0.vy -= ay;
    ball1.vx += ax;
    ball1.vy += ay;
}
```

Remember that this occurs once a collision is found between ball0 and ball1. Essentially, it starts out the same as the earlier example with the unmoving center ball. For now, let ball0 take the place of that center ball. You find the angle between the two, and get a target x and y. This is the point that you would need to place ball1 so that the two balls would not be touching. Based on that, you get the x and y acceleration that would cause ball1 to spring to that point. These are ax and ay.

But then you do something a little tricky. In this case, not only does ball1 need to spring away from ball0, but ball0 must spring away from ball1. The acceleration would be the same force and exactly the opposite direction. So rather than calculate it twice, you just add ax and ay to ball1's velocity, and subtract them from ball0's velocity! You get the same result, and you just saved a bunch of calculation right there. You might be thinking that this doubles the final acceleration, as it's being applied twice. That's true. To compensate, you make the spring variable quite a bit lower than usual.

While we're on the subject of optimization tricks, I'd like to mention another one here. The preceding code calculates the angle using Math.atan2, and then uses Math.cos and Math.sin to find the target point:

```
var angle:Number = Math.atan2(dy, dx);
var tx:Number = ball0.x + Math.cos(angle) * minDist;
var ty:Number = ball0.y + Math.sin(angle) * minDist;
```

But remember that sine is opposite over hypotenuse, and cosine is adjacent over hypotenuse. And realize that the opposite side of the angle is dy, the adjacent side is dx, and the hypotenuse is dist. Thus, you could actually shorten these three lines to just two:

```
var tx:Number = ball0.x + dx / dist * minDist;
var ty:Number = ball0.y + dy / dist * minDist;
```

Voila! You've just wiped out three calls to trig functions and replaced them with two simple divisions.

Before you move on, take some time to play with the springing bubbles example. You can adjust many variables. Try changing the spring, gravity, number, and size of the balls. You might want to try adding some friction or some mouse interaction.

Other methods of collision detection

The built-in hitTest methods and distance-based collision detection are not the only possible methods of finding out whether an object has hit another object, but between the two of them, they will get you through most of the situations where you need collision detection.

If you search around enough, however, you will find that some clever developers have come up with several other ingenious methods of determining when two things are touching. Grant Skinner, for example, has come up with a method of manipulating multiple BitmapData objects to determine when and where pixels of various objects are overlapping. You can find his work at www.gskinner.com.

Important formulas in this chapter

It's time to review the two important formulas presented in this chapter.

Distance-based collision detection:

```
// starting with spriteA and spriteB
// if using a plain sprite, or object without a radius property,
// you can use width or height divided by 2
var dx:Number = spriteB.x - spriteA.x;
var dy:Number = spriteB.y - spriteA.y;
var dist:Number = Math.sqrt(dx * dx + dy * dy);
if(dist < spriteA.radius + spriteB.radius)
{
    // handle collision
}
```

Multiple-object collision detection:

```
var numObjects:uint = 10; // for example
for(var i:uint = 0; i < numObjects - 1; i++)
{
    // evaluate reference using variable i. For example:
    var objectA = objects[i];

    for(var j:uint = i+1; j<numObjects;j++)
    {
        // evaluate reference using j. For example:
        var objectB = objects[j];

        // perform collision detection
        // between objectA and objectB
    }
}
```

Summary

This chapter covered just about everything you need to know about collision detection, including the built-in hitTest functions in all their variations, distance-based collision checking, and how to efficiently track collisions among many objects. You should know the pluses and minuses of each method, and situations where each works well or does not perform satisfactorily. You'll be using all of this material as you move forward in the book, and no doubt, you'll be using it extensively in your own projects.

In the next chapter, you'll look at collisions between objects and angled surfaces, using a technique known as coordinate rotation. This technique will also be used in Chapter 11, where you'll find out what to do to create a realistic reaction to the collisions you learned how to detect here.

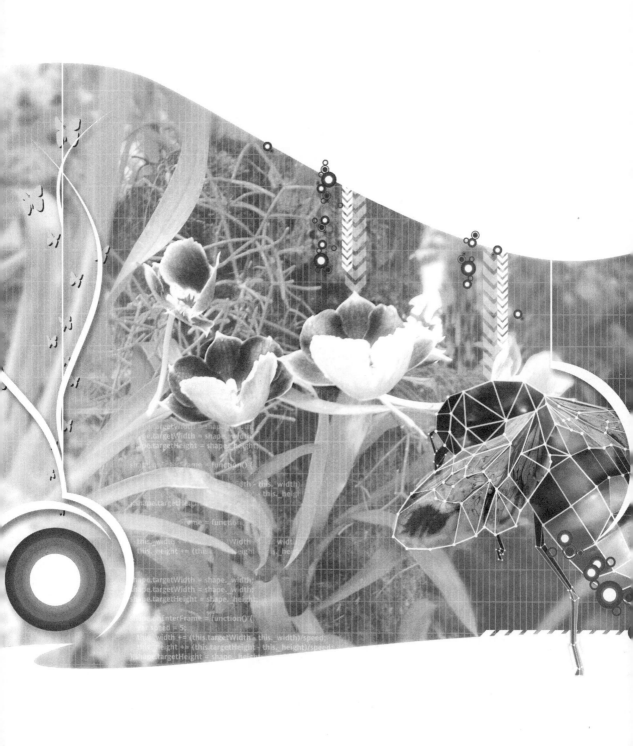

Chapter 10

COORDINATE ROTATION AND BOUNCING OFF ANGLES

What we'll cover in this chapter:

- Simple coordinate rotation
- Advanced coordinate rotation
- Bouncing off an angle
- Important formulas in this chapter

This chapter covers a particular technique known as *coordinate rotation*. As its name implies, this technique involves rotating a coordinate around a point. While useful all by itself, coordinate rotation is indispensable for several very interesting effects. One of those is the answer to a question that has continuously been asked on all the Flash boards for years: "How do I bounce something off an angled surface?" I'll cover how to do that in this chapter.

Another useful application of coordinate rotation is for calculating the reactions of two objects that bounce off each other. I'll show you how to do that in the next chapter, where I discuss the conservation of momentum. However, in that chapter, I'm going to assume you know about coordinate rotation already. So, if you're thinking of jumping ahead to that chapter, I recommend you sit tight and get through this one first.

Simple coordinate rotation

Although I covered the technique for simple coordinate rotation in Chapter 3's discussion of trigonometry, let's do a quick recap. You have a center point, an object, a radius, and an angle. You just keep increasing or decreasing the angle, and use basic trigonometry to place the object around the center point. You can set a variable such as vr (velocity of rotation) to control how much the angle is increased or decreased. And don't forget that the angle is in radians.

The structure of the code would be something like this pseudocode:

```
vr = 0.1;
angle = 0;
radius = 100;
centerX = 250;
centerY = 200;

// and in an enterFrame handler:
    sprite.x = centerX + cos(angle) * radius;
    sprite.y = centerY + sin(angle) * radius;
    angle += vr;
```

You're just using basic trig to set the x and y properties of the object based on the angle and the radius, and changing the angle on each frame. Let's make a couple of sample Flash movies to demonstrate this in action.

Here is the first example, document class Rotate1.as:

```
package
{
    import flash.display.Sprite;
    import flash.events.Event;

    public class Rotate1 extends Sprite
    {
        private var ball:Ball;
        private var angle:Number = 0;
        private var radius:Number = 150;
        private var vr:Number = .05;
```

```
public function Rotate1()
{
    init();
}

private function init():void
{
    ball = new Ball();
    addChild(ball);
    addEventListener(Event.ENTER_FRAME, onEnterFrame);
}

private function onEnterFrame(event:Event):void
{
    ball.x = stage.stageWidth / 2 + Math.cos(angle) * radius;
    ball.y = stage.stageHeight / 2 + Math.sin(angle) * radius;
    angle += vr;
}
    }
}
```

As you can see, this has nothing brand new to you in terms of code. Go ahead and try it out. This approach works great when you know or can specify the angle and radius from a center point.

But what if all you have is the position of the object and the center point? Well, naturally it isn't too hard to calculate the current angle and radius based on the x and y positions. Once you have them, you can carry on as before. The code would be something like this:

```
var dx:Number = ball.x - centerX;
var dy:Number = ball.y - centerY;
var angle:Number = Math.atan2(dy, dx);
var radius:Number = Math.sqrt(dx * dx + dy * dy);
```

This method of rotation based on coordinates might be fine for a single object, especially in a situation where you are just determining the angle and radius a single time. But in a more dynamic example, you could have many objects to rotate, and their relative positions to the center rotation point could be changing. So, for each object, you would need to compute its distance, angle, and radius, then add the vr to the angle, and finally calculate the new x, y position, on each frame. That's not too elegant, and probably not too efficient. Fortunately, there is a better way.

Advanced coordinate rotation

If you are going to be rotating objects around a point, and you are starting with just their positions, I've got a formula for you. The formula just needs the x, y position of the object in relation to the center point and the angle to rotate by. It returns the new x, y position of the object, relative to the center. Here's the basic formula:

```
x1 = cos(angle) * x - sin(angle) * y;
y1 = cos(angle) * y + sin(angle) * x;
```

If that just seems like a bunch of letters and symbols that happen to have a somewhat pleasing symmetry in the way they are arranged, don't feel bad. That's the way I felt about this formula when I first started using it. Actually, even though I use this formula quite often, I still feel pretty much that way about it. I have sat down a couple of times and figured out with diagrams exactly how the sines and cosines, x's and y's, pluses and minuses, and so forth work in terms of triangles and coordinates. And each time I did that, it made complete sense to me. And 30 minutes later, it looked like a bunch of symbols with nice symmetry.

So, although I usually strive to give you a complete conceptual understanding of the techniques I'm presenting, I'd be a hypocrite if I did that here. Because, personally, I've just memorized the formula so that I can type it in my sleep. The good news is that if you know more trigonometry than I do, you'll probably be able to get a deeper understanding of this technique; but even if you aren't a rocket scientist, you can memorize the formula and still get great results.

So, let's just look at what this formula is saying, which I've illustrated in Figure 10-1. The x and the y are, of course, the coordinates of the thing you are rotating. More specifically, they are the coordinates of that object in relation to the center point it is rotating around. Thus, if your center point is at 200, 100, and your object is at 300, 150, x will be 300 − 200, or 100, and y will be 150 − 100, or 50.

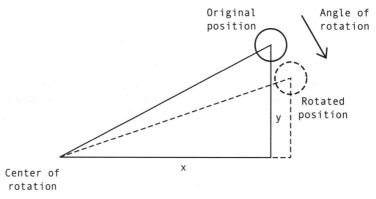

Figure 10-1. Rotating coordinates

The angle is how much you are rotating the object this particular time. It's not the current angle, or the resulting angle, but the difference between the two. In other words, talking in degrees for just a moment, if the object is at a 45-degree angle from the center point, and the angle here is 5 degrees, you will be rotating it another 5 degrees to put it at 50. Remember though, in this technique, you probably don't know, and don't really care about, the initial and final angles. You're just interested in how much rotation is occurring. Also, I'm sure I don't have to mention it, but as usual, this angle will be in radians, not degrees.

OK, so let's see it in action.

Rotating a single object

This example places a single ball at a random location and then uses the technique we just discussed to rotate it (document class Rotate2.as):

```
package
{
    import flash.display.Sprite;
    import flash.events.Event;

    public class Rotate2 extends Sprite
    {
        private var ball:Ball;
        private var vr:Number = .05;
        private var cos:Number = Math.cos(vr);
        private var sin:Number = Math.sin(vr);

        public function Rotate2()
        {
            init();
        }

        private function init():void
        {
            ball = new Ball();
            addChild(ball);
            ball.x = Math.random() * stage.stageWidth;
            ball.y = Math.random() * stage.stageHeight;
            addEventListener(Event.ENTER_FRAME, onEnterFrame);
        }

        private function onEnterFrame(event:Event):void
        {
            var x1:Number = ball.x - stage.stageWidth / 2;
            var y1:Number = ball.y - stage.stageHeight / 2;
            var x2:Number = cos * x1 - sin * y1;
            var y2:Number = cos * y1 + sin * x1;
            ball.x = stage.stageWidth / 2 + x2;
            ball.y = stage.stageHeight / 2 + y2;
        }
    }
}
```

Here, you are setting vr to the same value of .05 you used before. Then you're calculating the sine and cosine of that angle. Since it isn't going to change in this simple example, you can do it once at the top of the class, rather than recalculating it every frame. The x1 and y1 positions are calculated in relation to the point they will rotate around—the center of the stage. Then you apply the coordinate rotation formula as just described. This gives you x2 and y2, the new position of the ball. Again, this is in relation to the center point, so you need to add x2 and y2 to the center point to get the final position of the ball.

Try it out, and you'll see it should work exactly the same as the earlier version. Now, I'm sure you're thinking that if it works exactly the same, why bother going through this new formula, which actually looks more complex? Well, in a very simple situation like this, you'd probably be right. But let's look at some situations where this setup actually simplifies things. First, consider rotating multiple objects.

Rotating multiple objects

Suppose there are many objects to rotate, say a bunch of sprites in an array called sprites. The for loop would look something like this:

```
for(var i:uint = 0; i < numSprites; i++)
{
    var sprite:Sprite = sprites[i];
    var dx:Number = sprite.x - centerX;
    var dy:Number = sprite.y - centerY;
    var angle:Number = Math.atan2(dy, dx);
    var dist:Number = Math.sqrt(dx * dx + dy * dy);
    angle += vr;
    sprite.x = centerX + Math.cos(angle) * dist;
    sprite.y = centerY + Math.sin(angle) * dist;
}
```

whereas the advanced coordinate rotation method would look like this:

```
var cos:Number = Math.cos(vr);
var sin:Number = Math.sin(vr);
for(var i:uint = 0; i < numSprites; i++)
{
    var sprite:Sprite = sprites[i];
    var x1:Number = sprite.x - centerX;
    var y1:Number = sprite.y - centerY;
    var x2:Number = cos * x1 - sin * y1;
    var y2:Number = cos * y1 + sin * x1;
    sprite.x = centerX + x2;
    sprite.y = centerY + y2;
}
```

Notice that the first version includes four calls to Math functions within the loop, meaning that all four are executed once for each object being rotated. The second version has just two calls to Math functions, both outside the loop, meaning they are executed only once, regardless of how many objects there are. So, for example, if you have 30 sprites, you're looking at 120 Math calls on each frame with the first version, as compared to 2 with the second version. You decide which is going to be more efficient.

In the previous example, you were able to remove the sin and cos calculations right outside the enterFrame handler. This is because you were sticking with a fixed angle, so you could set it and forget it. In many cases, however, these angles of rotation may be changing, and you'll need to recalculate the sine and cosine each time it changes.

To demonstrate these latest concepts, let's build a quick example where the mouse position is controlling the speed of rotation of multiple objects. If the mouse is in the center of the screen, no rotation happens. As it moves to the left, the objects move faster and faster in a counterclockwise direction. As it moves to the right, they rotate in a clockwise direction. This example will start out quite similarly to the previous one, except you'll create multiple instances of Ball, storing them in an array named balls. Here's the document class (Rotation3.as):

```
package
{
    import flash.display.Sprite;
    import flash.events.Event;

    public class Rotate3 extends Sprite
    {
        private var balls:Array;
        private var numBalls:uint = 10;
        private var vr:Number = .05;

        public function Rotate3()
        {
            init();
        }

        private function init():void
        {
            balls = new Array();
            for(var i:uint = 0; i < numBalls; i++)
            {
                var ball:Ball = new Ball();
                balls.push(ball);
                addChild(ball);
                ball.x = Math.random() * stage.stageWidth;
                ball.y = Math.random() * stage.stageHeight;
            }
            addEventListener(Event.ENTER_FRAME, onEnterFrame);
        }

        private function onEnterFrame(event:Event):void
        {
            var angle:Number = (mouseX - stage.stageWidth / 2) * .001;
            var cos:Number = Math.cos(angle);
            var sin:Number = Math.sin(angle);
            for(var i:uint = 0; i < numBalls; i++)
            {
                var ball:Ball = balls[i];
                var x1:Number = ball.x - stage.stageWidth / 2;
                var y1:Number = ball.y - stage.stageHeight / 2;
                var x2:Number = cos * x1 - sin * y1;
                var y2:Number = cos * y1 + sin * x1;
                ball.x = stage.stageWidth / 2 + x2;
                ball.y = stage.stageHeight / 2 + y2;
            }
        }
    }
}
```

You can see that the code here isn't all that complex. If you're up to it, try recoding it using the angle and radius method, and see whether it looks better or worse and how it performs.

You'll revisit this formula when you get to the discussion of 3D in Chapter 15. In fact, you'll be using it twice within the same method, to rotate things around two axes and three dimensions. But don't let me scare you off yet. You have a lot to do before you get there.

Bouncing off an angle

I remember when I was first becoming addicted to Flash, math, and physics. I had figured out how to bounce things off a wall, floor, and ceiling. If a barrier was dead horizontal or vertical, I knew just what to do. But it didn't take too long for me to get bored. In real situations, things are not always horizontal or vertical. Sometimes, things are angled. And I couldn't figure out how to simulate this in Flash with the ease I could do bouncing off a flat surface. I went to the various online Flash forums and asked around. I wasn't the only one. I remember one board had three separate threads going with the exact title as this section: "Bouncing off an angle."

A few wise math gurus attempted answers. Something about the angle of reflection being equal to the angle of incidence. I remember a pretty straightforward formula that told you the angle at which a moving object would travel after hitting an angled surface. In and of itself, that was fine. But it solved only part of the problem. If you recall back to the discussion on bouncing off barriers, a few steps are involved:

1. Determine when you have passed a boundary.
2. Reset the object so it is resting directly on the boundary.
3. Reverse its velocity on the axis of the collision.

Knowing the final angle solved about half of step 3. But it didn't give me a way to discover when the collision with an angled surface had occurred, or where to position the object so it looked like it had stopped on the surface before bouncing. Nobody seemed to be able to answer all of those points. I tried everything I could think of. I drew enough diagrams to fill a warehouse and wrote enough test code to fill a hard drive. I was getting frustrated. It was so easy if the surfaces were flat. But when they were rotated, it was so complex. Perhaps you're starting to see where I'm going with this, and why I'm talking about this subject in this chapter.

At the time, Stuart Schoneveld of www.illogicz.com had an incredible physics engine online that handled such collisions smoothly and cleanly. I begged him for information on how he did it. Although he didn't show me any code, he gave me a general idea of what he did, in a sentence or two. It was one of those moments of revelation when the light comes shining through, and you feel like an idiot for not having seen it before.

What he told me was something like, "Bouncing off an angled surface? Just rotate the system so the surface is flat, do your bounce, and rotate it all back."

Wow! That was all I needed. You need to rotate the whole system to make your angle surface like a flat floor. This means rotating the surface, rotating the coordinates of the object in question, and rotating the object's velocity vector.

Now, rotating a velocity seems a bit complex, but think about it. You've been storing velocity in vx and vy variables. The vx and vy simply define a vector, which is an angle and a magnitude, or length. If you know the angle, you can rotate it directly. But if you just know the vx and vy, you can apply the advanced coordinate rotation formula to it and get the same result, just as you did for the position of the ball.

Some diagrams should help you visualize this a little better than words ever could. In Figure 10-2, you see the angled surface, the ball, which has obviously just hit the surface, and the vector arrow representing the ball's direction and speed.

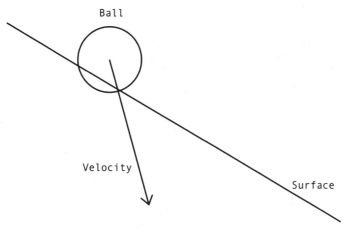

Figure 10-2. A ball hitting an angled surface

In Figure 10-3, you see that the whole thing has been rotated and the surface is now horizontal, just like the bottom barrier on the original bouncing example. Note that the velocity vector has been rotated right along with everything else.

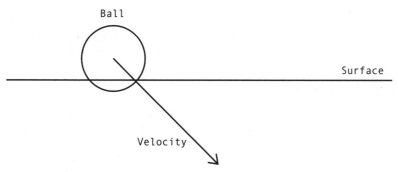

Figure 10-3. The same scene, rotated

The way the picture now looks, it's pretty simple to perform a bounce, right? Adjust the position, and change the y velocity, as in Figure 10-4.

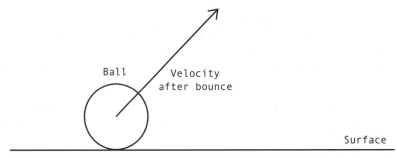

Figure 10-4. After the bounce

You now have a new position and velocity for the ball. Next, rotate everything back to the original angle, as shown in Figure 10-5.

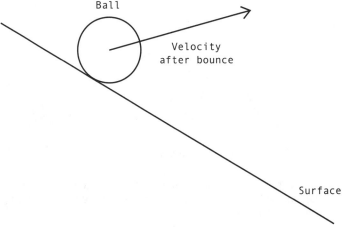

Figure 10-5. After rotating back

Voila! You've detected the collision, adjusted the position, and changed the velocity, all on an angled surface. Assuming that the pictures make sense to you, let's move on to some code and real graphics.

Performing the rotation

First, you need something to act as an angled surface. This is more for your eyes than for any mathematical necessity. For bouncing off of flat surfaces, you can use the boundaries of the stage, which inherently have a visible position. For an angled surface, it will help to have a real line at a real angle, so you can see the ball bouncing on it.

For this, you can just create a sprite, add it to the display list, and draw a horizontal line in it using the drawing API. Then you can rotate it a bit to make it an angled surface.

You'll also need the Ball class, which you should know to keep handy by now. When you position everything, make sure the ball is above the line, so it can fall onto it.

Here is the document class (AngleBounce.as):

```
package
{
    import flash.display.Sprite;
    import flash.events.Event;

    public class AngleBounce extends Sprite
    {
        private var ball:Ball;
        private var line:Sprite;
        private var gravity:Number = 0.3;
        private var bounce:Number = -0.6;

        public function AngleBounce()
        {
            init();
        }

        private function init():void
        {
            ball = new Ball();
            addChild(ball);
            ball.x = 100;
            ball.y = 100;

            line = new Sprite();
            line.graphics.lineStyle(1);
            line.graphics.lineTo(300, 0);
            addChild(line);
            line.x = 50;
            line.y = 200;
            line.rotation = 30;

            addEventListener(Event.ENTER_FRAME, onEnterFrame);
        }

        private function onEnterFrame(event:Event):void
        {
            // normal motion code
            ball.vy += gravity;
            ball.x += ball.vx;
            ball.y += ball.vy;
```

```
// get angle, sine, and cosine
var angle:Number = line.rotation * Math.PI / 180;
var cos:Number = Math.cos(angle);
var sin:Number = Math.sin(angle);

// get position of ball, relative to line
var x1:Number = ball.x - line.x;
var y1:Number = ball.y - line.y;

// rotate coordinates
var x2:Number = cos * x1 + sin * y1;
var y2:Number = cos * y1 - sin * x1;

// rotate velocity
var vx1:Number = cos * ball.vx + sin * ball.vy;
var vy1:Number = cos * ball.vy - sin * ball.vx;

// perform bounce with rotated values
if(y2 > -ball.height / 2)
{
    y2 = -ball.height / 2;
    vy1 *= bounce;
}

// rotate everything back;
x1 = cos * x2 - sin * y2;
y1 = cos * y2 + sin * x2;
ball.vx = cos * vx1 - sin * vy1;
ball.vy = cos * vy1 + sin * vx1;
ball.x = line.x + x1;
ball.y = line.y + y1;
        }
    }
}
```

You start out by declaring variables for the ball, the line, gravity, and bounce. The enterFrame handler begins with basic motion code.

You then get the angle of the line and convert it to radians. Once you have the angle, you get the sine and cosine of that angle.

Then you get the initial x, y position of the ball in relation to the line, by subtracting the line position from the ball position.

Finally, you're ready to rotate something! Now, when you look at the next couple of lines of code, you may notice something that seems wrong.

```
// rotate coordinates
var x2:Number = cos * x1 + sin * y1;
var y2:Number = cos * y1 - sin * x1;
```

The plus and minus are reversed from the original formula I gave you for coordinate rotation, which is as follows:

```
X1 = cos(angle) * x - sin(angle) * y;
y1 = cos(angle) * y + sin(angle) * x;
```

That's not a mistake. Think about what you're doing. Say the line is rotated 17 degrees. Using the original formula, you would wind up rotating it 17 degrees more, making it 34 degrees! Oops. You actually want to rotate it –17 degrees to put it at 0. Now, you could have calculated the sine and cosine to be Math.sin(-angle) and Math.cos(-angle), respectively. But eventually, you'll need the sine and cosine of the original angle, in order to rotate everything back.

So, rather than making two cosine and sine variables (at double the cost of calculation), you can use an alternative form of coordinate rotation to rotate everything in the opposite direction. It's as simple as reversing the plus and minus, as you just saw. If the line is at 17 degrees rotation, this will rotate everything –17 degrees, putting it at 0 degrees, or flat. Then do the same to the velocity.

Note that you don't need to actually rotate the line sprite. Again, it's mostly there for your eyes—to let you see where the ball is supposed to bounce. It's also a handy place to store the angle and position of the surface, since you can move and rotate with code.

Then you can perform the bounce. You do this using the x2, y2 position values and the vx1, vy1 velocity values. Realize that because y2 is in relation to the line sprite, the "bottom" boundary is the line itself, which will be 0. Taking into account the size of the ball, you check to see whether y2 is greater than 0 – ball.height / 2. This check is a shortcut to the following:

```
if(y2 > -ball.height / 2)
```

The rest of the bounce should be obvious.

Then you rotate everything back, using the original formula. This gives you updated values for x1, y1, ball.vx, and ball.vy. All you need to do at that point is reset the actual position of the ball instance by adding x1 and y1 to line.x and line.y.

Take some time to test this example. Try different rotations of the line, and different positions of both the line and ball. Make sure it all works fine.

Optimizing the code

You've already seen some examples of changing code a bit to make it more optimized. This usually involves doing things once instead of multiple times, or not doing them at all, unless you're really sure they need to be done.

I wrote the code in the previous example for clarity only. So, there is a lot happening on every frame that doesn't need to be. Most of that code needs to execute only when the ball has actually hit the line. Most of the time, you just need the basic motion code, and the bare minimum of calculation to check whether the ball has hit the line. In other words, all you need is the data that goes into the if statement:

```
if(y2 > -ball.height / 2)
```

So, you do need the y2 variable. And in order to get that, you need x1 and y1, and sin and cos. But if the ball hasn't hit the line, you don't need x2, or vx1 and vy1. So, those can go *inside* the if statement.

Also, if there's no hit, there's no need to rotate anything back or reset the ball position. So, all the stuff *after* the if statement can go inside the if statement as well. You wind up with this optimized version of the onEnterFrame method (which you'll find in AngleBounceOpt.as):

```
private function onEnterFrame(event:Event):void
{
    // normal motion code
    ball.vy += gravity;
    ball.x += ball.vx;
    ball.y += ball.vy;

    // get angle, sine, and cosine
    var angle:Number = line.rotation * Math.PI / 180;
    var cos:Number = Math.cos(angle);
    var sin:Number = Math.sin(angle);

    // get position of ball, relative to line
    var x1:Number = ball.x - line.x;
    var y1:Number = ball.y - line.y;

    // rotate coordinates
    var y2:Number = cos * y1 - sin * x1;

    // perform bounce with rotated values
    if(y2 > -ball.height / 2)
    {
        // rotate coordinates
        var x2:Number = cos * x1 + sin * y1;

        // rotate velocity
        var vx1:Number = cos * ball.vx + sin * ball.vy;
        var vy1:Number = cos * ball.vy - sin * ball.vx;

        y2 = -ball.height / 2;
        vy1 *= bounce;

        // rotate everything back;
        x1 = cos * x2 - sin * y2;
        y1 = cos * y2 + sin * x2;
        ball.vx = cos * vx1 - sin * vy1;
        ball.vy = cos * vy1 + sin * vx1;
        ball.x = line.x + x1;
        ball.y = line.y + y1;
    }
}
```

All the stuff in bold has been moved from outside the if statement to inside the statement, so it will happen only if a hit actually occurs, rather than every single frame. Can you imagine how many CPU cycles you just saved? It's pretty important to think about things like this, especially as your movies get more and more complex.

Making it dynamic

You can now start to make the action a little more dynamic. Let's adjust the angle of the line in real time, just to see how robust this thing is. You can do this with a single line of code, as the very first line inside the onEnterFrame method:

```
line.rotation = (stage.stageWidth/ 2 - mouseX) * .1;
```

Now you can move your mouse back and forth, and the line will tilt one way or the other. The ball should constantly adjust itself accordingly. You can find this code implemented in document class AngleBounceRotate.as.

Fixing the "falling off the edge" problem

What you're probably noticing now is that the ball will continue to roll along the angle of the line, even if it has gone past the edge of it. This may look a bit strange. But remember that the ball is not actually interacting with the line sprite at all. It's all done mathematically. But the results are so exact, it's easy to forget that nothing is actually "hitting" anything. And since the ball doesn't "know" anything about the line sprite, it doesn't know where it starts or ends. But you can tell it where the line is—using either a simple hit test or a more precise bounds check. Let's look at both methods, so you can decide which to use.

Hit testing

The easiest way to find the line's location is to wrap everything but the basic motion code inside an if statement with a hit test, as follows:

```
private function onEnterFrame(event:Event):void
{
    // normal motion code
    ball.vy += gravity;
    ball.x += ball.vx;
    ball.y += ball.vy;

    if(ball.hitTestObject(line)
    {
        // all the rest of the stuff that was in this function
    }
}
```

While that is pretty simple and might suffice for many implementations, there's another way to do it that's a little more exact, and which I prefer. Naturally, that means it's a little more complex and processor-intensive.

Bounds checking

I personally think that the getBounds method is one of the most underappreciated functions in ActionScript. I thought about mentioning it in Chapter 9, as it fits in nicely with collision detection, but I had enough to cover there, and one of the best uses I've found for it is exactly what I'm going to describe next. So I saved it for this chapter.

If you recall the discussion on hit testing, you should also remember what a bounding box is. In case your memory is like mine, I'll recap. The bounding box is the rectangle described by the visible graphic elements of a display object on stage. If you took any object and drew a rectangle around it so that the top edge touched the very top part of the object, the bottom edge touched the bottom part of the object, and the same with the left and right edges, you'd have the bounding box. In the Flash IDE, when you select a movie clip that is on stage, the blue rectangle you see is its bounding box.

This bounding box is used in both the hitTestObject and hitTestPoint functions. In those cases, the location of the bounding box is handled behind the scenes, and you get a true or a false as a return value from the function.

The getBounds function gives you direct access to the numerical values of the position and size of that box. Here's the basic signature of the function:

```
bounds = displayObject.getBounds(targetCoordinateSpace)
```

As you can see, it's called as a method of any display object, and it returns an instance of the flash.geom.Rectangle class, which is the obvious choice for describing the size and position of a rectangle. First, let's look at that single parameter, targetCoordinateSpace. What's that all about?

You use the targetCoordinateSpace parameter to specify from which viewpoint this bounding box will be described. In most cases, this will be the parent display object of the object in question. For example, if you have a sprite directly in your main document class, you could say sprite.getBounds(this), meaning, "Give me the bounding box for this sprite, in terms of the main movie's coordinates." On the other hand, if you were creating or attaching a sprite inside another sprite, you might want the bounding box in terms of the exterior sprite's location, as that might be different from the 0, 0 point of the stage. In that case, you could do something like this:

```
childSpite.getBounds(parentSprite);
```

This means you want the bounding box for the sprite named childSprite, which is inside the sprite named parentSprite, and you want it described in terms of parentSprite's coordinate space.

Naturally, the targetCoordinateSpace needs to be a display object, or an instance of some class that extends the DisplayObject class. And the main document class, Sprite, and MovieClip are display objects, so they all count.

Now, on to what the getBounds function returns. I said earlier that it returns a Rectangle instance that contains data about the bounding box. Earlier we dealt with the Rectangle class and saw that it contains four properties: x, y, width, and height. While we could use those here, it contains a few more properties that are even more useful: left, right, top, and bottom. I'm going to go out on a limb and say that you can probably guess what these refer to.

Let's try it out. Add an instance of the Ball class to the display list and then insert the following code (don't forget to import the flash.geom.Rectangle class):

```
var bounds:Rectangle = ball.getBounds(this);
trace(bounds.left);
trace(bounds.right);
trace(bounds.top);
trace(bounds.bottom);
```

For an interesting experiment, change the first line to read as follows:

```
var bounds:Rectangle = ball.getBounds(ball);
```

Now, you're getting the ball's bounds from its own viewpoint; in other words, in relationship to its own registration point. Since the ball was drawn with 0, 0 as its center, the left and top values should be negative and exactly equal to -right and -bottom. It's also worth mentioning that if you call getBounds without a parameter, you'll get the same result, as the object you are checking the bounds of will be used as the target coordinate space.

Just about now, you're probably starting to forget why I'm talking about bounds in the first place, so let's get back on track. We were trying to figure out when the ball has fallen off of the edge of the line, remember? So, you can call getBounds on the line, and find its left and right values. If the ball's x position is less than bounds.left, or if it is greater than bounds.right, it has gone over the edge. It's far more complex to describe than it is to just show, so here's the code:

```
private function onEnterFrame(event:Event):void
{
    line.rotation = (stage.stageWidth/ 2 - mouseX) * .1;

    // normal motion code
    ball.vy += gravity;
    ball.x += ball.vx;
    ball.y += ball.vy;

    var bounds:Rectangle = line.getBounds(this);
    if(ball.x > bounds.left && ball.x < bounds.right)
    {
        // all the rest of the stuff that was in this function
    }
}
```

You can see these changes implemented in the file AngleBounceBounds.as.

Fixing the "under the line" problem

In either method—hit testing or bounds checking—you're first finding out if the ball is in the vicinity of the line, and then doing coordinate rotation to get the adjusted positions and velocities. At that point, you check if the y2 rotated y position of the ball is past the line, and if so, perform a bounce.

But what if the ball passes *under* the line? Say the line is up in the middle of the stage, and the ball is bouncing around on the "floor." If either the hit test or the bounds check comes back true, Flash will think the ball has just bounced on the line, and will transport the ball from below the line to above it.

The way I've come up with to solve this is to compare vy1 with y2, and bounce only if vy1 is greater. How did I come up with that? Take a look at the diagram in Figure 10-6.

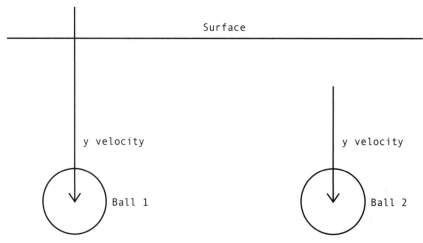

Figure 10-6. Did it go through or just pass under?

With the ball on the left, the y velocity is greater than the y position in relation to the line. This means that just before it moved, it had to be above the line. With the ball on the right, the velocity is less than the relative y position. In other words, it's below the line on this frame, and it was below the line on the last frame. So it's just moving underneath the frame. The only time you want to do a bounce is when the ball goes from above the line to below it. Now, let's look at how to fix the code to do that. Here's a section of the code out of the enterFrame handler:

```
// rotate coordinates
var y2:Number = cos * y1 - sin * x1;

// perform bounce with rotated values
if(y2 > -ball.height / 2)
{
    // rotate coordinates
    var x2:Number = cos * x1 + sin * y1;

    // rotate velocity
    var vx1:Number = cos * ball.vx + sin * ball.vy;
    var vy1:Number = cos * ball.vy - sin * ball.vx;
...
```

You just need to add that y2 < vy1 into your if statement:

```
if(y2 > -ball.height / 2 && y2 < vy1)
```

But in order to do that, you need to calculate vy1 beforehand. So that comes out of the `if` statement, and the snippet becomes corrected to this:

```
// rotate coordinates
var y2:Number = cos * y1 - sin * x1;

// rotate velocity
var vy1:Number = cos * ball.vy - sin * ball.vx;

// perform bounce with rotated values
if(y2 > -ball.height / 2 && y2 < vy1)
{
    // rotate coordinates
    var x2:Number = cos * x1 + sin * y1;

    // rotate velocity
    var vx1:Number = cos * ball.vx + sin * ball.vy;
...
```

So, you need to do a little extra calculation on each frame, with the payoff of greater accuracy and realism—that familiar trade-off. You can decide whether it's necessary. Say you have a setup where it's just not possible for the ball to go under a line. You don't need to worry about this, and you can move the vy1 calculation back inside the `if` statement and remove the extra check.

In the document class AngleBounceFinal.as, I added bouncing off the floors and walls, so that you can eventually see the ball go under the line. Try it with and without the code we just discussed to see the difference.

OK, we're bouncing, we're dynamic, we've got edges! Let's move on to the final, large-scale example of the chapter.

Bouncing off multiple angles

So far, you've just been dealing with a single line, or angled surface. Dealing with multiple surfaces is not really all that complicated. You just make a bunch of surfaces and loop through them. You can abstract the angle-bouncing code into its own function and just call that from within the loop.

Also, in all the examples in this chapter up to now, I've tried to keep things as simple as possible, giving you only the minimum amount of code necessary to demonstrate the principle at hand. However, the next example is a complete program, using all the techniques you've seen in prior chapters (with some comments to jar your memory).

The setup for this example is similar to the last few examples, with the same ball and basic line sprite, except I made the lines a bit smaller so there would be room for more of them. I've placed five lines and one ball on stage. The lines are put in an array named lines. I then positioned them around the stage. You can see the result in Figure 10-7.

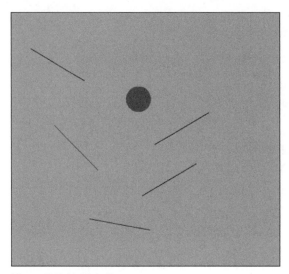

Figure 10-7. Multiple lines

Here's the code (which you'll find in MultiAngleBounce.as):

```
package
{
    import flash.display.Sprite;
    import flash.events.Event;
    import flash.geom.Rectangle;

    public class MultiAngleBounce extends Sprite
    {
        private var ball:Ball;
        private var lines:Array;
        private var numLines:uint = 5;
        private var gravity:Number = 0.3;
        private var bounce:Number = -0.6;

        public function MultiAngleBounce()
        {
            init();
        }

        private function init():void
        {
            ball = new Ball(20);
            addChild(ball);
            ball.x = 100;
            ball.y = 100;
```

```
    // create five lines
    lines = new Array();
    for(var i:uint = 0; i < numLines; i++)
    {
        var line:Sprite = new Sprite();
        line.graphics.lineStyle(1);
        line.graphics.moveTo(-50, 0)
        line.graphics.lineTo(50, 0);
        addChild(line);
        lines.push(line);
    }

    // position and rotate them
    lines[0].x = 100;
    lines[0].y = 100;
    lines[0].rotation = 30;

    lines[1].x = 100;
    lines[1].y = 230;
    lines[1].rotation = 45;

    lines[2].x = 250;
    lines[2].y = 180;
    lines[2].rotation = -30;

    lines[3].x = 150;
    lines[3].y = 330;
    lines[3].rotation = 10;

    lines[4].x = 230;
    lines[4].y = 250;
    lines[4].rotation = -30;

    addEventListener(Event.ENTER_FRAME, onEnterFrame);
}

private function onEnterFrame(event:Event):void
{
    // normal motion code
    ball.vy += gravity;
    ball.x += ball.vx;
    ball.y += ball.vy;

    // bounce off ceiling, floor, and walls
    if(ball.x + ball.radius > stage.stageWidth)
    {
        ball.x = stage.stageWidth - ball.radius;
```

```
            ball.vx *= bounce;
        }
        else if(ball.x - ball.radius < 0)
        {
            ball.x = ball.radius;
            ball.vx *= bounce;
        }
        if(ball.y + ball.radius > stage.stageHeight)
        {
            ball.y = stage.stageHeight - radius;
            ball.vy *= bounce;
        }
        else if(ball.y - ball.radius < 0)
        {
            ball.y = ball.radius;
            ball.vy *= bounce;
        }

        // check each line
        for(var i:uint = 0; i < numLines; i++)
        {
            checkLine(lines[i]);
        }
    }

    private function checkLine(line:Sprite):void
    {
        // get the bounding box of the line
        var bounds:Rectangle = line.getBounds(this);
        if(ball.x > bounds.left && ball.x < bounds.right)
        {

            // get angle, sine, and cosine
            var angle:Number = line.rotation * Math.PI / 180;
            var cos:Number = Math.cos(angle);
            var sin:Number = Math.sin(angle);

            // get position of ball, relative to line
            var x1:Number = ball.x - line.x;
            var y1:Number = ball.y - line.y;

            // rotate coordinates
            var y2:Number = cos * y1 - sin * x1;

            // rotate velocity
            var vy1:Number = cos * ball.vy - sin * ball.vx;
```

```
        // perform bounce with rotated values
        if(y2 > -ball.height / 2 && y2 < vy1)
        {
            // rotate coordinates
            var x2:Number = cos * x1 + sin * y1;

            // rotate velocity
            var vx1:Number = cos * ball.vx + sin * ball.vy;

            y2 = -ball.height / 2;
            vy1 *= bounce;

            // rotate everything back;
            x1 = cos * x2 - sin * y2;
            y1 = cos * y2 + sin * x2;
            ball.vx = cos * vx1 - sin * vy1;
            ball.vy = cos * vy1 + sin * vx1;
            ball.x = line.x + x1;
            ball.y = line.y + y1;
        }
    }
  }
 }
}
```

Yes, it's a lot of code, but as I've become fond of saying, it's all stuff you should recognize by now. Complex programs are not necessarily composed of complex pieces, but they are frequently built from a lot of familiar pieces, put together just right. In this case, the body of the checkLine method is identical to what was in onEnterFrame in the previous version. It's just being called five times from a for loop.

There is a bit of optimization you can try here if you are interested. Say you have many surfaces to check, and you are looping through them and checking each one. In many systems, once you have found a surface that the ball is hitting and handled that reaction, you don't need to continue checking all the other surfaces. So you could just break out of the for loop at that point. To do such a thing, you might want to have the checkLine function return true or false based on whether or not it has hit a line. Then your for loop in the onEnterFrame function could look like this:

```
for(var i:uint = 0; i < numLines; i++)
{
    if(checkLine(lines[i]))
    {
        break;
    }
}
```

In some cases though, particularly in a dense area of lines, you might want to check all of the lines on every frame. So, I'll leave it to you to decide whether such an optimization is appropriate.

Important formulas in this chapter

Here's a reminder of the two main formulas introduced in this chapter.

Coordinate rotation:

```
x1 = Math.cos(angle) * x - Math.sin(angle) * y;
y1 = Math.cos(angle) * y + Math.sin(angle) * x;
```

Reverse coordinate rotation:

```
x1 = Math.cos(angle) * x + Math.sin(angle) * y;
y1 = Math.cos(angle) * y - Math.sin(angle) * x;
```

Summary

As you've seen in this chapter, coordinate rotation can give you some very complex behavior, but it all boils down to a couple of formulas that never change. Once you're comfortable with the formulas, you can use them anywhere. I hope you're starting to see how you can create very complicated and richly realistic motion just by adding in more and more simple techniques.

You'll be using the coordinate rotation formula quite a bit in the next chapter, where you'll learn how to handle the results of collisions of objects with different velocities and masses.

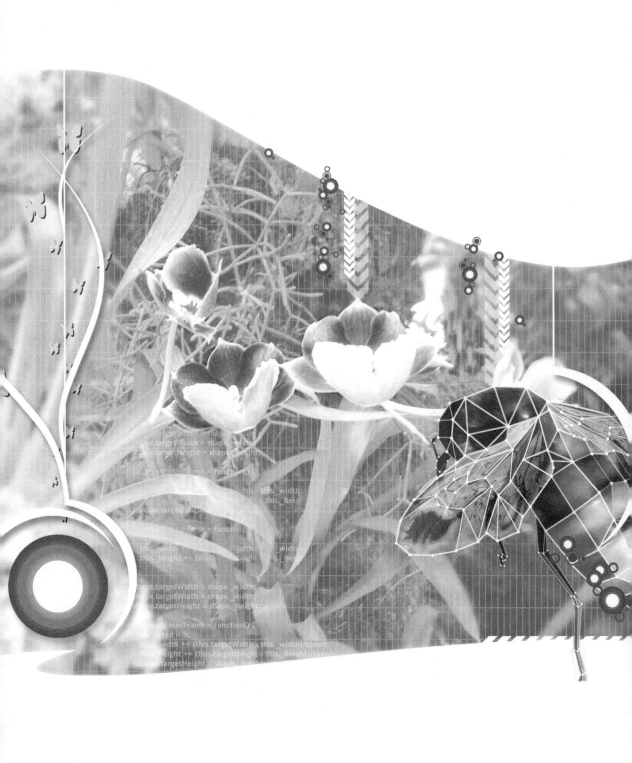

Chapter 11

BILLIARD BALL PHYSICS

What we'll cover in this chapter:

- Mass
- Momentum
- Conservation of momentum
- Important formulas in this chapter

As you might expect in a technical book like this, things start off simple and gradually become more complex. With this chapter, you reach a pinnacle of complexity. Not that the rest of the chapters after this are all downhill, but I think this one in particular requires that you have not skimped on the material that came earlier. That said, I'll walk you through the concepts step by step, and if you've followed along reasonably well up to now, you should be fine.

Specifically, this chapter will focus on momentum: What happens to the momentum of two objects that collide, the conservation of momentum, and how to apply this conservation of momentum in ActionScript to sprites.

As the objects used in these examples are all round, for simplicity's sake, this subject is often referred to as "billiard ball physics." And you'll soon see that these examples really do look like a bunch of different-sized billiard balls hitting each other.

As in previous chapters, when I get to the code, I'll start you out on one dimension to keep things simpler and easier to understand. Then I'll move into two dimensions, at which point you'll need to jump into some coordinate rotation (the subject of the previous chapter). Essentially, you'll be rotating the two-dimensional scene so it lies flat. You can then ignore one axis and treat it as a one-dimensional scene. But all that is just to whet your appetite for what's coming up. Let's start with the simple concepts of mass and momentum.

Mass

The earlier chapters of the book have gone into several aspects of motion: velocity, acceleration, vectors, friction, bouncing, easing, springing, and gravity. One thing that I have pretty successfully gotten away with ignoring is the concept of the mass of the object being moved around. Now, I'm going to reissue my standard disclaimer here, and say that there are probably several points in the book so far where, scientifically speaking, mass should have been in the equation. But I've generally concentrated on doing things *mostly* correctly, and kept the emphasis on making sure it *looks* right. Most important, the final result must be efficient enough that it won't totally kill Flash in the process.

Unfortunately, or maybe fortunately, I have reached a point where I just can't ignore mass any longer. Mass is just so tied up in the subject of momentum that I'm just going to have to confront it head on.

So just what is mass? Here on earth, we usually think of mass as how much something weighs. And that's pretty close, as weight is proportional to mass. The more mass something has, the more it weighs. In fact, we use the same terms to measure mass and weight: kilograms, pounds, and so on. Technically speaking though, mass is the measurement of how much an object resists change in velocity. Thus, the more mass an object has, the harder it is to move that object or to change how that object is moving (slow it down, speed it up, or change its direction).

This also relates to acceleration and force. The more mass something has, the more force you need to apply to it to produce a given acceleration. The engine in my Chevy Cavalier is designed to produce enough force to provide reasonable acceleration on the mass of a Chevy Cavalier (barely). It's not going to produce enough force to accelerate a large truck. The engine would need a lot more force, because the truck has a lot more mass.

Momentum

Now we move on to momentum. This is basically the product of an object's mass and velocity. In other words, mass *times* velocity. Momentum is usually indicated by the letter p, and mass by m. Thus, the following should be pretty self-explanatory:

    p = m * v

This means that something with a small mass and high velocity could have a similar momentum to something with a large mass and low velocity. The aforementioned large truck moving at a mere 20 miles an hour could easily kill you. A bullet, on the other hand, has a relatively tiny mass but a much higher velocity, and it's just as deadly.

Because velocity is a vector (direction and magnitude), momentum must also be a vector. The direction of the momentum vector is the same as the direction of the velocity vector. Thus, to fully describe momentum, you say something like this (where m/s is meters per second):

    5 kg * 20 m/s at 23 degrees

Pretty complex, eh? Now you know why I've waited until now to bring it up.

Conservation of momentum

Finally, we get to the meat of the chapter: conservation of momentum. What does that mean? Momentum is conserved? When? Where? How? OK, let's slow down. Momentum conservation has everything to do with collisions, which is something you're very familiar with by now. You've gone through a whole chapter on collision detection and even faked some collision reactions between two objects. Conservation of momentum is the exact principle you need to respond very realistically to a collision.

Conservation of momentum allows you to say, "This object was moving at velocity A and that object was moving at velocity B before the collision. Now, *after* the collision, this object will move at velocity C and that object will move at velocity D." To break it down further, knowing that velocity is speed and direction, you can say that if you know the speed and direction of two objects just before they collide, you can figure out the speed and direction they will move in after the collision. A very useful thing, as I'm sure you'll agree.

There's one catch though: You'll need to know each object's mass. Again, you see why I've put off this discussion until now. So, in reality, you're saying if you know the mass, speed, and direction of each object before the collision, you can figure out where and how fast the objects will go after they collide.

OK, so that's what conservation of momentum can do for you. But what is it? Basically, the Law of Conservation of Momentum says that the total momentum for a system before a collision will be equal to the total momentum after a collision. But what is this *system* the law refers to? This is just a collection of objects with momentum. Most discussions also specify that this would be a *closed system*, which is a system with no other forces or influences acting on it. In other words, you can just ignore anything but the actual collision itself. For our purposes, we will always be considering just the reaction between two objects, so our system will always be something like object A and object B.

The total momentum of the system is simply the combined momentum of all the objects in the system. For us, this will mean the combined momentum of object A and object B. So, if you combine the momentums before the collision, and combine the momentums afterward, the result should be the same. "Well, that's great," you say, "but it doesn't really tell me how to find out the new momentums." Patience, we're getting there. I told you we'll be walking through this step by step. A few paragraphs from now, you'll probably be wanting me to slow down, because here come the formulas!

Before I jump into the math, here's a suggestion. Don't worry too much at first about trying to figure out how to convert this to real code. You'll get to that soon enough. Just try to look at the next few formulas from a conceptual viewpoint. "This plus that equals that plus this. Sure, that makes sense." It will all translate very neatly into code by the end of this chapter.

OK, if combined momentum before and after the collision is the same, and momentum is velocity times mass, then for two objects—object 0 and object 1—you can come up with something like this:

```
momentum0 + momentum1 = momentum0Final + momentum1Final
```

or

```
(m0 * v0) + (m1 * v1) = (m0 * v0Final) + (m1 * v1Final)
```

Now, what you want to know is the final velocities for object 0 and object 1. Those would be v0Final and v1Final. The way to solve an equation with two unknowns is to find *another* equation that has the same two unknowns in it. It just so happens there is such an equation floating around the halls of the physics departments of the world. It has to do with kinetic energy. The funny thing is, you don't even have to know or even care what kinetic energy is all about. You just borrow the formula to help you solve your own problem, dust it off, and give it back when you're done. Here's the formula for kinetic energy:

```
KE = 0.5 * m * v²
```

Technically, kinetic energy is not a vector, so although you use the v for velocity in there, it deals with only the magnitude of the velocity. It doesn't care about the direction. But that won't hurt your calculations.

Now, it happens that the kinetic energy before and after a collision remains the same. So, you can do something like this:

```
KE0 + KE1 = KE0Final + KE1Final
```

or

```
(0.5 * m0 * v0²) + (0.5 * m1 * v1²) =
(0.5 * m0 * v0Final²) + (0.5 * m1 * v1Final²)
```

You can then factor out the 0.5 values to get this:

```
(m0 * v0²) + (m1 * v1²) = (m0 * v0Final²) + (m1 * v1Final²)
```

What do you know? You have a different equation with the same two unknown variables: v0final and v1Final. You can now factor these out and come up with a single equation for each unknown. I'll save us both a headache in the intervening algebra and just give you the formulas that you wind up with when all is said and done. If you're one of those people who actually like doing algebra equations, or you need some extra credit for school, I invite you to sit down with some paper and a few sharp pencils, and figure it out on your own. You will wind up with the equations that follow (if not, either you made a mistake or I'm in big trouble with my publisher).

$$v0Final = \frac{(m0 - m1) * v0 + 2 * m1 * v1}{m0 + m1}$$

$$v1Final = \frac{(m1 - m0) * v1 + 2 * m0 * v0}{m0 + m1}$$

And now you see why I said at the beginning of this chapter that you have reached a pinnacle of complexity. Actually, you haven't quite reached it yet. You're about to apply this to one axis, and after that, you're going to dive in and add coordinate rotation to it when you move to two axes. Hold on!

Conservation of momentum on one axis

Now that you've got some formulas, you can start making things move with them. For this first example, you'll again use the Ball class, but I've added a mass property to it. Here is the new code for that class (Ball.as):

```
package {
    import flash.display.Sprite;

    public class Ball extends Sprite {
        private var radius:Number;
        private var color:uint;
        public var vx:Number = 0;
        public var vy:Number = 0;
        public var mass:Number = 1;

        public function Ball(radius:Number=40, color:uint=0xff0000) {
            this.radius = radius;
            this.color = color;
            init();
        }
        public function init():void {
            graphics.beginFill(color);
            graphics.drawCircle(0, 0, radius);
            graphics.endFill();
        }
    }
}
```

You'll be creating two different instances of the class with different sizes, positions, and masses. You'll be ignoring the y axis this time around, so they'll both be in the same position vertically. So the basic setup when the movie starts will look something like Figure 11-1.

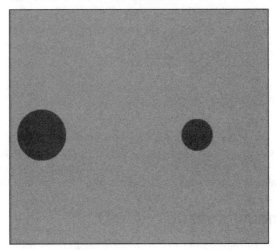

Figure 11-1. Setting the stage for conservation of momentum on one axis

The beginning of the class just creates the balls and positions them, and then does some basic motion code for one-axis velocity and simple distance-based collision detection:

```
package
{
    import flash.display.Sprite;
    import flash.events.Event;

    public class Billiard1 extends Sprite
    {
        private var ball0:Ball;
        private var ball1:Ball;

        public function Billiard1()
        {
            init();
        }

        private function init():void
        {
            ball0 = new Ball(40);
            ball0.mass = 2;
            ball0.x = 50;
            ball0.y = stage.stageHeight / 2;
            ball0.vx = 1;
            addChild(ball0);
```

```
            ball1 = new Ball(25);
            ball1.mass = 1
            ball1.x = 300;
            ball1.y = stage.stageHeight / 2;
            ball1.vx = -1;
            addChild(ball1);

            addEventListener(Event.ENTER_FRAME, onEnterFrame);
        }

        private function onEnterFrame(event:Event):void
        {
            ball0.x += ball0.vx;
            ball1.x += ball1.vx;
            var dist:Number = ball1.x - ball0.x;
            if(Math.abs(dist) < ball0.radius + ball1.radius)
            {
                // reaction will go here
            }
        }
    }
}
```

Now, the only question is how to code in the reaction. Well, let's take ball0 first. Considering that ball0 is object 0 and ball1 is object 1, you need to apply the following formula:

$$v0Final = \frac{(m0 - m1) * v0 + 2 * m1 * v1}{m0 + m1}$$

In ActionScript, this becomes the following code:

```
var vx0Final:Number = ((ball0.mass - ball1.mass) * ball0.vx +
                       2 * ball1.mass * ball1.vx) /
                       (ball0.mass + ball1.mass);
```

It shouldn't be too hard to see where that came from. You can then do the same thing with ball1, so this:

$$v1Final = \frac{(m1 - m0) * v1 + 2 * m0 * v0}{m0 + m1}$$

becomes this:

```
var vx1Final:Number = ((ball1.mass - ball0.mass) * ball1.vx +
                       2 * ball0.mass * ball0.vx) /
                       (ball0.mass + ball1.mass);
```

The final code for onEnterFrame winds up like this:

```
private function onEnterFrame(event:Event):void
{
    ball0.x += ball0.vx;
    ball1.x += ball1.vx;
    var dist:Number = ball1.x - ball0.x;
    if(Math.abs(dist) < ball0.radius + ball1.radius)
    {
        var vx0Final:Number = ((ball0.mass - ball1.mass) * ball0.vx +
                               2 * ball1.mass * ball1.vx) /
                               (ball0.mass + ball1.mass);
        var vx1Final:Number = ((ball1.mass - ball0.mass) * ball1.vx +
                               2 * ball0.mass * ball0.vx) /
                               (ball0.mass + ball1.mass);
        ball0.vx = vx0Final;
        ball1.vx = vx1Final;

        ball0.x += ball0.vx;
        ball1.x += ball1.vx;
    }
}
```

Note that the calculation for vx0Final uses ball1.vx and vice versa. Thus, I had to store both of them in temporary variables, rather than assigning them directly to the ball0.vx and ball1.vx properties.

Placing the objects

The last two lines of the preceding ActionScript deserve some explanation. After you figure out the new velocities for each ball, you add them back to the ball's position. That's something new. Why do that? Well, remember that in all previous bouncing examples, you needed to reposition the sprite so that it wasn't embedded in the wall. You just moved it out so it was touching the edge of the wall. You need to do the same thing here, but now you have two moving objects. You don't want them embedded in each other. That would not only look wrong, but it would usually result in the two objects becoming stuck together permanently.

You could place one of the balls just on the edge of the other one. But which one should you move? Whichever one you moved would kind of jump into its new position unnaturally, which would be especially noticeable at low speeds.

There are probably a number of ways to determine the correct placement of the balls, ranging from simple to complex and accurate to totally faked. The simple solution I used for this first example is just to add the new velocity back to the objects, moving them apart again. I've found that this is pretty realistic and quite simple—accomplished in two lines of code. Later, in the "Solving a potential problem" section, I'll show you a problem that can crop up with this method and give you a solution that's a little more robust.

Go ahead and compile and run the Billiard1.as document class. Then change the masses and velocities of each ball until you see what's going on. Change the sizes of each, too. Note that the size doesn't really have anything to do with the reaction. In most cases, the larger object would have a higher mass, and you could probably figure out the relative volume of the two balls and come up with realistic masses for their sizes. However, usually, I just mess around with numbers for mass until things look and feel right. I say something very scientific like, "Well, this ball is roughly twice as big, so I'll give it twice the mass."

Optimizing the code

The worst part of this solution is that huge equation right in the middle. Actually, the very worst part is the fact that the code has almost exactly the same equation in there twice. If you could somehow get rid of one of them, I'm sure you'd feel a lot better. The good news is that you can.

It's going to take a bit more math and algebra, which I'm not going to explain in mind-numbing detail. Basically, you need to find the total velocity of the two objects before the condition. Then, after you get the final velocity of one object, you can find the difference between it and the total velocity to get the final velocity for the other object.

You actually find the total velocity by *subtracting* the velocities of the two objects. That may seem strange, but think of it from the viewpoint of the system. Say the system is two cars on a highway. One is going at 50 mph and the other at 60 mph. Depending on which car you're in, you could see the other car going at 10 mph or –10 mph. In other words, it's either slowly moving ahead of you or falling behind you.

So, before you do anything in terms of collisions, you find out the total velocity (from ball1's viewpoint) by subtracting ball1.vx from ball0.vx.

```
var vxTotal:Number = ball0.vx - ball1.vx;
```

Finally, after calculating vx0Final, add that to vxTotal, and you'll have vx1Final. Again, this may seem counterintuitive, but try it out, and you'll see it works.

```
vx1Final = vxTotal + vx0Final;
```

Fantastic! That's better than that horrible double formula. Also, now that the formula for ball1.vx doesn't reference ball0.vx anymore, you can even get rid of the temporary variables. Here's the revised onEnterFrame method (from document class Billiard2.as):

```
private function onEnterFrame(event:Event):void
{
    ball0.x += ball0.vx;
    ball1.x += ball1.vx;
    var dist:Number = ball1.x - ball0.x;
    if(Math.abs(dist) < ball0.radius + ball1.radius)
    {
        var vxTotal:Number = ball0.vx - ball1.vx;
        ball0.vx = ((ball0.mass - ball1.mass) * ball0.vx +
                    2 * ball1.mass * ball1.vx) /
                    (ball0.mass + ball1.mass);
        ball1.vx = vxTotal + ball0.vx;
```

```
        ball0.x += ball0.vx;
        ball1.x += ball1.vx;
    }
}
```

You've gotten rid of quite a few math operations and still have the same result—not bad.

Now, this isn't one of those formulas that you're necessarily going to understand inside out, unless perhaps you have a physics background. You may not even memorize it, unless you're using it on a very regular basis. Personally, whenever I want to use this technique, I pull out the first version of this book and copy my own formulas!

Conservation of momentum on two axes

OK, take a deep breath. You're going to the next level. So far, you've applied a long-winded formula, but it's pretty much plug-and-play. You take the mass and the velocity of the two objects, plug them into the formula, and get your result.

Now I'm going to throw one more layer of complexity onto it—namely, another dimension. I've already given away the strategy at the beginning of the chapter, so you know that you'll be using coordinate rotation. Let's take a look at why.

Understanding the theory and strategy

Figure 11-2 illustrates the example you just saw: collision in one dimension.

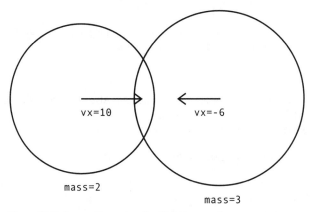

Figure 11-2. A one-dimensional collision

As you can see, the objects have different sizes, different masses, and different velocities. The velocities are represented by the arrows coming out from the center of each ball. These are vectors. To refresh your memory, a velocity vector points in the direction of the motion, and its length indicates the speed.

The one-dimensional example was pretty simple, because both velocity vectors were along the x axis. So, you could just add and subtract their magnitudes directly. Now, take a look at Figure 11-3, which shows two balls colliding in two dimensions.

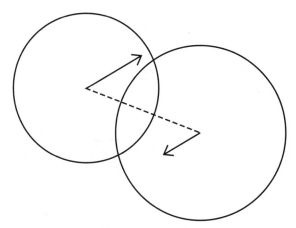

Figure 11-3. A two-dimensional collision

Now the velocities are in completely different directions. You can't just plug the velocities into the momentum-conservation formula. That would give you completely incorrect results. So, how do you solve this?

Well, you start by making the second diagram look a bit more like the first, by rotating it. First, figure out the angle formed by the positions of the two balls and rotate the whole scene—positions and velocities—counterclockwise by that amount. For example, if the angle is 30 degrees, rotate every-thing by –30. This is exactly the same thing you did in Chapter 10 to bounce off an angled surface. The resulting picture looks like Figure 11-4.

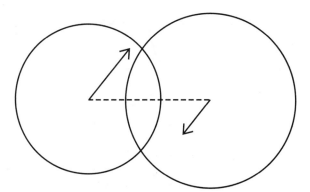

Figure 11-4. A two-dimensional collision, rotated

That angle between the two balls is pretty important, and not just to make things look pretty, either. That angle can be called the *angle of collision*. It's important because it's the only part of the ball's velocities that you care about—the portion of the velocity that lies on that angle.

Now, take a look at the diagram in Figure 11-5. Here, I've added in vector lines for the vx and vy for both velocities. Note that the vx for both balls lies exactly along the angle of collision.

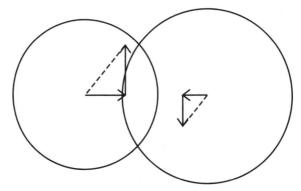

Figure 11-5. Draw in the x and y velocities.

As I just said, the only portion of the velocity you care about is the part that lies on the angle of collision. That is now your vx. In fact, you can just forget all about vy for now. I'll take it right out of the picture, as you can see in Figure 11-6.

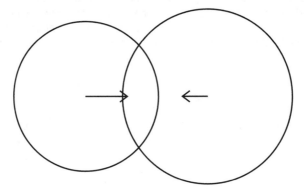

Figure 11-6. All you care about is the x velocity.

Does this look familiar? It's the first diagram again! You can easily solve this with the plug-and-play momentum formula. (Notice how I'm brainwashing you! You've already started agreeing with me that the formula for conservation of momentum is easy, haven't you?)

When you apply the formula, you wind up with two new vx values. Remember that the vy values never change. But the alteration of the vx alone changed the overall velocity to look something Figure 11-7.

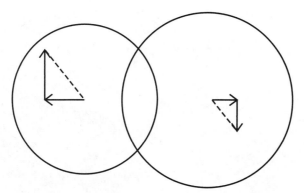

Figure 11-7. New x velocities, same y velocities, with the result of a new overall velocity

Have you already guessed what's next? You just rotate everything back again, as shown in Figure 11-8, and you have the final real vx and vy for each ball.

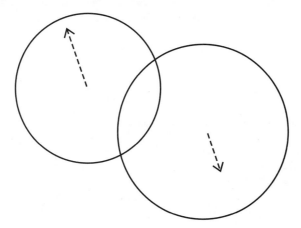

Figure 11-8. Everything rotated back

Well, that all looks very nice in a little line drawing, but now it's time to somehow convert all this into code. The hardest part for me is trying to continue to convince you that it's easy.

Writing the code

To begin, you need to make a base file that will allow two balls to move at any angle and eventually hit each other. Starting off with pretty much the same setup as before, you have two ball instances: ball0 and ball1. Let's make them a little larger now, like in Figure 11-9, so there's a good chance of them bumping into each other often.

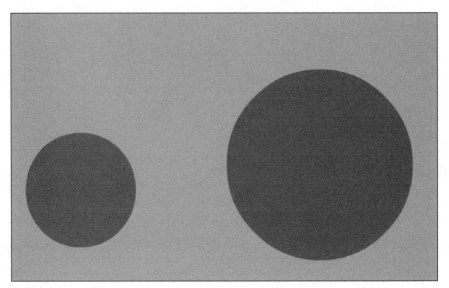

Figure 11-9. Setting the stage for conservation of momentum on two axes

```
package
{
    import flash.display.Sprite;
    import flash.events.Event;

    public class Billiard3 extends Sprite
    {
        private var ball0:Ball;
        private var ball1:Ball;
        private var bounce:Number = -1.0;

        public function Billiard3()
        {
            init();
        }

        private function init():void
        {
            ball0 = new Ball(150);
            ball0.mass = 2;
            ball0.x = stage.stageWidth - 200;
            ball0.y = stage.stageHeight - 200;
            ball0.vx = Math.random() * 10 - 5;
            ball0.vy = Math.random() * 10 - 5;
            addChild(ball0);
```

```
        ball1 = new Ball(90);
        ball1.mass = 1
        ball1.x = 100;
        ball1.y = 100;
        ball1.vx = Math.random() * 10 - 5;
        ball1.vy = Math.random() * 10 - 5;
        addChild(ball1);

        addEventListener(Event.ENTER_FRAME, onEnterFrame);
    }

    private function onEnterFrame(event:Event):void
    {
        ball0.x += ball0.vx;
        ball0.y += ball0.vy;
        ball1.x += ball1.vx;
        ball1.y += ball1.vy;

        checkWalls(ball0);
        checkWalls(ball1);
    }

    private function checkWalls(ball:Ball):void
    {
        if(ball.x + ball.radius > stage.stageWidth)
        {
            ball.x = stage.stageWidth - ball.radius;
            ball.vx *= bounce;
        }
        else if(ball.x - ball.radius < 0)
        {
            ball.x = ball.radius;
            ball.vx *= bounce;
        }
        if(ball.y + ball.radius > stage.stageHeight)
        {
            ball.y = stage.stageHeight - ball.radius;
            ball.vy *= bounce;
        }
        else if(ball.y - ball.radius < 0)
        {
            ball.y = ball.radius;
            ball.vy *= bounce;
        }
    }
  }
 }
}
```

Now, that's all stuff you should be able to do in your sleep by now. You set boundaries, set some random velocities, throw in some mass, move each ball according to its velocity, and check the boundaries. Notice that I pulled the boundary-checking stuff out into its own function, checkWalls, so I could use it twice without typing it in again.

I do the same thing with the collision-checking routine, putting it into a function called checkCollision. So, onEnterFrame becomes this:

```
private function onEnterFrame(event:Event):void
{
    ball0.x += ball0.vx;
    ball0.y += ball0.vy;
    ball1.x += ball1.vx;
    ball1.y += ball1.vy;
    checkCollision(ball0, ball1);
    checkWalls(ball0);
    checkWalls(ball1);
}
```

From this point on, I'll show you only the checkCollision function and any other functions I happen to come up with. The rest of the code doesn't change. If you want to see the finished product in all its glory, it's in Billiard3.as.

The beginning of that function is pretty simple. It's just a distance-based collision detection setup.

```
private function checkCollision(ball0:Ball, ball1:Ball):void
{
    var dx:Number = ball1.x - ball0.x;
    var dy:Number = ball1.y - ball0.y;
    var dist:Number = Math.sqrt(dx*dx + dy*dy);
    if(dist < ball0.radius + ball1.radius)
    {
        // collision handling code here
    }
}
```

See? You have about two-thirds of the code written already, and so far it has been a piece of cake!

The first thing that the collision-handling code needs to do is figure out the angle between the two balls. You can do that with Math.atan2(dy, dx). (If that didn't spring to your mind even as you were reading it, you might want to review the trigonometry in Chapter 3.) Then you store the cosine and sine calculations, as you'll be using them over and over.

```
// calculate angle, sine, and cosine
var angle:Number = Math.atan2(dy, dx);
var sin:Number = Math.sin(angle);
var cos:Number = Math.cos(angle);
```

Next, you need to do coordinate rotation for the velocity and position of both balls. Let's call the rotated positions x0, y0, x1, and y1 and the rotated velocities vx0, vy0, vx1, and vy1.

Since you are using ball0 as the "pivot point," its coordinates will be 0, 0. That won't change even after rotation, so you can just say this:

```
// rotate ball0's position
var x0:Number = 0;
var y0:Number = 0;
```

Next, ball1's position is in relation to ball0's position. This corresponds to the distance values you've already figured out, dx and dy. So, you can just rotate those to get ball1's rotated position:

```
// rotate ball1's position
var x1:Number = dx * cos + dy * sin;
var y1:Number = dy * cos - dx * sin;
```

Finally, rotate all the velocities. You should see a pattern forming:

```
// rotate ball0's velocity
var vx0:Number = ball0.vx * cos + ball0.vy * sin;
var vy0:Number = ball0.vy * cos - ball0.vx * sin;

// rotate ball1's velocity
var vx1:Number = ball1.vx * cos + ball1.vy * sin;
var vy1:Number = ball1.vy * cos - ball1.vx * sin;
```

Here's all the rotation code in place:

```
private function checkCollision(ball0:Ball, ball1:Ball):void
{
    var dx:Number = ball1.x - ball0.x;
    var dy:Number = ball1.y - ball0.y;
    var dist:Number = Math.sqrt(dx*dx + dy*dy);
    if(dist < ball0.radius + ball1.radius)
    {
        // calculate angle, sine, and cosine
        var angle:Number = Math.atan2(dy, dx);
        var sin:Number = Math.sin(angle);
        var cos:Number = Math.cos(angle);

        // rotate ball0's position
        var x0:Number = 0;
        var y0:Number = 0;

        // rotate ball1's position
        var x1:Number = dx * cos + dy * sin;
        var y1:Number = dy * cos - dx * sin;

        // rotate ball0's velocity
        var vx0:Number = ball0.vx * cos + ball0.vy * sin;
        var vy0:Number = ball0.vy * cos - ball0.vx * sin;
```

```
    // rotate ball1's velocity
    var vx1:Number = ball1.vx * cos + ball1.vy * sin;
    var vy1:Number = ball1.vy * cos - ball1.vx * sin;
  }
}
```

That's not so horrible yet, right? Well, hang in there. You're already one-third of the way through the painful stuff.

You can now do a simple one-dimensional collision reaction with vx0 and ball0.mass, and vx1 and ball1.mass. For the earlier one-dimensional example, you had the following code:

```
var vxTotal:Number = ball0.vx - ball1.vx;
ball0.vx = ((ball0.mass - ball1.mass) * ball0.vx +
            2 * ball1.mass * ball1.vx) /
           (ball0.mass + ball1.mass);
ball1.vx = vxTotal + ball0.vx;
```

You can now rewrite that as follows:

```
var vxTotal:Number = vx0 - vx1;
vx0 = ((ball0.mass - ball1.mass) * vx0 +
        2 * ball1.mass * vx1) /
       (ball0.mass + ball1.mass);
vx1 = vxTotal + vx0;
```

All you did was replace the ball0.vx and ball1.vx with the rotated versions, vx0 and vx1. Let's plug that into the function:

```
private function checkCollision(ball0:Ball, ball1:Ball):void
{
    var dx:Number = ball1.x - ball0.x;
    var dy:Number = ball1.y - ball0.y;
    var dist:Number = Math.sqrt(dx*dx + dy*dy);
    if(dist < ball0.radius + ball1.radius)
    {
        // calculate angle, sine, and cosine
        var angle:Number = Math.atan2(dy, dx);
        var sin:Number = Math.sin(angle);
        var cos:Number = Math.cos(angle);

        // rotate ball0's position
        var x0:Number = 0;
        var y0:Number = 0;

        // rotate ball1's position
        var x1:Number = dx * cos + dy * sin;
        var y1:Number = dy * cos - dx * sin;
```

```
            // rotate ball0's velocity
            var vx0:Number = ball0.vx * cos + ball0.vy * sin;
            var vy0:Number = ball0.vy * cos - ball0.vx * sin;

            // rotate ball1's velocity
            var vx1:Number = ball1.vx * cos + ball1.vy * sin;
            var vy1:Number = ball1.vy * cos - ball1.vx * sin;

            // collision reaction
            var vxTotal:Number = vx0 - vx1;
            vx0 = ((ball0.mass - ball1.mass) * vx0 +
                 2 * ball1.mass * vx1) /
                 (ball0.mass + ball1.mass);
            vx1 = vxTotal + vx0;
            x0 += vx0;
            x1 += vx1;
        }
    }
```

This code also adds the new x velocities to the x positions, to move them apart, as in the one-dimensional example.

Now that you have updated, post-collision positions and velocities, rotate everything back. Start by getting the unrotated, final positions.

```
    // rotate positions back
    var x0Final:Number = x0 * cos - y0 * sin;
    var y0Final:Number = y0 * cos + x0 * sin;
    var x1Final:Number = x1 * cos - y1 * sin;
    var y1Final:Number = y1 * cos + x1 * sin;
```

Remember to reverse the + and - in the rotation equations, as you are going in the other direction now. These "final" positions are actually not quite final. They are in relation to the pivot point of the system, which is ball0's original position. So, you need to add all of these to ball0's position to get the actual screen positions. Let's do ball1 first, so that it's using ball0's original position, not the updated one:

```
    // adjust positions to actual screen positions
    ball1.x = ball0.x + x1Final;
    ball1.y = ball0.y + y1Final;
    ball0.x = ball0.x + x0Final;
    ball0.y = ball0.y + y0Final;
```

Last, but not least, rotate back the velocities. These can be applied directly to the balls' vx and vy properties:

```
    // rotate velocities back
    ball0.vx = vx0 * cos - vy0 * sin;
    ball0.vy = vy0 * cos + vx0 * sin;
    ball1.vx = vx1 * cos - vy1 * sin;
    ball1.vy = vy1 * cos + vx1 * sin;
```

293

Let's take a look at the entire completed function:

```
private function checkCollision(ball0:Ball, ball1:Ball):void
{
    var dx:Number = ball1.x - ball0.x;
    var dy:Number = ball1.y - ball0.y;
    var dist:Number = Math.sqrt(dx*dx + dy*dy);
    if(dist < ball0.radius + ball1.radius)
    {
        // calculate angle, sine, and cosine
        var angle:Number = Math.atan2(dy, dx);
        var sin:Number = Math.sin(angle);
        var cos:Number = Math.cos(angle);

        // rotate ball0's position
        var x0:Number = 0;
        var y0:Number = 0;

        // rotate ball1's position
        var x1:Number = dx * cos + dy * sin;
        var y1:Number = dy * cos - dx * sin;

        // rotate ball0's velocity
        var vx0:Number = ball0.vx * cos + ball0.vy * sin;
        var vy0:Number = ball0.vy * cos - ball0.vx * sin;

        // rotate ball1's velocity
        var vx1:Number = ball1.vx * cos + ball1.vy * sin;
        var vy1:Number = ball1.vy * cos - ball1.vx * sin;

        // collision reaction
        var vxTotal:Number = vx0 - vx1;
        vx0 = ((ball0.mass - ball1.mass) * vx0 +
                2 * ball1.mass * vx1) /
                (ball0.mass + ball1.mass);
        vx1 = vxTotal + vx0;
        x0 += vx0;
        x1 += vx1;

        // rotate positions back
        var x0Final:Number = x0 * cos - y0 * sin;
        var y0Final:Number = y0 * cos + x0 * sin;
        var x1Final:Number = x1 * cos - y1 * sin;
        var y1Final:Number = y1 * cos + x1 * sin;

        // adjust positions to actual screen positions
        ball1.x = ball0.x + x1Final;
        ball1.y = ball0.y + y1Final;
        ball0.x = ball0.x + x0Final;
        ball0.y = ball0.y + y0Final;
```

```
            // rotate velocities back
            ball0.vx = vx0 * cos - vy0 * sin;
            ball0.vy = vy0 * cos + vx0 * sin;
            ball1.vx = vx1 * cos - vy1 * sin;
            ball1.vy = vy1 * cos + vx1 * sin;
        }
    }
```

Play around with this example. Change the size of the Ball instances, the initial velocities, masses, and so on. Become convinced that it works pretty well.

As for that checkCollision function, it's a doozy, yes. But if you read the comments, you see it's broken up into (relatively) simple chunks. You could probably optimize this, or you could refactor it a bit to remove some of the duplication. In fact, in the name of good practice, I've gone ahead and done this in Billiard4.as, which you can see here:

```
package
{
    import flash.display.Sprite;
    import flash.events.Event;
    import flash.geom.Point;

    public class Billiard4 extends Sprite
    {
        private var ball0:Ball;
        private var ball1:Ball;
        private var bounce:Number = -1.0;

        public function Billiard4()
        {
            init();
        }

        private function init():void
        {
            ball0 = new Ball(150);
            ball0.mass = 2;
            ball0.x = stage.stageWidth - 200;
            ball0.y = stage.stageHeight - 200;
            ball0.vx = Math.random() * 10 - 5;
            ball0.vy = Math.random() * 10 - 5;
            addChild(ball0);

            ball1 = new Ball(90);
            ball1.mass = 1
            ball1.x = 100;
            ball1.y = 100;
            ball1.vx = Math.random() * 10 - 5;
            ball1.vy = Math.random() * 10 - 5;
            addChild(ball1);
```

```
        addEventListener(Event.ENTER_FRAME, onEnterFrame);
}

private function onEnterFrame(event:Event):void
{
    ball0.x += ball0.vx;
    ball0.y += ball0.vy;
    ball1.x += ball1.vx;
    ball1.y += ball1.vy;
    checkCollision(ball0, ball1);
    checkWalls(ball0);
    checkWalls(ball1);
}

private function checkWalls(ball:Ball):void
{
    if(ball.x + ball.radius > stage.stageWidth)
    {
        ball.x = stage.stageWidth - ball.radius;
        ball.vx *= bounce;
    }
    else if(ball.x - ball.radius < 0)
    {
        ball.x = ball.radius;
        ball.vx *= bounce;
    }
    if(ball.y + ball.radius > stage.stageHeight)
    {
        ball.y = stage.stageHeight - ball.radius;
        ball.vy *= bounce;
    }
    else if(ball.y - ball.radius < 0)
    {
        ball.y = ball.radius;
        ball.vy *= bounce;
    }
}

private function checkCollision(ball0:Ball, ball1:Ball):void
{
    var dx:Number = ball1.x - ball0.x;
    var dy:Number = ball1.y - ball0.y;
    var dist:Number = Math.sqrt(dx*dx + dy*dy);
    if(dist < ball0.radius + ball1.radius)
    {
        // calculate angle, sine, and cosine
        var angle:Number = Math.atan2(dy, dx);
        var sin:Number = Math.sin(angle);
        var cos:Number = Math.cos(angle);
```

```
// rotate ball0's position
var pos0:Point = new Point(0, 0);

// rotate ball1's position
var pos1:Point = rotate(dx, dy, sin, cos, true);

// rotate ball0's velocity
var vel0:Point = rotate(ball0.vx,
                        ball0.vy,
                        sin,
                        cos,
                        true);

// rotate ball1's velocity
var vel1:Point = rotate(ball1.vx,
                        ball1.vy,
                        sin,
                        cos,
                        true);

// collision reaction
var vxTotal:Number = vel0.x - vel1.x;
vel0.x = ((ball0.mass - ball1.mass) * vel0.x +
         2 * ball1.mass * vel1.x) /
         (ball0.mass + ball1.mass);
vel1.x = vxTotal + vel0.x;

// update position
pos0.x += vel0.x;
pos1.x += vel1.x;

// rotate positions back
var pos0F:Object = rotate(pos0.x,
                          pos0.y,
                          sin,
                          cos,
                          false);

var pos1F:Object = rotate(pos1.x,
                          pos1.y,
                          sin,
                          cos,
                          false);

// adjust positions to actual screen positions
ball1.x = ball0.x + pos1F.x;
ball1.y = ball0.y + pos1F.y;
ball0.x = ball0.x + pos0F.x;
ball0.y = ball0.y + pos0F.y;
```

```
                        // rotate velocities back
                        var vel0F:Object = rotate(vel0.x,
                                                  vel0.y,
                                                  sin,
                                                  cos,
                                                  false);
                        var vel1F:Object = rotate(vel1.x,
                                                  vel1.y,
                                                  sin,
                                                  cos,
                                                  false);
                        ball0.vx = vel0F.x;
                        ball0.vy = vel0F.y;
                        ball1.vx = vel1F.x;
                        ball1.vy = vel1F.y;
                    }
                }

                private function rotate(x:Number,
                                        y:Number,
                                        sin:Number,
                                        cos:Number,
                                        reverse:Boolean):Point
                {
                    var result:Point = new Point();
                    if(reverse)
                    {
                        result.x = x * cos + y * sin;
                        result.y = y * cos - x * sin;
                    }
                    else
                    {
                        result.x = x * cos - y * sin;
                        result.y = y * cos + x * sin;
                    }
                    return result;
                }
            }
        }
```

Here, I've made a rotate function that takes in the values it needs and returns an instance of flash.geom.Point. This is an object that comes with a predefined x and y property (along with lots of other neat stuff we won't even use here). The returned point's x and y properties are rotated. This version isn't quite as easy to read when you're learning the principles involved, but it results in a lot less duplicated code.

Adding more objects

Now, having two sprites colliding and reacting was no easy task, but you made it. Congratulations. Now let's go for a few more colliding objects—say eight. That sounds like it's going to be four times more complex, but it's really not. The functions you have now just check two balls at a time, but that's all you really want to do anyway. You put more objects on stage, move them around, and check each one against all the others. And you've already done just that in the collision detection examples (Chapter 9). All you need to do is to plug in the checkCollision function where you would normally do the collision detection.

For this example (MultiBilliard.as), start with eight balls in an array, loop through them, and assign various properties to them:

```
package
{
    import flash.display.Sprite;
    import flash.events.Event;
    import flash.geom.Point;

    public class MultiBilliard extends Sprite
    {
        private var balls:Array;
        private var numBalls:uint = 8;
        private var bounce:Number = -1.0;

        public function MultiBilliard()
        {
            init();
        }

        private function init():void
        {
            balls = new Array();
            for(var i:uint = 0; i < numBalls; i++)
            {
                var radius:Number = Math.random() * 20 + 20;
                var ball:Ball = new Ball(radius);
                ball.mass = radius;
                ball.x = i * 100
                ball.y = i * 50;
                ball.vx = Math.random() * 10 - 5;
                ball.vy = Math.random() * 10 - 5;
                addChild(ball);
                balls.push(ball);
            }

            addEventListener(Event.ENTER_FRAME, onEnterFrame);
        }

        private function onEnterFrame(event:Event):void
        {
            // coming soon...
        }
```

```
        // checkWalls, checkCollision, and rotate methods are not
        // listed but are exactly the same as in the previous example
    }
}
```

You might notice that I spaced out the initial x and y positions of each ball to ensure that they were not touching each other to start with. If so, they could get stuck together.

The onEnterFrame method is surprisingly simple. It has just two loops: one for basic movement and one for collision detection.

```
private function onEnterFrame(event:Event):void
{
    for(var i:uint = 0; i < numBalls; i++)
    {
        var ball:Ball = balls[i];
        ball.x += ball.vx;
        ball.y += ball.vy;
        checkWalls(ball);
    }
    for(i = 0; i < numBalls - 1; i++)
    {
        var ballA:Ball = balls[i];
        for(var j:Number = i + 1; j < numBalls; j++)
        {
            var ballB:Ball = balls[j];
            checkCollision(ballA, ballB);
        }
    }
}
```

The first for loop just runs through each ball on stage, moving it and bouncing it off the walls. Then you have a nested loop that compares each ball with every other one, as I covered in the discussion of collision detection (in Chapter 9). In this, you get a reference to two of the balls at a time, name them ballA and ballB, and pass these to the checkCollision function. And, amazingly enough, that's all there is to it! The checkWalls, checkCollision, and rotate functions are exactly the same, and therefore are not repeated here.

To add more balls, just update the numBalls variable to the new total, and make sure they are positioned to not touch originally.

Solving a potential problem

One word of warning regarding the setup I've described in this chapter: It's still possible for a pair of objects to get kind of stuck together. This mostly happens in a crowded environment with many sprites bouncing off each other, and it seems worse when they are moving at high speeds. You can also occasionally see this behavior if two or three balls collide in a corner of the stage.

Say you have three balls on stage—ball0, ball1, and ball2—and they all happen to be really close together. Here's basically what happens:

- The code moves all three according to their velocities.
- The code checks ball0 vs. ball1, and ball0 vs. ball2. It finds no collision.
- The code checks ball1 vs. ball2. These two happen to be hitting, so it does all the calculations for their new velocities and updates their positions so that they are no longer touching. This inadvertently puts ball1 in contact with ball0. However, this particular combination has already been checked for a collision, so it now goes unnoticed.
- On the next loop, the code again moves each according to its velocity. This potentially drives ball0 and ball1 even further together.
- Now the code does notice that ball0 and ball1 are hitting. It calculates their new velocities and adds the new velocities to the positions, to move them apart. But, since they were already touching, this might not be enough to actually separate them. They become stuck.

Again, this mostly occurs when you have a lot of objects in a small space, moving at higher speeds. It will also happen if the objects are already touching at the start of the movie. As you may see this issue crop up now and then, it's good to know where the problem lies. The exact point is in the checkCollision function, specifically the following lines:

```
// update position
pos0.x += vel0.x;
pos1.x += vel1.x;
```

This just assumes that the collision occurred due to only the two ball's own velocities, and that adding back on the new velocities will separate them. Most of the time, this is true. But the situations I just described are exceptions. If you are running into this situation, you need something more stringent in ensuring that the sprites are definitely separated before moving on. I came up with the following method:

```
// update position
var absV:Number = Math.abs(vel0.x) + Math.abs(vel1.x);
var overlap:Number = (ball0.radius + ball1.radius)
                     - Math.abs(pos0.x - pos1.x);
pos0.x += vel0.x / absV * overlap;
pos1.x += vel1.x / absV * overlap;
```

This is totally my own creation, so I'm not sure how accurate it is, but it seems to work pretty well. It first determines the absolute velocity (a term I made up!). This is the sum of the absolute values of both velocities. For instance, if one velocity is –5 and the other is 10, the absolute values are 5 and 10, and the total is 5 + 10, or 15.

Next, it determines how much the balls are actually overlapping. It does this by getting their total radii, and subtracting their distance.

Then it moves each ball a portion of the overlap, according to their percent of the absolute velocity. The result is that the balls should be exactly touching each other, with no overlap. It's a bit more complex than the earlier version, but it pretty much clears up the bugs.

In fact, in the next version, `MultiBilliard2.as`, I created 20 balls, made them a bit larger, and randomly placed them on stage. The ones that overlap still freak out for a few frames, but eventually, due to this new code, they all settle down.

Of course, you're free to investigate your own solutions to the problem, and if you come up with something that is simpler, more efficient, and more accurate, please share!

Important formulas in this chapter

The important formula in this chapter is the one for conservation of momentum.

Conservation of momentum, in straight mathematical terms:

```
             (m0 - m1) * v0 + 2 * m1 * v1
v0Final = ---------------------------
                   m0 + m1
```

```
             (m1 - m0) * v1 + 2 * m0 * v0
v1Final = ---------------------------
                   m0 + m1
```

Conservation of momentum in ActionScript, with a shortcut:

```
var vxTotal:Number = vx0 - vx1;
vx0 = ((ball0.mass - ball1.mass) * vx0 +
    2 * ball1.mass * vx1) /
    (ball0.mass + ball1.mass);
vx1 = vxTotal + vx0;
```

Summary

Congratulations! You've made it through what will probably be the heaviest math in the book. You now have in your repertoire the methods for handling accurate collision reactions. This is one of the most common things that people write to me asking about. With what you have under your belt right now, you could whip up a pretty decent game of billiards, which would be a fitting thing to do with billiard ball physics! One thing I've totally ignored in these examples, just to keep them simple, is the concept of friction. You might want to try adding that into the system. You certainly know enough at this point to do so. You might also want to check out Chapter 19, where I give you a little trick to use in the case that both objects have the same mass.

In the next chapter, I'll tone things down a bit and look into particle attraction, though adding in some billiard ball physics to the examples there would be quite fitting.

Chapter 12

PARTICLE ATTRACTION AND GRAVITY

What we'll cover in this chapter:

- Particles
- Gravity
- Springs
- Important formulas in this chapter

I'm pretty happy with how the progression of these chapters has turned out. Each chapter adds a new concept that generally seems to progress in terms of interaction. At first, you just had things moving around. Then things started interacting with the environment, then the user, and then each other through collisions. In this chapter, I'll expand on the ways objects interact with each other, particularly from a distance. Specifically, I'll cover particles, gravity (a little differently this time), springs (again!), and the world-famous Node Garden. Let's dive right in!

Particles

I guess I should define what I mean by a particle. For me, and for the purposes of this chapter, a *particle* is simply a single unit, generally in the company of several (or many) other similar units. Thus, a particle could be a speck of dust, a beach ball, or a planet.

Particles generally share a common type of behavior, but also can have their own individuality. Followers of object-oriented programming will see an analogy here to *objects*. All objects of a particular class usually share the same behavior, defined by the methods of the class, and individual instances are customized by assigning values to various properties. You've already seen how this works with the instances of the Ball class you've been using in the examples. Each had its own properties: velocity, mass, size, color, and so on, but all of the balls moved with the same rules.

You already have the Ball class, which has pretty much all the functionality you'll need here. In this case, as in the examples so far, the particle instance will merely hold properties. The document class will take care of moving each particle and handling any reactions. Another strategy would be to move the behavior code into the particle class. Thus each particle would have its own enterFrame handler or timer for animation, and would take responsibility for moving itself and handling any reactions. Either method will work, and both have their plusses and minuses. In the examples in this book, you'll keep the animation in the document class just for simplicity's sake.

The general setup will be the same in each of the examples here. Most of the variations will be in the interaction and attraction between the particles, and they will come in the onEnterFrame method. The setup basically consists of creating a bunch of particles and sprinkling them randomly around the screen. Here's that code:

```
package {
    import flash.display.Sprite;
    import flash.events.Event;

    public class ClassName extends Sprite
    {
        private var particles:Array;
        private var numParticles:uint = 30;

        public function ClassName()
        {
            init();
        }
```

```
        private function init():void
        {
            particles = new Array();
            for(var i:uint = 0; i < numParticles; i++)
            {
                var particle:Ball = new Ball(5);
                particle.x = Math.random() * stage.stageWidth;
                particle.y = Math.random() * stage.stageHeight;
                particle.mass = 1;
                addChild(particle);
                particles.push(particle);
            }

            addEventListener(Event.ENTER_FRAME, onEnterFrame);
        }

        private function onEnterFrame(event:Event):void
        {

        }
    }
}
```

Here, you initialize each particle's radius to 5 and set the mass to 1. You'll probably want to try changing that around to get different effects later. You might also want to start off the particles with a random velocity or randomly size them.

All the rest of the examples in this chapter assume this basic setup and will occasionally add something to it. But mainly I'll be describing the onEnterFrame method and any other functions that need to be written. First, I'll describe some background theory, but hold on to the file you just created, because you'll be getting back to it very soon.

Gravity

The first kind of particle attraction I'm going to talk about is gravity. Now, I can hear you saying, "Didn't you cover that way back in Part Two of the book?" True, I did, but that was gravity as seen from very close up.

Standing on earth, gravity has a pretty simple description: It pulls things down. In fact, it pulls things down at a very specific rate. The acceleration it applies is equal to about 32 feet per second per second. One way of expressing acceleration is by how much velocity it adds over a specific time period. Gravity makes things go 32 feet per second faster, every second it pulls on them. You can go to the tallest mountain or the lowest valley, and that number 32 isn't going to change enough for you to notice (that is, without some sensitive instruments).

Gravitational force

When you start stepping back, you see that actually, the farther away you are from a planet or large body, the less the gravity becomes. This is a very good thing. Otherwise, we would all be sucked into the sun, which would be sucked into every other sun and planet, which would all wind up smashed together pretty quickly. So, when you get out to the point where you can refer to planets as particles, the distance between them very much affects the gravitational pull.

How much the distance affects the force is very easy to describe. It's inversely proportional to the square of the distance. Well, maybe that needs some explanation. First, gravity is also very tied in with mass. The more mass something has, the more force it will pull on other things, and the more it will be pulled by them. There is also something called the *gravitational constant* (abbreviated as G) that fits in there. Here's the full equation for the force of gravity:

$$force = G * m1 * m2 / distance^2$$

In plain English, the force of gravity on an object by another object is equal to this gravitational constant, times both masses, divided by the square of the distance between them. Hmmm . . . that looks pretty simple. You just need to know what this gravitational constant is, and you'll be all set. Well, here's the official definition of it:

$$G = (6.6742 \pm 0.0010) * 10^{-11} * m^3 * kg^{-1} * s^{-2}$$

Now, if you want to figure out coding that in ActionScript, go for it. For me, when I see something like that, I immediately know I'm going to be doing some faking soon. You want to know how I usually fake it? I write my gravity formula like this:

$$force = m1 * m2 / distance^2$$

Yup, that's right, I ignore G. And now I'll plug in my usual disclaimer. If you are doing a Flash-based space shuttle guidance system for NASA, you should probably leave G in there. But if you're coding up the next great online space wars game, you're probably going to be able to live without it.

Now that you have a formula, let's put it into code. Set up the onEnterFrame function first, and have it call a gravitate function so you can separate the code that handles gravity:

```
private function onEnterFrame(event:Event):void
{
    for(var i:uint = 0; i < numParticles; i++)
    {
        var particle:Ball = particles[i];
        particle.x += particle.vx;
        particle.y += particle.vy;
    }
    for(i=0; i < numParticles - 1; i++)
    {
        var partA:Ball = particles[i];
        for(var j:uint = i + 1; j < numParticles; j++)
        {
```

```
            var partB:Ball = particles[j];
            gravitate(partA, partB);
        }
    }
}
```

Here, you're just moving all the particles with basic motion code in a single for loop, and then doing a double for loop to get their interactions. Once you have partA and partB, you pass these two particles to the gravitate function. Here's that function:

```
private function gravitate(partA:Ball, partB:Ball):void
{
    var dx:Number = partB.x - partA.x;
    var dy:Number = partB.y - partA.y;
    var distSQ:Number = dx * dx + dy * dy;
    var dist:Number = Math.sqrt(distSQ);
    var force:Number = partA.mass * partB.mass / distSQ;
    var ax:Number = force * dx / dist;
    var ay:Number = force * dy / dist;
    partA.vx += ax / partA.mass;
    partA.vy += ay / partA.mass;
    partB.vx -= ax / partB.mass;
    partB.vy -= ay / partB.mass;
}
```

First, you find the dx and dy between the two particles, and the total distance. Remember that the formula for gravity—force = G × m1 × m2 / distance2—contains the distance squared. Normally, I would calculate distance all at once using dist = Math.sqrt(dx*dx + dy*dy). But then to get distance squared, I would be squaring something that was a square root! That's double work. If I just use the variable distSQ to grab a reference to dx*dx + dy*dy before I take the square root, I save myself that calculation.

Next I find the total force by multiplying the masses and dividing by the distance squared. Then I figure out the total acceleration on the x and y axes. Again, I'm using the shortcut I discussed at the very end of Chapter 9, using dx / dist instead of Math.cos(angle) and dy / dist instead of Math.sin(angle). This saves me from needing to use Math.atan2(dy, dx) to find the angle in the first place.

Now, notice that I keep talking about the *total* force and the *total* acceleration. This is the combined force acting between the two objects. You need to divvy it up between the two, based on their masses. If you think of the earth and the sun, there is a particular force between them. It is the product of their masses, divided by the square of their distance. So, they are pulling toward each other with that total force. The earth is being pulled toward the sun, and the sun is being pulled toward the earth. Obviously, the earth gets a lot more of that acceleration because it has much less mass than the sun. So, to get the individual acceleration for either object in the system, you divide the total acceleration by that object's mass. Thus, you have the last four lines of the formula. Notice that partA gets the acceleration added, and partB gets it subtracted. This is merely due to the order of subtraction I used to get dx and dy.

The final code for this example can be found in `Gravity.as`. Go ahead and test it. You should see that the particles start out motionless, but are slowly attracted to each other, something like what you see in Figure 12-1. Occasionally, a couple of them will start sort of orbiting around each other. But mostly what happens is that they hit and fly off in opposite directions.

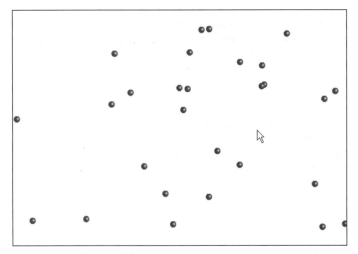

Figure 12-1. We have particles!

Is this speeding off a bug? Well, yes and no. It's not a bug in the code. It's actually expected behavior, and is something called the *slingshot effect*. It's what NASA uses to send probes into deep space. As an object gets closer and closer to a planet, it feels more and more acceleration, and it starts traveling with a very high velocity. If you aim it just right, so it comes very close to the planet, but just misses it, that object will whip off into space too fast for the planet's gravity to capture it. All that speed with zero fuel—now that's efficiency.

But back to Flash. What is happening here is that the objects are getting to within a very small distance of each other—almost zero distance. Thus, the force between them becomes huge, almost infinite. So, mathematically, it's correct, but from a simulation viewpoint, it's unrealistic. What should happen is that if the objects get close enough together, they collide. If you aimed that space probe directly at the planet, it would not zoom past it at infinite speed. It would make a crater.

Collision detection and reaction

So, for your particles, you need to have some kind of collision detection and reaction. What you do is up to you. You could have them explode and disappear. You could have one particle disappear and add its mass to the other one, as if they had joined.

For this example, I realized that I had some very nice collision and reaction code left over from the previous chapter, in a function called checkCollision. Let's just plug that right in here, like so:

```
private function onEnterFrame(event:Event):void
{
    for(var i:uint = 0; i < numParticles; i++)
    {
        var particle:Ball = particles[i];
        particle.x += particle.vx;
        particle.y += particle.vy;
    }
    for(i=0; i < numParticles - 1; i++)
    {
        var partA:Ball = particles[i];
        for(var j:uint = i + 1; j < numParticles; j++)
        {
            var partB:Ball = particles[j];
            checkCollision(partA, partB);
            gravitate(partA, partB);
        }
    }
}
```

Only that one line in bold has changed. Plus, of course, I copied and pasted the checkCollision and rotate functions into the file. (Don't forget to import the flash.geom.Point function as well, as that is used by these other functions.) This code can be found in GravityBounce.as.

Now the particles are attracted to each other, but bounce off when they hit. Try changing the mass of the particles and see how they attract differently. You can even do bizarre things like giving the particles negative mass and watching them repel each other!

In the file GravityRandom.as, I kept everything the same, but added a line and changed a couple more in the init method:

```
private function init():void
{
    particles = new Array();
    for(var i:uint = 0; i < numParticles; i++)
    {
        var size:Number = Math.random() * 25 + 5;
        var particle:Ball = new Ball(size);
        particle.x = Math.random() * stage.stageWidth;
        particle.y = Math.random() * stage.stageHeight;
        particle.mass = size;
        addChild(particle);
        particles.push(particle);
    }

    addEventListener(Event.ENTER_FRAME, onEnterFrame);
}
```

This just gives each particle a random size and a mass based on that size, as you can see in Figure 12-2. Things start to get interesting.

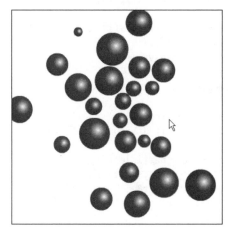

Figure 12-2. Colliding planets?

Orbiting

Finally, just to show you how realistic this gets, let's set up a simple planetary system, with a sun and planet. Make a large sun with a mass of 10,000, and a planet with a mass of 1. Then move the planet a distance away from the sun and give it some velocity perpendicular to the line between it and the sun. The setup looks something like Figure 12-3.

Figure 12-3. Setting up the stage

If you get the masses, distance, and velocity just right, you should be able to get the planet into orbit. It took some trial and error, but I came up with what's in Orbit.as. All I'm going to show you here is the init code. The only other change to the file was to set the numParticles variable to 2.

```
private function init():void
{
    particles = new Array();

    var sun:Ball = new Ball(100, 0xffff00);
    sun.x = stage.stageWidth / 2;
    sun.y = stage.stageHeight / 2;
    sun.mass = 10000;
    addChild(sun);
    particles.push(sun);

    var planet:Ball = new Ball(10, 0x00ff00);
    planet.x = stage.stageWidth / 2 + 200;
    planet.y = stage.stageHeight / 2;
    planet.vy = 7;
```

```
        planet.mass = 1;
        addChild(planet);
        particles.push(planet);

        addEventListener(Event.ENTER_FRAME, onEnterFrame);
    }
```

As an extra example, check out OrbitDraw.as, which draws a line tracing the orbit. You can wind up with some interesting patterns.

Springs

The other kind of particle attraction you probably want to try is springs. Yes, springs, my favorite subject! Recall that in Chapter 8, you tried out chains of springs and objects springing to each other. Here, you'll look at a broader application, where you have many particles, all springing to each other, as in the gravity examples you just saw.

The inspiration for this example came from a piece Jared Tarbell did at www.levitated.net, called the Node Garden, shown in Figure 12-4. The idea is that you could have a field of these nodes (particles), and they could each have various types of interactions with any other nodes that were nearby. I think it was my idea to have one of those reactions be a spring.

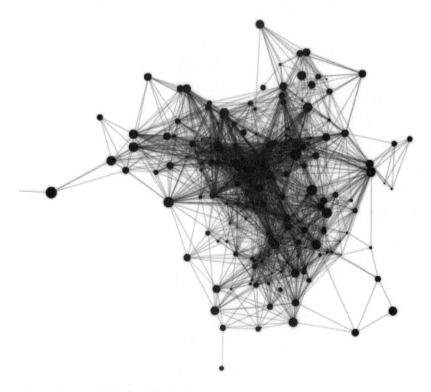

Figure 12-4. Jared Tarbell's Node Garden

Gravity vs. springs

If you look at gravity and springs, you see they are very similar, yet almost exactly opposite. Both apply acceleration to two objects to pull them together. But in gravity, the farther apart the objects are, the less acceleration there is. In a spring, the acceleration gets *larger* as the distance increases.

So, while you could just swap out the gravity code and plug the spring code into the previous examples, the effect might not be too interesting, because the particles would eventually just lump into a mass. Springs can't tolerate distance. If gravity's motto is "out of sight, out of mind," a spring's credo is "absence makes the spring grow fonder."

So you have a dilemma. You want to have particles attract with a spring force, but you want them to tolerate some distance and not be pulling themselves together. My solution for this was to come up with a minimum distance variable. Mathematically speaking, it might be more like a maximum distance, because it is the largest distance at which a reaction will still take place. But minimum distance always seemed right to my brain, because it means that particles must be at *least* this close together to react. If they are farther apart, they ignore each other.

A springy node garden

Let's get started making our own springy node garden. In the interest of making this look as close as possible to the example in the original version of this book, I changed the background of the movie to black and made the particles white. It's not perfect, but short of going off on a tangent with complex gradient fill code or embedding external graphics, it will have to do. I'll leave the fancy graphics stuff to you.

On to the code. You'll find it in NodeGarden.as, but let's go through it step by step. First, set some variables for number of particles, the minimum distance I just talked about, and a spring value.

```
var numParticles:uint = 30;
var minDist:Number = 100;
var springAmount:Number = .001;
```

In the earlier spring examples in Chapter 8, you used something like 0.2 for a spring amount. You need to use something much lower here, as a lot more particles are interacting. If you go too high, the velocity will build up much too fast. However, if you go too low, the particles will just meander about the screen, seemingly unaware of each other.

Then initialize things:

```
private function init():void
{
    particles = new Array();
    for(var i:uint = 0; i < numParticles; i++)
    {
        var particle:Ball = new Ball(5, 0xffffff);
        particle.x = Math.random() * stage.stageWidth;
        particle.y = Math.random() * stage.stageHeight;
        particle.vx = Math.random() * 6 - 3;
        particle.vy = Math.random() * 6 - 3;
```

```
            addChild(particle);
            particles.push(particle);
        }

        addEventListener(Event.ENTER_FRAME, onEnterFrame);
    }
```

This just creates a bunch of particles, throws them around the screen, and gives them random velocities. Note that I got rid of mass for this example. Later, in the "Nodes with mass" section, I'll show you
an experiment with adding mass back in.

Next comes the onEnterFrame method:

```
    private function onEnterFrame(event:Event):void
    {
        for(var i:uint = 0; i < numParticles; i++)
        {
            var particle:Ball = particles[i];
            particle.x += particle.vx;
            particle.y += particle.vy;
            if(particle.x > stage.stageWidth)
            {
                particle.x = 0;
            }
            else if(particle.x < 0)
            {
                particle.x = stage.stageWidth;
            }
            if(particle.y > stage.stageHeight)
            {
                particle.y = 0;
            }
            else if(particle.y < 0)
            {
                particle.y = stage.stageHeight;
            }
        }

        for(i=0; i < numParticles - 1; i++)
        {
            var partA:Ball = particles[i];
            for(var j:uint = i + 1; j < numParticles; j++)
            {
                var partB:Ball = particles[j];
                spring(partA, partB);
            }
        }
    }
```

This should look pretty familiar. It's pretty similar to the earlier examples. I just added in screen wrapping and called a spring function instead of gravitate.

Now to the meat of it, the spring function itself:

```
private function spring(partA:Ball, partB:Ball):void
{
    var dx:Number = partB.x - partA.x;
    var dy:Number = partB.y - partA.y;
    var dist:Number = Math.sqrt(dx * dx + dy * dy);
    if(dist < minDist)
    {
        var ax:Number = dx * springAmount;
        var ay:Number = dy * springAmount;
        partA.vx += ax;
        partA.vy += ay;
        partB.vx -= ax;
        partB.vy -= ay;
    }
}
```

First, you find the distance between the two particles. If it's not less than minDist, you move on. If it is less, however, you figure out the acceleration on each axis, based on the distance and springValue. You add that acceleration to partA's velocity and subtract it from partB's velocity. This pulls the particles together.

Go ahead and try it out. You'll see something like Figure 12-5. Notice how the particles kind of clump together like flies buzzing around a . . . whatever flies like to buzz around. But even those clumps move around, break up, join other clumps, and so on. It's interesting emergent behavior. Try changing the minDist and springValue values to see what happens.

Figure 12-5. Nodes in action

Nodes with connections

While it is pretty obvious that something is going on between the nodes here, I wanted to really point out the specific interaction between each pair of nodes. What better way than to draw a line between any two nodes that are interacting? That's simple enough to do. I just altered the spring function a little bit:

```
private function spring(partA:Ball, partB:Ball):void
{
    var dx:Number = partB.x - partA.x;
    var dy:Number = partB.y - partA.y;
    var dist:Number = Math.sqrt(dx * dx + dy * dy);
    if(dist < minDist)
    {
        graphics.lineStyle(1, 0xffffff);
        graphics.moveTo(partA.x, partA.y);
        graphics.lineTo(partB.x, partB.y);
        var ax:Number = dx * springAmount;
        var ay:Number = dy * springAmount;
        partA.vx += ax;
        partA.vy += ay;
        partB.vx -= ax;
        partB.vy -= ay;
    }
}
```

If two nodes are interacting, this function sets a line style and draws a line between them. You should also add the following as the first line in the onEnterFrame method, so you are starting fresh each frame:

```
graphics.clear();
```

So, the nodes are now connected, as shown in Figure 12-6. This is OK, but I don't like the way the lines kind of snap on and off as nodes come in and out of range of each other.

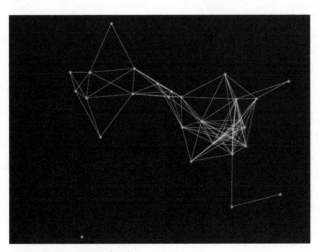

Figure 12-6. Connect the dots

317

I want a more gradient approach. I figure that if two nodes are just under `minDist` apart, the line should be almost completely transparent. As they get closer and closer, the line should become brighter and brighter. So, if I say `dist / minDist`, this gives me a fraction from 0 to 1 for alpha. But this is backward, because if `dist` equals `minDist`, alpha will be 1, and as `dist` approaches 0, alpha will approach 0. OK, so take that number and *subtract* it from 1, which effectively reverses the effect. Here's the final line-drawing code:

```
graphics.lineStyle(1, 0xffffff, 1 - dist / minDist);
graphics.moveTo(partA.x, partA.y);
graphics.lineTo(partB.x, partB.y);
```

This, to me, is a very beautiful effect, as shown in Figure 12-7. The result is in `NodeGardenLines.as`.

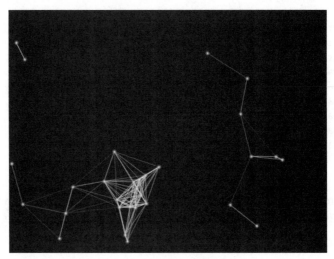

Figure 12-7. Subtle change, but a world of difference

Nodes with mass

While writing the chapter, I intrigued myself with the idea of nodes having mass, something I never thought of before. So, I tried it out and came up with `NodesMass.as`. In it, I assign each node a random scale and mass based on that scale.

```
private function init():void
{
    particles = new Array();
    for(var i:uint = 0; i < numParticles; i++)
    {
        var size:Number = Math.random() * 10 + 2;
        var particle:Ball = new Ball(size, 0xffffff);
        particle.x = Math.random() * stage.stageWidth;
        particle.y = Math.random() * stage.stageHeight;
        particle.vx = Math.random() * 6 - 3;
        particle.vy = Math.random() * 6 - 3;
```

```
        particle.mass = size;
        addChild(particle);
        particles.push(particle);
    }
    addEventListener(Event.ENTER_FRAME, onEnterFrame);
}
```

This is used only when I'm adding in the velocities in the spring function. I divide the velocity by the mass of each particle. This gives the larger ones more inertia.

```
private function spring(partA:Ball, partB:Ball):void
{
    var dx:Number = partB.x - partA.x;
    var dy:Number = partB.y - partA.y;
    var dist:Number = Math.sqrt(dx * dx + dy * dy);
    if(dist < minDist)
    {
        graphics.lineStyle(1, 0xffffff, 1 - dist / minDist);
        graphics.moveTo(partA.x, partA.y);
        graphics.lineTo(partB.x, partB.y);
        var ax:Number = dx * springAmount;
        var ay:Number = dy * springAmount;
        partA.vx += ax / partA.mass;
        partA.vy += ay / partA.mass;
        partB.vx -= ax / partB.mass;
        partB.vy -= ay / partB.mass;
    }
}
```

Since I was cutting down the overall effect of the spring, I increased the springValue to .0025. I like the overall effect, which you can see in Figure 12-8.

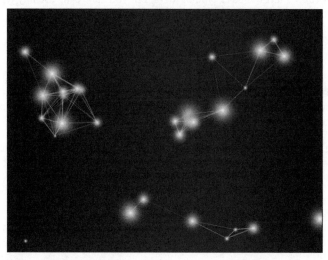

Figure 12-8. One more for the road

So what can you use nodes for? Personally, I think they are pretty cool to look at, and I even made a nice screensaver with them once. But I can imagine all kinds of game scenarios you could build with them for starters. Throw an *Asteroids*-type spaceship in there, and try to make it avoid the nodes. I bet that would be a nice challenge!

Important formulas in this chapter

Obviously, the big formula here is gravity.

Basic gravity:

```
force = G * m1 * m2 / distance2
```

ActionScript-friendly gravity implementation:

```
function gravitate(partA:Ball, partB:Ball):void
{
        var dx:Number = partB.x - partA.x;
        var dy:Number = partB.y - partA.y;
        var distSQ:Number = dx * dx + dy * dy;
        var dist:Number = Math.sqrt(distSQ);
        var force:Number = partA.mass * partB.mass / distSQ;
        var ax:Number = force * dx / dist;
        var ay:Number = force * dy / dist;
        partA.vx += ax / partA.mass;
        partA.vy += ay / partA.mass;
        partB.vx -= ax / partB.mass;
        partB.vy -= ay / partB.mass;
}
```

Note that in the function, I left the Ball type in there, but you can really use any type of custom class, as long as it can store values for velocity, mass, and position.

Summary

This chapter covered interaction between particles at a distance, and how you can use gravity and springing for interesting effects. As a result, you have two new ways to make some *very* dynamic motion graphics involving many objects.

In the next couple of chapters, I'm going to talk about some very new subjects: *forward kinematics* and *inverse kinematics*. These techniques allow you to make cool things like robot arms and walking figures.

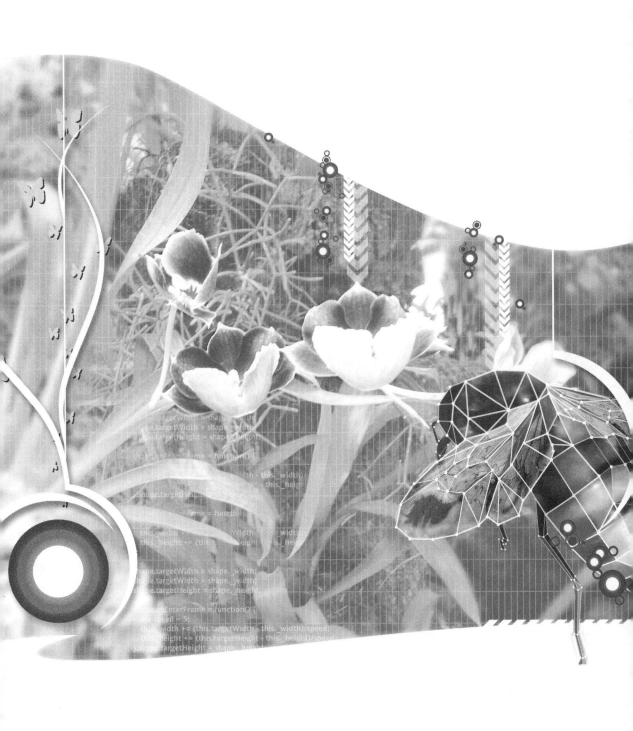

Chapter 13

FORWARD KINEMATICS: MAKING THINGS WALK

What we'll cover in this chapter:

- Introducing forward and inverse kinematics
- Getting started programming forward kinematics
- Automating the process
- Making it really walk

Up to now, you've been going down a particular path, and it has all flowed very nicely. In fact, the previous chapters covered just about all the basics of interactive ActionScripted animation, even all the very advanced "basics." Now, I'm going to branch off to some other interesting techniques that use kinematics.

So, what exactly is this thing called *kinematics*? It always seemed kind of scary when I tried to find out about it. I know it's built into some advanced 3D animation programs, and if you look it up online, you'll find some pages that will barrage you with strange symbols in equations that make anything you've done so far in this book look like first-grade arithmetic. So, first, I want to say that it's really not that tough. The previous chapters covered just about all the concepts you need. You just have to put them together in the right way.

Kinematics is basically the branch of mathematics that deals with the motion of objects without regard for force or mass. So, it's speed, direction, and velocity. Sounds pretty basic, eh? Well, that's a pretty simple definition, and I'm sure it gets into some complex stuff, but for our purposes, yeah, that's pretty much it.

When people in computer science, graphics, games, and so on start talking about kinematics, they are talking about two specific branches of kinematics: forward kinematics and inverse kinematics. Let's start there.

Introducing forward and inverse kinematics

Forward and inverse kinematics generally have to do with a system of connected parts, such as a chain or a jointed arm. They have to do with how that system moves, and how each part moves in relation to the other parts and to the whole.

Often, a kinematics system has two ends: the base and the free end. A jointed arm is usually attached to something fixed at one end, and the other end moves around to reach and grab things. A chain might be attached to something on one or both ends, or not at all.

Forward kinematics (FK) deals with motion that originates at the base of the system and moves out to the free end. *Inverse kinematics* (IK) deals with the opposite: motion originating at, or determined by, the free end and going back to the base, if there is one.

Some examples are in order. In most cases, the limbs of a body in a walk cycle will be done with *forward* kinematics. The thigh moves, which moves the calf. The calf moves, which moves the foot. The foot moves. In this case, the foot isn't determining anything. It winds up wherever it winds up, based on the positions of all the limbs before it.

An example of *inverse* kinematics would be pulling someone by the hand. Here, the force applied on the free end—the hand—controls the position and movements of the hand, forearm, upper arm, and eventually the whole body.

Another, more subtle, example of inverse kinematics is an arm reaching for something. Again, the hand is what is driving the system. Of course, you can say that, in this example, the upper arm and forearm are moving, and they control the position of the hand. That's true, but there is a direct intention to put that hand in a specific place. That is the driving force. In this case, it's not a physical force, but an intention. The forearm and upper arm are simply arranging themselves in whatever configuration necessary to position that hand.

The differences will become clearer as you go through the examples in this and the next chapter. But for now, remember that dragging and reaching are generally inverse kinematics, while a repeated cycle of motion, such as walking, is usually forward kinematics, which is the subject of this chapter.

Getting started programming forward kinematics

Programming both types of kinematics involves a few basic elements:

- The parts of the system. I'll call them *segments*.
- The position of each segment.
- The rotation of each segment.

Each segment in these examples will be an oblong shape like a forearm or an upper arm, or any part of a leg. Of course, the last segment could be some other shape, such as a hand, a foot, a gripper, a stinger, or a device that shoots green laser beams at intruders.

Each segment will have a pivot point at one end, around which it can rotate. If that segment has any subsegments, they will pivot on the opposite end of that segment. Just like your upper arm pivots on your shoulder, your forearm pivots on your elbow, and your hand pivots on your wrist.

Of course, in many real systems, that pivoting can be in many directions. Think of how many ways you can move your wrist. By the end of this book, you might want to try to do something like that in Flash on your own, but right now, the system is going to be strictly two-dimensional.

Moving one segment

Let's start with a single segment and get it moving somehow. First, you need something to use as a segment. If you're guessing that might be a custom class that extends Sprite, you're right. A sprite can have graphics, it can have a position, it can be rotated, and it can be added to the display list. We'll take it. Here is the class I came up with, Segment.as:

```
package
{
    import flash.display.Sprite;
    import flash.geom.Point;

    public class Segment extends Sprite
    {
        private var color:uint;
        private var segmentWidth:Number;
        private var segmentHeight:Number;

        public var vx:Number = 0;
        public var vy:Number = 0;

        public function Segment(segmentWidth:Number,
                                segmentHeight:Number,
                                color:uint = 0xffffff)
```

```
        {
            this.segmentWidth = segmentWidth;
            this.segmentHeight = segmentHeight;
            this.color = color;
            init();
        }

        public function init():void
        {
            // draw the segment itself
            graphics.lineStyle(0);
            graphics.beginFill(color);
            graphics.drawRoundRect(-segmentHeight / 2,
                                   -segmentHeight / 2,
                                   segmentWidth + segmentHeight,
                                   segmentHeight,
                                   segmentHeight,
                                   segmentHeight);
            graphics.endFill();

            // draw the two "pins"
            graphics.drawCircle(0, 0, 2);
            graphics.drawCircle(segmentWidth, 0, 2);
        }

        public function getPin():Point
        {
            var angle:Number = rotation * Math.PI / 180;
            var xPos:Number = x + Math.cos(angle) * segmentWidth;
            var yPos:Number = y + Math.sin(angle) * segmentWidth;
            return new Point(xPos, yPos);
        }
    }
}
```

This basically takes a width, height, and color and draws a rounded rectangle as the segment. It also draws a small circle at the registration point of the segment (0, 0) and one at the end point. These are the two "pins," where the segments will attach to other segments. (You'll also notice a couple of public variables, vx and vy. More on those later in the "Handling the reaction" section of this chapter.)

The following snippet creates a few segments with different widths and heights to give you an idea how the Segment class is used:

```
var segment:Segment = new Segment(100, 20);
addChild(segment);
segment.x = 100;
segment.y = 50;
var segment1:Segment = new Segment(200, 10);
addChild(segment1);
segment1.x = 100;
```

```
segment1.y = 80;
var segment2:Segment = new Segment(80, 40);
addChild(segment2);
segment2.x = 100;
segment2.y =120;
```

Figure 13-1 shows what this snippet creates.

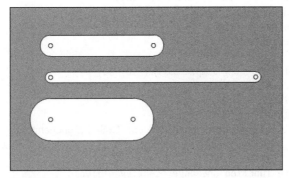

Figure 13-1. Some sample segments

One major point to notice in Figure 13-1 is that the segment width winds up being the distance between the two pins. The actual width of the segment goes beyond that in both directions. You can see that each segment is placed at an x position of 100. Although their left edges do not line up, all of the pins on the left do. When you rotate the segment, it will rotate around that left-hand pin.

You'll also notice in the code for the Segment class that there is a public getPin() method that returns an instance of flash.geom.Point. This will return the x, y position of the right-hand pin. This will obviously change as the segment is rotated, so we use some basic trigonometry to calculate that position. This is where the next segment will be attached—which you will see in the next section of this chapter.

For the first example, SingleSegment.as, I've created a . . . well, a single segment and put it on the stage. I'm also using a slider class, SimpleSlider.as, which I created and added to the project. You can download this from this book's download page at www.friendsofed.com, which you're free to use for whatever you want. It's pretty useful for adjusting numeric values on the fly. For this slider, you can set minimum, maximum, and value parameters in the constructor. You'll see that I set minimum to –90, maximum to 90, and value to 0. Here's the class file itself that ties it all together:

```
package {
    import flash.display.Sprite;
    import flash.events.Event;

    public class SingleSegment extends Sprite
    {
        private var slider:SimpleSlider;
        private var segment:Segment;
```

```
public function SingleSegment()
{
    init();
}

private function init():void
{
    segment = new Segment(100, 20);
    addChild(segment);
    segment.x = 100;
    segment.y = 100;

    slider = new SimpleSlider(-90, 90, 0);
    addChild(slider);
    slider.x = 300;
    slider.y = 20;
    slider.addEventListener(Event.CHANGE, onChange);
}

private function onChange(event:Event):void
{
    segment.rotation = slider.value;
}
    }
}
```

This just says that whenever the value of the slider changes, it will call the onChange method, which sets the rotation of segment0 to the slider's value. Try that out, and you should see something like Figure 13-2. If it all works, you've completed the first phase of forward kinematics.

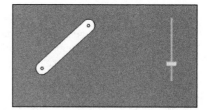

Figure 13-2. It moves!

Moving two segments

Working with one segment was very simple and rather boring, but necessary. It's time to move on. The original slider and segment will be named slider0 and segment0. Create another instance of Segment, and name it segment1. Also create another slider instance down there and call it slider1. The new slider will control the rotation of the new segment, which will be positioned at the point returned by segment0's getPin() method.

Here's the code, which you'll also find in TwoSegments.as:

```
package {
    import flash.display.Sprite;
    import flash.events.Event;

    public class TwoSegments extends Sprite
    {
```

```
    private var slider0:SimpleSlider;
    private var slider1:SimpleSlider;
    private var segment0:Segment;
    private var segment1:Segment;

    public function TwoSegments()
    {
        init();
    }

    private function init():void
    {
        segment0 = new Segment(100, 20);
        addChild(segment0);
        segment0.x = 100;
        segment0.y = 100;

        segment1 = new Segment(100, 20);
        addChild(segment1);
        segment1.x = segment0.getPin().x;
        segment1.y = segment0.getPin().y;

        slider0 = new SimpleSlider(-90, 90, 0);
        addChild(slider0);
        slider0.x = 320;
        slider0.y = 20;
        slider0.addEventListener(Event.CHANGE, onChange);

        slider1 = new SimpleSlider(-90, 90, 0);
        addChild(slider1);
        slider1.x = 340;
        slider1.y = 20;
        slider1.addEventListener(Event.CHANGE, onChange);
    }

    private function onChange(event:Event):void
    {
        segment0.rotation = slider0.value;
        segment1.rotation = slider1.value;
        segment1.x = segment0.getPin().x;
        segment1.y = segment0.getPin().y;
    }
  }
}
```

Take a quick look down at the bottom of the onChange method, and you'll see that it now contains code to position segment1 based on the return value of segment0.getPin(). This is the same code that is used when the segment is first created, to make sure it is positioned properly to start.

You set up slider1 to call the onChange method in the same way as slider0. And, obviously, you have segment1's rotation now based on slider1.

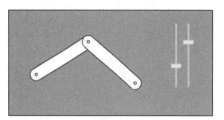

Figure 13-3. Forward kinematics with two segments

If you test this file, you'll see that as you rotate segment0 around, segment1 remains attached to the end of it, as shown in Figure 13-3. Realize that there is no actual physical attachment between the two segments. It's all being done with math. You can also rotate segment1 independently with its slider. For some fun, change the height and width of either or both of the segments. See that it all still works perfectly.

One thing that looks a bit strange is that while segment1 *moves* with segment0; it doesn't *rotate* with it. It's like there's some gyro-stabilizer inside of it, holding its orientation steady. I don't know about you, but my forearm doesn't have a gyro-stabilizer in it (though that might be kind of cool), so to me, this looks unnatural. What really should be happening is that segment1's rotation should be segment0's rotation plus the value of slider1. The TwoSegments2.as document class handles this with the following code:

```
private function onChange(event:Event):void
{
    segment0.rotation = slider0.value;
    segment1.rotation = segment0.rotation + slider1.value;
    segment1.x = segment0.getPin().x;
    segment1.y = segment0.getPin().y;
}
```

Now, that looks more like a real arm. Of course, if you're talking about a human arm, you might not like the way the elbow can bend in both directions. Just change the range of slider1 so minimum is something like –160 and maximum is 0, as in the following code, and that should look more normal.

```
slider1 = new SimpleSlider(-160, 0, 0);
```

This might be a good time to reflect on the term *forward kinematics* again. The base of this system is the pivot point of segment0. The free end is the other end of segment1. If you want, you can imagine a hand there. The rotation and position of the base determine the position of segment1. And segment1's rotation and position determine the position of the free end. The free end has no say at all in where it is, should be, or would like to be. It just goes along for the ride. Thus, control is moving forward from the base to the free end.

Automating the process

All these sliders for rotation give you a lot of control, but what you've created is something like a piece of construction machinery with hydraulic levers to move around the parts. If you want to make something really walk, you're going to have to step back and give it some self-control.

You just need a way for each segment to smoothly swing back and forth, and then somehow synchronize them all. That sounds like a job for a sine wave.

In Walking1.as, I've replaced the sliders with a trig function. It takes the sine of the cycle variable (which is initialized to 0) and multiplies it by 90, resulting in a value from 90 to –90. The cycle variable is constantly increased, so you get an oscillation. For now, I've used the resulting angle variable to control both segments. I added an enterFrame handler that controls the action, so the motion is continuous.

```
package {
    import flash.display.Sprite;
    import flash.events.Event;

    public class Walking1 extends Sprite
    {
        private var segment0:Segment;
        private var segment1:Segment;
        private var cycle:Number = 0;

        public function Walking1()
        {
            init();
        }

        private function init():void
        {
            segment0 = new Segment(100, 20);
            addChild(segment0);
            segment0.x = 200;
            segment0.y = 200;

            segment1 = new Segment(100, 20);
            addChild(segment1);
            segment1.x = segment0.getPin().x;
            segment1.y = segment0.getPin().y;

            addEventListener(Event.ENTER_FRAME, onEnterFrame);
        }

        private function onEnterFrame(event:Event):void
        {
            cycle += .05;
            var angle:Number = Math.sin(cycle) * 90;
            segment0.rotation = angle;
            segment1.rotation = segment0.rotation + angle;
            segment1.x = segment0.getPin().x;
            segment1.y = segment0.getPin().y;
        }
    }
}
```

Building a natural walk cycle

OK, now you have something moving around looking vaguely arm-like. Let's turn it into a leg. Start with the following changes:

1. Make the system point down by adding 90 to segment0's rotation and reducing its range of motion from 90 degrees in both directions to 45 degrees.

2. Use a separate angle for each segment, so you'll have angle0 and angle1.

3. Reduce angle1's range to 45, and then add 45 to it. This makes its final range 0 to 90, so that it bends in only one direction, like a real knee. If that isn't totally clear, try it with and without the added 45 to see what it's doing, and try some other numbers in there, until you get a feel for how it all fits together.

You end up with the following from Walking2.as. I'm only showing the onEnterFrame method, as nothing else has changed:

```
private function onEnterFrame(event:Event):void
{
    cycle += .05;
    var angle0:Number = Math.sin(cycle) * 45 + 90;
    var angle1:Number = Math.sin(cycle) * 45 + 45;
    segment0.rotation = angle0;
    segment1.rotation = segment0.rotation + angle1;
    segment1.x = segment0.getPin().x;
    segment1.y = segment0.getPin().y;
}
```

Well, you're getting there, as shown in Figure 13-4. This is starting to look like a leg, or at least starting to move like one.

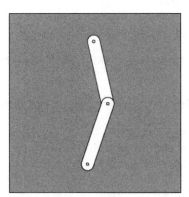

Figure 13-4. The beginnings of a walk cycle

The problem is it doesn't really look like it's walking. Maybe it's kicking a half-hearted field goal, or perhaps practicing some ballet moves, but it's not walking. What's happening now is that both segments are moving in the same direction at the same time. They are totally in sync, which, if you were to analyze an actual walk cycle, is not how it works.

The segments are in sync because they are both using the cycle variable to calculate their angle. To throw them out of sync, you could resort to using cycle0 and cycle1 variables, but you don't need to go that far with it. Instead, you can just offset cycle a bit when using it to find angle1, like so:

```
var angle1:Number = Math.sin(cycle + offset) * 45 + 45;
```

Of course, you'll need to define offset earlier in the code. But how much should offset be? I don't know that there's any set amount. Experiment until you find something that looks good. I'll give you a hint: It should be something between Math.PI and -Math.PI (or 3.14 and –3.14). Anything more or less than that is just going to kind of double back on itself. For instance, I used -Math.PI / 2, which puts it a quarter of a cycle behind angle0. Of course, -Math.PI / 2 is about –1.57, so you might want to try other numbers around that value, like –1.7 or –1.3, and see whether that looks better or worse. A little later, I'll throw in a slider to do it all dynamically. The file with this offset in it is Walking3.as.

Now, this whole "one leg walking" thing sounds a bit too Zen for me, so let's add another leg. You'll start by throwing in two more segments, named segment2 and segment3. The segment2 object should be in the exact same position as segment0, as it will also be the top level, or base, of the whole leg, and segment3 should be positioned using segment1's getPin() method.

Now, rather than duplicate all the code that makes segment0 and segment1 walk, I abstracted it into its own method, called walk:

```
private function walk(segA:Segment, segB:Segment, cyc:Number):void
{
    var angleA:Number = Math.sin(cyc) * 45 + 90;
    var angleB:Number = Math.sin(cyc + offset) * 45 + 45;
    segA.rotation = angleA;
    segB.rotation = segA.rotation + angleB;
    segB.x = segA.getPin().x;
    segB.y = segA.getPin().y;
}
```

Notice that the function takes three parameters: two segments, segA and segB, and cyc, which stands for cycle. The rest of the code is pretty much what you've been using. Now, to make segment0 and segment1 walk, just call it like this:

```
walk(segment0, segment1, cycle);
```

By now, you see where I'm going with this, and you're ready to make segment2 and segment3 walk as well. If you jump right into it, you'll end up with this as your onEnterFrame method:

```
private function onEnterFrame(event:Event):void
{
    walk(segment0, segment1, cycle);
    walk(segment2, segment3, cycle);
    cycle += .05;
}
```

But if you try that, you're going to be wondering where the second leg is. The problem is that both legs are moving exactly in sync, so they appear as one. Once again, you need to desynchronize. Last time, you offset the bottom segment's position on the cycle from the top segment's position. This time, you'll offset the second leg from the first. Again, this comes down to changing the value it's using for cycle. And once again, rather than keeping track of two different variables, just add something to or subtract something from cycle before you send it into the walk method. So the onEnterFrame method becomes this:

```
private function onEnterFrame(event:Event):void
{
    walk(segment0, segment1, cycle);
    walk(segment2, segment3, cycle + Math.PI);
    cycle += .05;
}
```

Why Math.PI? The long answer is that value puts the second leg 180 degrees out of sync with the first, so the first leg will move forward while the second is moving back, and vice versa. The short answer is because it works! You can try it out with some different values, say Math.PI / 2, and see that it looks a lot more like a gallop than a walk or run. But keep that in mind—you may need to make something gallop someday!

The file as it stands is available as Walking4.as and looks like Figure 13-5. Notice that I also made the base segments (the "thighs") a bit larger than the lower segments (the "calves"). Again, remember that due to the dynamic way everything is set up, it will all work no matter what the sizes are. In the next version, you're going to make a lot more things dynamic with sliders, but I highly recommend that you play around with some of these variables now manually, by changing the values in the code and seeing how the values affect things.

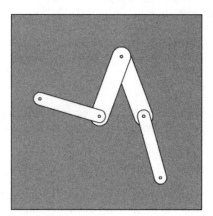

Figure 13-5. Behold! It walks!

Making it dynamic

Next, let's really play around with this walk cycle and see just how much you can change it by altering the various values that go into it. The Walking5.as file brings back the Slider class so you can start changing some of these variables on the fly.

In this example, I created and positioned five of these sliders across the top of the movie, as shown in Figure 13-6.

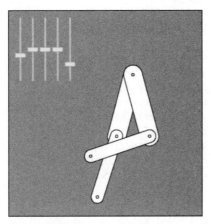

Figure 13-6. Adding the sliders

Table 13-1 shows the slider names (from left to right), what they do, and the settings to use for them. These are just ranges and values I found to work well. By all means, feel free to experiment with other values.

Table 13-1. The Sliders for Controlling the Walk Cycle

Instance	Description	Settings
speedSlider	Controls the speed at which the system moves.	minimum: 0, maximum: 0.3, value: 0.12
thighRangeSlider	Controls how far back and forth the top-level segments (thighs) can move.	minimum: 0, maximum: 90, value: 45
thighBaseSlider	Controls the base angle of the top-level segments. So far, this has been 90, meaning that the legs will point straight down and move back and forth from there. But you can get some interesting effects by changing this value.	minimum: 0, maximum: 180, value: 90
calfRangeSlider	Controls how much range of motion the lower segments (calves) have.	minimum: 0, maximum: 90, value: 45
calfOffsetSlider	Controls the offset value (you've been using -Math.PI / 2).	minimum: -3.14, maximum: 3.14, value: -1.57

Now, you need to go in and change the code so that it uses the values provided by the sliders, rather than hard-coded values.

```
package {
    import flash.display.Sprite;
    import flash.events.Event;

    public class Walking5 extends Sprite
    {
        private var segment0:Segment;
        private var segment1:Segment;
        private var segment2:Segment;
        private var segment3:Segment;
        private var speedSlider:SimpleSlider;
        private var thighRangeSlider:SimpleSlider;
        private var thighBaseSlider:SimpleSlider;
        private var calfRangeSlider:SimpleSlider;
        private var calfOffsetSlider:SimpleSlider;
        private var cycle:Number = 0;

        public function Walking5()
        {
            init();
        }

        private function init():void
        {
            segment0 = new Segment(100, 30);
            addChild(segment0);
            segment0.x = 200;
            segment0.y = 100;

            segment1 = new Segment(100, 20);
            addChild(segment1);
            segment1.x = segment0.getPin().x;
            segment1.y = segment0.getPin().y;

            segment2 = new Segment(100, 30);
            addChild(segment2);
            segment2.x = 200;
            segment2.y = 100;

            segment3 = new Segment(100, 20);
            addChild(segment3);
            segment3.x = segment2.getPin().x;
            segment3.y = segment2.getPin().y;

            speedSlider = new SimpleSlider(0, 0.3, 0.12);
            addChild(speedSlider);
            speedSlider.x = 10;
            speedSlider.y = 10;
```

```
            thighRangeSlider = new SimpleSlider(0, 90, 45);
            addChild(thighRangeSlider);
            thighRangeSlider.x = 30;
            thighRangeSlider.y = 10;

            thighBaseSlider = new SimpleSlider(0, 180, 90);
            addChild(thighBaseSlider);
            thighBaseSlider.x = 50;
            thighBaseSlider.y = 10;

            calfRangeSlider = new SimpleSlider(0, 90, 45);
            addChild(calfRangeSlider);
            calfRangeSlider.x = 70;
            calfRangeSlider.y = 10;

            calfOffsetSlider = new SimpleSlider(-3.14, 3.14, -1.57);
            addChild(calfOffsetSlider);
            calfOffsetSlider.x = 90;
            calfOffsetSlider.y = 10;

            addEventListener(Event.ENTER_FRAME, onEnterFrame);
        }

        private function onEnterFrame(event:Event):void
        {
            walk(segment0, segment1, cycle);
            walk(segment2, segment3, cycle + Math.PI);
            cycle += speedSlider.value;
        }

        private function walk(segA:Segment, segB:Segment,
                              cyc:Number):void
        {
            var angleA:Number = Math.sin(cyc) *
                            thighRangeSlider.value +
                            thighBaseSlider.value;
            var angleB:Number = Math.sin(cyc +
                            calfOffsetSlider.value) *
                            calfRangeSlider.value +
                            calfRangeSlider.value;
            segA.rotation = angleA;
            segB.rotation = segA.rotation + angleB;
            segB.x = segA.getPin().x;
            segB.y = segA.getPin().y;
        }

    }
}
```

This code is exactly as it was before, but now it's using the slider values rather than values hard-coded into the file. I'm sure you can have a lot of fun with this file, exploring different variations of the walk cycle.

Making it really walk

So far, you have a couple of legs moving around in a manner that looks pretty realistic. But they are just kind of floating in space there. Earlier in the book, you got something moving with velocity and acceleration, and then had it interact with the environment. It's time to do the same thing here.

This portion of the chapter gets pretty complex, so I'll go through the code one concept at a time. The final file, with all of these concepts incorporated, is RealWalk.as.

Giving it some space

Since this thing is actually going to be walking around and so forth, let's make all the parts a bit smaller so that there is room for it to move around. I took the original four segments and made them half of what they were, getting this, for example:

```
segment0 = new Segment(50, 15);
```

Next, because it will be moving around and reacting with boundaries, define variables for vx and vy:

```
private var vx:Number = 0;
private var vy:Number = 0;
```

At this point, if you were to run the example, you'd have a miniature, working version of the previous file.

Adding gravity

Next, you need to create some gravity. Otherwise, even if you program in the boundary reaction, the legs are just going to float in space anyway. You'll even make the gravity variable at runtime, with another slider! So, create a new slider instance and name it gravitySlider. Set minimum to 0, maximum to 1, and value to 0.2. Here's the piece of code that creates that last slider:

```
gravitySlider = new SimpleSlider(0, 1, 0.2);
addChild(gravitySlider);
gravitySlider.x = 110;
gravitySlider.y = 10;
```

Now, you need to do the velocity calculations, along with the gravity acceleration. Rather than jamming all this into the onEnterFrame method, just make a call to another method called doVelocity:

```
private function onEnterFrame(event:Event):void
{
    doVelocity();
    walk(segment0, segment1, cycle);
    walk(segment2, segment3, cycle + Math.PI);
    cycle += speedSlider.value;
}
```

And in that method, just add gravity to vy, and then add vx and vy to the position of segment0 and segment2. Remember that you don't need to worry about segment1 and segment3, as their positions are calculated in relationship to the higher-level segments.

```
private function doVelocity():void
{
    vy += gravitySlider.value;
    segment0.x += vx;
    segment0.y += vy;
    segment2.x += vx;
    segment2.y += vy;
}
```

You can test this version if you want, but it won't be very exciting. There's no x velocity happening yet, and gravity just pulls the legs right through the floor. So, you need to check the floor to see whether the legs have hit it. That means it's time for collision detection.

Handling the collision

To start, make onEnterFrame call another method, checkFloor. This will happen after the calls to walk, so it's operating on the latest positions. Generally speaking, you'll need to check only segment1 and segment3—the lower-level segments—to see whether they hit the floor. So, call checkFloor with both of them.

```
private function onEnterFrame(event:Event):void
{
    doVelocity();
    walk(segment0, segment1, cycle);
    walk(segment2, segment3, cycle + Math.PI);
    cycle += speedSlider.value;
    checkFloor(segment1);
    checkFloor(segment3);
}
```

Now comes the first interesting part: the collision detection. Note that I said "interesting" and not "impossibly difficult." It's really pretty simple. You want to know whether any part of the segment in question has gone below the bottom boundary (as specified by the bottom variable).

Probably the easiest way to do this is by calling getBounds on the segment and seeing whether the bounds' bottom property is greater than the height of the stage. That's how you'll start the checkFloor method:

```
private function checkFloor(seg:Segment):void
{
    var yMax:Number = seg.getBounds(this).bottom;
    if(yMax > stage.stageHeight)
    {

    }
}
```

I took a little shortcut there in the first line of the function, which may look a bit odd to you.

```
var yMax:Number = seg.getBounds(this).bottom;
```

Normally, you might expect to do that in two steps, like so:

```
var bounds:Rectangle = seg.getBounds(this);
var yMax:Number = bounds.bottom;
```

But what not everyone realizes is that since seg.getBounds(this) is a statement that returns a Rectangle, you can directly access the properties of that Rectangle from that statement like so: seg.getBounds(this).bottom. Flash first evaluates the call to setBounds as a Rectangle, and then it sees the dot and property, and looks for that property of that object. If that syntax is confusing to you, go ahead and use the two-line method, remembering to import the flash.geom.Rectangle class. If you were going to do anything else with the bounds object, such as read additional properties, you would want to store it first. But in this case, you're interested in only bottom, so you grab it right off the bat and don't have an extra variable sitting around.

OK, now say you've determined that yMax is indeed greater than stage.stageHeight, or in real-world terms, the leg has hit the floor. What do you do? Well, just as in other boundary collisions, you first want to move the object so it's resting right on the boundary. Realize that if yMax is the lowest edge of the segment, and stage.stageHeight is the floor, you need to move the segment back up exactly the distance between them. In other words, say stage.stageHeight is 600, and yMax is 620, you'll need to change the segment's y position by −20. But you don't just want to move the segment. You want to move *all* the segments by that amount, since they are all part of the same body and must move as one. So, you get something like this:

```
private function checkFloor(seg:Segment):void
{
    var yMax:Number = seg.getBounds(this).bottom;
    if(yMax > stage.stageHeight)
    {
        var dy:Number = yMax - stage.stageHeight;
        segment0.y -= dy;
        segment1.y -= dy;
        segment2.y -= dy;
        segment3.y -= dy;
    }
}
```

This iteration is worth playing with some more. Adjust the slider values to see the different walk cycles in action. You'll get more of a feel for them with the legs actually interacting with the environment. Of course, it's still not really walking yet. That's up next.

Handling the reaction

Now, you have the legs successfully colliding with the floor, but other than repositioning themselves, there's no real reaction. The whole reason you walk is to get some horizontal motion going—x velocity, in this case. Furthermore, your walk cycle should give you a bit of y velocity as well—at least enough to counteract gravity briefly. You see this more in a fast run, where you might get slightly airborne for a brief period of the cycle.

One way of looking at this is that your foot is moving down. When it hits the floor, it can't move down any more, so that vertical momentum goes back up to your body, moving it up. The stronger your foot is moving down, the more lift you get. Likewise, if your foot is moving backward when it hits, that horizontal momentum goes back to your body, moving it forward. The faster your foot is moving back, the more horizontal thrust you get.

OK, we have a theory here. If you can keep track of the "foot's" x and y velocity, then when you get a collision, you can subtract that x and y velocity from the vx and vy values.

The first problem you run into is that you don't have any feet yet. Actually, although you are free to add some physical feet yourself, figuring out their locations the same way you did the positions for the second segments, I'm not going to use real feet in this example. Instead, I'm just going to calculate the position of the virtual feet, which, you may have guessed, is the value returned by getPin() on the lower segments.

If you keep track of where that pin is before the segment moves, and where it is after the segment moves, you can subtract the two and get the "foot's" velocity on both x and y. You can do that right in the walk method and store the values in the public vx and vy properties of the segment (now you see where those come in). Note that since you are using the Point class, you'll need to import flash.geom.Point.

```
private function walk(segA:Segment, segB:Segment, cyc:Number):void
{
    var foot:Point = segB.getPin();
    var angleA:Number = Math.sin(cyc) *
                        thighRangeSlider.value +
                        thighBaseSlider.value;
    var angleB:Number = Math.sin(cyc + calfOffsetSlider.value) *
                        calfRangeSlider.value +
                        calfRangeSlider.value;
    segA.rotation = angleA;
    segB.rotation = segA.rotation + angleB;
    segB.x = segA.getPin().x;
    segB.y = segA.getPin().y;
    segB.vx = segB.getPin().x - foot.x;
    segB.vy = segB.getPin().y - foot.y;
}
```

Now each bottom segment has a vx and vy property, which represents not the velocity of the segment itself, but the velocity of that bottom pivot point, or virtual foot.

So, what do you do with this velocity? Well, you wait until you have a collision with the floor, and then you subtract it from the overall velocity. In other words, if the foot is moving down at 3 pixels per frame (a vy of 3) when it hits, you'll subtract 3 from the overall vy. You'll do the same with the vx. In code, it's really simple:

```
private function checkFloor(seg:Segment):void
{
    var yMax:Number = seg.getBounds(this).bottom;
    if(yMax > stage.stageHeight)
    {
        var dy:Number = yMax - stage.stageHeight;
        segment0.y -= dy;
        segment1.y -= dy;
        segment2.y -= dy;
        segment3.y -= dy;
        vx -= seg.vx;
        vy -= seg.vy;
    }
}
```

At this point, I'll throw in my usual disclaimer about how this is an extremely simplified and probably totally inaccurate representation of how the forces involved in walking actually work. But then I'll smile and say "test the movie." See if you like the effect. It looks pretty darned cool to me. I've got a pair of legs walking across my screen!

Screen wrapping, revisited

You've probably noticed that the legs walk off screen, never to return. A little screen wrapping will fix that. When the legs go off to the right, you move them back to the left. It's a little more complex than before, because now you're moving four pieces around in unison, instead of a single object. But then again, remember that you need to check only either one of the two top segments, as they are always in the same position, and the lower segments' positions are totally determined by the upper ones. Add a call to a method named checkWalls at the end of onEnterFrame:

```
private function onEnterFrame(event:Event):void
{
    doVelocity();
    walk(segment0, segment1, cycle);
    walk(segment2, segment3, cycle + Math.PI);
    cycle += speedSlider.value;
    checkFloor(segment1);
    checkFloor(segment3);
    checkWalls();
}
```

Let's leave a general margin of 100 pixels, so that either leg can go 100 pixels off the right of the stage before wrapping. If it goes past that, you reposition everything way over to the left. How far to the left? The width of the stage plus 200, for the 100-pixel margin on each side. So, start your if statement in the checkWalls method like so:

```
private function checkWalls():void
{
    var w:Number = stage.stageWidth + 200;
    if(segment0.x > stage.stageWidth + 100)
    {
        segment0.x -= w;
        segment1.x -= w;
        segment2.x -= w;
        segment3.x -= w;
    }
}
```

Then do the exact same thing for the left edge, as some walk cycles can actually make the legs go backward. Here's the final checkWalls method:

```
private function checkWalls():void
{
    var w:Number = stage.stageWidth + 200;
    if(segment0.x > stage.stageWidth + 100)
    {
        segment0.x -= w;
        segment1.x -= w;
        segment2.x -= w;
        segment3.x -= w;
    }
    else if(segment0.x < -100)
    {
        segment0.x += w;
        segment1.x += w;
        segment2.x += w;
        segment3.x += w;
    }
}
```

And there you have it. In case it got confusing, the code for the whole thing follows (and can be found in RealWalk.as).

```
package {
    import flash.display.Sprite;
    import flash.events.Event;
    import flash.geom.Point;

    public class RealWalk extends Sprite
    {
        private var segment0:Segment;
        private var segment1:Segment;
        private var segment2:Segment;
```

```
private var segment3:Segment;
private var speedSlider:SimpleSlider;
private var thighRangeSlider:SimpleSlider;
private var thighBaseSlider:SimpleSlider;
private var calfRangeSlider:SimpleSlider;
private var calfOffsetSlider:SimpleSlider;
private var gravitySlider:SimpleSlider;
private var cycle:Number = 0;
private var vx:Number = 0;
private var vy:Number = 0;

public function RealWalk()
{
    init();
}

private function init():void
{
    segment0 = new Segment(50, 15);
    addChild(segment0);
    segment0.x = 200;
    segment0.y = 100;

    segment1 = new Segment(50, 10);
    addChild(segment1);
    segment1.x = segment0.getPin().x;
    segment1.y = segment0.getPin().y;

    segment2 = new Segment(50, 15);
    addChild(segment2);
    segment2.x = 200;
    segment2.y = 100;

    segment3 = new Segment(50, 10);
    addChild(segment3);
    segment3.x = segment2.getPin().x;
    segment3.y = segment2.getPin().y;

    speedSlider = new SimpleSlider(0, 0.3, 0.12);
    addChild(speedSlider);
    speedSlider.x = 10;
    speedSlider.y = 10;

    thighRangeSlider = new SimpleSlider(0, 90, 45);
    addChild(thighRangeSlider);
    thighRangeSlider.x = 30;
    thighRangeSlider.y = 10;
```

```
    thighBaseSlider = new SimpleSlider(0, 180, 90);
    addChild(thighBaseSlider);
    thighBaseSlider.x = 50;
    thighBaseSlider.y = 10;

    calfRangeSlider = new SimpleSlider(0, 90, 45);
    addChild(calfRangeSlider);
    calfRangeSlider.x = 70;
    calfRangeSlider.y = 10;

    calfOffsetSlider = new SimpleSlider(-3.14, 3.14, -1.57);
    addChild(calfOffsetSlider);
    calfOffsetSlider.x = 90;
    calfOffsetSlider.y = 10;

    gravitySlider = new SimpleSlider(0, 1, 0.2);
    addChild(gravitySlider);
    gravitySlider.x = 110;
    gravitySlider.y = 10;

    addEventListener(Event.ENTER_FRAME, onEnterFrame);
}

private function onEnterFrame(event:Event):void
{
    doVelocity();
    walk(segment0, segment1, cycle);
    walk(segment2, segment3, cycle + Math.PI);
    cycle += speedSlider.value;
    checkFloor(segment1);
    checkFloor(segment3);
    checkWalls();
}

private function walk(segA:Segment, segB:Segment,
                      cyc:Number):void
{
    var foot:Point = segB.getPin();
    var angleA:Number = Math.sin(cyc) *
                        thighRangeSlider.value +
                        thighBaseSlider.value;
    var angleB:Number = Math.sin(cyc +
                        calfOffsetSlider.value) *
                        calfRangeSlider.value +
                        calfRangeSlider.value;
    segA.rotation = angleA;
    segB.rotation = segA.rotation + angleB;
    segB.x = segA.getPin().x;
```

```
            segB.y = segA.getPin().y;
            segB.vx = segB.getPin().x - foot.x;
            segB.vy = segB.getPin().y - foot.y;
        }

        private function doVelocity():void
        {
            vy += gravitySlider.value;
            segment0.x += vx;
            segment0.y += vy;
            segment2.x += vx;
            segment2.y += vy;
        }

        private function checkFloor(seg:Segment):void
        {
            var yMax:Number = seg.getBounds(this).bottom;
            if(yMax > stage.stageHeight)
            {
                var dy:Number = yMax - stage.stageHeight;
                segment0.y -= dy;
                segment1.y -= dy;
                segment2.y -= dy;
                segment3.y -= dy;
                vx -= seg.vx;
                vy -= seg.vy;
            }
        }

        private function checkWalls():void
        {
            var w:Number = stage.stageWidth + 200;
            if(segment0.x > stage.stageWidth + 100)
            {
                segment0.x -= w;
                segment1.x -= w;
                segment2.x -= w;
                segment3.x -= w;
            }
            else if(segment0.x < -100)
            {
                segment0.x += w;
                segment1.x += w;
                segment2.x += w;
                segment3.x += w;
            }
        }
    }
}
```

Summary

You've done some pretty powerful stuff in this chapter, conquering the basics of forward kinematics. Note that the methods I gave you here are probably not the only solutions to the subject. They're obviously tailored toward a particular application of the technology: making something walk. Feel free to leave things out, change things, or add whatever you want to this system. Experiment and see what you can come up with.

Next up, you'll look at the other side of the coin: inverse kinematics.

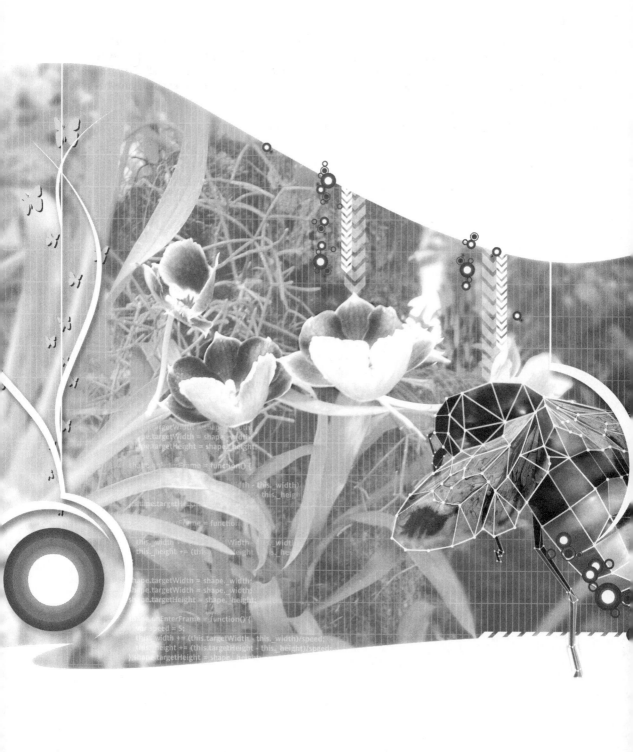

Chapter 14

INVERSE KINEMATICS: DRAGGING AND REACHING

What we'll cover in this chapter:

- Reaching and dragging single segments
- Dragging multiple segments
- Reaching with multiple segments
- Using the standard inverse kinematics method
- Important formulas in this chapter

In Chapter 13, I covered some of the basics of kinematics and the difference between inverse and forward kinematics. That chapter went into forward kinematics. Now, you're ready for its close relative, inverse kinematics. The movements involved are dragging and reaching.

As with the forward kinematics examples, the examples in this chapter build systems from individual segments. You'll begin with single segments, and then move on to multiple segments. First, I'll show you the simplest method for calculating the various angles and positions. This just approximates measurements using the basic trigonometry you've already seen in action. Finally, I'll briefly cover another method using something called the law of cosines, which can be more accurate at the cost of being more complex—that familiar trade-off.

Reaching and dragging single segments

As I mentioned in the previous chapter, inverse kinematics systems can be broken down into a couple of different types: reaching and dragging.

When the free end of the system is reaching for a target, the other end of the system, the base, may be unmovable, so the free end may never be able to get all the way to the target if it is out of range. An example of this is when you're trying to grab hold of something. Your fingers move toward the object, your wrist pivots to put your fingers as close as possible, and your elbow, shoulder, and the rest of your body move in whatever way they can to try to give you as much reach as possible. Sometimes, the combination of all these positions will put your fingers in contact with the object; sometimes, you won't be able to reach it. If the object were to move from side to side, all your limbs would constantly reposition themselves to keep your fingers reaching as close as they could to the object. Inverse kinematics will show you how to position all those pieces to give the best reach.

The other type of inverse kinematics is when something is being dragged. In this case, the free end is being moved by some external force. Wherever it is, the rest of the parts of the system follow along behind it, positioning themselves in whatever way is physically possible. For this, imagine an unconscious or dead body (sorry, that's all I could come up with). You grab it by the hand and drag it around. The force you apply to the hand causes the wrist, elbow, shoulder, and rest of the body to pivot and move in whatever way they can as they are dragged along. In this case, inverse kinematics will show you how those pieces will fall into the correct positions as they are dragged.

To give you a quick idea of the difference between these two methods, let's run through an example of each one with a single segment. You'll need the Segment class we used in the last chapter, so make sure that is in your project or class path.

Reaching with a single segment

For reaching, all the segment will be able to do is turn toward the target. The target, if you haven't read my mind already, will be the mouse. To turn the segment toward the target, you need the distance between the two, on the x and y axes. You then can use Math.atan2 to get the angle between them in radians. Converting that to degrees, you know how to rotate the segment. Here's the code (which you'll also find in OneSegment.as):

```
package {
    import flash.display.Sprite;
    import flash.events.Event;

    public class OneSegment extends Sprite
    {
        private var segment0:Segment;

        public function OneSegment()
        {
            init();
        }

        private function init():void
        {
            segment0 = new Segment(100, 20);
            addChild(segment0);
            segment0.x = stage.stageWidth / 2;
            segment0.y = stage.stageHeight / 2;

            addEventListener(Event.ENTER_FRAME, onEnterFrame);
        }

        private function onEnterFrame(event:Event):void
        {
            var dx:Number = mouseX - segment0.x;
            var dy:Number = mouseY - segment0.y;
            var angle:Number = Math.atan2(dy, dx);
            segment0.rotation = angle * 180 / Math.PI;
        }
    }
}
```

Figure 14-1 shows the result. Test this and watch how the segment follows the mouse around. Even if the segment is too far away, you can see how it seems to be reaching for the mouse.

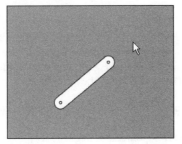

Figure 14-1. A single segment reaching toward the mouse

Dragging with a single segment

Now, let's try dragging. Here, you're not actually dragging using the startDrag and stopDrag methods (though you could conceivably do it that way). Instead, you'll just assume that the segment is attached to the mouse right at that second pivot point.

The first part of the dragging method is exactly the same as the reaching method: You rotate the sprite toward the mouse. But then you go a step further and move the segment to a position that will place the second pivot point exactly where the mouse is. To do that, you need to know the distance between the two pins on each axis. You can get this by getting the difference (on each axis) between the segment's getPin() point and its actual x, y location. We'll call these w and h. Then just subtract w and h from the current mouse location, and you'll know where to put the segment. Here's the onEnterFrame method from OneSegmentDrag.as, the only part that has changed:

```
    private function onEnterFrame(event:Event):void
    {
        var dx:Number = mouseX - segment0.x;
        var dy:Number = mouseY - segment0.y;
        var angle:Number = Math.atan2(dy, dx);
        segment0.rotation = angle * 180 / Math.PI;

        var w:Number = segment0.getPin().x - segment0.x;
        var h:Number = segment0.getPin().y - segment0.y;
        segment0.x = mouseX - w;
        segment0.y = mouseY - h;
    }
```

You can see how the segment is permanently attached to the mouse and rotates to drag along behind it. You can even push the segment around in the opposite direction.

Dragging multiple segments

Dragging a system with inverse kinematics is actually a bit simpler than reaching, so I'll cover that first. Let's begin with a couple of segments.

Dragging two segments

Starting with the previous example, create another segment, name it segment1, and add it to the display list. The strategy is pretty simple. You already have segment0 dragging on the mouse position. You just have segment1 drag on segment0. To start with, you can simply copy and paste the code, and change some of the references. The new code is shown in bold.

```
    private function onEnterFrame(event:Event):void
    {
        var dx:Number = mouseX - segment0.x;
        var dy:Number = mouseY - segment0.y;
        var angle:Number = Math.atan2(dy, dx);
        segment0.rotation = angle * 180 / Math.PI;
```

```
            var w:Number = segment0.getPin().x - segment0.x;
            var h:Number = segment0.getPin().y - segment0.y;
            segment0.x = mouseX - w;
            segment0.y = mouseY - h;

            dx = segment0.x - segment1.x;
            dy = segment0.y - segment1.y;
            angle = Math.atan2(dy, dx);
            segment1.rotation = angle * 180 / Math.PI;

            w = segment1.getPin().x - segment1.x;
            h = segment1.getPin().y - segment1.y;
            segment1.x = segment0.x - w;
            segment1.y = segment0.y - h;
        }
    }
}
```

You see how in the new block of code, you figure the distance from segment1 to segment0, and use that for the angle and rotation and position of segment1. You can test this example and see how it's a pretty realistic two-segment system.

Now, you have a lot of duplicated code there, which is not good. If you wanted to add more segments, this file would get longer and longer, all with the same code repeated. The solution is to move the duplicated code out into its own function, called drag. This function needs to know what segment to drag and what x, y point to drag to. Then you can drag segment0 to mouseX, mouseY and segment1 to segment0.x, segment0.y. Here's the full code (which also appears in TwoSegmentDrag.as):

```
package {
    import flash.display.Sprite;
    import flash.events.Event;

    public class TwoSegmentDrag extends Sprite
    {
        private var segment0:Segment;
        private var segment1:Segment;

        public function TwoSegmentDrag()
        {
            init();
        }

        private function init():void
        {
            segment0 = new Segment(100, 20);
            addChild(segment0);
            segment1 = new Segment(100, 20);
            addChild(segment1);
```

```
        addEventListener(Event.ENTER_FRAME, onEnterFrame);
    }

    private function onEnterFrame(event:Event):void
    {
        drag(segment0, mouseX, mouseY);
        drag(segment1, segment0.x, segment0.y);
    }

    private function drag(segment:Segment,
                          xpos:Number,
                          ypos:Number):void
    {
        var dx:Number = xpos - segment.x;
        var dy:Number = ypos - segment.y;
        var angle:Number = Math.atan2(dy, dx);
        segment.rotation = angle * 180 / Math.PI;

        var w:Number = segment.getPin().x - segment.x;
        var h:Number = segment.getPin().y - segment.y;
        segment.x = xpos - w;
        segment.y = ypos - h;
    }
    }
}
```

Dragging more segments

Now you can add as many segments as you want. Say you throw down a total of six segments, named segment0 through segment5, and put them in an array. You can then use a for loop to call the drag function for each segment. You can find this example in MultiSegmentDrag.as. Here's code for that file:

```
package {
    import flash.display.Sprite;
    import flash.events.Event;

    public class MultiSegmentDrag extends Sprite
    {
        private var segments:Array;
        private var numSegments:uint = 6;

        public function MultiSegmentDrag()
        {
            init();
        }
```

```
private function init():void
{
    segments = new Array();
    for(var i:uint = 0; i < numSegments; i++)
    {
        var segment:Segment = new Segment(50, 10);
        addChild(segment);
        segments.push(segment);
    }
    addEventListener(Event.ENTER_FRAME, onEnterFrame);
}

private function onEnterFrame(event:Event):void
{
    drag(segments[0], mouseX, mouseY);
    for(var i:uint = 1; i < numSegments; i++)
    {
        var segmentA:Segment = segments[i];
        var segmentB:Segment = segments[i - 1];
        drag(segmentA, segmentB.x, segmentB.y);
    }
}

private function drag(segment:Segment,
                      xpos:Number,
                      ypos:Number):void
{
    var dx:Number = xpos - segment.x;
    var dy:Number = ypos - segment.y;
    var angle:Number = Math.atan2(dy, dx);
    segment.rotation = angle * 180 / Math.PI;

    var w:Number = segment.getPin().x - segment.x;
    var h:Number = segment.getPin().y - segment.y;
    segment.x = xpos - w;
    segment.y = ypos - h;
}
    }
}
```

Here, segmentB is the segment being dragged to, and segmentA is the next segment in line—the one that is being dragged. You just pass these to the drag function. Figure 14-2 shows the result.

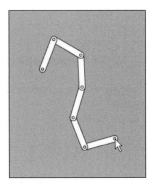

Figure 14-2. Multiple-segment dragging

Well, there you have the basics of inverse kinematics. That's not too complex, huh? You can add as many segments as you want just by changing the numSegments variable. In Figure 14-3, you can see 50 segments, demonstrating just how robust this system is.

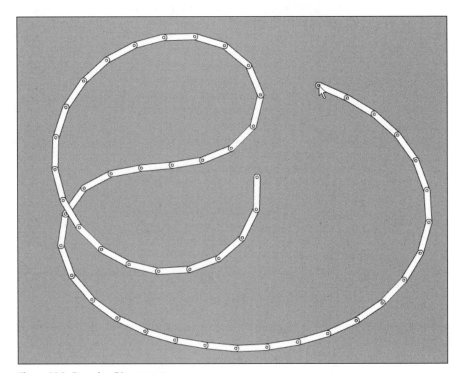

Figure 14-3. Dragging 50 segments

Reaching with multiple segments

To start with inverse kinematics reaching, you'll take this chapter's initial example, OneSegment.as, and add to that. That file simply had the segment rotating to a target, which was the mouse position.

Reaching for the mouse

First, you need to determine where the segment should be to exactly touch that target. This is the same calculation you use to position the segment when you're dragging. However, in this case, you don't actually move the segment. You just find that position. So, what do you do with that position? You use that as the target of the next segment up the line, and have that segment rotate to that position. When you reach the base of the system, you then work back down, positioning each piece on the end of its parent. Figure 14-4 illustrates how this works.

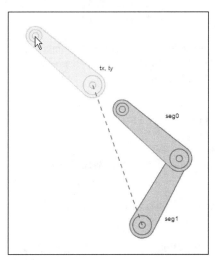

Figure 14-4. segment0 rotates to the mouse. tx, ty is where it would like to be. segment1 will rotate to tx, ty.

The first file from this chapter, OneSegment.as, had a single segment, segment0, reaching for the mouse. We'll create another one, named segment1, and add it to the display list. The next step is to find the target point where segment0 would be hitting the target. Once again, this is the same point you moved the segment to in the dragging examples. But don't move it, just store the position. So, you get this:

```
private function onEnterFrame(event:Event):void
{
    var dx:Number = mouseX - segment0.x;
    var dy:Number = mouseY - segment0.y;
    var angle:Number = Math.atan2(dy, dx);
    segment0.rotation = angle * 180 / Math.PI;
```

```
    var w:Number = segment0.getPin().x - segment0.x;
    var h:Number = segment0.getPin().y - segment0.y;
    var tx:Number = mouseX - w;
    var ty:Number = mouseY - h;
}
```

I called that point tx, ty, because it will be the target for segment1 to rotate to.

Next, you can copy and paste and adjust the rotation code to have segment1 rotate to its target:

```
private function onEnterFrame(event:Event):void
{
    var dx:Number = mouseX - segment0.x;
    var dy:Number = mouseY - segment0.y;
    var angle:Number = Math.atan2(dy, dx);
    segment0.rotation = angle * 180 / Math.PI;

    var w:Number = segment0.getPin().x - segment0.x;
    var h:Number = segment0.getPin().y - segment0.y;
    var tx:Number = mouseX - w;
    var ty:Number = mouseY - h;

    dx = tx - segment1.x;
    dy = ty - segment1.y;
    angle = Math.atan2(dy, dx);
    segment1.rotation = angle * 180 / Math.PI;
}
```

This code is the same as the first four lines of the function, but using a different segment and different target.

Finally, reposition segment0 so it's sitting on the end of segment1, since segment1 has now rotated to a different position.

```
private function onEnterFrame(event:Event):void
{
    var dx:Number = mouseX - segment0.x;
    var dy:Number = mouseY - segment0.y;
    var angle:Number = Math.atan2(dy, dx);
    segment0.rotation = angle * 180 / Math.PI;

    var w:Number = segment0.getPin().x - segment0.x;
    var h:Number = segment0.getPin().y - segment0.y;
    var tx:Number = mouseX - w;
    var ty:Number = mouseY - h;

    dx = tx - segment1.x;
    dy = ty - segment1.y;
    angle = Math.atan2(dy, dx);
    segment1.rotation = angle * 180 / Math.PI;
```

```
    segment0.x = segment1.getPin().x;
    segment0.y = segment1.getPin().y;
}
```

When you test this example, you'll see that the segments do work as a unit to reach for the mouse. Now, let's clean up the code so you can add more segments to it easily. First, let's move all of the rotation stuff into its own function, called reach.

```
private function reach(segment:Segment, xpos:Number, ypos:Number):Point
{
    var dx:Number = xpos - segment.x;
    var dy:Number = ypos - segment.y;
    var angle:Number = Math.atan2(dy, dx);
    segment.rotation = angle * 180 / Math.PI;

    var w:Number = segment.getPin().x - segment.x;
    var h:Number = segment.getPin().y - segment.y;
    var tx:Number = xpos - w;
    var ty:Number = ypos - h;
    return new Point(tx, ty);
}
```

Note that the return type of the function is Point, and the last line creates and returns a Point based on tx and ty. This allows you to call the reach function to rotate the segment, and it will return the target, which you can pass to the next call. Don't forget to import the Point class. So, the onEnterFrame function becomes this:

```
private function onEnterFrame(event:Event):void
{
    var target:Point = reach(segment0, mouseX, mouseY);
    reach(segment1, target.x, target.y);
    segment0.x = segment1.getPin().x;
    segment0.y = segment1.getPin().y;
}
```

Here, segment0 always reaches toward the mouse, and segment1 reaches toward segment0. We can then move that positioning code into its own method, position:

```
private function position(segmentA:Segment, segmentB:Segment):void
{
    segmentA.x = segmentB.getPin().x;
    segmentA.y = segmentB.getPin().y;
}
```

Then you can position segment0 on the end of segment1 by using

```
position(segment0, segment1);
```

Here's the final code for TwoSegmentReach.as:

```
package {
    import flash.display.Sprite;
    import flash.events.Event;
    import flash.geom.Point;

    public class TwoSegmentReach extends Sprite
    {
        private var segment0:Segment;
        private var segment1:Segment;

        public function TwoSegmentReach()
        {
            init();
        }

        private function init():void
        {
            segment0 = new Segment(100, 20);
            addChild(segment0);

            segment1 = new Segment(100, 20);
            addChild(segment1);
            segment1.x = stage.stageWidth / 2;
            segment1.y = stage.stageHeight / 2;

            addEventListener(Event.ENTER_FRAME, onEnterFrame);
        }

        private function onEnterFrame(event:Event):void
        {
            var target:Point = reach(segment0, mouseX, mouseY);
            reach(segment1, target.x, target.y);
            position(segment0, segment1);
        }

        private function reach(segment:Segment,
                               xpos:Number,
                               ypos:Number):Point
        {
            var dx:Number = xpos - segment.x;
            var dy:Number = ypos - segment.y;
            var angle:Number = Math.atan2(dy, dx);
            segment.rotation = angle * 180 / Math.PI;
```

```
                var w:Number = segment.getPin().x - segment.x;
                var h:Number = segment.getPin().y - segment.y;
                var tx:Number = xpos - w;
                var ty:Number = ypos - h;
                return new Point(tx, ty);
            }

            private function position(segmentA:Segment,
                                     segmentB:Segment):void
            {
                segmentA.x = segmentB.getPin().x;
                segmentA.y = segmentB.getPin().y;
            }
        }
    }
```

With all that in place, it's easy enough to create an array to hold as many segments as you want to create. MultiSegmentReach.as does just that:

```
package {
    import flash.display.Sprite;
    import flash.events.Event;
    import flash.geom.Point;

    public class MultiSegmentReach extends Sprite
    {
        private var segments:Array;
        private var numSegments:uint = 6;

        public function MultiSegmentReach()
        {
            init();
        }

        private function init():void
        {
            segments = new Array();
            for(var i:uint = 0; i < numSegments; i++)
            {
                var segment:Segment = new Segment(50, 10);
                addChild(segment);
                segments.push(segment);
            }
            // center the last one
            segment.x = stage.stageWidth / 2;
            segment.y = stage.stageHeight / 2;
            addEventListener(Event.ENTER_FRAME, onEnterFrame);
        }
```

```
private function onEnterFrame(event:Event):void
{
    var target:Point = reach(segments[0], mouseX, mouseY);
    for(var i:uint = 1; i < numSegments; i++)
    {
        var segment:Segment = segments[i];
        target = reach(segment, target.x, target.y);
    }
    for(i = numSegments - 1; i > 0; i--)
    {
        var segmentA:Segment = segments[i];
        var segmentB:Segment = segments[i - 1];
        position(segmentB, segmentA);
    }
}

private function reach(segment:Segment,
                      xpos:Number,
                      ypos:Number):Point
{
    var dx:Number = xpos - segment.x;
    var dy:Number = ypos - segment.y;
    var angle:Number = Math.atan2(dy, dx);
    segment.rotation = angle * 180 / Math.PI;

    var w:Number = segment.getPin().x - segment.x;
    var h:Number = segment.getPin().y - segment.y;
    var tx:Number = xpos - w;
    var ty:Number = ypos - h;
    return new Point(tx, ty);
}

private function position(segmentA:Segment,
                         segmentB:Segment):void
{
    segmentA.x = segmentB.getPin().x;
    segmentA.y = segmentB.getPin().y;
}
        }
    }
```

You can see the results of this in Figure 14-5. Now, this is a lot better than what you started out with. But why does the segment chain have to chase the mouse all day? It seems to have some will of its own. Let's see what happens if you give it a toy!

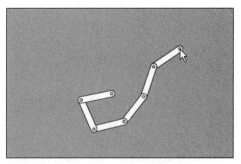

Figure 14-5. Multiple-segment reaching

Reaching for an object

For the next example, I resurrected the Ball class, so get that into your project or class path.

Then create some new variables for the ball to use as it moves around. Note that this code builds on the last example, so you can just add the following:

```
private var ball:Ball;
private var gravity:Number = 0.5;
private var bounce:Number = -0.9;
```

Then, in the init method, create an instance of Ball and add it to the display list.

```
private function init():void
{
    ball = new Ball();
    ball.vx = 10;
    addChild(ball);
    segments = new Array();
    for(var i:uint = 0; i < numSegments; i++)
    {
        var segment:Segment = new Segment(50, 10);
        addChild(segment);
        segments.push(segment);
    }
    segment.x = stage.stageWidth / 2;
    segment.y = stage.stageHeight;
    addEventListener(Event.ENTER_FRAME, onEnterFrame);
}
```

In onEnterFrame, you call a function named moveBall. This just separates all the ball-moving code so it doesn't clutter things up:

```
private function onEnterFrame(event:Event):void
{
    moveBall();
    var target:Point = reach(segments[0], mouseX, mouseY);
    for(var i:uint = 1; i < numSegments; i++)
    {
        var segment:Segment = segments[i];
        target = reach(segment, target.x, target.y);
    }
    for(i = numSegments - 1; i > 0; i--)
    {
        var segmentA:Segment = segments[i];
        var segmentB:Segment = segments[i - 1];
        position(segmentB, segmentA);
    }
}
```

And here is that function:

```
private function moveBall():void
{
    ball.vy += gravity;
    ball.x += ball.vx;
    ball.y += ball.vy;
    if(ball.x + ball.radius > stage.stageWidth)
    {
        ball.x = stage.stageWidth - ball.radius;
        ball.vx *= bounce;
    }
    else if(ball.x - ball.radius < 0)
    {
        ball.x = ball.radius;
        ball.vx *= bounce;
    }
    if(ball.y + ball.radius > stage.stageHeight)
    {
        ball.y = stage.stageHeight - ball.radius;
        ball.vy *= bounce;
    }
    else if(ball.y - ball.radius < 0)
    {
        ball.y = ball.radius;
        ball.vy *= bounce;
    }
}
```

Then change the second line of the onEnterFrame function to have it reach for the ball instead of the mouse:

```
var target:Point = reach(segments[0], ball.x, ball.y);
```

And that's all there is to it. You should see something like Figure 14-6. The ball now bounces around, and the arm follows it. Pretty amazing, right?

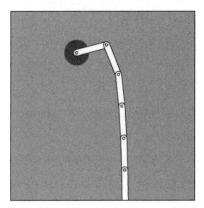

Figure 14-6. It likes to play ball.

But, you can do better. Right now, the arm does well at touching the ball, but the ball completely ignores the arm. Let's have them interact.

Adding some interaction

How the ball and the arm interact depends on what you want them to do. But, no matter what you do, the first thing you need is some collision detection. Then you can have the reaction if there is a collision. Again, you'll pull all that stuff into its own function and call it from onEnterFrame.

```
private function onEnterFrame(event:Event):void
{
    moveBall();
    var target:Point = reach(segments[0], ball.x, ball.y);
    for(var i:uint = 1; i < numSegments; i++)
    {
        var segment:Segment = segments[i];
        target = reach(segment, target.x, target.y);
    }
    for(i = numSegments - 1; i > 0; i--)
    {
        var segmentA:Segment = segments[i];
        var segmentB:Segment = segments[i - 1];
        position(segmentB, segmentA);
    }
    checkHit();
}
```

I've named this function checkHit, and placed it last in the function, so everything is in its final position. Here's the start of the checkHit function:

```
public function checkHit():void
{
    var segment:Segment = segments[0];
    var dx:Number = segment.getPin().x - ball.x;
    var dy:Number = segment.getPin().y - ball.y;
    var dist:Number = Math.sqrt(dx * dx + dy * dy);
    if(dist < ball.radius)
    {
        // reaction goes here
    }
}
```

The first thing you do is get the distance from the end pin of the first arm to the ball, and use distance-based collision detection to see whether it's hitting the ball.

Now we get back to the question of what to do when you do get a hit. Here's my plan: The arm will throw the ball up in the air (negative y velocity) and move it randomly on the x axis (random x velocity), like so:

```
public function checkHit():void
{
    var segment:Segment = segments[0];
    var dx:Number = segment.getPin().x - ball.x;
    var dy:Number = segment.getPin().y - ball.y;
    var dist:Number = Math.sqrt(dx * dx + dy * dy);
    if(dist < ball.radius)
    {
        ball.vx += Math.random() * 2 - 1;
        ball.vy -= 1;
    }
}
```

This works out pretty well, and the final code can be found in PlayBall.as. I actually left it running overnight, and the next morning, the arm was still happily playing with its toy! But don't take it as anything "standard" that you are supposed to do. You might want to have it catch the ball and throw it toward a target. A game of basketball maybe? Or have two arms play catch? Play around with different reactions. You surely have enough tools under your belt now to do something interesting in there.

Using the standard inverse kinematics method

I'll be perfectly honest with you. The method of calculating inverse kinematics I've described so far is something I came up with completely on my own. I think the first time I did it, I didn't even know that what I was doing was called inverse kinematics. I simply wanted something to reach for something else, and I worked out what each piece had to do in order to accomplish that, fooled around with it, got it working, and got it down to a system that I could easily duplicate and describe to others. It works pretty well, looks pretty good, and doesn't kill the CPU, so I'm happy with it. I hope you are too.

But, shocking as this may seem to you, I was not the first one to consider this problem. Many others, with much larger IQs and much more formal training in math, have tackled this problem and come up with alternative solutions that are probably much more in line with how physical objects actually move. So let's take a look at the "standard" way of doing inverse kinematics. Then you'll have a couple different methods at your disposal and can choose whichever one you like.

Introducing the law of cosines

The usual way for doing inverse kinematics uses, as the section title implies, something called the *law of cosines*. Uh-oh, more trigonometry? Yup. Recall that in Chapter 3, all the examples use right triangles—triangles with one right angle (90 degrees). The rules for such triangles are fairly simple: sine equals opposite over hypotenuse, cosine equals adjacent over hypotenuse, and so on. I've used these rules quite extensively throughout the book.

But what if you have a triangle that doesn't have a 90-degree angle? Are you just left out in the cold? No, the ancient Greeks thought of that one, too, and gave us the law of cosines to help us figure out the various angles and lengths of even this kind of shape. Of course, it is a little more complex, but if you have enough information about the triangle, you can use this law to figure out the rest.

The question you should be asking now is "What the heck does this have to do with inverse kinematics?" Well, take a look at the diagram in Figure 14-7.

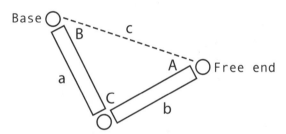

Figure 14-7. Two segments form a triangle with sides a, b, c, and angles A, B, C.

Here, you have two segments. The one on the left is the base. It's fixed, so you know that location. You want to put the free end at the location shown. You've formed an arbitrary triangle.

What do you know about this triangle? You can easily find out the distance between the two ends— side c. And you know the length of each segment—sides a and b. So, you know all three lengths.

What do you need to know about this triangle? You just need to know the two angles of the two segments—angles B and C. This is what the law of cosines helps you discover. Let me introduce you to it:

$$c^2 = a^2 + b^2 - 2 * a * b * \cos C$$

Now, you need to know angle C, so you can isolate that on one side. I won't go through every step, as it's pretty basic algebra. You should wind up with this:

C = acos ((a2 + b2 - c2) / (2 * a * b))

The acos there is arccosine, or inverse cosine. The cosine of an angle gives you a ratio, or decimal. The arccosine of that ratio gives you back the angle. The Flash function for this is Math.acos(). Since you know sides a, b, and c, you can now find angle C. Similarly, you need to know angle B. The law of cosines says this:

b^2 = a^2 + c^2 - 2 * a * c * cos B

And that boils down to this:

B = acos((a^2 + c^2 - b^2)/ (2 * a * c))

Converting to ActionScript gives you something like this:

```
B = Math.acos((a * a + c * c - b * b) / (2 * a * c));
C = Math.acos((a * a + b * b - c * c) / (2 * a * b));
```

Now you have *almost* everything you need to start positioning things. Almost, because the angles B and C aren't really the angles of rotation you'll be using for the segments. Look at the next diagram in Figure 14-8.

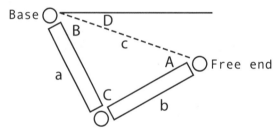

Figure 14-8. Figuring the rotation of seg1

While you know angle B, what you need to determine is how much to actually rotate seg1. This is how far from zero, or horizontal, it's going to be, and is represented by angles D plus B. Luckily, you can get angle D by figuring out the angle between the base and free end, as illustrated in Figure 14-9.

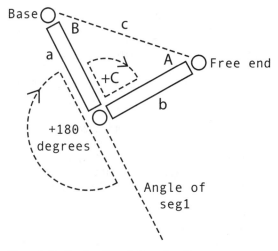

Figure 14-9. Figuring the rotation of seg0

Then you know angle C, but that is only in relation to seg1. What you need for rotation is seg1's rotation, plus 180, plus C. I'll call that angle E.

OK, enough talk. Let's see it in code, and it will all become clear.

ActionScripting the law of cosines

I'm just going to give you the inverse kinematics code in one big lump, and then explain it. Here's the code (which you can also find in Cosines.as):

```
package {
    import flash.display.Sprite;
    import flash.events.Event;
    import flash.geom.Point;

    public class Cosines extends Sprite
    {
        private var segment0:Segment;
        private var segment1:Segment;

        public function Cosines()
        {
            init();
        }

        private function init():void
        {
            segment0 = new Segment(100, 20);
            addChild(segment0);
```

```
        segment1 = new Segment(100, 20);
        addChild(segment1);
        segment1.x = stage.stageWidth / 2;
        segment1.y = stage.stageHeight / 2;

        addEventListener(Event.ENTER_FRAME, onEnterFrame);
    }

    private function onEnterFrame(event:Event):void
    {
        var dx:Number = mouseX - segment1.x;
        var dy:Number = mouseY - segment1.y;
        var dist:Number = Math.sqrt(dx * dx + dy * dy);

        var a:Number = 100;
        var b:Number = 100;
        var c:Number = Math.min(dist, a + b);

        var B:Number = Math.acos((b * b - a * a - c * c) /
                                (-2 * a * c));
        var C:Number = Math.acos((c * c - a * a - b * b) /
                                (-2 * a * b));
        var D:Number = Math.atan2(dy, dx);
        var E:Number = D + B + Math.PI + C;

        segment1.rotation = (D + B) * 180 / Math.PI;

        segment0.x = segment1.getPin().x;
        segment0.y = segment1.getPin().y;
        segment0.rotation = E * 180 / Math.PI;
    }
  }
}
```

Here's the procedure:

1. Get the distance from segment1 to the mouse.

2. Get the three sides' lengths. Sides a and b are easy. They are equal to 100, since that's how long we made the segments. (You can remove the magic number 100 and make the code more dynamic; I'm just trying to keep things simple.) Side c is equal to dist or a + b, whichever is smaller. This is because one side of a triangle can't be longer than the other two sides added together. If you don't believe me, try to draw such a shape. This also gets back into the reaching paradigm. If the distance from the base to the mouse is 200, but the length of the two segments adds up to only 120, it just isn't going to make it.

3. Figure out angles B and C using the law of cosines formula, and angle D using `Math.atan2`. E, as mentioned, is D + B + 180 + C. Of course, in code, you substitute `Math.PI` radians for 180 degrees.

4. Just as the diagram in Figure 14-9 shows, convert angle D + B to degrees, and that's seg1's rotation. Use the same angle to find the end point of seg1 and position seg0 on it.

5. Finally, seg0's rotation is E, converted to degrees.

There you have it: inverse kinematics using the law of cosines. You might notice that the joint always bends the same way. This might be good if you're building something like an elbow or a knee that can bend only one way.

When you're figuring out the angles analytically like this, there are two solutions to the problem: It could bend this way, or it could bend that way. You've hard-coded it to bend one way by *adding* D and B, and then *adding* C. If you subtracted them all, you'd get the same effect, but the limb would bend in the other direction.

```
private function onEnterFrame(event:Event):void
{
    var dx:Number = mouseX - segment1.x;
    var dy:Number = mouseY - segment1.y;
    var dist:Number = Math.sqrt(dx * dx + dy * dy);

    var a:Number = 100;
    var b:Number = 100;
    var c:Number = Math.min(dist, a + b);

    var B:Number = Math.acos((b * b - a * a - c * c) / (-2 * a * c));
    var C:Number = Math.acos((c * c - a * a - b * b) / (-2 * a * b));
    var D:Number = Math.atan2(dy, dx);
    var E:Number = D - B + Math.PI - C;

    segment1.rotation = (D - B) * 180 / Math.PI;

    segment0.x = segment1.getPin().x;
    segment0.y = segment1.getPin().y;
    segment0.rotation = E * 180 / Math.PI;
}
```

If you want it to bend either way, you'll need to figure out some kind of conditional logic to say, "If it's in this position, bend this way; otherwise, bend that way." Unfortunately, I have only enough space to give you this brief introduction to the law of cosines method. But if this is the kind of thing you're interested in doing, I'm sure you'll be able to find plenty of additional data on the subject. A quick web search for "inverse kinematics" just gave me more than 90,000 results. So yeah, you'll be able to dig up something!

Important formulas in this chapter

For the standard form of inverse kinematics, you use the law of cosines formula.

Law of cosines:

$$a^2 = b^2 + c^2 - 2 * b * c * \cos A$$
$$b^2 = a^2 + c^2 - 2 * a * c * \cos B$$
$$c^2 = a^2 + b^2 - 2 * a * b * \cos C$$

Law of cosines in ActionScript:

```
A = Math.acos((b * b + c * c - a * a) / (2 * b * c));
B = Math.acos((a * a + c * c - b * b) / (2 * a * c));
C = Math.acos((a * a + b * b - c * c) / (2 * a * b));
```

Summary

Inverse kinematics is a vast subject—far more than could ever be covered in a single chapter. Even so, I think this chapter described some pretty cool and useful things. You saw how to set up an inverse kinematics system and two ways of looking at it: dragging and reaching. If nothing else, I hope I've at least sparked some excitement in you for the subject. The main ideas I've tried to convey are that you can do some really fun stuff with it, and it doesn't have to be all that complex. There's much more that can be done in Flash with inverse kinematics, and I'm sure that you're now ready to go discover it and put it to use.

In the next chapter, you're going to enter a whole new dimension, which will allow you to add some depth to your movies. Yes, we're going 3D.

Part Four

3D ANIMATION

Chapter 15

3D BASICS

What we'll cover in this chapter:

- The third dimension and perspective
- Velocity and acceleration
- Bouncing
- Gravity
- Wrapping
- Easing and springing
- Coordinate rotation
- Collision detection
- Important formulas in this chapter

Everything you've done so far in the book has been in just two (and sometimes only one) dimension, and you've done some pretty cool stuff. Now, let's take it to the next level.

Creating graphics in 3D is always exciting. That extra dimension seems to make things really come to life. How to do 3D in Flash has been covered in innumerable books and tutorials. So, while I don't plan on skimping on anything, I'm going to move through the basics pretty quickly. After that, I'll explain how the motion effects discussed in the previous chapters can be done with a third dimension. Specifically, this chapter covers velocity, acceleration, friction, gravity, bouncing, wrapping, easing, springing, coordinate rotation, and collision detection.

For now, you'll primarily be concerned with taking a sprite and moving it around in 3D space, using perspective to calculate its size and position on the screen. The sprite itself will be flat, of course. It won't have a back, side, top, or bottom that you can see. In the next couple of chapters, you'll do some modeling of points, lines, shapes, and solids in 3D.

The third dimension and perspective

It goes without saying that the main concept behind 3D is the existence of another dimension beyond x and y. This is the dimension of depth, and it is usually labeled z.

Flash does not have a built-in z dimension, but it isn't too difficult to create one with ActionScript. It's actually far less complex than a lot of the stuff you've just done in the previous chapters!

The z axis

To begin with, you need to decide which direction the z axis is going to go: in or out. Let me explain. If you recall back to Chapter 3's discussion of Flash's coordinate system, you'll remember that it is in some ways opposite to most other common coordinate systems. The y axis goes down instead of up, and angles are measured clockwise instead of counterclockwise.

So, should you make the z axis so that as an object's z position increases, it is going away from you or toward you? Neither way is necessarily more *correct* than the other. In fact, this subject has been addressed enough times that there are even names to describe the two methods: left-hand system and right-hand system.

Take your right hand and form an *L* with your thumb and forefinger, and then bend your middle finger 90 degrees from your index finger, each one will be pointing in another dimension. Now point your index finger in the direction the positive x axis goes, and your middle finger in the direction of the positive y axis. In a right-hand system, your thumb will now be pointing in the direction of the positive z axis. For Flash, this means the z axis will increase as it goes away from the viewer, and decrease as it goes toward the viewer, as shown in Figure 15-1.

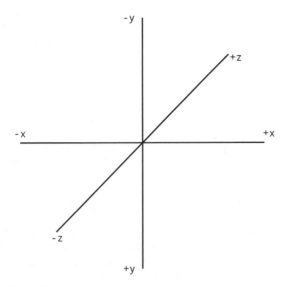

Figure 15-1. Right-hand coordinate system

If you try it with your left hand, you'll get the opposite result. Figure 15-2 shows the left-hand coordinate system.

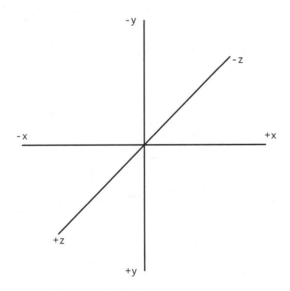

Figure 15-2. Left-hand coordinate system

I use the right-hand coordinate system (Figure 15-1) for the examples here. There's no reason that you couldn't make a left-hand system, but it seems to fall together a little better to make the z axis go in.

The next step in creating a third (z) dimension in Flash is to figure out how to simulate perspective.

Perspective

Perspective is how we tell if something is closer to us or farther away. Or, to put it another way, how we make something look like it is closer or farther. While the field of fine arts has a number of techniques for presenting perspective, I'll be concentrating on two here:

- Things get smaller as they get farther away.
- Things converge on a vanishing point as they get farther away.

I won't beat the point to death—I'm sure you've seen enough examples of train tracks coming to a point on the horizon. So basically, when you move something on the z axis, you need to do two things:

- Scale it up or down.
- Move it closer to or further away from the vanishing point.

In working with only two dimensions, you can generally get away with using the screen x and y coordinates for your object's x and y position. You just do a one-to-one mapping. This isn't going to work in 3D, because two objects can have the same x and y position, and yet, due to their depth, have a different position on the screen. So, each object you move in 3D will need to have its own x, y, and z coordinates that have nothing to do with the screen position. These now describe a location in virtual space. The perspective calculation will tell you where to put the object on the screen.

The perspective formula

The basic idea is that as something gets further away (z increases), its scale approaches 0 and its x, y position converges on the 0, 0 of the vanishing point. The good news is that the ratio of distance to scale is the same as the ratio of distance to convergence. So, you just need to figure out what that ratio is for a given distance and use it in both places. The diagram in Figure 15-3 helps to explain this concept.

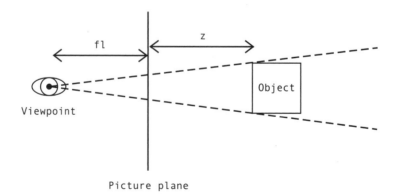

Figure 15-3. Perspective seen from the side

You have an object off in the distance. You have a viewpoint: your eyes. And you have a picture plane, which you can consider the computer screen. You have the distance of the object to the picture plane, which is the z value, and, finally, you have the distance from the viewpoint to the picture point. This last one is the key. It's not exactly the same as the focal length of a camera lens, but it is analogous, so I usually use the variable fl to represent it.

Here's the formula:

```
scale = fl / (fl + z)
```

This will usually yield a number between 0.0 and 1.0, which is your ratio for scaling and converging on the vanishing point. However, as z goes negative, fl + z approaches 0 and scale approaches infinity. This is the ActionScript equivalent to being poked in the eye.

So, what do you do with this scale value? Well, assuming you are dealing with a sprite (or subclass of the Sprite class), you assign that value to the sprite's scaleX and scaleY. You then multiply the object's x and y position by this factor to find its screen x and y position.

Let's look at an example. Usual values of fl are around 200 to 300. Let's use 250. If z is zero—in other words, the object is exactly on the picture plane—then scale will be 250 / (250 + 0). This comes out to exactly 1.0. That's your scaleX and scaleY (remember that for scaleX and scaleY, 1.0 means 100%). Multiplying 1.0 by the object's x and y positions gives the same numbers back as a result, so the object's screen position is exactly equal to its x and y.

Now move it out so that z is 250. That makes scale 250 / (250 + 250), or 0.5 for scaleX and scaleY. It also moves the object's screen position. If the object were at 200, 300 on x, y, its screen position would now be 100, 150. So, it has moved halfway to the vanishing point. (Actually, the screen position would be in relation to the vanishing point, which you'll see shortly.)

Now, move z way out to 9750. This makes scale 250 / 10000, or 0.025 for scaleX and scaleY. The object will become just a speck, very close to the vanishing point.

OK, enough theory. Time for some code.

Perspective in ActionScript

As you might have guessed, I'm going to use the Ball class again. Of course, you are free to use whatever you want as an object, but I'm going to concentrate on the code and leave the cool graphics to you. For interaction, let's get fancy and use the mouse *and* keyboard. You'll use the mouse to control the ball's x and y position, and the up and down keys to move it forward and back on the z axis. Note that because the variables x and y are now taken by ActionScript, we'll use xpos, ypos, and zpos to represent the 3D position.

Here's the code for document class Perspective1.as:

```
package {
    import flash.display.Sprite;
    import flash.events.Event;
    import flash.events.KeyboardEvent;
    import flash.ui.Keyboard;

    public class Perspective1 extends Sprite
    {
        private var ball:Ball;
```

```
private var xpos:Number = 0;
private var ypos:Number = 0;
private var zpos:Number = 0;
private var fl:Number = 250;
private var vpX:Number = stage.stageWidth / 2;
private var vpY:Number = stage.stageHeight / 2;

public function Perspective1()
{
    init();
}

private function init():void
{
    ball = new Ball();
    addChild(ball);
    addEventListener(Event.ENTER_FRAME, onEnterFrame);
    stage.addEventListener(KeyboardEvent.KEY_DOWN, onKeyDown);
}

private function onEnterFrame(event:Event):void
{
    xpos = mouseX - vpX;
    ypos = mouseY - vpY;
    var scale:Number = fl / (fl + zpos);
    ball.scaleX = ball.scaleY = scale;
    ball.x = vpX + xpos * scale;
    ball.y = vpY + ypos * scale;
}

private function onKeyDown(event:KeyboardEvent):void
{
    if(event.keyCode == Keyboard.UP)
    {
        zpos += 5;
    }
    else if(event.keyCode == Keyboard.DOWN)
    {
        zpos -= 5;
    }
}
}
}
```

First, you create variables for xpos, ypos, and zpos, as well as fl. Then you create a vanishing point, vpX, vpY. Remember that as things go off in the distance, they converge on 0, 0. If you don't offset this somehow, everything will converge at the top-left corner of the screen, which is not what you want. You'll use vpX, vpY to make the center of the stage the vanishing point.

Next, in onEnterFrame, set xpos and ypos to equal the mouse position, as offset by the vanishing point. In other words, if the mouse is 200 pixels right of center, x will be 200. If it's 200 pixels left of center, x will be −200.

Then add a listener for the keyDown event and change zpos accordingly. If the up key is being pressed, zpos increases, and pressing the down key decreases it. This will make the ball move farther from or closer to the viewer.

Finally, calculate scale using the formula I just covered, and size and position the ball accordingly. Note that the screen x and y positions of the ball are calculated from the vanishing point, adding on the xpos and ypos times the scale. Thus, as scale becomes very small, the ball will converge on the vanishing point.

When you test it, at first it looks like you're simply dragging the ball with the mouse. This is because zpos is zero, making scale 1.0. So, no noticeable perspective is being applied. As you press the up cursor key, the ball appears to slide into the distance, as shown in Figure 15-4. Now as you move the mouse around, the ball moves with it, but much less, giving you a parallax effect.

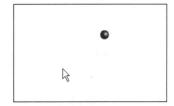

Figure 15-4. Perspective in action

One thing you might notice is that if you hold down the cursor key too long, the ball starts getting very large. This is fine. If you held a pebble up close to your eye, it would look like a boulder. If you keep holding the key down, though, you'll see that it grows to an infinite size and then shrinks down again, but now it's upside down and reversed. What has happened is that the ball has gone behind the viewpoint. So, I guess this must be what you would see if your eyes could look behind you.

Mathematically, what happens is that when zpos is equal to -fl, the formula scale = fl / (fl + zpos) becomes scale = fl / 0. In many languages, dividing by zero gives you an error. In Flash, it gives you Infinity. As you decrease zpos even more, you're now dividing fl by a negative number. Scale becomes negative, which is why your ball goes upside down and backward.

How can you handle this? A simple way is to just make the ball invisible if it goes past a certain point. If zpos is less than or equal to -fl, you'll have a problem, so you can test for that condition and handle it in the following enterFrame handler from Perspective2.as (the rest of the class is the same as Perspective1.as):

```
private function onEnterFrame(event:Event):void
{
    if(zpos > -fl)
    {
        xpos = mouseX - vpX;
        ypos = mouseY - vpY;
        var scale:Number = fl / (fl + zpos);
        ball.scaleX = ball.scaleY = scale;
        ball.x = vpX + xpos * scale;
        ball.y = vpY + ypos * scale;
        ball.visible = true;
    }
    else
```

```
        {
            ball.visible = false;
        }
    }
```

Note that if the ball is not visible, you don't need to worry about scaling and positioning it. Also note that if the ball is in visible range, you need to make sure it is visible. It adds a little extra overhead, but it's necessary overall.

Well, there you have it, the barebones basics of 3D. Not so painful, is it? Make sure you play around with this example a bit to get a good feel for it. In particular, try changing the value for fl and see the different effects you get. This is equivalent to changing the lens of a camera. High values for fl are like a telephoto lens, giving you a small field of view, with less visible perspective. A low fl value will create a wide-angle lens, with exaggerated perspective.

The rest of the chapter is devoted to ActionScripting the various motion effects covered in previous chapters, but now in 3D.

Velocity and acceleration

Accomplishing velocity and acceleration in 3D is surprisingly easy. For 2D, you had vx and vy variables to represent velocity on two axes. You just need to add a vz for the third dimension. Similarly, if you have something like ax and ay for acceleration, you just add an az variable.

You can alter the last example to make it work sort of like the *Asteroids* spaceship, but in 3D. Let's make it all keyboard-controlled now. Cursor keys can provide thrust on the x and y axes, and we'll grab a couple other keys, say Shift and Ctrl, for z thrust.

Here's the code (which you'll also find in Velocity3D.as):

```
package {
    import flash.display.Sprite;
    import flash.events.Event;
    import flash.events.KeyboardEvent;
    import flash.ui.Keyboard;

    public class Velocity3D extends Sprite
    {
        private var ball:Ball;
        private var xpos:Number = 0;
        private var ypos:Number = 0;
        private var zpos:Number = 0;
        private var vx:Number = 0;
        private var vy:Number = 0;
        private var vz:Number = 0;
        private var friction:Number = .98;
        private var fl:Number = 250;
        private var vpX:Number = stage.stageWidth / 2;
        private var vpY:Number = stage.stageHeight / 2;
```

```
public function Velocity3D()
{
    init();
}

private function init():void
{
    ball = new Ball();
    addChild(ball);
    addEventListener(Event.ENTER_FRAME, onEnterFrame);
    stage.addEventListener(KeyboardEvent.KEY_DOWN, onKeyDown);
}

private function onEnterFrame(event:Event):void
{
    xpos += vx;
    ypos += vy;
    zpos += vz;

    vx *= friction;
    vy *= friction;
    vz *= friction;

    if(zpos > -fl)
    {
        var scale:Number = fl / (fl + zpos);
        ball.scaleX = ball.scaleY = scale;
        ball.x = vpX + xpos * scale;
        ball.y = vpY + ypos * scale;
        ball.visible = true;
    }
    else
    {
        ball.visible = false;
    }
}

private function onKeyDown(event:KeyboardEvent):void
{
    switch(event.keyCode)
    {
        case Keyboard.UP :
        vy -= 1;
        break;

        case Keyboard.DOWN :
        vy += 1;
        break;
```

```
                    case Keyboard.LEFT :
                    vx -= 1;
                    break;

                    case Keyboard.RIGHT :
                    vx += 1;
                    break;

                    case Keyboard.SHIFT :
                    vz += 1;
                    break;

                    case Keyboard.CONTROL :
                    vz -= 1;
                    break;

                    default :
                    break;
                }
            }
        }
    }
```

All you've done here is add variables for velocity on each axis and some friction. When one of the six keys is pressed, it adds or subtracts from the appropriate velocity (remember that acceleration changes velocity). Then it adds the velocity to the position on each axis and computes friction.

Now you have a 3D object moving with acceleration, velocity, and friction. Wow, three birds with one stone. I told you it was easy.

Bouncing

For the purposes of this section, I'll be talking about bouncing off a flat surface—in other words, one that aligns perfectly with the x, y, or z axis. This is analogous to the bouncing off the sides of the screen you did in 2D.

Single object bouncing

With bouncing in 3D, again you detect when the object has gone past a boundary, adjust it to sit on that boundary, and then reverse its velocity on the appropriate axis. One of the differences with 3D is in how you decide where the boundaries are. In 2D, you generally use the stage coordinates or some other visible rectangular area. In 3D, things aren't quite so simple. There is no real concept of a visible edge, unless you draw one in 3D. You'll get to drawing in 3D in the next chapter, so for now, you'll be bouncing off arbitrarily placed invisible walls.

So, you set up your boundaries the same as before, but now you are setting them up in a 3D space, which means that they can be negative as well as positive. You also have the option of setting up a boundary on the z axis. The boundaries look something like this:

```
    private var top:Number = -250;
    private var bottom:Number = 250;
    private var left:Number = -250;
    private var right:Number = 250;
    private var front:Number = 250;
    private var back:Number = -250;
```

Then, after determining the object's new position, you need to check it against all six boundaries. Remember that you take half of the object's width into account in checking for the collision, and that you've already stored that value in a property of the Ball class called radius. Here's the full code for 3D bouncing (which also appears in Bounce3D.as):

```
package {
    import flash.display.Sprite;
    import flash.events.Event;

    public class Bounce3D extends Sprite
    {
        private var ball:Ball;
        private var xpos:Number = 0;
        private var ypos:Number = 0;
        private var zpos:Number = 0;
        private var vx:Number = Math.random() * 10 - 5;
        private var vy:Number = Math.random() * 10 - 5;
        private var vz:Number = Math.random() * 10 - 5;
        private var fl:Number = 250;
        private var vpX:Number = stage.stageWidth / 2;
        private var vpY:Number = stage.stageHeight / 2;
        private var top:Number = -100;
        private var bottom:Number = 100;
        private var left:Number = -100;
        private var right:Number = 100;
        private var front:Number = 100;
        private var back:Number = -100;

        public function Bounce3D()
        {
            init();
        }

        private function init():void
        {
            ball = new Ball(15);
            addChild(ball);
            addEventListener(Event.ENTER_FRAME, onEnterFrame);
        }
```

```
private function onEnterFrame(event:Event):void
{
    xpos += vx;
    ypos += vy;
    zpos += vz;

    var radius:Number =  ball.radius;
    if(xpos + radius > right)
    {
        xpos = right - radius;
        vx *= -1;
    }
    else if(xpos - radius < left)
    {
        xpos = left + radius;
        vx *= -1;
    }
    if(ypos + radius > bottom)
    {
        ypos = bottom - radius;
        vy *= -1;
    }
    else if(ypos - radius < top)
    {
        ypos = top + radius;
        vy *= -1;
    }
    if(zpos + radius > front)
    {
        zpos = front - radius;
        vz *= -1;
    }
    else if(zpos - radius < back)
    {
        zpos = back + radius;
        vz *= -1;
    }

    if(zpos > -fl)
    {
        var scale:Number = fl / (fl + zpos);
        ball.scaleX = ball.scaleY = scale;
        ball.x = vpX + xpos * scale;
        ball.y = vpY + ypos * scale;
        ball.visible = true;
    }
    else
    {
```

```
                ball.visible = false;
            }
        }
    }
}
```

Note that I removed all of the key-handling stuff and just gave the ball a random velocity on each axis. Now you can see it is definitely bouncing around, but you can't really tell what it is bouncing against— as I said, these are arbitrarily placed invisible boundaries.

Multiple object bouncing

One thing you could do to help visualize the walls a little better would be to fill up the space with more objects. To do this, we'll need multiple instances of the Ball class. But then each instance will need its own xpos, ypos, zpos, and velocities on each axis as well. It could get messy trying to keep track of all of that in the main class, so I've created a new class, Ball3D, which you can see here:

```
package {
    import flash.display.Sprite;

    public class Ball3D extends Sprite {
        public var radius:Number;
        private var color:uint;
        public var xpos:Number = 0;
        public var ypos:Number = 0;
        public var zpos:Number = 0;
        public var vx:Number = 0;
        public var vy:Number = 0;
        public var vz:Number = 0;
        public var mass:Number = 1;

        public function Ball3D(radius:Number=40, color:uint=0xff0000) {
            this.radius = radius;
            this.color = color;
            init();
        }
        public function init():void {
            graphics.beginFill(color);
            graphics.drawCircle(0, 0, radius);
            graphics.endFill();
        }
    }
}
```

As you can see, all this does is add properties for position and velocity on each axis. Again, just throwing on public properties to a class is a pretty bad practice for object-oriented programming, but we'll just keep things simple for now, to demonstrate the formulas. In MultiBounce3D.as, I've created 50 instances of this new class. Each one now has its own xpos, ypos, and zpos, and vx, vy, vz. The onEnterFrame method now loops through, gets a reference to each Ball3D, and passes it to a move method. This method does the same thing to each ball that the original onEnterFrame code did to just one. Here's the code (which you'll also find in MultiBounce3D.as):

```
package {
    import flash.display.Sprite;
    import flash.events.Event;

    public class MultiBounce3D extends Sprite
    {
        private var balls:Array;
        private var numBalls:uint = 50;
        private var fl:Number = 250;
        private var vpX:Number = stage.stageWidth / 2;
        private var vpY:Number = stage.stageHeight / 2;
        private var top:Number = -100;
        private var bottom:Number = 100;
        private var left:Number = -100;
        private var right:Number = 100;
        private var front:Number = 100;
        private var back:Number = -100;

        public function MultiBounce3D()
        {
            init();
        }

        private function init():void
        {
            balls = new Array();
            for(var i:uint = 0; i < numBalls; i++)
            {
                var ball:Ball3D = new Ball3D(15);
                balls.push(ball);
                ball.vx = Math.random() * 10 - 5;
                ball.vy = Math.random() * 10 - 5;
                ball.vz = Math.random() * 10 - 5;
                addChild(ball);
            }
            addEventListener(Event.ENTER_FRAME, onEnterFrame);
        }

        private function onEnterFrame(event:Event):void
        {
            for(var i:uint = 0; i < numBalls; i++)
            {
                var ball:Ball3D = balls[i];
                move(ball);
            }
        }
```

```
private function move(ball:Ball3D):void
{
    var radius:Number =  ball.radius;

    ball.xpos += ball.vx;
    ball.ypos += ball.vy;
    ball.zpos += ball.vz;

    if(ball.xpos + radius > right)
    {
        ball.xpos = right - radius;
        ball.vx *= -1;
    }
    else if(ball.xpos - radius < left)
    {
        ball.xpos = left + radius;
        ball.vx *= -1;
    }
    if(ball.ypos + radius > bottom)
    {
        ball.ypos = bottom - radius;
        ball.vy *= -1;
    }
    else if(ball.ypos - radius < top)
    {
        ball.ypos = top + radius;
        ball.vy *= -1;
    }
    if(ball.zpos + radius > front)
    {
        ball.zpos = front - radius;
        ball.vz *= -1;
    }
    else if(ball.zpos - radius < back)
    {
        ball.zpos = back + radius;
        ball.vz *= -1;
    }

    if(ball.zpos > -fl)
    {
        var scale:Number = fl / (fl + ball.zpos);
        ball.scaleX = ball.scaleY = scale;
        ball.x = vpX + ball.xpos * scale;
        ball.y = vpY + ball.ypos * scale;
        ball.visible = true;
    }
    else
    {
```

```
                                        ball.visible = false;
                        }
                    }
                }
            }
```

When you run this file, the balls largely fill up the space between the six boundaries, as shown in Figure 15-5, and you can get an idea of the shape of this space.

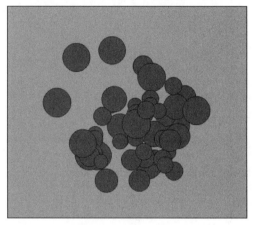

Figure 15-5. Bouncing 3D balls

Z-sorting

Now, this addition of multiple objects brings up an issue lacking in the code you have so far—something called *z-sorting*. Z-sorting is pretty much what it sounds like: how things are sorted on the z axis, or which one goes in front of another one. It's actually not very apparent right now, due to the fact that the objects we are using are a flat color. To make it a little more apparent, change the Ball3D's init method to the following, and run the last example again:

```
public function init():void {
    graphics.lineStyle(0);
    graphics.beginFill(color);
    graphics.drawCircle(0, 0, radius);
    graphics.endFill();
}
```

By adding an outline to the ball, you can see which ball is on top of which. This pretty much ruins the whole 3D effect, as smaller objects are now appearing in front of larger ones. Z-sorting handles this, but it's not automatic. Flash doesn't know that you are simulating 3D. It just knows that you're moving and scaling sprites. And it certainly doesn't know whether you're using a left-hand or right-hand coordinate system. So, it has no idea that because this ball is farther away, it should appear behind this other one that is closer. It just sorts them according to their relative indexes in the display list.

In AS 2, z-sorting was easily handled by changing the depth of the movie clip with movieClip. swapDepths(depth). Movie clips with a higher depth appeared in front of ones with a lower depth.

In AS 3, however, things are a bit more complex. There isn't a special depth value for display objects that can be arbitrarily set. The display list works more like an array. Each display object on the list has an index. The indexes start at zero, and go up to the number of objects on that part of the list. For example, say you added three sprites, A, B, and C, to your class. They would be at indexes 0, 1, and 2. There is no way, for instance, to place one of them at index 100, much less –100. Furthermore, if you removed sprite B, sprites A and C would now be at indexes 0 and 1. You get the idea. There are never any "spaces" in the list.

In terms of depth, index 0 is the bottom, and any display objects with a higher number will appear in front of objects with a lower number. You can change depths of objects with a few different methods:

- setChildIndex(child:DisplayObject, index:int) moves the specified object to the specified index. Simple.

- swapChildren(child1:DisplayObject, child2:DisplayObject) switches the two specified objects.

- swapChildrenAt(index1:int, index2:int) switches whatever two objects happen to be at the specified indexes.

The easiest one for your use is setChildIndex. You already have all the balls in an array. If you can sort that array from the highest depth (furthest away) to lowest (closest), you can then run through it and set the indexes for each of the balls from 0 (again, farthest away) to 49 (again, closest). The following method does just that:

```
private function sortZ():void
{
    balls.sortOn("zpos", Array.DESCENDING | Array.NUMERIC);
    for(var i:uint = 0; i < numBalls; i++)
    {
        var ball:Ball3D = balls[i];
        setChildIndex(ball, i);
    }
}
```

This sorts the array based on the zpos property of each object in it. Because it specifies Array. DESCENDING and Array.NUMERIC, it will sort it in reverse numerical order—in other words, high to low. The result is that the ball that is furthest away (highest zpos value) will be first in the array, and the closest one will be last.

Then it loops through the array, setting the display list index for each ball to the same order they now have in the array.

Once this method is in the class, you just need to call it after you've moved all the balls, right at the end of the onEnterFrame method:

```
private function onEnterFrame(event:Event):void
{
    for(var i:uint = 0; i < numBalls; i++)
    {
        var ball:Ball3D = balls[i];
        move(ball);
    }
    sortZ();
}
```

The rest of the code remains the same as the last example. The full code can be found in Zsort.as.

Gravity

I should mention that here I'm talking about simple gravity as seen from the earth's surface, and as described in Chapter 5. In this case, gravity works pretty much the same in 3D as it does in 2D. All you need to do is choose a number for the force gravity is exerting on the object, and add that number to the object's y velocity on each frame or iteration.

Since gravity in 3D is so simple, I could be tempted to gloss it over and say, "Yup, same as 2D. OK, next subject." But I decided to throw in a nice example that demonstrates how something so simple can create a really great effect, like 3D fireworks.

To start with, you need an object to represent a single "firework"—you know, one of those dots of glowing light that can be combined with others to make a big explosion. Our trusty Ball3D class, with a smaller radius, will serve the purpose just fine. We'll just make each one a random color for a nice display. It will also help if you make your movie's background black. I did this in the class with a SWF metadata statement, but if you are working in the Flash CS3 IDE, you can simply set the background color in the document properties.

Since I'm sure you can handle it by now, I'm going to dump the entire code listing on you (Fireworks.as), and then explain it.

```
package {
    import flash.display.Sprite;
    import flash.events.Event;

    [SWF(backgroundColor=0x000000)]
    public class Fireworks extends Sprite
    {
        private var balls:Array;
        private var numBalls:uint = 100;
        private var fl:Number = 250;
        private var vpX:Number = stage.stageWidth / 2;
        private var vpY:Number = stage.stageHeight / 2;
```

```
private var gravity:Number = 0.2;
private var floor:Number = 200;
private var bounce:Number = -0.6;

public function Fireworks()
{
    init();
}

private function init():void
{
    balls = new Array();
    for(var i:uint = 0; i < numBalls; i++)
    {
        var ball:Ball3D = new Ball3D(3, Math.random() *
                                       0xffffff);
        balls.push(ball);
        ball.ypos = -100;
        ball.vx = Math.random() * 6 - 3;
        ball.vy = Math.random() * 6 - 6;
        ball.vz = Math.random() * 6 - 3;
        addChild(ball);
    }
    addEventListener(Event.ENTER_FRAME, onEnterFrame);
}

private function onEnterFrame(event:Event):void
{
    for(var i:uint = 0; i < numBalls; i++)
    {
        var ball:Ball3D = balls[i];
        move(ball);
    }
    sortZ();
}

private function move(ball:Ball3D):void
{
    ball.vy += gravity;
    ball.xpos += ball.vx;
    ball.ypos += ball.vy;
    ball.zpos += ball.vz;

    if(ball.ypos > floor)
    {
        ball.ypos = floor;
        ball.vy *= bounce;
    }
```

```
            if(ball.zpos > -fl)
            {
                var scale:Number = fl / (fl + ball.zpos);
                ball.scaleX = ball.scaleY = scale;
                ball.x = vpX + ball.xpos * scale;
                ball.y = vpY + ball.ypos * scale;
                ball.visible = true;
            }
            else
            {
                ball.visible = false;
            }
        }

        private function sortZ():void
        {
            balls.sortOn("zpos", Array.DESCENDING | Array.NUMERIC);
            for(var i:uint = 0; i < numBalls; i++)
            {
                var ball:Ball3D = balls[i];
                setChildIndex(ball, i);
            }
        }
    }
}
```

First, add a few properties: gravity, bounce, and floor. The first two you should know by now. The floor property is just that—the bottom-most y value that the objects can hit before they bounce.

Other than the one line that adds gravity to each ball's vy property, and the bouncing when each one hits the floor, there's not a whole lot going on here that we haven't covered, but things are starting to look pretty cool, huh?

The result looks something like Figure 15-6.

Figure 15-6. Fireworks! (Trust me, it looks much better in motion.)

Wrapping

If you can remember back to Chapter 6, I talked about three possible reactions when an object hits a boundary. I just covered bouncing. There was also wrapping and regeneration. For 3D, I have found wrapping to be pretty useful, but really only on the z axis.

In 2D wrapping, you check whether the object went off the screen on the x or y axes. This works pretty well, because when the object goes beyond one of those boundaries, you can't see it anymore, so you can easily reposition it without jarring the viewer's attention. You don't have that luxury in 3D.

With 3D, there are really only two points where it's safe to remove and reposition an object. One is when the object has gone behind the viewpoint. The previous examples test for this and turn the object invisible in such a case. The other is when the object is so far in the distance and shrunk to such a small size that it's invisible or nearly so. This means that you can safely wrap on the z axis. When something goes behind you, you toss it way out in front of you, and let it come at you again. Or, if something has gone so far out that you can barely see it, remove it and replace it behind you. If you want, you can try wrapping on the x or y axis as well, but in most cases, you're going to wind up with an unnatural popping in and out of existence effect.

The good news is that z-axis wrapping can be pretty useful. I've used it to create a realistic 3D racing-type game, which I'll partially re-create here.

The idea is to place various 3D objects out in front of the viewpoint. Then you move those objects toward the viewpoint. In other words, you give them some negative z velocity. Depending on how you set it up, this can either look like a lot of objects coming toward you or it can trick the eye to look like you're moving toward the objects. Once an object has gone behind the viewpoint, you'll replace it way out in the distance. That way, there is a never-ending supply of objects to drive past.

The objects I used in this example are simple stylized trees, creating a basic tree structure with randomized branch positions. I'm sure you can do better!

The code to draw the tree is in a class named Tree, which, as you can see here, simply has the three position properties and code to draw a somewhat random stick figure tree.

```
package {
    import flash.display.Sprite;

    public class Tree extends Sprite {
        public var xpos:Number = 0;
        public var ypos:Number = 0;
        public var zpos:Number = 0;

        public function Tree() {
            init();
        }
        public function init():void {
            graphics.lineStyle(0, 0xffffff);
            graphics.lineTo(0, -140 - Math.random() * 20);
            graphics.moveTo(0, -30 - Math.random() * 30);
            graphics.lineTo(Math.random() * 80 - 40,
                            -100 - Math.random() * 40);
            graphics.moveTo(0, -60 - Math.random() * 40);
            graphics.lineTo(Math.random() * 60 - 30,
                            -110 - Math.random() * 20);
        }
    }
}
```

Again, I went with white on a black background, using SWF metadata for the background color. But you can make any kind of objects you want, and make them as complex as you want. The document class merely creates a whole bunch (100 to be exact) of these trees. They are spread out randomly on the x axis, 1,000 pixels in either direction. They are also spread out on the z axis, from 0 to 10,000. They all have the same y position though, based on the floor property, which gives the impression of a ground plane.

Here's the code (which you can also find in Trees.as):

```
package {
    import flash.display.Sprite;
    import flash.events.Event;
    import flash.events.KeyboardEvent;
    import flash.ui.Keyboard;

    [SWF(backgroundColor=0x000000)]
    public class Trees extends Sprite
    {
        private var trees:Array;
        private var numTrees:uint = 100;
```

```
private var fl:Number = 250;
private var vpX:Number = stage.stageWidth / 2;
private var vpY:Number = stage.stageHeight / 2;
private var floor:Number = 50;
private var vz:Number = 0;
private var friction:Number = 0.98;

public function Trees()
{
    init();
}

private function init():void
{
    trees = new Array();
    for(var i:uint = 0; i < numTrees; i++)
    {
        var tree:Tree = new Tree();
        trees.push(tree);
        tree.xpos = Math.random() * 2000 - 1000;
        tree.ypos = floor;
        tree.zpos = Math.random() * 10000;
        addChild(tree);
    }
    addEventListener(Event.ENTER_FRAME, onEnterFrame);
    stage.addEventListener(KeyboardEvent.KEY_DOWN, onKeyDown);
}

private function onEnterFrame(event:Event):void
{
    for(var i:uint = 0; i < numTrees; i++)
    {
        var tree:Tree = trees[i];
        move(tree);
    }
    vz *= friction;
    sortZ();
}

private function onKeyDown(event:KeyboardEvent):void
{
    if(event.keyCode == Keyboard.UP)
    {
        vz -= 1;
    }
    else if(event.keyCode == Keyboard.DOWN)
    {
        vz += 1;
    }
}
```

```
private function move(tree:Tree):void
{
    tree.zpos += vz;

    if(tree.zpos < -fl)
    {
        tree.zpos += 10000;
    }
    if(tree.zpos > 10000 - fl)
    {
        tree.zpos -= 10000;
    }

    var scale:Number = fl / (fl + tree.zpos);
    tree.scaleX = tree.scaleY = scale;
    tree.x = vpX + tree.xpos * scale;
    tree.y = vpY + tree.ypos * scale;
    tree.alpha = scale;
}

private function sortZ():void
{
    trees.sortOn("zpos", Array.DESCENDING | Array.NUMERIC);
    for(var i:uint = 0; i < numTrees; i++)
    {
        var tree:Tree = trees[i];
        setChildIndex(tree, i);
    }
}
    }
}
```

Notice that now there is only a single variable for z velocity, as the trees won't be moving on the x or y axis, and all will be moving in unison on the z axis. In the onEnterFrame method, you check for the up or down cursor key being pressed and increment or decrement vz accordingly. A little friction keeps the speed from increasing infinitely, and slows you down if no key is being pressed.

The code then loops through each tree, updating its z position with the current z velocity. Then it checks whether a tree has gone behind you. If so, rather than turning it invisible, it moves the tree 10,000 pixels into the z axis. Likewise, if it has gone past 10,000 – fl, it moves the tree back 10,000.

You then do the standard perspective actions. Here, I also added another little tidbit to further enhance the illusion of depth:

```
tree.alpha = scale;
```

This sets the transparency of the tree in relation to its depth on the z axis. The farther away it goes, the more it fades out. This is atmospheric perspective, simulating the effect of the atmosphere between the viewer and the object. This is particularly effective when you have objects moving way out in the distance, as in this example.

This specific calculation gives the effect of a dark, spooky night. You might want to try something like the following:

```
tree.alpha = scale * .7 + .3;
```

This will give the trees an opacity of at least 30%. Not quite so foggy. There are no right or wrong values for most of this stuff—just different values that create different effects.

You might notice also that I left the z-sorting method in there. In this particular case, it doesn't make much of a visual difference because the trees are just simple lines of the same color, but if you were to draw more complex, overlapping objects, it would be pretty vital.

You can see the result of this file in Figure 15-7.

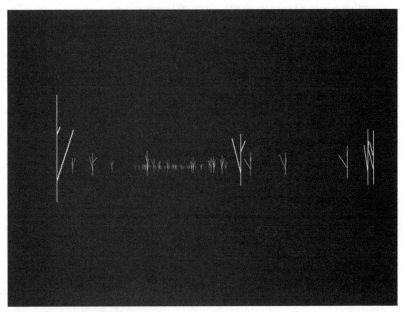

Figure 15-7. Watch out for the trees!

I liked this example so much that I added a few enhancements beyond the scope of the subject of wrapping, just to give you an idea of where this could go. Here is the result (which can also be found in Trees2.as):

```
package {
    import flash.display.Sprite;
    import flash.events.Event;
    import flash.events.KeyboardEvent;
    import flash.ui.Keyboard;

    [SWF(backgroundColor=0x000000)]
    public class Trees2 extends Sprite
    {
```

```
private var trees:Array;
private var numTrees:uint = 100;
private var fl:Number = 250;
private var vpX:Number = stage.stageWidth / 2;
private var vpY:Number = stage.stageHeight / 2;
private var floor:Number = 50;
private var ax:Number = 0;
private var ay:Number = 0;
private var az:Number = 0;
private var vx:Number = 0;
private var vy:Number = 0;
private var vz:Number = 0;
private var gravity:Number = 0.3;
private var friction:Number = 0.98;

public function Trees2()
{
    init();
}

private function init():void
{
    trees = new Array();
    for(var i:uint = 0; i < numTrees; i++)
    {
        var tree:Tree = new Tree();
        trees.push(tree);
        tree.xpos = Math.random() * 2000 - 1000;
        tree.ypos = floor;
        tree.zpos = Math.random() * 10000;
        addChild(tree);
    }
    addEventListener(Event.ENTER_FRAME, onEnterFrame);
    stage.addEventListener(KeyboardEvent.KEY_DOWN, onKeyDown);
    stage.addEventListener(KeyboardEvent.KEY_UP, onKeyUp);
}

private function onEnterFrame(event:Event):void
{
    vx += ax;
    vy += ay;
    vz += az;
    vy -= gravity;
    for(var i:uint = 0; i < numTrees; i++)
    {
        var tree:Tree = trees[i];
        move(tree);
    }
    vx *= friction;
```

```
            vy *= friction;
            vz *= friction;
        sortZ();
    }

    private function onKeyDown(event:KeyboardEvent):void
    {
        switch(event.keyCode)
        {
            case Keyboard.UP :
            az = -1;
            break;

            case Keyboard.DOWN :
            az = 1;
            break;

            case Keyboard.LEFT :
            ax = 1;
            break;

            case Keyboard.RIGHT :
            ax = -1;
            break;

            case Keyboard.SPACE :
            ay = 1;
            break;

            default :
            break;
        }
    }

    private function onKeyUp(event:KeyboardEvent):void
    {
        switch(event.keyCode)
        {
            case Keyboard.UP :
            case Keyboard.DOWN :
            az = 0;
            break;

            case Keyboard.LEFT :
            case Keyboard.RIGHT :
            ax = 0;
            break;
```

```
                    case Keyboard.SPACE :
                    ay = 0;
                    break;

                    default :
                    break;
            }
        }

        private function move(tree:Tree):void
        {
            tree.xpos += vx;
            tree.ypos += vy;
            tree.zpos += vz;

            if(tree.ypos < floor)
            {
                tree.ypos = floor;
            }

            if(tree.zpos < -fl)
            {
                tree.zpos += 10000;
            }
            if(tree.zpos > 10000 - fl)
            {
                tree.zpos -= 10000;
            }

            var scale:Number = fl / (fl + tree.zpos);
            tree.scaleX = tree.scaleY = scale;
            tree.x = vpX + tree.xpos * scale;
            tree.y = vpY + tree.ypos * scale;
            tree.alpha = scale;
        }

        private function sortZ():void
        {
            trees.sortOn("zpos", Array.DESCENDING | Array.NUMERIC);
            for(var i:uint = 0; i < numTrees; i++)
            {
                var tree:Tree = trees[i];
                setChildIndex(tree, i);
            }
        }
    }
}
```

Here, I've added velocity for the x and y axes, as well as some gravity. I also had to do some fancy foot-work to be able to catch multiple keys. One thing I really miss about AS 2 is the Key.isDown() method, which you could call at any time to find out whether a particular key was being pressed. Since we can only know the last key that was pressed or released in AS 3, I had to check which key had been pressed and set the acceleration on the appropriate axis to 1 or –1. Then when that key was released, I set the acceleration back to 0. The acceleration for each axis gets added to the velocity on that axis at the beginning of onEnterFrame. The left and right cursor keys were obvious choices for the x veloc-ity, and I used the spacebar for y. One interesting point is that I am actually *subtracting* gravity from vy. This is because I want it to seem like the *viewer* is the one who is falling down to where the trees are, as shown in Figure 15-8. Really, the trees are "falling up" to where the viewpoint is, but it winds up looking the same. Notice also that I limit the trees' y position to 50, which makes it look like you've landed on the ground.

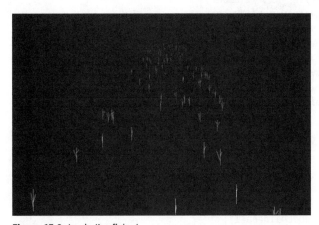

Figure 15-8. Look, I'm flying!

I didn't do anything to limit movement on the x axis, which means you can go way off to the side of the forest if you want. It wouldn't be too hard for you to set up some limitation, but I think I've done enough here to get you started.

Easing and springing

Easing and springing are also not much more complex in 3D than they are in 2D (the subject of Chapter 8). You mainly need to add in another variable or two for the z axis, and you're all set.

Easing

There's not a whole lot to cover on easing. In 2D, you have tx and ty as a target point. You just add tz for the z axis. On each frame, you measure the distance from the object to the target on each axis, and move it a fraction of the way there.

Let's look at a simple example that eases an object to a random target, and when it gets there, it picks another target and moves the object there. Note that I went back to the Ball3D class for the next couple of examples. Here's the code (which can also be found in Easing3D.as):

```
package {
    import flash.display.Sprite;
    import flash.events.Event;

    public class Easing3D extends Sprite
    {
        private var ball:Ball3D;
        private var tx:Number;
        private var ty:Number;
        private var tz:Number;
        private var easing:Number = .1;
        private var fl:Number = 250;
        private var vpX:Number = stage.stageWidth / 2;
        private var vpY:Number = stage.stageHeight / 2;

        public function Easing3D()
        {
            init();
        }

        private function init():void
        {
            ball = new Ball3D();
            addChild(ball);

            tx = Math.random() * 500 - 250;
            ty = Math.random() * 500 - 250;
            tz = Math.random() * 500

            addEventListener(Event.ENTER_FRAME, onEnterFrame);
        }

        private function onEnterFrame(event:Event):void
        {
            var dx:Number = tx - ball.xpos;
            var dy:Number = ty - ball.ypos;
            var dz:Number = tz - ball.zpos;
            ball.xpos += dx * easing;
            ball.ypos += dy * easing;
            ball.zpos += dz * easing;

            var dist:Number = Math.sqrt(dx*dx + dy*dy + dz*dz);

            if(dist < 1)
            {
```

```
            tx = Math.random() * 500 - 250;
            ty = Math.random() * 500 - 250;
            tz = Math.random() * 500
        }

        if(ball.zpos > -fl)
        {
            var scale:Number = fl / (fl + ball.zpos);
            ball.scaleX = ball.scaleY = scale;
            ball.x = vpX + ball.xpos * scale;
            ball.y = vpY + ball.ypos * scale;
            ball.visible = true;
        }
        else
        {
            ball.visible = false;
        }
    }
  }
}
```

The most interesting point of this code is the following line:

```
var dist:Number = Math.sqrt(dx*dx + dy*dy + dz*dz);
```

If you remember, in 2D, you measure the distance between two points by the following equation:

```
var dist:Number = Math.sqrt(dx*dx + dy*dy);
```

To move into 3D distances, just add the square of the distance on the third axis. This always strikes me as too simple. It seems like I should be using a cube root instead of a square root, now that I've added on an extra term. But it doesn't work that way.

Springing

Springing, being a close cousin to easing, requires a similar adjustment for 3D. You just use the distance to the target to change the velocity, rather than the position. I'll give you another quick example. In this one (file Spring3D.as), clicking the mouse will create a new random target for the ball to spring to.

```
package {
    import flash.display.Sprite;
    import flash.events.Event;
    import flash.events.MouseEvent;

    public class Spring3D extends Sprite
    {
        private var ball:Ball3D;
        private var tx:Number;
        private var ty:Number;
```

```
private var tz:Number;
private var spring:Number = .1;
private var friction:Number = .94;
private var fl:Number = 250;
private var vpX:Number = stage.stageWidth / 2;
private var vpY:Number = stage.stageHeight / 2;

public function Spring3D()
{
    init();
}

private function init():void
{
    ball = new Ball3D();
    addChild(ball);

    tx = Math.random() * 500 - 250;
    ty = Math.random() * 500 - 250;
    tz = Math.random() * 500

    addEventListener(Event.ENTER_FRAME, onEnterFrame);
    stage.addEventListener(MouseEvent.MOUSE_DOWN, onMouseDown);
}

private function onEnterFrame(event:Event):void
{
    var dx:Number = tx - ball.xpos;
    var dy:Number = ty - ball.ypos;
    var dz:Number = tz - ball.zpos;
    ball.vx += dx * spring;
    ball.vy += dy * spring;
    ball.vz += dz * spring;
    ball.xpos += ball.vx;
    ball.ypos += ball.vy;
    ball.zpos += ball.vz;
    ball.vx *= friction;
    ball.vy *= friction;
    ball.vz *= friction;

    if(ball.zpos > -fl)
    {
        var scale:Number = fl / (fl + ball.zpos);
        ball.scaleX = ball.scaleY = scale;
        ball.x = vpX + ball.xpos * scale;
        ball.y = vpY + ball.ypos * scale;
        ball.visible = true;
    }
```

```
        else
        {
            ball.visible = false;
        }
    }

    private function onMouseDown(event:MouseEvent):void
    {
        tx = Math.random() * 500 - 250;
        ty = Math.random() * 500 - 250;
        tz = Math.random() * 500
    }
  }
}
```

As you can see, this uses the basic spring formula (from Chapter 8) with a third axis.

Coordinate rotation

Next up is coordinate rotation in 3D. This does get a bit more complex than 2D, which you saw in Chapters 10 and 11. Not only can you choose between three different axes to rotate on, you can even rotate on more than one of them at once.

In 2D coordinate rotation, the points are rotated around the z axis, as shown in Figure 15-9. Think of a *Wheel of Fortune*–type spinning wheel with an axle through the center. The axle is the z axis. Only the x and y coordinates change.

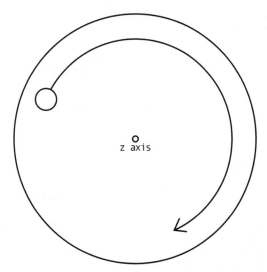

Figure 15-9. Rotation on the z axis

In 3D, you can also rotate on the x or y axis. An x-axis rotation would look like a car tire rolling toward you, as shown in Figure 15-10. The axle is on the x axis. Points rotate around that and change their y and z positions.

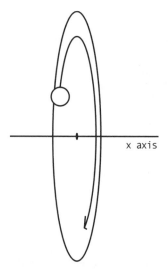

Figure 15-10. Rotation on the x axis

For y-axis rotation, imagine an old record player, something like Figure 15-11. The spindle is the y axis. Points change on the x and z axes.

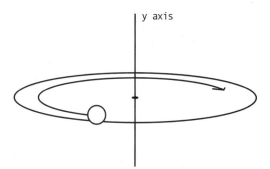

Figure 15-11. Rotation on the y axis

Thus, for 3D, when you rotate an object on one axis, its position will change on the other two axes.

If you check back to Chapter 10, you'll find the following formula for 2D rotation:

```
x1 = cos(angle) * x - sin(angle) * y;
y1 = cos(angle) * y + sin(angle) * x;
```

In 3D, you do basically the same thing, but you need to specify *which* angle you're talking about: x, y, or z. Thus, you get the following three formulas:

```
x1 = cos(angleZ) * x - sin(angleZ) * y;
y1 = cos(angleZ) * y + sin(angleZ) * x;

x1 = cos(angleY) * x - sin(angleY) * z;
z1 = cos(angleY) * z + sin(angleY) * x;

y1 = cos(angleX) * y - sin(angleX) * z;
z1 = cos(angleX) * z + sin(angleX) * y;
```

Let's try a y-axis rotation. The following code can be found in RotateY.as. It creates 50 instances of Ball3D and randomly positions them. Then it gets a y angle based on the mouse's x position. The further right the mouse goes, the higher the number for the angle. This makes the objects seem to follow the mouse in their rotation.

```
package {
    import flash.display.Sprite;
    import flash.events.Event;

    public class RotateY extends Sprite
    {
        private var balls:Array;
        private var numBalls:uint = 50;
        private var fl:Number = 250;
        private var vpX:Number = stage.stageWidth / 2;
        private var vpY:Number = stage.stageHeight / 2;

        public function RotateY()
        {
            init();
        }

        private function init():void
        {
            balls = new Array();
            for(var i:uint = 0; i < numBalls; i++)
            {
                var ball:Ball3D = new Ball3D(15);
                balls.push(ball);
                ball.xpos = Math.random() * 200 - 100;
                ball.ypos = Math.random() * 200 - 100;
                ball.zpos = Math.random() * 200 - 100;
                addChild(ball);
            }
            addEventListener(Event.ENTER_FRAME, onEnterFrame);
        }
```

```
private function onEnterFrame(event:Event):void
{
    var angleY:Number = (mouseX - vpX) * .001;
    for(var i:uint = 0; i < numBalls; i++)
    {
        var ball:Ball3D = balls[i];
        rotateY(ball, angleY);
    }
    sortZ();
}

private function rotateY(ball:Ball3D, angleY:Number):void
{
    var cosY:Number = Math.cos(angleY);
    var sinY:Number = Math.sin(angleY);

    var x1:Number = ball.xpos * cosY - ball.zpos * sinY;
    var z1:Number = ball.zpos * cosY + ball.xpos * sinY;

    ball.xpos = x1;
    ball.zpos = z1;

    if(ball.zpos > -fl)
    {
        var scale:Number = fl / (fl + ball.zpos);
        ball.scaleX = ball.scaleY = scale;
        ball.x = vpX + ball.xpos * scale;
        ball.y = vpY + ball.ypos * scale;
        ball.visible = true;
    }
    else
    {
        ball.visible = false;
    }
}

private function sortZ():void
{
    balls.sortOn("zpos", Array.DESCENDING | Array.NUMERIC);
    for(var i:uint = 0; i < numBalls; i++)
    {
        var ball:Ball3D = balls[i];
        setChildIndex(ball, i);
    }
}
```

The important parts are in bold. You get an angle and call the rotateY method on each ball with that angle. Inside that method, you get the sine and cosine of the angle, do the rotation, and assign x1 and z1 back to ball.xpos and ball.zpos. After that, it's just standard perspective and z-sorting. Figure 15-12 shows the result.

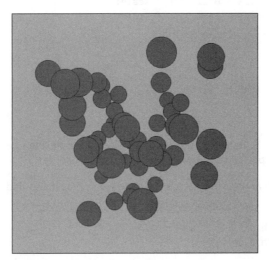

Figure 15-12. Rotation on the y axis

Once you've tried that, you can try switching it over to x-axis rotation. Just change the onEnterFrame method and add a rotateX method:

```
private function onEnterFrame(event:Event):void
{
    var angleX:Number = (mouseY - vpY) * .001;
    for(var i:uint = 0; i < numBalls; i++)
    {
        var ball:Ball3D = balls[i];
        rotateX(ball, angleX);
    }
    sortZ();
}

private function rotateX(ball:Ball3D, angleX:Number):void
{
    var cosX:Number = Math.cos(angleX);
    var sinX:Number = Math.sin(angleX);

    var y1:Number = ball.ypos * cosX - ball.zpos * sinX;
    var z1:Number = ball.zpos * cosX + ball.ypos * sinX;

    ball.ypos = y1;
    ball.zpos = z1;
```

```
            if(ball.zpos > -fl)
            {
                var scale:Number = fl / (fl + ball.zpos);
                ball.scaleX = ball.scaleY = scale;
                ball.x = vpX + ball.xpos * scale;
                ball.y = vpY + ball.ypos * scale;
                ball.visible = true;
            }
            else
            {
                ball.visible = false;
            }
        }
```

Now, angleX is based on the mouse's y position. You take the cosine and sine of that, and use them to get y1 and z1, which are passed to the ball's ypos and zpos properties.

Next, let's combine the two rotations. Here's the code (which you'll also find in RotateXY.as):

```
package {
    import flash.display.Sprite;
    import flash.events.Event;

    public class RotateXY extends Sprite
    {
        private var balls:Array;
        private var numBalls:uint = 50;
        private var fl:Number = 250;
        private var vpX:Number = stage.stageWidth / 2;
        private var vpY:Number = stage.stageHeight / 2;

        public function RotateXY()
        {
            init();
        }

        private function init():void
        {
            balls = new Array();
            for(var i:uint = 0; i < numBalls; i++)
            {
                var ball:Ball3D = new Ball3D(15);
                balls.push(ball);
                ball.xpos = Math.random() * 200 - 100;
                ball.ypos = Math.random() * 200 - 100;
                ball.zpos = Math.random() * 200 - 100;
                addChild(ball);
            }
            addEventListener(Event.ENTER_FRAME, onEnterFrame);
        }
```

```
private function onEnterFrame(event:Event):void
{
    var angleX:Number = (mouseY - vpY) * .001;
    var angleY:Number = (mouseX - vpX) * .001;
    for(var i:uint = 0; i < numBalls; i++)
    {
        var ball:Ball3D = balls[i];
        rotateX(ball, angleX);
        rotateY(ball, angleY);
        doPerspective(ball);
    }
    sortZ();
}

private function rotateX(ball:Ball3D, angleX:Number):void
{
    var cosX:Number = Math.cos(angleX);
    var sinX:Number = Math.sin(angleX);

    var y1:Number = ball.ypos * cosX - ball.zpos * sinX;
    var z1:Number = ball.zpos * cosX + ball.ypos * sinX;

    ball.ypos = y1;
    ball.zpos = z1;
}

private function rotateY(ball:Ball3D, angleY:Number):void
{
    var cosY:Number = Math.cos(angleY);
    var sinY:Number = Math.sin(angleY);

    var x1:Number = ball.xpos * cosY - ball.zpos * sinY;
    var z1:Number = ball.zpos * cosY + ball.xpos * sinY;

    ball.xpos = x1;
    ball.zpos = z1;
}

private function doPerspective(ball:Ball3D):void
{
    if(ball.zpos > -fl)
    {
        var scale:Number = fl / (fl + ball.zpos);
        ball.scaleX = ball.scaleY = scale;
        ball.x = vpX + ball.xpos * scale;
        ball.y = vpY + ball.ypos * scale;
        ball.visible = true;
    }
    else
```

```
        {
            ball.visible = false;
        }
    }

    private function sortZ():void
    {
        balls.sortOn("zpos", Array.DESCENDING | Array.NUMERIC);
        for(var i:uint = 0; i < numBalls; i++)
        {
            var ball:Ball3D = balls[i];
            setChildIndex(ball, i);
        }
    }
}
}
```

The main changes from the previous examples are in bold. Now, you find both angleY and angleX, and call both rotateX and rotateY on each ball. Note that I moved the perspective code out of the rotate methods and into its own method, as it does not have to be called twice. I'm sure you can easily add a rotateZ method based on what you have just learned and the preceding formulas.

Play around with this one. By combining 3D coordinate rotation with some of the concepts from the racing game examples in the "Wrapping" section earlier in this chapter, you can create some rich, interactive 3D environments.

Collision detection

The last thing I want to cover in this introduction to 3D is collision detection. The only feasible way of doing collision detection in 3D in Flash is distance-based. This is not too much different from collision detection in 2D. You find the distance between two objects (using the 3D distance formula), and if that is less than the sum of their radii, you have a hit.

For a 3D collision detection example, I altered one of the earlier 3D bouncing examples, giving it fewer objects and more space. In the code, I first do the normal 3D motion and perspective, and then do a double for loop to compare all the balls' locations. If any are less distance apart than twice their radius, I use some color transform code to turn them both blue. It's pretty simple. Here's the code (file Collision3D.as):

```
package {
    import flash.display.Sprite;
    import flash.events.Event;
    import flash.geom.ColorTransform;

    public class Collision3D extends Sprite
    {
        private var balls:Array;
        private var numBalls:uint = 20;
```

```
private var fl:Number = 250;
private var vpX:Number = stage.stageWidth / 2;
private var vpY:Number = stage.stageHeight / 2;
private var top:Number = -200;
private var bottom:Number = 200;
private var left:Number = -200;
private var right:Number = 200;
private var front:Number = 200;
private var back:Number = -200;

public function Collision3D()
{
    init();
}

private function init():void
{
    balls = new Array();
    for(var i:uint = 0; i < numBalls; i++)
    {
        var ball:Ball3D = new Ball3D(15);
        balls.push(ball);
        ball.xpos = Math.random() * 400 - 200;
        ball.ypos = Math.random() * 400 - 200;
        ball.zpos = Math.random() * 400 - 200;
        ball.vx = Math.random() * 10 - 5;
        ball.vy = Math.random() * 10 - 5;
        ball.vz = Math.random() * 10 - 5;
        addChild(ball);
    }
    addEventListener(Event.ENTER_FRAME, onEnterFrame);
}

private function onEnterFrame(event:Event):void
{
    for(var i:uint = 0; i < numBalls; i++)
    {
        var ball:Ball3D = balls[i];
        move(ball);
    }
    for(i = 0; i < numBalls - 1; i++)
    {
        var ballA:Ball3D = balls[i];
        for(var j:uint = i + 1; j < numBalls; j++)
        {
            var ballB:Ball3D = balls[j];
            var dx:Number = ballA.xpos - ballB.xpos;
            var dy:Number = ballA.ypos - ballB.ypos;
            var dz:Number = ballA.zpos - ballB.zpos;
```

415

```
                var dist:Number = Math.sqrt(dx*dx + dy*dy + dz*dz);
                if(dist < ballA.radius + ballB.radius)
                {
                    var blueTransform:ColorTransform =
                        new ColorTransform(0, 1, 1, 1,
                                               0, 0, 255, 0);
                    ballA.transform.colorTransform = blueTransform;
                    ballB.transform.colorTransform = blueTransform;
                }
            }
        }
        sortZ();
    }

    private function move(ball:Ball3D):void
    {
        var radius:Number =  ball.radius;

        ball.xpos += ball.vx;
        ball.ypos += ball.vy;
        ball.zpos += ball.vz;

        if(ball.xpos + radius > right)
        {
            ball.xpos = right - radius;
            ball.vx *= -1;
        }
        else if(ball.xpos - radius < left)
        {
            ball.xpos = left + radius;
            ball.vx *= -1;
        }
        if(ball.ypos + radius > bottom)
        {
            ball.ypos = bottom - radius;
            ball.vy *= -1;
        }
        else if(ball.ypos - radius < top)
        {
            ball.ypos = top + radius;
            ball.vy *= -1;
        }
        if(ball.zpos + radius > front)
        {
            ball.zpos = front - radius;
            ball.vz *= -1;
        }
        else if(ball.zpos - radius < back)
        {
```

```
        ball.zpos = back + radius;
        ball.vz *= -1;
    }

    if(ball.zpos > -fl)
    {
        var scale:Number = fl / (fl + ball.zpos);
        ball.scaleX = ball.scaleY = scale;
        ball.x = vpX + ball.xpos * scale;
        ball.y = vpY + ball.ypos * scale;
        ball.visible = true;
    }
    else
    {
        ball.visible = false;
    }
}

private function sortZ():void
{
    balls.sortOn("zpos", Array.DESCENDING | Array.NUMERIC);
    for(var i:uint = 0; i < numBalls; i++)
    {
        var ball:Ball3D = balls[i];
        setChildIndex(ball, i);
    }
}
    }
}
```

The key part is in bold. The balls start out all red, and as they collide, they change color. Before long, all are blue.

Important formulas in this chapter

The important formulas in this chapter are those for 3D perspective, coordinate rotation, and distance.

Basic perspective:

```
scale = fl / (fl + zpos);
sprite.scaleX = sprite.scaleY = scale;
sprite.alpha = scale;     // optional
sprite.x = vanishingPointX + xpos * scale;
sprite.y = vanishingPointY + ypos * scale;
```

Z-sorting:

```
// assumes an array of 3D objects with a zpos property
objectArray.sortOn("zpos", Array.DESCENDING | Array.NUMERIC);
for(var i:uint = 0; i < numObjects; i++)
{
    setChildIndex(objectArray[i], i);
}
```

Coordinate rotation:

```
x1 = cos(angleZ) * xpos - sin(angleZ) * ypos;
y1 = cos(angleZ) * ypos + sin(angleZ) * xpos;

x1 = cos(angleY) * xpos - sin(angleY) * zpos;
z1 = cos(angleY) * zpos + sin(angleY) * xpos;

y1 = cos(angleX) * ypos - sin(angleX) * zpos;
z1 = cos(angleX) * zpos + sin(angleX) * ypos;
```

3D distance:

```
dist = Math.sqrt(dx * dx + dy * dy + dz * dz);
```

Summary

You now have the basics of 3D under your belt, and you've seen most of the basic motion code adapted for 3D. I have to say I kind of surprised myself by the number of times I was able to say, "This is the same as 2D, you just have to add a z variable . . . ," or something of the sort. I thought there would be more complex stuff to explain here, but most of it turned out to be rather simple.

You'll use a lot of what you learned here in the next chapter, where you actually begin to sculpt 3D forms with points and lines.

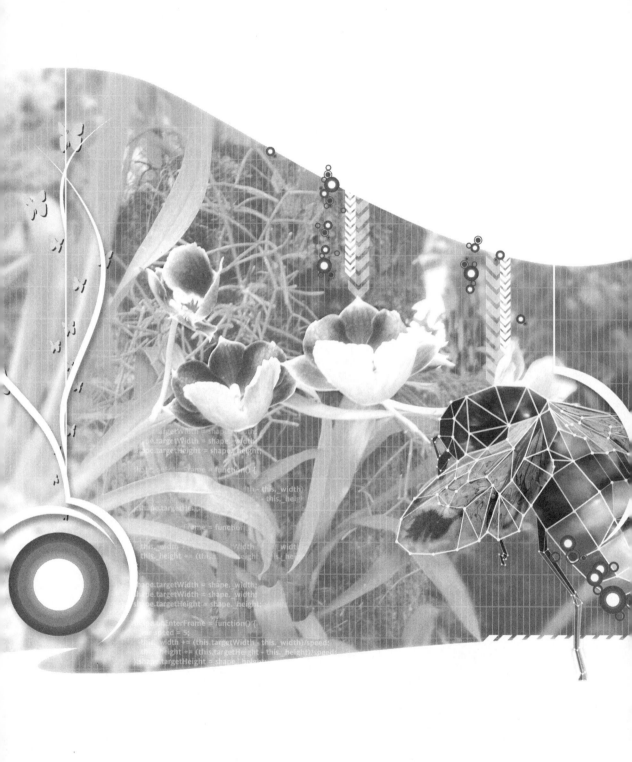

Chapter 16

3D LINES AND FILLS

What we'll cover in this chapter:

- Creating points and lines
- Making shapes
- Creating 3D fills
- Modeling 3D solids
- Moving 3D solids

Chapter 15 presented an introduction to 3D, but took you only as far as positioning objects in a 3D space and figuring out their size and screen position. The objects themselves were actually 2D. It is kind of like those older 3D games where you could walk around an object or a character and it would seem to turn to face you. That object or character was not actually turning—but it appeared that way because it was a 2D object and that's the only view of it you had.

In this chapter, you're going to actually start doing 3D modeling in Flash. In particular, you'll learn about how to create and use 3D points, lines, fills, and solids. When you've finished this chapter, you'll be able to create a variety of shapes, move them, and rotate them, all in 3D.

Creating points and lines

It doesn't make much sense to make points in 3D without making some 3D lines, too. Since a point, by definition, has no dimension, it would be invisible. To start off with, though, you'll continue to use instances of the Ball3D class, with very small radii, as points just so you can see where they are. From there, you simply need to draw some lines to connect the balls. Pretty easy. You've already done similar things, but now the points will have perspective applied to them, to put them in a 3D space.

You can make a point instance black and, say, 10 pixels across. You'll create a few of these points, rotate them based on the mouse position (as in some of the later examples in the previous chapter), and then draw some lines between them. The code itself is almost identical to that in the file RotateXY.as from the last chapter. The main difference is the last part of the onEnterFrame, where you loop through drawing a line from the first point, through all the rest, to the last one. I also removed the sortZ method, as it doesn't make a difference here. Here's the full code from Lines3D1.as; Figure 16-1 shows the result.

```
package {
    import flash.display.Sprite;
    import flash.events.Event;

    public class Lines3D1 extends Sprite
    {
        private var balls:Array;
        private var numBalls:uint = 50;
        private var fl:Number = 250;
        private var vpX:Number = stage.stageWidth / 2;
        private var vpY:Number = stage.stageHeight / 2;

        public function Lines3D1()
        {
            init();
        }

        private function init():void
        {
            balls = new Array();
            for(var i:uint = 0; i < numBalls; i++)
            {
```

```
            var ball:Ball3D = new Ball3D(5, 0);
            balls.push(ball);
            ball.xpos = Math.random() * 200 - 100;
            ball.ypos = Math.random() * 200 - 100;
            ball.zpos = Math.random() * 200 - 100;
            addChild(ball);
        }
        addEventListener(Event.ENTER_FRAME, onEnterFrame);
    }

    private function onEnterFrame(event:Event):void
    {
        var angleX:Number = (mouseY - vpY) * .001;
        var angleY:Number = (mouseX - vpX) * .001;
        for(var i:uint = 0; i < numBalls; i++)
        {
            var ball:Ball3D = balls[i];
            rotateX(ball, angleX);
            rotateY(ball, angleY);
            doPerspective(ball);
        }
        graphics.clear();
        graphics.lineStyle(0);
        graphics.moveTo(balls[0].x, balls[0].y);
        for(i = 1; i < numBalls; i++)
        {
            graphics.lineTo(balls[i].x, balls[i].y);
        }
    }

    private function rotateX(ball:Ball3D, angleX:Number):void
    {
        var cosX:Number = Math.cos(angleX);
        var sinX:Number = Math.sin(angleX);

        var y1:Number = ball.ypos * cosX - ball.zpos * sinX;
        var z1:Number = ball.zpos * cosX + ball.ypos * sinX;

        ball.ypos = y1;
        ball.zpos = z1;
    }
    private function rotateY(ball:Ball3D, angleY:Number):void
    {
        var cosY:Number = Math.cos(angleY);
        var sinY:Number = Math.sin(angleY);

        var x1:Number = ball.xpos * cosY - ball.zpos * sinY;
        var z1:Number = ball.zpos * cosY + ball.xpos * sinY;
```

```
        ball.xpos = x1;
        ball.zpos = z1;
    }

    private function doPerspective(ball:Ball3D):void
    {
        if(ball.zpos > -fl)
        {
            var scale:Number = fl / (fl + ball.zpos);
            ball.scaleX = ball.scaleY = scale;
            ball.x = vpX + ball.xpos * scale;
            ball.y = vpY + ball.ypos * scale;
            ball.visible = true;
        }
        else
        {
            ball.visible = false;
        }
    }
}
}
```

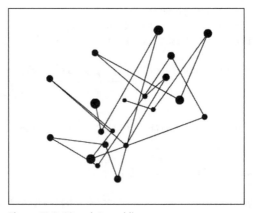

Figure 16-1. 3D points and lines

Now that's pretty cool. And there's not a whole lot to it, actually.

If you're moving toward modeling 3D solids, you're going to want to eventually get rid of all those black dots. The first attempt at this is pretty basic. Just set the radius of each Ball3D instance to 0 when it is created, like so:

```
    var ball:Ball3D = new Ball3D(0);
```

You can see the results of this in Figure 16-2.

If you look at the earlier code listing, you'll see that some parts of it are now superfluous. The parts about scaleX, scaleY, and visible are completely irrelevant for an invisible point. There's nothing there to see or scale. You can follow this line of thought a little further and realize that we have this whole custom class that extends the Sprite class currently being used only as a holder for five variables: xpos, ypos, zpos, x, and y. That is really overkill. A sprite has many capabilities—event dispatching, graphics, the ability to contain other display objects, etc.—and uses up a fair amount of resources. Using a sprite in this way is like driving a tank down to the corner store to pick up a loaf of bread.

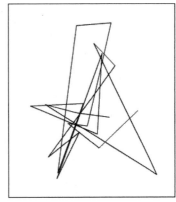

Figure 16-2. 3D lines with invisible points

If all we're doing is storing those variables I just mentioned, let's make a class that just has those variables as its only properties. I've done just that. In fact, rather than just having it contain a few properties, I've even moved the perspective and coordinate rotation methods into it! Ladies and gentlemen, I present to you the Point3D class:

```
package
{
    public class Point3D
    {
        public var fl:Number = 250;
        private var vpX:Number = 0;
        private var vpY:Number = 0;
        private var cX:Number = 0;
        private var cY:Number = 0;
        private var cZ:Number = 0;
        public var x:Number = 0;
        public var y:Number = 0;
        public var z:Number = 0;

        public function Point3D(x:Number=0, y:Number=0, z:Number=0)
        {
            this.x = x;
            this.y = y;
            this.z = z;
        }

        public function setVanishingPoint(vpX:Number, vpY:Number):void
        {
            this.vpX = vpX;
            this.vpY = vpY;
        }

        public function setCenter(cX:Number,
                                  cY:Number,
                                  cZ:Number=0):void
```

```
    {
        this.cX = cX;
        this.cY     = cY;
        this.cZ = cZ;
    }

    public function get screenX():Number
    {
        var scale:Number = fl / (fl + z + cZ);
        return vpX + (cX + x) * scale;
    }

    public function get screenY():Number
    {
        var scale:Number = fl / (fl + z + cZ);
        return vpY + (cY + y) * scale;
    }

    public function rotateX(angleX:Number):void
    {
        var cosX:Number = Math.cos(angleX);
        var sinX:Number = Math.sin(angleX);

        var y1:Number = y * cosX - z * sinX;
        var z1:Number = z * cosX + y * sinX;

        y = y1;
        z = z1;
    }

    public function rotateY(angleY:Number):void
    {
        var cosY:Number = Math.cos(angleY);
        var sinY:Number = Math.sin(angleY);

        var x1:Number = x * cosY - z * sinY;
        var z1:Number = z * cosY + x * sinY;

        x = x1;
        z = z1;
    }

    public function rotateZ(angleZ:Number):void
    {
        var cosZ:Number = Math.cos(angleZ);
        var sinZ:Number = Math.sin(angleZ);

        var x1:Number = x * cosZ - y * sinZ;
        var y1:Number = y * cosZ + x * sinZ;
```

```
            x = x1;
            y = y1;
        }
    }
}
```

Using this class, you can now pass in x, y, and z positions when you create a 3D point, or set them later with the public x, y, and z properties. It also contains a default fl property, and properties to hold the vanishing point, settable by the setVanishingPoint() method. You can rotate the point around its center on any axis with the three rotate methods. In addition, there is a setCenter method, which you can use to change the center. You'll see that in use shortly. Finally, it handles all the perspective stuff for you as well. When you've positioned and rotated the point, just grab screenX and screenY to get the screen position of the point with all the perspective calculations applied. While I've tried to shy away from giving you ready-built classes like this, it's going to make things a whole lot easier over the next couple of chapters.

When you refactor the rotating lines program using this new class, it becomes amazingly simple, as you can see in Lines3D2.as:

```
package {
    import flash.display.Sprite;
    import flash.events.Event;

    public class Lines3D2 extends Sprite
    {
        private var points:Array;
        private var numPoints:uint = 50;
        private var fl:Number = 250;
        private var vpX:Number = stage.stageWidth / 2;
        private var vpY:Number = stage.stageHeight / 2;

        public function Lines3D2()
        {
            init();
        }

        private function init():void
        {
            points = new Array();
            for(var i:uint = 0; i < numPoints; i++)
            {
                var point:Point3D =
                    new Point3D(Math.random() * 200 - 100,
                                Math.random() * 200 - 100,
                                Math.random() * 200 - 100);
                point.setVanishingPoint(vpX, vpY);
                points.push(point);
            }
            addEventListener(Event.ENTER_FRAME, onEnterFrame);
        }
```

```
private function onEnterFrame(event:Event):void
{
    var angleX:Number = (mouseY - vpY) * .001;
    var angleY:Number = (mouseX - vpX) * .001;
    for(var i:uint = 0; i < numPoints; i++)
    {
        var point:Point3D = points[i];
        point.rotateX(angleX);
        point.rotateY(angleY);
    }

    graphics.clear();
    graphics.lineStyle(0);
    graphics.moveTo(points[0].screenX, points[0].screenY);
    for(i = 1; i < numPoints; i++)
    {
        graphics.lineTo(points[i].screenX, points[i].screenY);
    }
}
}
}
```

The main changes are in bold. You should be able to follow them pretty easily.

Making shapes

Random lines are cool for demonstration purposes, but there's no reason you can't impose a bit of order on that mess. All it takes is getting rid of the initial loop that creates random x, y, and z values for those points and replacing it with some specific, predetermined values. For example, let's make a square. Figure 16-3 shows the square you'll draw and the 3D locations of its four corners.

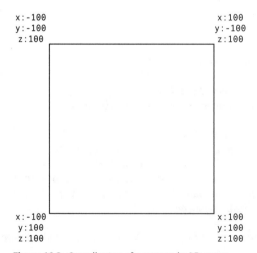

Figure 16-3. Coordinates of a square in 3D space

Note that all the z values are the same. This is because a square lies on a plane. The easiest way to keep the square on the plane is to give all of its points the same measurement on one axis (here I chose the z axis) and define the square on the other two (x and y axes).

Here's the code that will replace the random point-creating loop:

```
points[0] = new Point3D(-100, -100,  100);
points[1] = new Point3D( 100, -100,  100);
points[2] = new Point3D( 100,  100,  100);
points[3] = new Point3D(-100,  100,  100);
```

You will have to then manually set the vanishing point for each point. Doing this in a loop is easiest:

```
for(var i:uint = 0; i < numPoints; i++)
{
    points[i].setVanishingPoint(vpX, vpY);
}
```

Also, since you're down to just four points now, you'll have to change numPoints to 4. The rest of the code should work just fine, but you'll make one addition: a line to connect the last point with the first, to close the shape. Here's the full code as found in Square3D.as (Figure 16-4 shows the result):

```
package {
    import flash.display.Sprite;
    import flash.events.Event;

    public class Square3D extends Sprite
    {
        private var points:Array;
        private var numPoints:uint = 4;
        private var fl:Number = 250;
        private var vpX:Number = stage.stageWidth / 2;
        private var vpY:Number = stage.stageHeight / 2;

        public function Square3D()
        {
            init();
        }

        private function init():void
        {
            points = new Array();
            points[0] = new Point3D(-100, -100,  100);
            points[1] = new Point3D( 100, -100,  100);
            points[2] = new Point3D( 100,  100,  100);
            points[3] = new Point3D(-100,  100,  100);
            for(var i:uint = 0; i < numPoints; i++)
            {
                points[i].setVanishingPoint(vpX, vpY);
            }
```

```
            addEventListener(Event.ENTER_FRAME, onEnterFrame);
        }

        private function onEnterFrame(event:Event):void
        {
            var angleX:Number = (mouseY - vpY) * .001;
            var angleY:Number = (mouseX - vpX) * .001;
            for(var i:uint = 0; i < numPoints; i++)
            {
                var point:Point3D = points[i];
                point.rotateX(angleX);
                point.rotateY(angleY);
            }

            graphics.clear();
            graphics.lineStyle(0);
            graphics.moveTo(points[0].screenX, points[0].screenY);
            for(i = 1; i < numPoints; i++)
            {
                graphics.lineTo(points[i].screenX, points[i].screenY);
            }
            graphics.lineTo(points[0].screenX, points[0].screenY);
        }
    }
}
```

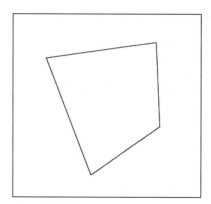

Figure 16-4. 3D spinning square

Fantastic—a spinning square! You should be able to create just about any flat shape now. I often plot out the points on a piece of graph paper beforehand (as shown in Figure 16-5) to help me out.

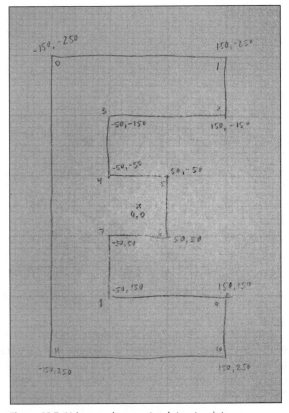

Figure 16-5. Using graph paper to plot out points

From this sketch, I can create my points like so:

```
points[0]  =  new Point3D(-150, -250, 100);
points[1]  =  new Point3D( 150, -250, 100);
points[2]  =  new Point3D( 150, -150, 100);
points[3]  =  new Point3D( -50, -150, 100);
points[4]  =  new Point3D( -50,  -50, 100);
points[5]  =  new Point3D(  50,  -50, 100);
points[6]  =  new Point3D(  50,   50, 100);
points[7]  =  new Point3D( -50,   50, 100);
points[8]  =  new Point3D( -50,  150, 100);
points[9]  =  new Point3D( 150,  150, 100);
points[10] = new Point3D( 150,  250, 100);
points[11] = new Point3D(-150,  250, 100);
```

and wind up with a spinning E as seen in SpinningE.as and in Figure 16-6. Don't forget to change numPoints to 12 now. Later you'll make this value dynamic by using points.length.

When you run this example, you'll notice that as the E shape moves toward you, some of the points get too close and do that inversion thing you saw in the very first 3D examples. Your first thought might be to just increase the z value of all the points, but that would actually make the effect worse. For example, say I made z 500. As it rotated, z would go from 500 to –500, putting some of the points even further behind the viewpoint and making an even worse mess of things. Instead, use the setCenter method to push the whole set of points out on the z axis, like so:

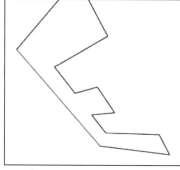

Figure 16-6. 3D spinning letter

```
for(var i:uint = 0; i < numPoints; i++)
{
    points[i].setVanishingPoint(vpX, vpY);
    points[i].setCenter(0, 0, 200);
}
```

If you look back at the Point3D class, you'll see that this is used when figuring the scale:

```
var scale:Number = fl / (fl + z + cZ);
```

This pushes the entire system, including the rotation of the system, out 200 pixels. The value for z will remain the same, but because perspective is calculated on higher values, everything will be well in front of the viewer. Try using other values and see how it works. A little later, we'll play with moving the shape around on the other axes.

Creating 3D fills

As you might imagine, a large part of the work for fills has already been done. You've already created the points for a shape and connected them from one end to the other with a line. All you really need to do is add a beginFill and endFill to the drawing code. The code in the FilledE.as file does just that; see Figure 16-7 for the results. Here's the relevant section of code with the changes in bold:

```
graphics.clear();
graphics.lineStyle(0);
graphics.beginFill(0xffcccc);
graphics.moveTo(points[0].screenX, points[0].screenY);
for(i = 1; i < numPoints; i++)
{
    graphics.lineTo(points[i].screenX, points[i].screenY);
}
graphics.lineTo(points[0].screenX, points[0].screenY);
graphics.endFill();
```

This comes right at the end of the onEnterFrame function.

At this point, it's a good idea to look at how traditional 3D programs model shapes and solids. In the previous examples, both the square and the letter E are *polygons*. A polygon is simply a closed shape made of at least three line segments. Thus, a triangle is the simplest polygon. You'll find that in many 3D modeling and rendering programs—even those that use patches, meshes, nurbs, and complex polygons—all 3D forms are finally reduced to a set of triangles just prior to being rendered.

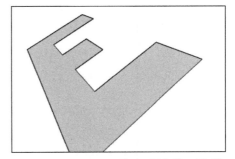

Figure 16-7. First 3D fills

Using triangles

There are a number of advantages to using triangles—probably more than I know, but I'll cover a few here. First, with a triangle, you can be sure that all the points of the polygon are always on the same plane, since a triangle *defines* a plane. If you are still not sure why this is important, take the letter E example and randomly change around some of the z values of its points. While you may get some interesting results, they can also quickly become unexpected and unpredictable.

Second, using triangles, it is sometimes easier to draw complex shapes. Consider Figure 16-8, for example.

This type of shape would be kind of tough to create with a single polygon. You'd have to double back on yourself at least once. You'd also get into the situation where every polygon you create would have a different number of points and require special handling. On the other hand, with triangles, you can model the A as shown in Figure 16-9.

You can then set up a function that takes three points and renders a single triangle. You just need a list of points and then a list of triangles. One loop goes through the list of points, positions them, and applies perspective. Another loop goes through the triangle list and renders each one.

This isn't to say that you have to go with a triangle-only approach. You could make a function that dynamically renders a polygon of any number of sides. But to keep

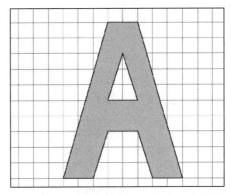

Figure 16-8. More complex 3D shape

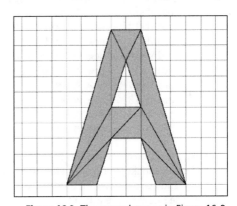

Figure 16-9. The same shape as in Figure 16-8, rendered with triangles

things simple and flexible here, let's go with the triangles. Let's try it out with the letter A example. First, you need to define all of your points and triangles. As shown in Figure 16-10, I've laid out the shape, and numbered all of its points and each of its triangles.

433

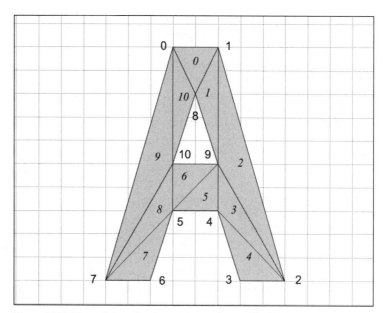

Figure 16-10. The points and polygons that make up this shape

When you graph out all the points, you get the following values:

```
points[0] = new Point3D( -50, -250, 100);
points[1] = new Point3D(  50, -250, 100);
points[2] = new Point3D( 200,  250, 100);
points[3] = new Point3D( 100,  250, 100);
points[4] = new Point3D(  50,  100, 100);
points[5] = new Point3D( -50,  100, 100);
points[6] = new Point3D(-100,  250, 100);
points[7] = new Point3D(-200,  250, 100);
points[8] = new Point3D(   0, -150, 100);
points[9] = new Point3D(  50,    0, 100);
points[10] = new Point3D(-50,    0, 100);
```

Next, you need to define the triangles. Each triangle is simply a list of three points; let's call them a, b, and c. Let's make a Triangle class to keep track of the points for each triangle. We can even get really fancy and have a draw method for each triangle so it knows how to draw itself. I'll list it here, and you'll see how to use it in a moment.

```
package
{
    import flash.display.Graphics;

    public class Triangle
    {
        private var pointA:Point3D;
        private var pointB:Point3D;
        private var pointC:Point3D;
```

```
        private var color:uint;

        public function Triangle(a:Point3D,
                                 b:Point3D,
                                 c:Point3D, color:uint)
        {
            pointA = a;
            pointB = b;
            pointC = c;
            this.color = color;
        }

        public function draw(g:Graphics):void
        {
            g.beginFill(color);
            g.moveTo(pointA.screenX, pointA.screenY);
            g.lineTo(pointB.screenX, pointB.screenY);
            g.lineTo(pointC.screenX, pointC.screenY);
            g.lineTo(pointA.screenX, pointA.screenY);
            g.endFill();
        }
    }
}
```

Now we'll need another array to hold the list of triangles. So, up at the top of the class, define the array:

```
    private var triangles:Array;
```

Then, in the init function, after defining all the points, you define the triangles. Note that each triangle is also created with a specific color.

```
triangles = new Array();
triangles[0] =  new Triangle(points[0], points[1],
                             points[8], 0xffcccc);
triangles[1] =  new Triangle(points[1], points[9],
                             points[8], 0xffcccc);
triangles[2] =  new Triangle(points[1], points[2],
                             points[9], 0xffcccc);
triangles[3] =  new Triangle(points[2], points[4],
                             points[9], 0xffcccc);
triangles[4] =  new Triangle(points[2], points[3],
                             points[4], 0xffcccc);
triangles[5] =  new Triangle(points[4], points[5],
                             points[9], 0xffcccc);
triangles[6] =  new Triangle(points[9], points[5],
                             points[10],0xffcccc);
triangles[7] =  new Triangle(points[5], points[6],
                             points[7], 0xffcccc);
triangles[8] =  new Triangle(points[5], points[7],
                             points[10],0xffcccc);
```

```
triangles[9] =  new Triangle(points[0], points[10],
                             points[7], 0xffcccc);
triangles[10] = new Triangle(points[0], points[8],
                             points[10],0xffcccc);
```

One thing you'll notice is that I ordered the points of each triangle to go in a clockwise direction. That isn't important at this stage of the game, but it will become very important in the next chapter, so it's a good habit to get into.

> By the way, if you're thinking that plotting and entering all these points and triangles by hand is tedious, that's because it is tedious. And it's going to get worse when you get into modeling solid forms. That's why most 3D programs have visual modeling front ends to them, which give you all kinds of tools to create forms and extract all the points and polygons for you. Creating such a modeling front end might be possible in Flash, but it's well beyond the scope of this book!

Now, your rendering loop will look like this (don't worry, I'm going to give you the whole thing to look at in a bit):

```
graphics.clear();
for(i = 0; i < triangles.length; i++)
{
     triangles[i].draw(graphics);
}
```

You see that this uses the draw method defined in the Triangle class, passing in a reference to graphics. That's all there is to it! The triangle begins a fill based on its defined color, moves to the position of the first point, draws its shape, and ends the fill. Quite elegant, you might say.

Actually, it's at points like this that I wonder about people who say that object-oriented programming makes programming more complex. The Triangle class is very easy to understand, and the part of the main class that uses it couldn't be any simpler. Compare that to the linear solution I used in the earlier version of the book, which was far more complex and took quite a bit of explanation.

You can see the results of this example in Figure 16-11.

Figure 16-11. The A shape

And, just to keep you up to date on things, here's the code found in Triangles.as:

```
package {
    import flash.display.Sprite;
    import flash.events.Event;

    public class Triangles extends Sprite
    {
        private var points:Array;
        private var triangles:Array;
        private var fl:Number = 250;
        private var vpX:Number = stage.stageWidth / 2;
        private var vpY:Number = stage.stageHeight / 2;

        public function Triangles()
        {
            init();
        }

        private function init():void
        {
            points = new Array();
            points[0] = new Point3D( -50, -250, 100);
            points[1] = new Point3D(  50, -250, 100);
            points[2] = new Point3D( 200,  250, 100);
            points[3] = new Point3D( 100,  250, 100);
            points[4] = new Point3D(  50,  100, 100);
            points[5] = new Point3D( -50,  100, 100);
            points[6] = new Point3D(-100,  250, 100);
            points[7] = new Point3D(-200,  250, 100);
            points[8] = new Point3D(   0, -150, 100);
            points[9] = new Point3D(  50,    0, 100);
            points[10] = new Point3D(-50,    0, 100);
            for(var i:uint = 0; i < points.length; i++)
            {
                points[i].setVanishingPoint(vpX, vpY);
                points[i].setCenter(0, 0, 200);
            }
            triangles = new Array();
            triangles[0] = new Triangle(points[0], points[1],
                                        points[8], 0xffcccc);
            triangles[1] = new Triangle(points[1], points[9],
                                        points[8], 0xffcccc);
            triangles[2] = new Triangle(points[1], points[2],
                                        points[9], 0xffcccc);
            triangles[3] = new Triangle(points[2], points[4],
                                        points[9], 0xffcccc);
            triangles[4] = new Triangle(points[2], points[3],
                                        points[4], 0xffcccc);
```

```
            triangles[5] = new Triangle(points[4], points[5],
                                          points[9], 0xffcccc);
            triangles[6] = new Triangle(points[9], points[5],
                                          points[10],0xffcccc);
            triangles[7] = new Triangle(points[5], points[6],
                                          points[7], 0xffcccc);
            triangles[8] = new Triangle(points[5], points[7],
                                          points[10],0xffcccc);
            triangles[9] = new Triangle(points[0], points[10],
                                          points[7], 0xffcccc);
            triangles[10] =new Triangle(points[0], points[8],
                                          points[10],0xffcccc);

            addEventListener(Event.ENTER_FRAME, onEnterFrame);
        }

        private function onEnterFrame(event:Event):void
        {
            var angleX:Number = (mouseY - vpY) * .001;
            var angleY:Number = (mouseX - vpX) * .001;
            for(var i:uint = 0; i < points.length; i++)
            {
                var point:Point3D = points[i];
                point.rotateX(angleX);
                point.rotateY(angleY);
            }

            graphics.clear();
            for(i = 0; i < triangles.length; i++)
            {
                triangles[i].draw(graphics);
            }
        }
    }
}
```

Modeling 3D solids

Well, we finally get down to where this chapter was originally headed: creating 3D solids in Flash!

In the computing world, the first example in any book or tutorial is almost always "Hello, World," a program that will in one way or another print those words to the screen. In programming 3D solids, the equivalent seems to be a spinning cube. Let's not break from tradition.

Modeling a spinning cube

First of all, you need eight points to define the eight corners of the cube. These are shown in Figure 16-12.

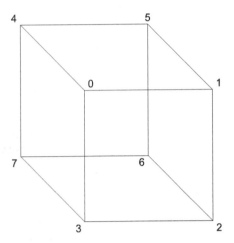

Figure 16-12. The points of a 3D cube

The points are defined like this in the code:

```
// front four corners
points[0] = new Point3D(-100, -100, -100);
points[1] = new Point3D( 100, -100, -100);
points[2] = new Point3D( 100,  100, -100);
points[3] = new Point3D(-100,  100, -100);
// back four corners
points[4] = new Point3D(-100, -100,  100);
points[5] = new Point3D( 100, -100,  100);
points[6] = new Point3D( 100,  100,  100);
points[7] = new Point3D(-100,  100,  100);
```

Then you need to define the triangles. Each face of the cube will consist of two triangles. There will be 12 triangles altogether—two each for the six faces. Again, I'm going to list the points for each triangle in a clockwise direction, as seen from the outer face of that triangle. It gets a little tricky, but try to rotate the cube in your mind so that the triangle you're defining is facing you, and then list the points in clockwise order from that viewpoint. For example, the front face is easy; Figure 16-13 shows the two triangles.

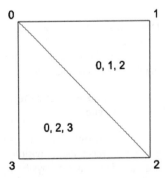

Figure 16-13. The front face of the cube

439

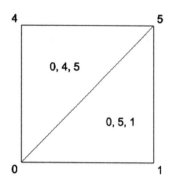

Figure 16-14. The top face of the cube

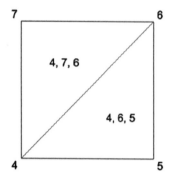

Figure 16-15. The back face of the cube

Figure 16-14 shows the top face.

And Figure 16-15 shows the back.

Continuing around with each face, you come up with the following triangle definitions:

```
// front
triangles[0] = new Triangle(points[0], points[1],
                            points[2], 0x6666cc);
triangles[1] = new Triangle(points[0], points[2],
                            points[3], 0x6666cc);
// top
triangles[2] = new Triangle(points[0], points[5],
                            points[1], 0x66cc66);
triangles[3] = new Triangle(points[0], points[4],
                            points[5], 0x66cc66);
//back
triangles[4] = new Triangle(points[4], points[6],
                            points[5], 0xcc6666);
triangles[5] = new Triangle(points[4], points[7],
                            points[6], 0xcc6666);
// bottom
triangles[6] = new Triangle(points[3], points[2],
                            points[6], 0xcc66cc);
triangles[7] = new Triangle(points[3], points[6],
                            points[7], 0xcc66cc);
// right
triangles[8] = new Triangle(points[1], points[5],
                            points[6], 0x66cccc);
triangles[9] = new Triangle(points[1], points[6],
                            points[2], 0x66cccc);
// left
triangles[10] =new Triangle(points[4], points[0],
                            points[3], 0xcccc66);
triangles[11] =new Triangle(points[4], points[3],
                            points[7], 0xcccc66);
```

Notice also that each face has a different color, as the two triangles that make up that face are the same color. Again, this clockwise orientation doesn't matter a whole lot right now, but in the next chapter, you'll use this for something called *backface culling*. This term refers to a way of determining which surfaces are facing you and which are facing away. You'll see why this is important in a moment.

The Cube.as file is exactly the same as Triangles.as, with these new point and triangle definitions in the init function.

Go ahead and run this. Whoa—it's all messed up! You can see some of the back faces, some of the time. Other faces seem invisible all the time. What's going on? Well, the faces on the back of the cube (the back faces) are always being drawn. And the triangles are being drawn in the same order, based on their position in the triangles array. So the faces at the bottom of the list always draw over the faces at the top of the list, and you get bizarre, unpredictable results like this. You need to *cull*, or weed out and get rid of, those back faces, since you don't need to render them.

Again, backface culling will be covered in detail in the next chapter, and you'll also learn how to apply some basic lighting on each surface, based on its angle.

As a temporary fix for the rest of this chapter, you can go into the draw method of the Triangle class and set the fill transparency to 0.5:

```
public function draw(g:Graphics):void
{
    g.beginFill(color, .5);
    g.moveTo(pointA.screenX, pointA.screenY);
    g.lineTo(pointB.screenX, pointB.screenY);
    g.lineTo(pointC.screenX, pointC.screenY);
    g.lineTo(pointA.screenX, pointA.screenY);
    g.endFill();
}
```

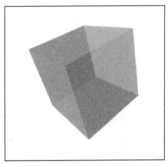

This allows you to see through any side, and makes the whole solid look like it's made from colored glass. Again, this is a temporary workaround until we get to backface culling.

Figure 16-16 shows the finished 3D cube.

Figure 16-16. The resulting 3D cube

Modeling other shapes

Congratulations! You've mastered the spinning cube. Now you can move on to model all kinds of shapes. Just draw them out on a piece of graph paper, mark up the points and triangles, and put them into the arrays. It often helps to draw several views of the object, rotated so you can see each face and what points make up the triangles. This section offers a few to get you started.

Pyramid

Here's the code for a 3D pyramid (which you can also find in Pyramid.as). First the points:

```
points[0] = new Point3D(   0, -200,    0);
points[1] = new Point3D( 200,  200, -200);
points[2] = new Point3D(-200,  200, -200);
points[3] = new Point3D(-200,  200,  200);
points[4] = new Point3D( 200,  200,  200);
```

And then the triangles:

```
triangles[0] = new Triangle(points[0], points[1], points[2], 0x6666cc);
triangles[1] = new Triangle(points[0], points[2], points[3], 0x66cc66);
triangles[2] = new Triangle(points[0], points[3], points[4], 0xcc6666);
triangles[3] = new Triangle(points[0], points[4], points[1], 0x66cccc);
triangles[4] = new Triangle(points[1], points[3], points[2], 0xcc66cc);
triangles[5] = new Triangle(points[1], points[4], points[3], 0xcc66cc);
```

Figure 16-17 shows the result.

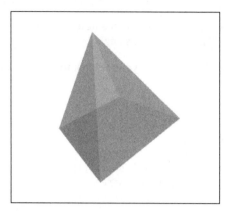

Figure 16-17. A 3D pyramid

Extruded letter A

In ExtrudedA.as, I went all out and extruded the earlier letter A example. This meant copying the first 11 points, moving one set to a z of –50 and the other set to +50, then creating triangles for the second set (making sure they were still going clockwise as seen from the back), and finally making triangles to join the two sides. Tedious? You bet! But a nice effect when it was done:

```
points[0] = new Point3D( -50, -250,  -50);
points[1] = new Point3D(  50, -250,  -50);
points[2] = new Point3D( 200,  250,  -50);
points[3] = new Point3D( 100,  250,  -50);
points[4] = new Point3D(  50,  100,  -50);
points[5] = new Point3D( -50,  100,  -50);
points[6] = new Point3D(-100,  250,  -50);
points[7] = new Point3D(-200,  250,  -50);
points[8] = new Point3D(   0, -150,  -50);
points[9] = new Point3D(  50,    0,  -50);
points[10] = new Point3D( -50,    0,  -50);

points[11] = new Point3D( -50, -250,  50);
points[12] = new Point3D(  50, -250,  50);
points[13] = new Point3D( 200,  250,  50);
points[14] = new Point3D( 100,  250,  50);
points[15] = new Point3D(  50,  100,  50);
points[16] = new Point3D( -50,  100,  50);
points[17] = new Point3D(-100,  250,  50);
points[18] = new Point3D(-200,  250,  50);
points[19] = new Point3D(   0, -150,  50);
points[20] = new Point3D(  50,    0,  50);
points[21] = new Point3D( -50,    0,  50);
```

```
triangles[0] =new Triangle(points[0],    points[1],
                          points[8],   0x6666cc);
triangles[1] =new Triangle(points[1],    points[9],
                          points[8],   0x6666cc);
triangles[2] =new Triangle(points[1],    points[2],
                          points[9],   0x6666cc);
triangles[3] =new Triangle(points[2],    points[4],
                          points[9],   0x6666cc);
triangles[4] =new Triangle(points[2],    points[3],
                          points[4],   0x6666cc);
triangles[5] =new Triangle(points[4],    points[5],
                          points[9],   0x6666cc);
triangles[6] =new Triangle(points[9],    points[5],
                          points[10],  0x6666cc);
triangles[7] =new Triangle(points[5],    points[6],
                          points[7],   0x6666cc);
triangles[8] =new Triangle(points[5],    points[7],
                          points[10],  0x6666cc);
triangles[9] =new Triangle(points[0],    points[10],
                          points[7],   0x6666cc);
triangles[10] = new Triangle(points[0], points[8],
                          points[10], 0x6666cc);
triangles[11] = new Triangle(points[11], points[19],
                          points[12], 0xcc6666);
triangles[12] = new Triangle(points[12], points[19],
                          points[20], 0xcc6666);
triangles[13] = new Triangle(points[12], points[20],
                          points[13], 0xcc6666);
triangles[14] = new Triangle(points[13], points[20],
                          points[15], 0xcc6666);
triangles[15] = new Triangle(points[13], points[15],
                          points[14], 0xcc6666);
triangles[16] = new Triangle(points[15], points[20],
                          points[16], 0xcc6666);
triangles[17] = new Triangle(points[20], points[21],
                          points[16], 0xcc6666);
triangles[18] = new Triangle(points[16], points[18],
                          points[17], 0xcc6666);
triangles[19] = new Triangle(points[16], points[21],
                          points[18], 0xcc6666);
triangles[20] = new Triangle(points[11], points[18],
                          points[21], 0xcc6666);
triangles[21] = new Triangle(points[11], points[21],
                          points[19], 0xcc6666);
triangles[22] = new Triangle(points[0],  points[11],
                          points[1],  0xcccc66);
triangles[23] = new Triangle(points[11], points[12],
                          points[1],  0xcccc66);
```

```
triangles[24] = new Triangle(points[1],  points[12],
                             points[2],  0xcccc66);
triangles[25] = new Triangle(points[12], points[13],
                             points[2],  0xcccc66);
triangles[26] = new Triangle(points[3],  points[2],
                             points[14], 0xcccc66);
triangles[27] = new Triangle(points[2],  points[13],
                             points[14], 0xcccc66);
triangles[28] = new Triangle(points[4],  points[3],
                             points[15], 0xcccc66);
triangles[29] = new Triangle(points[3],  points[14],
                             points[15], 0xcccc66);
triangles[30] = new Triangle(points[5],  points[4],
                             points[16], 0xcccc66);
triangles[31] = new Triangle(points[4],  points[15],
                             points[16], 0xcccc66);
triangles[32] = new Triangle(points[6],  points[5],
                             points[17], 0xcccc66);
triangles[33] = new Triangle(points[5],  points[16],
                             points[17], 0xcccc66);
triangles[34] = new Triangle(points[7],  points[6],
                             points[18], 0xcccc66);
triangles[35] = new Triangle(points[6],  points[17],
                             points[18], 0xcccc66);
triangles[36] = new Triangle(points[0],  points[7],
                             points[11], 0xcccc66);
triangles[37] = new Triangle(points[7],  points[18],
                             points[11], 0xcccc66);
triangles[38] = new Triangle(points[8],  points[9],
                             points[19], 0xcccc66);
triangles[39] = new Triangle(points[9],  points[20],
                             points[19], 0xcccc66);
triangles[40] = new Triangle(points[9],  points[10],
                             points[20], 0xcccc66);
triangles[41] = new Triangle(points[10], points[21],
                             points[20], 0xcccc66);
triangles[42] = new Triangle(points[10], points[8],
                             points[21], 0xcccc66);
triangles[43] = new Triangle(points[8],  points[19],
                             points[21], 0xcccc66);
```

Figure 16-18 shows the result.

As you can see, these things build up quickly. The original, flat A had 11 triangles. Extruding it somehow quadrupled that! This code still runs pretty smoothly, but you aren't going to get any massive 3D worlds with thousands of polygons in Flash. Still, you can do some pretty cool things. This same program ran nicely in AS 2. With AS 3 being far faster, I don't think we are even close to pushing its limits here. And with Flash Player improving in performance with each release, who knows what the future holds?

Figure 16-18. An extruded letter A

Cylinder

One more shape example. This time I'm going to show you how you can create points and triangles with some math. The only thing I changed in Cylinder.as was the init function (and I added a numFaces variable at the top). Instead of defining points and triangles by hand, I created an algorithm to do it for me and make a cylinder. Here's that init function:

```
private var numFaces:uint = 20;

private function init():void
{

    points = new Array();
    triangles = new Array();

    var index:uint = 0;
    for(var i:uint = 0; i < numFaces; i++)
    {
        var angle:Number = Math.PI * 2 / numFaces * i;
        var xpos:Number = Math.cos(angle) * 200;
        var ypos:Number = Math.sin(angle) * 200;
        points[index] =     new Point3D(xpos, ypos, -100);
        points[index + 1] = new Point3D(xpos, ypos,  100);
        index += 2;
    }
    for(i = 0; i < points.length; i++)
    {
        points[i].setVanishingPoint(vpX, vpY);
        points[i].setCenter(0, 0, 200);
    }
    index = 0;
    for(i = 0; i < numFaces - 1; i++)
    {
```

```
            triangles[index] =     new Triangle(points[index],
                                                 points[index + 3],
                                                 points[index + 1],
                                                 0x6666cc);
            triangles[index + 1] = new Triangle(points[index],
                                                 points[index + 2],
                                                 points[index + 3],
                                                 0x6666cc);
            index += 2;
        }

        triangles[index] =     new Triangle(points[index],
                                             points[1],
                                             points[index + 1],
                                             0x6666cc);
        triangles[index+1] = new Triangle(points[index],
                                          points[0],
                                          points[1],
                                          0x6666cc);

        addEventListener(Event.ENTER_FRAME, onEnterFrame);
    }
```

Now, I know this isn't the most lucid code, so let's go through it with some explanation and maybe a diagram or two.

You're going to loop around in a full circle and create points at certain intervals. For each loop, you first get an angle, which is the full circle, divided by the number of faces, times the particular segment you're working on.

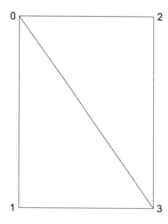

You use that angle, with some trigonometry you should be well used to by now, to determine the x, y point for that point on the circle. You then make two points, one with a z of –100 and one with a z of +100. When this loop is done, you'll have two circles of dots, one close to you and one a bit farther away. Now you just need to connect them with triangles.

Again, you loop through for each face. This time, you create two triangles. Seen from the side, the first face looks like Figure 16-19.

This makes the two triangles:

0, 3, 1
0, 2, 3

Figure 16-19. The first face of the cylinder

Since the `index` variable is 0, you can also define these like so:

```
index, index + 3, index + 1
index, index + 2, index + 3
```

which is exactly how you define the two triangles. You then increase index by 2 to handle the next face with points 2, 3, 4, and 5.

You do that up to the second-to-last face, and then connect the last one back to the first two points, 0 and 1, as shown in Figure 16-20.

These wind up as follows:

```
index, 1, index + 1
index, 0, 1
```

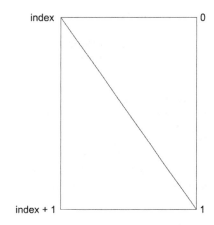

Figure 16-20. The last face of the cylinder

with the result shown in Figure 16-21. If you want to make the form a little more clear, you can go into the `Triangle` class and add in a `lineStyle` statement to the code that draws each triangle.

Figure 16-21. The resulting 3D cylinder

Moving 3D solids

Moving one of the 3D solids is pretty easy now that you have the `Point3D` class. Just change its center with the `setCenter` method. You've already been doing just that to move the shape out on the z axis. Just do the same thing with the other axes. But let's take a quick look at what the code is doing when we change those values. It's all in the `screenX` and `screenY` methods of the `Point3D` class:

```
public function get screenX():Number
{
    var scale:Number = fl / (fl + z + cZ);
    return vpX + (cX + x) * scale;
}
```

```
public function get screenY():Number
{
    var scale:Number = fl / (fl + z + cZ);
    return vpY + (cY + y) * scale;
}
```

The center z property, cZ, is added to the z position value, but only when the scale is calculated, effectively pushing the point out into the distance without actually altering the z position itself.

The same thing happens with cX and cY. They are added to the x and y position values just before scale is applied. This pushes the point off in one of those directions, again without permanently altering it. Because we are not changing any of these values, the point—and thus the larger shape that it is part of—will continue to rotate around its own center, rather than orbiting around the center of the world.

Let's see this in action. Go back to the Cube.as class, and add two class properties at the top of the class:

```
private var offsetX:Number = 0;
private var offsetY:Number = 0;
```

and in the init method, add the following line:

```
stage.addEventListener(KeyboardEvent.KEY_DOWN, onKeyDown);
```

Then create the handler method:

```
private function onKeyDown(event:KeyboardEvent):void
{
    if(event.keyCode == Keyboard.LEFT)
    {
        offsetX = -5;
    }
    else if(event.keyCode == Keyboard.RIGHT)
    {
        offsetX = 5;
    }
    else if(event.keyCode == Keyboard.UP)
    {
        offsetY = -5;
    }
    else if(event.keyCode == Keyboard.DOWN)
    {
        offsetY = 5;
    }
    for(var i:Number = 0; i < points.length; i++)
    {
        points[i].x += offsetX;
        points[i].y += offsetY;
    }
}
```

Don't forget to import the KeyboardEvent and Keyboard classes.

This merely loops through each point and adds or subtracts 5 from its value. Since the actual positions of all the points are changing, the model now kind of orbits around the center of the 3D space. This may or may not be what you wanted it to do. If you just want to move the whole model, and still have it rotate around its own center, that's where the setCenter method comes in. Change the onKeyDown code to the following:

```
private function onKeyDown(event:KeyboardEvent):void
{
    if(event.keyCode == Keyboard.LEFT)
    {
        offsetX -= 5;
    }
    else if(event.keyCode == Keyboard.RIGHT)
    {
        offsetX += 5;
    }
    else if(event.keyCode == Keyboard.UP)
    {
        offsetY -= 5;
    }
    else if(event.keyCode == Keyboard.DOWN)
    {
        offsetY += 5;
    }
    for(var i:Number = 0; i < points.length; i++)
    {
        points[i].setCenter(offsetX, offsetY, 200);
    }
}
```

Now the entire cube moves as a whole, and continues to rotate around its center, not orbit around the world's center.

Summary

With what you've learned in this chapter, you should be well on your way to modeling your own 3D shapes in ActionScript and manipulating them in 3D space.

This chapter concentrated on the modeling aspect and on how to draw the lines and fills. In the next chapter, you'll explore how to create more solid-looking solids. All that material builds on the foundation of points, lines, and fills that you've covered here. So, when you're ready, let's move on!

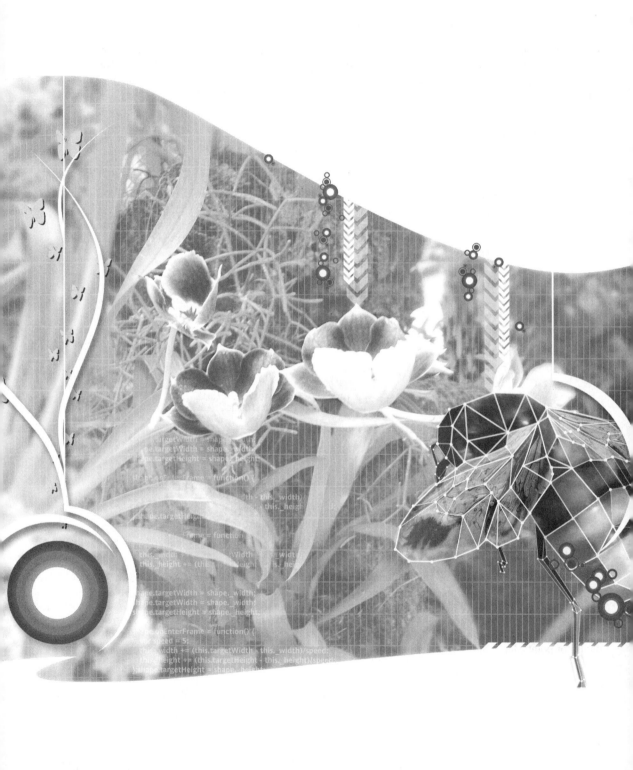

Chapter 17

BACKFACE CULLING AND 3D LIGHTING

What we'll cover in this chapter:

- Backface culling
- Depth sorting
- 3D lighting

In Chapter 16, I covered all the basics of modeling 3D solids: how to create the points, lines, and polygons that make up a form, even how to give each polygon a color. But if you recall, you just left that color with a 50% transparency, so you could see right through it. So while it was cool to be able to model complex 3D solids, you're still lacking a lot in terms of realism.

In this chapter, I'm going to remedy that by introducing you to backface culling (not drawing the polygons facing away from you), depth sorting (I covered this a bit in Chapter 15, but we'll take a new look at it in terms of polygons), and 3D lighting.

I think you will be amazed at the results on your 3D models once these three techniques are applied. After the first two, you will be able to create 3D solids that actually look solid. With 3D lighting, they will really come alive.

Before we begin, I want to give credit where it is due. Almost all of the code in this chapter was derived from techniques introduced by Todd Yard in Chapter 10 of *Macromedia Flash MX Studio* (friends of ED, 2002). (Todd is also the technical reviewer on this book, so it's not like I was going to sneak anything past him!) That particular chapter of *Macromedia Flash MX Studio* is probably the best single resource I've found anywhere on these subjects, and I've referred to it every time I've needed to apply any of these advanced 3D techniques. As that book is now more than four years old (ancient in terms of technical books) and three versions of Flash behind, I'm really happy to be able to pull the information forward and keep it available and current.

For the examples in this chapter, I am going to build on the rotating, extruded, 3D letter A that was created near the end of the last chapter. This serves as a sufficiently complex model that it will be pretty obvious if you do something wrong, and look pretty darn cool when you do everything right!

Backface culling

Backface culling was alluded to a couple of times in the last chapter, and now you are going to find out what it is all about and exactly how it works.

Remember that in the earlier models, you made all the fills semitransparent. The reason for this was that you were always drawing every polygon, and you had no control over what order they were drawn in. So a polygon on the back of the model might get drawn on top of one on the front of the model, creating some odd results. Giving them all an alpha value of 50% made them all relatively equal and let me put off this discussion while you concentrated on your modeling techniques. Now you are going to deal with it.

In principle, backface culling is pretty simple. You draw the polygons that are facing you, and you don't draw the ones that are facing away from you. The tricky part is determining which are which.

You should also remember that I was constantly reminding you to define the points of each polygon in a clockwise direction. Even though that is completely unnecessary for what you've been doing so far, you'll now see why this was so important, and why it was good to get into that habit from the start.

It's a neat little observation that if the points of a polygon are arranged in a clockwise fashion when that triangle is facing you, they will be counterclockwise when that polygon is facing away from you. You can see this demonstrated in Figure 17-1, which has a triangle facing you. (Since all the polygons you will be using will be triangles, I will occasionally mix the two terms. For the most part, I'll use "polygon" as a general term, and "triangle" to discuss a specific triangular polygon under discussion.)

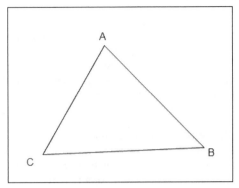

Figure 17-1. A triangle facing you has points in a clockwise direction.

And in Figure 17-2, I've rotated the triangle so it is facing in the opposite direction.

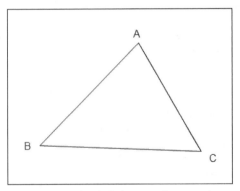

Figure 17-2. A triangle facing away from you has points in a counterclockwise direction.

Now you see that points go around in a counterclockwise direction.

There are a few points of clarification to make here. First of all, what do I mean when I say a polygon is "facing you"? I mean that the *exterior* side of the polygon is facing you. Although it's not obvious when I show a single triangle, remember that I'm talking about 3D solids here. In that case, each polygon has one exterior side and one interior side.

Another point is that when determining clockwise or counterclockwise, I'm talking about the *screen* positions of the points. Not the 3D x, y, and z positions, but the screenX, screenY position that is determined by applying perspective.

Finally, it should be noted that you could reverse the setup and make a system where counterclockwise polygons were the facing ones, and clockwise ones faced away. Either way works as long as you are consistent.

So again, we get back to the question, how do you determine whether three points are arranged in a clockwise or counterclockwise direction? Think about it for a while. It's such an easy thing for your eyes to pick out, but when it comes down to putting it in code, it suddenly seems like a very abstract concept.

As I mentioned, the solution I'm going to give you here is based on the one given in *Macromedia Flash MX Studio*. But just to make sure I was providing the best method possible, I decided to see whether I could come up with my own function to distinguish clockwise from counterclockwise. While I did manage to put something together that worked perfectly, it was twice as long as the existing solution and far more complex, involving coordinate rotation and lots of trig. Since I'm generally a nice guy, I decided to give you the simple one. And don't worry, it's just as accurate as my overly complex one!

What you're going to do is add a method to the Triangle class, called isBackFace. This will evaluate the three points that make up the triangle, and return true if they are counterclockwise and false if they are clockwise. Here is the class with that new function. Notice also that the call to beginFill no longer uses .5 for alpha. We're going to draw opaque shapes here.

```
package
{
    import flash.display.Graphics;

    public class Triangle
    {
        private var pointA:Point3D;
        private var pointB:Point3D;
        private var pointC:Point3D;
        private var color:uint;

        public function Triangle(a:Point3D, b:Point3D,
                                 c:Point3D, color:uint)
        {
            pointA = a;
            pointB = b;
            pointC = c;
            this.color = color;
        }

        public function draw(g:Graphics):void
        {
            if(isBackFace())
            {
                return;
            }
            g.beginFill(color);
            g.moveTo(pointA.screenX, pointA.screenY);
            g.lineTo(pointB.screenX, pointB.screenY);
            g.lineTo(pointC.screenX, pointC.screenY);
            g.lineTo(pointA.screenX, pointA.screenY);
            g.endFill();
        }
```

```
private function isBackFace():Boolean
{
    // see http://www.jurjans.lv/flash/shape.html
    var cax:Number = pointC.screenX - pointA.screenX;
    var cay:Number = pointC.screenY - pointA.screenY;

    var bcx:Number = pointB.screenX - pointC.screenX;
    var bcy:Number = pointB.screenY - pointC.screenY;

    return cax * bcy > cay * bcx;
}
    }
}
```

You see the link to the website, http://www.jurjans.lv/flash/shape.html. Todd Yard credited this site in *Macromedia Flash MX Studio*, so I'll pass it on. In addition to giving credit where it is due, the site has some excellent reference material and tutorials on many similar subjects.

For a quick explanation, the function calculates the lengths of two sides of the triangle, and with some sleight-of-hand multiplication and comparison, is able to tell which direction they are going. If you are interested in the specifics of why this works, see the site just mentioned, or do a search for "backface culling." I'm sure you'll find plenty of reading material. For now, though, I'm going to just say it is simple, quick, efficient, and 100% workable, and leave it at that!

So, how do you use this method? You don't really need to think about it. It is a private method, meaning it can only be called from within the Triangle class itself. It is called as the first statement of the draw method. If it returns true, the triangle is a back face and should not be drawn, so the draw method just stops there and returns. If isBackFace returns false, the triangle is facing forward, and will be drawn as usual.

Now, you can run ExtrudedA.as, or any other 3D model you've created, and you'll see that things are quite a bit different. As you rotate the shape around, you'll see that as soon as a particular face is facing the other way, it is no longer drawn. Things aren't perfect yet, as there are still parts that are further away drawing on top of parts that are closer, but we are getting there. If the term "z-sorting," or "depth sorting," just came to mind, you are right on track. That's what's coming up next.

Figure 17-3. Backface culling in action

Right now you should be looking at something similar to what appears in Figure 17-3.

Depth sorting

Depth sorting, or z-sorting, is something we've already discussed in Chapter 15, when you were just applying perspective to sprites. In that case, you sorted the array of sprites (actually subclasses of Sprite that had 3D properties) by their zpos property.

At this point however, you are not dealing with multiple sprites. All of the polygons are being drawn within the same graphics object of the main document class. Thus, whenever a particular polygon is drawn, it will be drawn on top of any that have been drawn earlier. So, rather than swapping anything's depth, you just need to determine which polygon gets drawn when. Specifically, you want to draw the ones that are farthest away first; then you draw the rest, working your way forward, so that the closest polygons are drawn last, covering anything they might be in front of.

So how do you do that? Well, you have all the polygons in an array called triangles. And when you draw the shape, you loop through triangles, drawing each triangle from zero through to the end. What you need to do is sort this array so that the triangle that is furthest away is in element zero of the array, and the one closest to the viewer is in the very last element.

This is pretty similar to what we did when sorting the array of sprites. But in this case, triangles are just a collection of three Point3D objects. They don't have a single property that describes the overall depth of the triangle. However, it is easy enough to create such a property. It turns out that the value that works best is the minimum z value of the three points within a triangle. In other words, if a triangle had three points with depths 200, 250, and 300, we should say this triangle is at a z position of 200.

We can use the Math.min method to determine the minimum z value of all three points. But we'll have to use it twice, as you can only pass two values to it at a time. We'll do this within a new get depth method of the Triangle class. Here's the updated class:

```
package
{
    import flash.display.Graphics;

    public class Triangle
    {
        private var pointA:Point3D;
        private var pointB:Point3D;
        private var pointC:Point3D;
        private var color:uint;

        public function Triangle(a:Point3D, b:Point3D,
                                 c:Point3D, color:uint)
        {
            pointA = a;
            pointB = b;
            pointC = c;
            this.color = color;
        }

        public function draw(g:Graphics):void
        {
            if(isBackFace())
            {
                return;
            }
            g.beginFill(color);
            g.moveTo(pointA.screenX, pointA.screenY);
```

```
            g.lineTo(pointB.screenX, pointB.screenY);
            g.lineTo(pointC.screenX, pointC.screenY);
            g.lineTo(pointA.screenX, pointA.screenY);
            g.endFill();
        }

        private function isBackFace():Boolean
        {
            // see http://www.jurjans.lv/flash/shape.html
            var cax:Number = pointC.screenX - pointA.screenX;
            var cay:Number = pointC.screenY - pointA.screenY;

            var bcx:Number = pointB.screenX - pointC.screenX;
            var bcy:Number = pointB.screenY - pointC.screenY;

            return cax * bcy > cay * bcx;
        }

        public function get depth():Number
        {
            var zpos:Number = Math.min(pointA.z, pointB.z);
            zpos = Math.min(zpos, pointC.z);
            return zpos;
        }
    }
}
```

Now you can sort the triangles array and know which to draw first and which to draw last. Again, you'll want to sort it in descending order so that the one with the highest depth (furthest away) is first. You'll have to do this in your main class, and you'll have to do it just before you draw any of the triangles. I'm using the ExtrudedA class, so the onEnterFrame method of this class will now look like this:

```
private function onEnterFrame(event:Event):void
{
    var angleX:Number = (mouseY - vpY) * .001;
    var angleY:Number = (mouseX - vpX) * .001;
    for(var i:uint = 0; i < points.length; i++)
    {
        var point:Point3D = points[i];
        point.rotateX(angleX);
        point.rotateY(angleY);
    }

    triangles.sortOn("depth", Array.DESCENDING | Array.NUMERIC);
    graphics.clear();
    for(i = 0; i < triangles.length; i++)
    {
        triangles[i].draw(graphics);
    }
}
```

You see it's just that one line that changes. Again, the wonders of object-oriented programming making life easier for us!

When you run this, you should have a perfectly rendered solid, as shown in Figure 17-4. You are really getting someplace now. The next step will boost you right over the top in terms of coolness!

3D lighting

While the last example is pretty close to perfect in terms of rendering, it still kind of lacks something. It's a bit flat. OK, OK, you already know where I'm heading with this, because it says so right in the section title, so let's add some 3D lighting.

Figure 17-4. Sorting the depths puts it all right!

Like backface culling, the specifics behind 3D lighting can get pretty complex and math intensive. I don't really have the space to get into a detailed discussion of all the finer points, but a quick web search will turn up more information on the subject than you could probably read in a lifetime. What I'm going to give you here are the basics, along with some functions you can use and adapt as needed.

First of all, you need a light source. A light source at its simplest has two properties: location and brightness. In more complex 3D systems, it may also be able to point in a certain direction, have a color of its own, have falloff rates, conical areas, etc. But all that is beyond the scope of what you are doing here.

Let's start out by making a Light class. It will hold the properties I just mentioned—location and brightness.

```
package
{
    public class Light
    {
        public var x:Number;
        public var y:Number;
        public var z:Number;
        private var _brightness:Number;

        public function Light(x:Number = -100,
                              y:Number = -100,
                              z:Number = -100,
                              brightness:Number = 1)
        {
            this.x = x;
            this.y = y;
            this.z = z;
            this.brightness = brightness;
        }
```

```
        public function set brightness(b:Number):void
        {
            _brightness = Math.max(b, 0);
            _brightness = Math.min(_brightness, 1);
        }

        public function get brightness():Number
        {
            return _brightness;
        }
    }
}
```

Now, in the init method of your main class, you can create a new default light like so:

```
var light:Light = new Light();
```

Or, you could create a light with a particular position and location like this:

```
var light:Light = new Light(100, 200, 300, .5);
```

Two things important to note here. One is that the position is used to calculate the angle of the light only. The strength of the light you are creating does not fall off with distance. Thus changing the x, y, and z to –1,000,000 or down to –1 would make no difference in terms of how brightly the object is lit. Only the brightness property will change that characteristic of the light. You could certainly add this functionality, altering the brightness value based on the distance from the light to the area it is hitting. It wouldn't even be that hard, but I have enough to cover here, so I'll leave that to you.

Also, brightness must be a number from 0.0 to 1.0. If you go outside of that range, you can wind up with some odd results. For this reason, we make _brightness a private property, and allow access through the public getter and setter, brightness. This allows us to validate the number that is passed in, to make sure it is within range.

Ideally, a class would have no public properties at all, only private properties accessed through getter and setter functions, even if those properties don't need to be validated. I've cut a lot of corners in order to make the code simple and highlight the animation principles. But in this case, there's good reason to go the extra step.

Now, what the light source is going to do is change the brightness of the color of a triangle, based on the angle of the light that is falling on that polygon. So if the polygon is facing directly at the light, it will display the full value of its color. As it turns away from the light, it will get darker and darker. Finally, when it is facing completely away from the light source, it will be completely in shadow and colored black.

Since members of the Triangle class keep track of their own color, and know how to draw themselves, it seems like each triangle is going to need access to this light to perform its drawing function. So, let's give the triangles a light property. We'll cut some more corners and just make it a public property:

```
public var light:Light;
```

Then in the main class, after you create the triangles, just loop through them and give each one a reference to the light:

```
var light:Light = new Light();
for(i = 0; i < triangles.length; i++)
{
    triangles[i].light = light;
}
```

Alternatively, you could make light an additional parameter to the Triangle constructor, which would ensure that every triangle always has a light source. I'll leave that choice up to you.

So, what Triangle now needs is a function that will look at its base color and the angle and brightness of the light, and return an adjusted color. Here is that function:

```
function getAdjustedColor():uint
{
    var red:Number =   color >> 16;
    var green:Number = color >> 8 & 0xff;
    var blue:Number =  color & 0xff;

    var lightFactor:Number = getLightFactor();

    red *= lightFactor;
    green *= lightFactor;
    blue *= lightFactor;

    return red << 16 | green << 8 | blue;
}
```

This function first splits the triangle's base color into red, green, and blue components (see Chapter 4). It then calls another method, getLightFactor. You'll see that function in a moment. For now, you just need to know that it returns a number from 0.0 to 1.0. This is how much it needs to alter the color of that particular triangle, 1.0 being full brightness, and 0.0 being black.

It then multiplies each of the component colors by that light factor, joins them back into a single 24-bit color value, and returns that as the adjusted color. That's going to be the color of the triangle, based on its lighting.

Now, how do you come up with this lightFactor? Let's look:

```
private function getLightFactor():Number
{
    var ab:Object = new Object();
    ab.x = pointA.x - pointB.x;
    ab.y = pointA.y - pointB.y;
    ab.z = pointA.z - pointB.z;

    var bc:Object = new Object();
    bc.x = pointB.x - pointC.x;
    bc.y = pointB.y - pointC.y;
    bc.z = pointB.z - pointC.z;
```

```
        var norm:Object = new Object();
        norm.x = (ab.y * bc.z) - (ab.z * bc.y);
        norm.y = -((ab.x * bc.z) - (ab.z * bc.x));
        norm.z = (ab.x * bc.y) - (ab.y * bc.x);

        var dotProd:Number = norm.x * light.x +
                             norm.y * light.y +
                             norm.z * light.z;

        var normMag:Number = Math.sqrt(norm.x * norm.x +
                                       norm.y * norm.y +
                                       norm.z * norm.z);

        var lightMag:Number = Math.sqrt(light.x * light.x +
                                        light.y * light.y +
                                        light.z * light.z);

        return (Math.acos(dotProd / (normMag * lightMag)) / Math.PI)
               * light.brightness;
    }
```

Whoa, that is quite a function, huh? To *fully* understand all that's going on here, you'd have to have a good grasp on advanced vector math, but I'll try to walk through the bare basics of it.

First of all you need to find the *normal* of the triangle. This is a vector that is perpendicular to the surface of the triangle, as depicted in Figure 17-5. Imagine you had a triangular piece of wood and you put a nail through the back of it so it stuck out directly through the face. That nail would represent the normal of that surface. If you study anything about 3D rendering and lighting, you are going to see all kinds of references to normals.

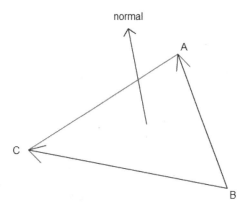

Figure 17-5. The normal is perpendicular to the surface of the triangle.

You can find the normal of a surface by taking two vectors that make up that surface plane and calculating their *cross product*. A cross product of two vectors is a new vector, which is perpendicular to those two. The two vectors you will use will be the lines between points A and B, and points B and C. Each vector will be held in a generic object with x, y, and z properties.

```
var ab:Object = new Object();
ab.x = pointA.x - pointB.x;
ab.y = pointA.y - pointB.y;
ab.z = pointA.z - pointB.z;

var bc:Object = new Object();
bc.x = pointB.x - pointC.x;
bc.y = pointB.y - pointC.y;
bc.z = pointB.z - pointC.z;
```

Then you calculate the normal, which is another vector. You'll call this object norm. The following code computes the cross product of the vectors ab and bc:

```
var norm:Object = new Object();
norm.x = (ab.y * bc.z) - (ab.z * bc.y);
norm.y = -((ab.x * bc.z) - (ab.z * bc.x));
norm.z = (ab.x * bc.y) - (ab.y * bc.x);
```

Again, I don't have the space to cover the details of why this is calculated this way, but this is the standard formula for calculating a cross product. If you are interested in how this is derived, you can check any decent reference on linear algebra.

Now you need to know how closely that normal aligns with the angle of the light. Another bit of vector math goodness is called the *dot product*, which is the difference between two vectors. You have the vector of the normal, and the vector of the light. The following calculates that dot product:

```
var dotProd:Number = norm.x * light.x +
                     norm.y * light.y +
                     norm.z * light.z;
```

As you can see, dot products are a bit simpler than cross products!

OK, you are almost there! Next, you calculate the magnitude of the normal, and the magnitude of the light, which you might recognize as the 3D version of the Pythagorean Theorem:

```
var normMag:Number = Math.sqrt(norm.x * norm.x +
                               norm.y * norm.y +
                               norm.z * norm.z);

var lightMag:Number = Math.sqrt(light.x * light.x +
                                light.y * light.y +
                                light.z * light.z);
```

Note that this lightMag variable is calculated every time a triangle is rendered, which allows for a moving light source. If you know that the light source is going to be fixed, you could create this variable at the beginning of the code and calculate it one time as soon as the light was created or assigned to the triangle. Alternatively, you could add a lightMag property to the Light class. This could be calculated any time its x, y, or z properties actually changed. See, I'm leaving all kinds of room for you to improve things!

Finally, you take all these bits you've just calculated, and put them into the magic formula:

```
return (Math.acos(dotProd / (normMag * lightMag)) / Math.PI)
        * light.brightness;
```

Basically, dotProd is one measurement and normMag * lightMag is another. Dividing these two gives you a ratio. Recall from our discussion in Chapter 3 that the cosine of an angle gives you a ratio, and the arccosine of a ratio gives you an angle. So using Math.acos here on this ratio of measurements gives you an angle. This is essentially the angle at which the light is striking the surface of the polygon. It will be in the range of 0 to Math.PI radians (0 to 180 degrees), meaning it's either hitting head on or completely from behind.

Dividing this angle by Math.PI gives you a percentage, and multiplying that by the percentage of brightness gives you your final light factor, which you use to alter the base color.

OK, now all this was just to get a new color for the surface! Implementing it in your existing code is actually pretty easy. Where you wind up using it is in the draw method. Instead of using the base color, use the adjusted color, like so:

```
g.beginFill(getAdjustedColor());
```

To wrap things up, here is the full and final code for Triangle.as and ExtrudedA.as, showing all the changes that we made in this chapter.

First Triangle:

```
package
{
    import flash.display.Graphics;

    public class Triangle
    {
        private var pointA:Point3D;
        private var pointB:Point3D;
        private var pointC:Point3D;
        private var color:uint;
        public var light:Light;

        public function Triangle(a:Point3D, b:Point3D,
                                 c:Point3D, color:uint)
        {
            pointA = a;
            pointB = b;
            pointC = c;
            this.color = color;
        }
```

```
public function draw(g:Graphics):void
{
    if(isBackFace())
    {
        return;
    }
    g.beginFill(getAdjustedColor());
    g.moveTo(pointA.screenX, pointA.screenY);
    g.lineTo(pointB.screenX, pointB.screenY);
    g.lineTo(pointC.screenX, pointC.screenY);
    g.lineTo(pointA.screenX, pointA.screenY);
    g.endFill();
}

private function getAdjustedColor():uint
{
    var red:Number = color >> 16;
    var green:Number = color >> 8 & 0xff;
    var blue:Number =color & 0xff;

    var lightFactor:Number = getLightFactor();

    red *= lightFactor;
    green *= lightFactor;
    blue *= lightFactor;

    return red << 16 | green << 8 | blue;
}

private function getLightFactor():Number
{
    var ab:Object = new Object();
    ab.x = pointA.x - pointB.x;
    ab.y = pointA.y - pointB.y;
    ab.z = pointA.z - pointB.z;

    var bc:Object = new Object();
    bc.x = pointB.x - pointC.x;
    bc.y = pointB.y - pointC.y;
    bc.z = pointB.z - pointC.z;

    var norm:Object = new Object();
    norm.x = (ab.y * bc.z) - (ab.z * bc.y);
    norm.y = -((ab.x * bc.z) - (ab.z * bc.x));
    norm.z = (ab.x * bc.y) - (ab.y * bc.x);

    var dotProd:Number = norm.x * light.x +
                         norm.y * light.y +
                         norm.z * light.z;
```

```
                    var normMag:Number = Math.sqrt(norm.x * norm.x +
                                                   norm.y * norm.y +
                                                   norm.z * norm.z);

                    var lightMag:Number = Math.sqrt(light.x * light.x +
                                                    light.y * light.y +
                                                    light.z * light.z);

                    return (Math.acos(dotProd / (normMag * lightMag)) /
                            Math.PI) * light.brightness;
                }

                private function isBackFace():Boolean
                {
                    // see http://www.jurjans.lv/flash/shape.html
                    var cax:Number = pointC.screenX - pointA.screenX;
                    var cay:Number = pointC.screenY - pointA.screenY;

                    var bcx:Number = pointB.screenX - pointC.screenX;
                    var bcy:Number = pointB.screenY - pointC.screenY;

                    return cax * bcy > cay * bcx;
                }

                public function get depth():Number
                {
                    var zpos:Number = Math.min(pointA.z, pointB.z);
                    zpos = Math.min(zpos, pointC.z);
                    return zpos;
                }
            }
        }
    }
```

And then ExtrudedA:

```
    package {
        import flash.display.Sprite;
        import flash.events.Event;

        public class ExtrudedA extends Sprite
        {
            private var points:Array;
            private var triangles:Array;
            private var fl:Number = 250;
            private var vpX:Number = stage.stageWidth / 2;
            private var vpY:Number = stage.stageHeight / 2;

            public function ExtrudedA()
            {
```

```
            init();
        }

        private function init():void
        {
            points = new Array();
            points[0] = new Point3D( -50, -250,  -50);
            points[1] = new Point3D(  50, -250,  -50);
            points[2] = new Point3D( 200,  250,  -50);
            points[3] = new Point3D( 100,  250,  -50);
            points[4] = new Point3D(  50,  100,  -50);
            points[5] = new Point3D( -50,  100,  -50);
            points[6] = new Point3D(-100,  250,  -50);
            points[7] = new Point3D(-200,  250,  -50);
            points[8] = new Point3D(   0, -150,  -50);
            points[9] = new Point3D(  50,    0,  -50);
            points[10] = new Point3D( -50,    0,  -50);

            points[11] = new Point3D( -50, -250,  50);
            points[12] = new Point3D(  50, -250,  50);
            points[13] = new Point3D( 200,  250,  50);
            points[14] = new Point3D( 100,  250,  50);
            points[15] = new Point3D(  50,  100,  50);
            points[16] = new Point3D( -50,  100,  50);
            points[17] = new Point3D(-100,  250,  50);
            points[18] = new Point3D(-200,  250,  50);
            points[19] = new Point3D(   0, -150,  50);
            points[20] = new Point3D(  50,    0,  50);
            points[21] = new Point3D( -50,    0,  50);
            for(var i:uint = 0; i < points.length; i++)
            {
                points[i].setVanishingPoint(vpX, vpY);
                points[i].setCenter(0, 0, 200);
            }

            triangles = new Array();
            triangles[0] =new Triangle(points[0],    points[1],
                                       points[8],    0xcccccc);
            triangles[1] =new Triangle(points[1],    points[9],
                                       points[8],    0xcccccc);
            triangles[2] =new Triangle(points[1],    points[2],
                                       points[9],    0xcccccc);
            triangles[3] =new Triangle(points[2],    points[4],
                                       points[9],    0xcccccc);
            triangles[4] =new Triangle(points[2],    points[3],
                                       points[4],    0xcccccc);
            triangles[5] =new Triangle(points[4],    points[5],
                                       points[9],    0xcccccc);
            triangles[6] =new Triangle(points[9],    points[5],
```

```
                                  points[10],  0xcccccc);
triangles[7] =new Triangle(points[5],   points[6],
                                  points[7],   0xcccccc);
triangles[8] =new Triangle(points[5],   points[7],
                                  points[10],  0xcccccc);
triangles[9] =new Triangle(points[0],   points[10],
                                  points[7],   0xcccccc);
triangles[10] =new Triangle(points[0],   points[8],
                                  points[10],  0xcccccc);
triangles[11] =new Triangle(points[11], points[19],
                                  points[12], 0xcccccc);
triangles[12] =new Triangle(points[12], points[19],
                                  points[20], 0xcccccc);
triangles[13] =new Triangle(points[12], points[20],
                                  points[13], 0xcccccc);
triangles[14] =new Triangle(points[13], points[20],
                                  points[15], 0xcccccc);
triangles[15] =new Triangle(points[13], points[15],
                                  points[14], 0xcccccc);
triangles[16] =new Triangle(points[15], points[20],
                                  points[16], 0xcccccc);
triangles[17] =new Triangle(points[20], points[21],
                                  points[16], 0xcccccc);
triangles[18] =new Triangle(points[16], points[18],
                                  points[17], 0xcccccc);
triangles[19] =new Triangle(points[16], points[21],
                                  points[18], 0xcccccc);
triangles[20] =new Triangle(points[11], points[18],
                                  points[21], 0xcccccc);
triangles[21] =new Triangle(points[11], points[21],
                                  points[19], 0xcccccc);
triangles[22] =new Triangle(points[0],   points[11],
                                  points[1],   0xcccccc);
triangles[23] =new Triangle(points[11], points[12],
                                  points[1],   0xcccccc);
triangles[24] =new Triangle(points[1],   points[12],
                                  points[2],   0xcccccc);
triangles[25] =new Triangle(points[12], points[13],
                                  points[2],   0xcccccc);
triangles[26] =new Triangle(points[3],   points[2],
                                  points[14], 0xcccccc);
triangles[27] =new Triangle(points[2],   points[13],
                                  points[14], 0xcccccc);
triangles[28] =new Triangle(points[4],   points[3],
                                  points[15], 0xcccccc);
triangles[29] =new Triangle(points[3],   points[14],
                                  points[15], 0xcccccc);
triangles[30] =new Triangle(points[5],   points[4],
                                  points[16], 0xcccccc);
```

```
triangles[31] =new Triangle(points[4],  points[15],
                            points[16], 0xcccccc);
triangles[32] =new Triangle(points[6],  points[5],
                            points[17], 0xcccccc);
triangles[33] =new Triangle(points[5],  points[16],
                            points[17], 0xcccccc);
triangles[34] =new Triangle(points[7],  points[6],
                            points[18], 0xcccccc);
triangles[35] =new Triangle(points[6],  points[17],
                            points[18], 0xcccccc);
triangles[36] =new Triangle(points[0],  points[7],
                            points[11], 0xcccccc);
triangles[37] =new Triangle(points[7],  points[18],
                            points[11], 0xcccccc);
triangles[38] =new Triangle(points[8],  points[9],
                            points[19], 0xcccccc);
triangles[39] =new Triangle(points[9],  points[20],
                            points[19], 0xcccccc);
triangles[40] =new Triangle(points[9],  points[10],
                            points[20], 0xcccccc);
triangles[41] =new Triangle(points[10], points[21],
                            points[20], 0xcccccc);
triangles[42] =new Triangle(points[10], points[8],
                            points[21], 0xcccccc);
triangles[43] =new Triangle(points[8],  points[19],
                            points[21], 0xcccccc);

    var light:Light = new Light();
    for(i = 0; i < triangles.length; i++)
    {
        triangles[i].light = light;
    }

    addEventListener(Event.ENTER_FRAME, onEnterFrame);
}

private function onEnterFrame(event:Event):void
{
    var angleX:Number = (mouseY - vpY) * .001;
    var angleY:Number = (mouseX - vpX) * .001;
    for(var i:uint = 0; i < points.length; i++)
    {
        var point:Point3D = points[i];
        point.rotateX(angleX);
        point.rotateY(angleY);
    }
    triangles.sortOn("depth", Array.DESCENDING |
                            Array.NUMERIC);
```

```
            graphics.clear();
            for(i = 0; i < triangles.length; i++)
            {
                triangles[i].draw(graphics);
            }
        }
    }
}
```

As you can see, there were only two minor changes to the document class. Most of the work happened in Triangle. However, I did change it so that all the triangles are the same color, which I think shows off the effect of the lighting much better (see Figure 17-6).

Figure 17-6. 3D solid with backface culling, depth sorting, and 3D lighting

Summary

Wow! That was a lot to cover in just a few pages! But I think the results are pretty incredible. You now have the tools to make some stunning 3D movies. And it goes without saying that there are a lot of variations you can throw in here. For instance, in the last example, the light is stationary and the object moves. Try moving the light around instead. (It's just a matter of altering its x, y, and/or z positions.)

That about wraps up our main discussion of 3D. In the next chapter, you'll be looking at matrix math, which is often used as an alternative to some of the scaling and rotation methods you've been using so far, and thus is something you'll often see in 3D programming.

Part Five

ADDITIONAL TECHNIQUES

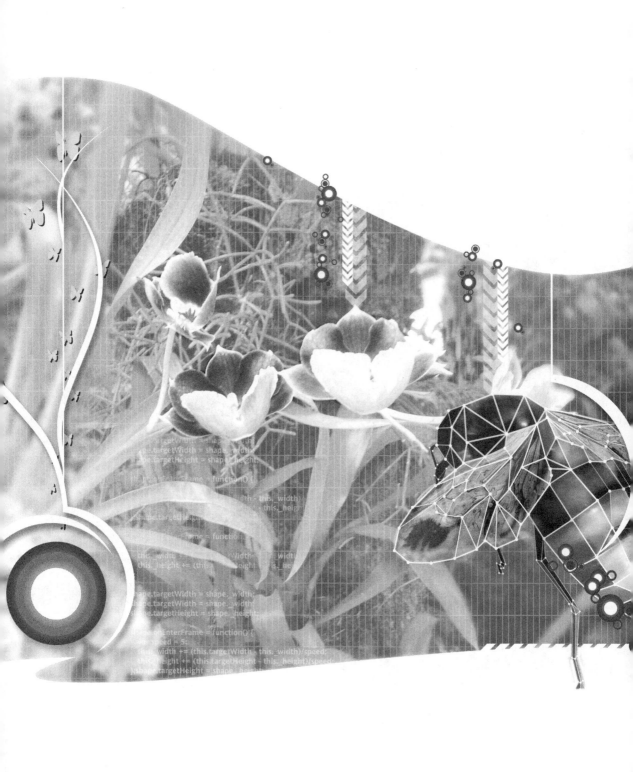

Chapter 18

MATRIX MATH

What we'll cover in this chapter:

- Matrix basics
- Matrix operations
- The Matrix class

In this chapter, I'm not necessarily going to introduce any new types of motion or physics or methods of rendering graphics. What I am going to do is give you an introduction to *matrices*, which provide an alternative way of doing a lot of the things you've already been doing.

Matrices are used quite often in 3D systems for rotating, scaling, and translating (moving) 3D points. They are also used quite a bit in various 2D graphics transformations. You might recall that the beginGradientFill method uses a matrix to position, size, and rotate the gradient.

In this chapter, you'll see how to create a system of 3D matrices to manipulate sprites in 3D and look into several built-in uses of matrices in Flash. Oh, and I'm quite proud of myself for not having made a single corny reference to any Keanu Reeves movie yet. Let's see how long I can restrain myself.

Matrix basics

A matrix, by simplest definition, is a grid of numbers. It can have one or more horizontal rows and one or more vertical columns. Figure 18-1 shows some matrices.

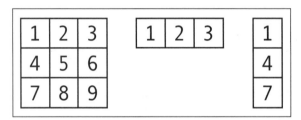

Figure 18-1. A 3×3 matrix, a 1×3 matrix, and a 3×1 matrix

Any particular matrix is usually represented by some variable, such as M. To refer to a specific cell in a matrix, you use the variable name with the row and column number in subscript. For example, if the 3×3 matrix in Figure 18-1 is called M, then $M_{2,3}$ is equal to 6, as it refers to the second row, third column.

The cells of a matrix can contain not only simple numbers, but also formulas and variables. If you've ever used a spreadsheet, that is basically one big matrix. You can have one cell hold the sum of a column, and another cell multiplies that sum by some fraction that's held in another cell, and so forth. So you see that matrices can be pretty useful.

Matrix operations

Now, where a spreadsheet is kind of a free-form matrix, the matrices we'll be dealing with are a lot more structured, and have all kinds of rules associated with them for what we can do with them and how to do it.

Most instructional material on matrix math that I've seen takes one of two approaches. The first school describes how to do the operations in detail, using matrices full of seemingly random numbers. You learn the rules, but you have no idea why you are doing certain things or what the result means. It's like playing a game where you arrange the numbers in a pretty pattern.

The second approach is to describe the contents of the matrices in detail and skim over the operation, with vague instructions such as "and then you just multiply these two matrices together and get this . . . ," leaving the reader with no idea how this multiplication is done.

To ensure you understand how matrices work, I've chosen to walk the line between these two methods, starting with presenting some matrices containing meaningful values, and then describing how to manipulate them.

Matrix addition

One of the more common uses of matrices is manipulating 3D points. A 3D point contains a value for x, y, and z positions. We can easily view this as a 1✕3 matrix like so:

    x y z

Now say you want to move this point in space, also called *translating* the point. What you need to know is how far to move it on each axis. You can put this in a *translation matrix*. This is another 1✕3 matrix that looks something like this:

    dx dy dz

Here, dx, dy, and dz are the distances to move on each axis. Now you need to somehow apply the transformation matrix to the point matrix. This is done with matrix addition, which is pretty simple. You just add each corresponding cell together to make a new matrix containing the sum of each cell. Obviously, to add two matrices, they need to be the same size. For translation, you do this:

    x y z   +   dx dy dz   = (x + dx) (y + dy) (z + dz)

Here, the resulting matrix could be called x1, y1, z1, and contains the new position of the point after it has been translated. Let's try it with some actual numbers. Say your point was at 100, 50, 75 on x, y, z, and you wanted to move it -10, 20, -35. Here's how that would look:

    100 50 75   +   -10 20 -35   =   (100 - 10) (50 + 20) (75 - 35)

Thus, when you perform the addition, you get 90, 70, 40 as the point's new position. Pretty simple, right? You probably already noticed the correlation to velocity, where the velocity on each axis is added to the position on that axis. Same deal here. We're just looking at it a bit differently.

If you had a larger matrix, you would still carry on the same way, matching up the cells. We won't be dealing with matrix addition for anything larger than 3✕1 matrices here, but I'll give you an abstract example:

    a b c   j k l   (a + j) (b + k) (c + l)
    d e f   +   m n o   =   (d + m) (e + n) (f + o)
    g h i   p q r   (g + p) (h + q) (i + r)

And that's about all you need to know about matrix addition. After I cover matrix multiplication, I'll show you how to put together some actual functions to use in a matrix-based 3D engine.

Matrix multiplication

Much more common for doing 3D transformations is *matrix multiplication*, which is usually used for scaling and rotating. We won't actually be using 3D scaling in this book, as the examples cover using either points, which can't be scaled, or sprites, which do not have any 3D "thickness" and are therefore only scaled in two dimensions. Of course, you could build a more complex engine that could scale an entire 3D solid. You'd then need to write additional functions that would alter the 3D points making up the solid based on the new size. That's beyond the scope of what we're doing here, but since scaling is a very simple and clear demonstration of matrix multiplication, I'll run you through an example.

Scaling with a matrix

First you'll need to know an object's existing width, height, and depth—in other words, its measurement of size on each of the three axes. This of course creates a 3×1 matrix:

w h d

As you probably realize, w, h, and d stand for width, height, and depth. Next you need a scaling matrix like the following:

sx   0   0
 0 sy   0
 0   0 sz

Here, sx, sy, and sz are the percentages to scale on that particular axis. These would be in terms of a fraction or decimal, so that 1.0 is 100%, 2.0 is 200%, 0.5 is 50%, etc. You'll see why the matrix is laid out this way in a minute.

One thing you need to know about matrix multiplication is that in order to multiply two matrices, the first matrix must have the same number of *columns* as the second one has *rows*. The first one can have any number of rows, and the second can have any number of columns, as long as these criteria have been met. In this case, you are fine, as the first matrix has three columns (w, h, d), and the scaling matrix has three rows.

So, how do you multiply these things? Let me just go ahead and do it and see if you can see the pattern:

```
                sx   0   0
    w  h  d  *   0  sy   0
                 0   0  sz
```

This produces the following matrix as a result:

(w*sx + h*0 + d*0)   (w*0 + h*sy + d*0)   (w*0 + h*0 + d*sz)

When you get rid of all the zeros, it winds up as this:

(w*sx)   (h*sy)   (d*sz)

This is pretty logical, as you are multiplying the width (x axis measurement) by the x scaling factor, the height by the y scaling factor, and the depth by the z scaling factor. But, what exactly did we do there? All those zeros are kind of occluding things, so let's abstract it a bit so the pattern is clearer.

```
               a  b  c
   u   v   w  *  d  e  f
               g  h  i
```

Now you can see the pattern emerge in this result:

```
   (u*a + v*d  + w*g)  (u*b  + v*e + w*h)  (u*c  + v*f  + w*i)
```

You can see that you move across the first row of the first matrix (u, v, w) and multiply by each first element in each row of the second (a, d, g). Adding those together gives you the first element for the first row of the result. Doing the same with the second column of the second matrix (b, e, h) gives you the second column result.

If you have more than one row in the first matrix, you then repeat the actions with that second row, which gives you the second row of the result:

```
   u   v   w      a  b  c
   x   y   z   *  d  e  f
                  g  h  i
```

which gives you this 3×2 matrix as a result:

```
   (u*a + v*d  + w*g)  (u*b  + v*e + w*h)  (u*c  + v*f  + w*i)
   (x*a + y*d  + z*g)  (x*b  + y*e + z*h)  (x*c  + y*f  + z*i)
```

Now let's see some matrix multiplication in something that you will actually use—coordinate rotation. Hopefully the scaling example will make it more clear what we're doing.

Coordinate rotation with a matrix

First of all, you need to dig up your 3D point matrix:

```
   x  y  z
```

This will hold the coordinates of the point you want to rotate. Now of course, you need a rotation matrix. As you know, you can rotate on any one of three axes. You'll create each of these types of rotation as separate matrices. Let's start with an x axis rotation matrix:

```
   1    0    0
   0    cos  sin
   0    -sin cos
```

Now you have some sines and cosines in there, and the obvious question might be, "The sine or cosine of what?" Well, it's the sine or cosine of whatever angle you're rotating by. If you're rotating that point by 45 degrees, it would be the sine and cosine of 45 degrees. (Of course, in code, you'd use radians.)

Now, let's perform matrix multiplication with this and a 3D point matrix and see what results you get.

```
                1    0    0
x   y   z   *   0   cos  sin
                0  -sin  cos
```

For that, you get

```
(x*1 + y*0  + z*0)  (x*0  + y*cos - z*sin)  (x*0  + y*sin  + z*cos)
```

Cleaning that up gives you

```
(x)  (y*cos - z*sin)  (z*cos + y*sin)
```

This translates roughly to the following in ActionScript:

```
x = x;
y = Math.cos(angle) * y - Math.sin(angle) * z;
z = Math.cos(angle) * z + Math.sin(angle) * y;
```

Now, if you think back to Chapter 10, where I discussed coordinate rotation, you'll see this is exactly how you were accomplishing x axis rotation. This isn't a big surprise, as matrix math is just a different way of looking at and organizing various formulas and equations.

From here, you can easily create a matrix for y axis rotation:

```
 cos  0  sin
   0  1   0
-sin  0  cos
```

And finally, one for rotation on the z axis:

```
 cos  sin  0
-sin  cos  0
   0    0  1
```

It would be good practice to go ahead and multiply each of these by an x, y, z matrix and verify that you get the same formulas you used for coordinate rotation on those two axes in Chapter 10.

Coding with matrices

OK, you know enough of the basics to start putting this stuff into code. You'll be reusing and altering the RotateXY.as class from Chapter 15, so open that up. That class had a rotateX and rotateY method to perform the 3D coordinate rotation. We'll be changing how those work to make them use matrices.

Start with the rotateX function. This will take the ball's x, y, z coordinates, put these in a 1×3 matrix, and then create an x rotation matrix based on the given angle. These matrices will be in the form of arrays. Finally, it will multiply these two matrices together using the matrixMultiply function, which you also need to create! The result of the multiplication will be another array, so you have to assign those values back to the ball's x, y, and z coordinates. Here's the new version of that method:

```
    private function rotateX(ball:Ball3D, angleX:Number):void
    {
        var position:Array = [ball.xpos, ball.ypos, ball.zpos];

        var sin:Number = Math.sin(angleX);
        var cos:Number = Math.cos(angleX);
        var xRotMatrix:Array = new Array();
        xRotMatrix[0] = [1,    0,    0];
        xRotMatrix[1] = [0,  cos, sin];
        xRotMatrix[2] = [0, -sin, cos]

        var result:Array = matrixMultiply(position, xRotMatrix);
        ball.xpos = result[0];
        ball.ypos = result[1];
        ball.zpos = result[2];
    }
```

And here is the matrix multiplication function:

```
    private function matrixMultiply(matrixA:Array, matrixB:Array):Array
    {
        var result:Array = new Array();
        result[0] = matrixA[0] * matrixB[0][0] +
                    matrixA[1] * matrixB[1][0] +
                    matrixA[2] * matrixB[2][0];

        result[1] = matrixA[0] * matrixB[0][1] +
                    matrixA[1] * matrixB[1][1] +
                    matrixA[2] * matrixB[2][1];

        result[2] = matrixA[0] * matrixB[0][2] +
                    matrixA[1] * matrixB[1][2] +
                    matrixA[2] * matrixB[2][2];
        return result;
    }
```

Now this particular matrix multiplication function is hard-coded to multiply a 1×3 matrix by a 3×3 matrix, since that's what you'll be doing in each case. You could use for loops to make a more dynamic function that could handle any sized matrices, but let's keep things simple here.

Finally, create your rotateY function. If you understand the rotateX function, this one should look pretty obvious. You just create a y rotation matrix instead of an x rotation matrix.

```
    private function rotateY(ball:Ball3D, angleY:Number):void
    {
        var position:Array = [ball.xpos, ball.ypos, ball.zpos];

        var sin:Number = Math.sin(angleY);
        var cos:Number = Math.cos(angleY);
        var yRotMatrix:Array = new Array();
```

```
            yRotMatrix[0] = [ cos, 0, sin];
            yRotMatrix[1] = [   0, 1,   0];
            yRotMatrix[2] = [-sin, 0, cos]

            var result:Array = matrixMultiply(position, yRotMatrix);
            ball.xpos = result[0];
            ball.ypos = result[1];
            ball.zpos = result[2];
        }
```

And there you have it. You could also create a rotateZ function if you want. Since we don't actually need that for this example, I'll leave it as an exercise for you to do on your own.

Now if you run RotateXY.as and compare it to Chapter 15's version, they should look exactly the same. In AS 2, I found that the nonmatrix version ran quite a bit more smoothly. The reason for this is that you're already performing quite extensive math for the 3D rotations, scaling, etc. When you get into matrix math, you wind up doing a whole lot of extra calculations. When you start multiplying the matrices, you're actually doing four multiply-times-zero operations, and adding the four results to other numbers. That's eight math operations that essentially do nothing at all. Multiply that times 50 objects, and two rotations per frame, and you get 800 superfluous calculations per frame! It's a statement to the power of Flash CS3 and AS 3 that both versions now run with no noticeable difference. But I'm sure as you add more and more objects, you will reach a point where those excess calculations take their toll. Then again, the matrix code I gave you is very basic. You could probably optimize it quite a bit, and get even more performance out of it.

Even if you don't use matrices for 3D, you'll still find them useful for other purposes, and I'll cover these next. Use of matrices in 3D provides a nice introduction, as you can see how they relate to formulas you already know. Also, matrices are used extensively for 3D in other languages that are far more efficient than ActionScript currently. In these languages, you can afford to spend a few CPU cycles in order to gain the neat organization that matrices can offer your code. If you wind up attempting 3D animation in anything other than Flash, you are bound to run into matrices again. And, who knows where the Flash player will be in a few years? There may come a day when these techniques are perfectly suitable for Flash.

The Matrix class

As mentioned, one good reason for knowing about matrices is that they are used in several places in core ActionScript classes. In fact, there's even a built-in Matrix class. If you take a look at the Flash help files for the flash.geom.Matrix class, you'll find that they are quite clear and informative. If you've understood everything up to now in this chapter, you should have no problem grasping that material. Since it is so well written, I won't waste space rehashing it all, but I will give a quick summary and a couple of examples.

A matrix is used mainly to transform (rotate, scale, and translate) a display object. Any display object (sprite, movie clip, text field, and so on) now has a property called transform. This is an instance of the flash.geom.Transform class, and it contains another property called matrix. If you create an instance of the Matrix class and assign it to this transform.matrix property, it will alter the form, size, or position of that display object. You'll see some concrete examples very shortly.

Basically, the matrix in the Matrix class is a 3X3 matrix set up like so:

```
a   b   tx
c   d   ty
u   v   w
```

The u, v, and w are set to 0, 0, and 1 automatically and are used internally. They are unchangeable, so you don't have to worry about them. (More explanation on what they actually are and do appears in the help files.) You can create a new Matrix with the following syntax:

```
import flash.geom.Matrix;
var myMatrix:Matrix = new Matrix(a, b, c, d, tx, ty);
```

So what do all these letters mean? Well, tx and ty are pretty easy. These control the position of the display object by translating it on the x and y axis. The a, b, c, and d are a little trickier because they are so dependent on each other. If you set b and c to 0, you can use a and d to scale the object on the x and y axes. If you set a and d to 1, you can use b and c to skew the object on the y and x axes, respectively. Finally, you can use a, b, c, and d together in a way that I'm sure you'll find very familiar. In this case, they would be laid out like this:

```
 cos   sin   tx
-sin   cos   ty
  u     v    w
```

Of course, you can see that this contains a rotation matrix, and it will indeed rotate the object. Naturally, cos and sin in this example refer to the cosine and sine of a particular angle (in radians) that you wish to rotate the sprite by. Let's try that one out.

Here you can see MatrixRotate.as, which creates a simple sprite with a red box in it. It then sets up an enterFrame handler, where all the action takes place:

```
package
{
    import flash.display.Sprite;
    import flash.events.Event;
    import flash.geom.Matrix;

    public class MatrixRotate extends Sprite
    {
        private var angle:Number = 0;
        private var box:Sprite;

        public function MatrixRotate()
        {
            init();
        }

        private function init():void
        {
            box = new Sprite();
            box.graphics.beginFill(0xff0000);
```

```
            box.graphics.drawRect(-50, -50, 100, 100);
            box.graphics.endFill();
            addChild(box);
            addEventListener(Event.ENTER_FRAME, onEnterFrame);
        }

        private function onEnterFrame(event:Event):void
        {
            angle += .05;
            var cos:Number = Math.cos(angle);
            var sin:Number = Math.sin(angle);
            box.transform.matrix = new Matrix(cos, sin,
                                             -sin, cos,
                                              stage.stageWidth / 2,
                                              stage.stageHeight / 2);
        }
    }
}
```

Here you have an angle variable that increases on each frame. The code finds the sine and cosine of that angle and feeds them into a new `Matrix` object, in the way specified for rotation. I've also applied a translation, based on the stage width and height, which centers the sprite. The new matrix is assigned to the `transform.matrix` property of the sprite. Test this and you have a spinning box.

Now, you may be wondering why you don't just change the rotation property of the sprite. It's true that in this simple case, that would be a much simpler solution. But there may be many cases where you are dealing with a lot of angles and radians and sines and cosines, and it might actually be much easier to just assign a matrix like this, rather than converting everything back to degrees and changing the rotation.

But for another, far more practical demonstration, let's try skewing. *Skewing* means stretching something out on one axis so that one part goes one way and the other part goes the other way. *Italic letters* are an example of a skew. The top part of the letters goes to the right and the bottom part to the left. This is something that has always been notoriously tricky in Flash, but is incredibly easy with the Matrix class. As I said earlier, you set a and d of the matrix to 1. The b property is the amount to skew on the y axis, and the c controls the skew on the x axis. Let's try an x skew first. In SkewX.as, I used almost the exact same setup as the last example, but changed the way the matrix is created in the onEnterFrame method.

```
        private function onEnterFrame(event:Event):void
        {
            var skewX:Number = (mouseX - stage.stageWidth / 2) * .01;
            box.transform.matrix = new Matrix(1,      0,
                                             skewX, 1,
                                             stage.stageWidth / 2,
                                             stage.stageHeight / 2);
        }
```

Here I made the skewX variable relative to the mouse's x position, offset from the center of the stage. I then multiplied that by .01 to keep the skew in a manageable range, and fed that into the matrix.

Now when you test this movie, you will see how you can skew an entire sprite, as you see in Figure 18-2. While this was possible before the Matrix class, if you know anyone who has tried it, show them the preceding code, and watch them start drooling! Or, if you tried it yourself, you already know what I mean.

Figure 18-2. Sprite skewed on the x axis

In SkewXY, I did the same thing with the y axis:

```
private function onEnterFrame(event:Event):void
{
    var skewX:Number = (mouseX - stage.stageWidth / 2) * .01;
    var skewY:Number = (mouseY - stage.stageHeight / 2) * .01;
    box.transform.matrix = new Matrix(1,       skewY,
                                      skewX, 1,
                                      stage.stageWidth / 2,
                                      stage.stageHeight / 2);
}
```

Figure 18-3 gives you a feel for how skewing a sprite on two axes turns out.

Figure 18-3. Sprite skewed on both axes

It's pretty amazing to be able to do this kind of effect so easily. If you aren't sure where you would use this kind of effect, I'll tell you that skewing is used quite often for pseudo-3D. As you move your mouse around in the last example, you can probably already see how it appears to have some perspective, as if the shape was leaning over and spinning around. It's not particularly accurate 3D, but it can be used for some pretty convincing effects. There are a few tutorials out there on the Web that show you how to accomplish this kind of pseudo-3D with skewing. Use of the Matrix class will probably cut the code in those examples in half.

Again, be sure to check out the help files for the Matrix class, as there are a *lot* of other goodies in there. Also, realize that that is not the only place AS 3 utilizes matrices. You might want to take a look at ColorMatrixFilter, ConvolutionFilter, the various drawing API fill and gradient methods, and the flash.geom.Transform class. Matrices galore in there!

Summary

I've covered the basics of what matrices are, how to use them and combine them, and created some pretty cool effects with them in this chapter. Now that you have the concepts in your head, you're ready to take advantage of the power that matrices can offer, and hopefully won't shy away from using them when you encounter them in the built-in methods of AS 3, as you surely will.

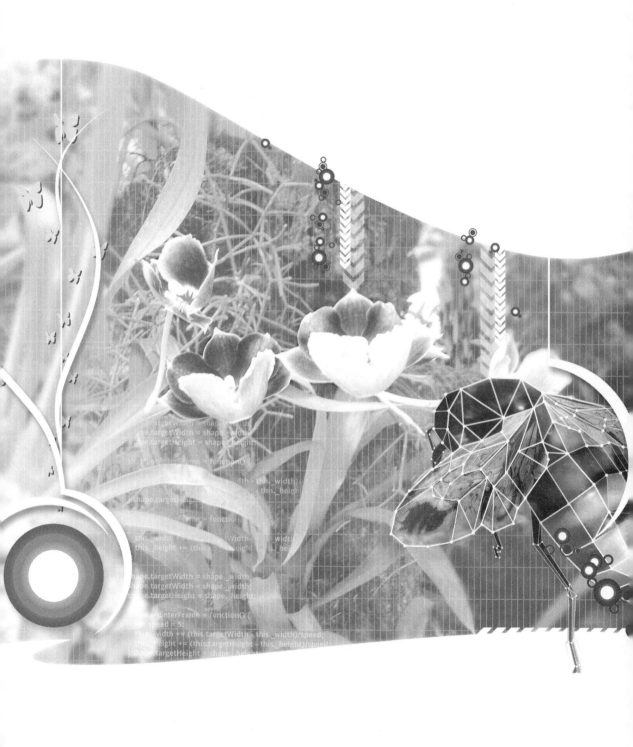

Chapter 19

TIPS AND TRICKS

What we'll cover in this chapter:

- Brownian (random) motion
- Random distribution
- Interval- and timer-based animation
- Collisions between same-mass objects
- Integrating sound
- Useful formulas

Well, you made it to the last chapter. This one I set aside for all the little things I really wanted to tell you about, but didn't really fit in anywhere else, or would have distracted from the main points I was trying to get across in some other chapter.

I'm also going to regroup all the formulas we've been coming up with and listing at the end of each chapter, so this can serve as a single point of reference for them.

As these various subjects are just random bits and pieces (albeit useful bits), there's not a whole lot of organizing I can do here. Thus each section will be a stand-alone unit. So, without further ado, here we go.

Brownian (random) motion

First some history. One day, a botanist named Robert Brown was trying to look at some grains of pollen in a drop of water and found that they were randomly moving around. Even though there was no current or motion in the water, those little grains just never settled down. He found the same thing happened with dust particles, so it wasn't like the pollen was swimming. Even though he hadn't the slightest idea why they did this, and neither he nor anyone else really offered an explanation for several decades, he somehow got the phenomenon named after him—just for noticing it!

The way Brownian motion is explained these days is that the zillions of water molecules in a drop of water are in constant motion, even if the water appears to be still. These molecules collide with the pollen or dust particle, and in doing so, transfer some of their momentum to it. Since even a speck of dust is a million times heavier than a single water molecule, each collision doesn't do much. But when you have so many millions of collisions per second, it starts to add up.

Now some of the molecules might be hitting on one side, and some on the other. Overall, they are going to generally average out. But over time, you are going to see fluctuations, where more are hitting, say, on the left side, and it's enough to start the particle moving a bit to the right. Then more might hit on the bottom, and the particle starts to move upward. Again, these eventually average out, so it doesn't usually result in much momentum in any one direction. You get this random floating-around action.

You can easily simulate this in Flash. On each frame, you just calculate random numbers to add to the x and y velocity of a moving object. The random numbers should be calculated to be either positive or negative, and usually quite small, say in a range from –0.1 to +0.1. You can do that like so:

```
vx += Math.random() * 0.2 - 0.1;
vy += Math.random() * 0.2 - 0.1;
```

Multiplying the random decimal by 0.2 gives you a number from 0.0 to 0.2. Subtracting 0.1 makes it –0.1 to 0.1. It's important to add some friction into this, otherwise the velocities tend to build up, and things start zipping around unnaturally. In Brownian1.as, I've created 50 particles and have them floating around with Brownian motion. The particles are instances of our old familiar Ball class, made small and black. Here is the code:

```
package {
    import flash.display.Sprite;
    import flash.events.Event;

    public class Brownian1 extends Sprite
    {
        private var numDots:uint = 50;
        private var friction:Number = 0.95;
        private var dots:Array;

        public function Brownian1()
        {
            init();
        }

        private function init():void
        {
            dots = new Array();
            for(var i:uint = 0; i < numDots; i++)
            {
                var dot:Ball = new Ball(1, 0);
                dot.x = Math.random() * stage.stageWidth;
                dot.y = Math.random() * stage.stageHeight;
                dot.vx = 0;
                dot.vy = 0;
                addChild(dot);
                dots.push(dot);
            }
            addEventListener(Event.ENTER_FRAME, onEnterFrame);
        }

        private function onEnterFrame(event:Event):void
        {
            for(var i:uint = 0; i <numDots; i++)
            {
                var dot:Ball = dots[i];
                dot.vx += Math.random() * 0.2 - 0.1;
                dot.vy += Math.random() * 0.2 - 0.1;
                dot.x += dot.vx;
                dot.y += dot.vy;
                dot.vx *= friction;
                dot.vy *= friction;

                if(dot.x > stage.stageWidth)
                {
                    dot.x = 0;
                }
                else if(dot.x < 0)
                {
```

```
            dot.x = stage.stageWidth;
        }
        if(dot.y > stage.stageHeight)
        {
            dot.y = 0;
        }
        else if(dot.y < 0)
        {
            dot.y = stage.stageHeight;
        }
    }
  }
 }
}
```

Most of this is old news to you, so I've put the relevant bits in bold.

Figure 19-1 shows how running this code appears on screen.

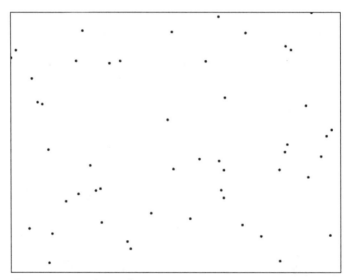

Figure 19-1. Brownian motion

In Brownian2.as, I reduced the number of dots to 20. I then added the line

```
graphics.lineStyle(0, 0, .5);
```

to the init function, and changed the first part of onEnterFrame to include some drawing code.

```
private function onEnterFrame(event:Event):void
{
    for(var i:uint = 0; i < numDots; i++)
    {
        var dot:Ball = dots[i];
        graphics.moveTo(dot.x, dot.y);
        dot.vx += Math.random() * 0.2 - 0.1;
        dot.vy += Math.random() * 0.2 - 0.1;
        dot.x += dot.vx;
        dot.y += dot.vy;
        dot.vx *= friction;
        dot.vy *= friction;
        graphics.lineTo(dot.x, dot.y);
```

This draws a line from where each dot is before it moves to where it is after it moves. So it draws its own path, as shown in Figure 19-2. You'll often see these kinds of diagrams if you look up the term "Brownian motion."

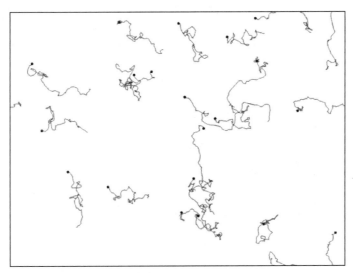

Figure 19-2. Brownian motion with trails

Brownian motion is useful any time you want something to be moving around as if it were floating with no volition of its own, with no forces really acting on it. You can also add it to a sprite that has some other motion applied to it, to give it a sense of randomness. An example would be a fly or bee that's buzzing around. You might have it moving along in some path, but adding in some random motion could make it look much more lifelike.

Random distribution

From time to time, you may want to create a bunch of objects and place them at random positions. You've seen how this is done many times throughout the book, but here we'll focus on a few different methods of doing this, and the different results that they will give you.

Square distribution

If you want the objects to randomly cover the entire stage, that's pretty simple. Just choose a random number up to the stage's width for x, and a random number up to its height for y. In fact, you did just that in the preceding section:

```
for(var i:uint = 0; i < numDots; i++)
{
    var dot:Ball = new Ball(1, 0);
    dot.x = Math.random() * stage.stageWidth;
    dot.y = Math.random() * stage.stageHeight;
    ...
```

But say you wanted to kind of clump the dots in near the center of the stage, say 100 pixels to either side, top, or bottom of the center. You could do something like the following, which is in Random1.as:

```
package {
    import flash.display.Sprite;

    public class Random1 extends Sprite
    {
        private var numDots:uint = 50;

        public function Random1()
        {
            init();
        }

        private function init():void
        {

            for(var i:uint = 0; i < numDots; i++)
            {
                var dot:Ball = new Ball(1, 0);
                dot.x = stage.stageWidth / 2 +
                        Math.random() * 200 - 100;
                dot.y = stage.stageHeight / 2 +
                        Math.random() * 200 - 100;
                addChild(dot);
            }
        }
    }
}
```

This creates a random number from −100 to +100 and adds it to the center point of the stage, so all of the dots will be no farther than 100 pixels on either axis from the center. Figure 19-3 shows what that gives you.

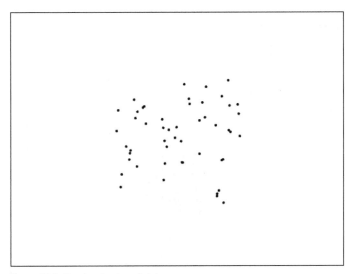

Figure 19-3. Randomly placed dots

Not too bad. But if you crowd them in a bit more by making a lot more dots (300) and reducing the area to 100 by 100, you'll notice something odd starting to happen. Here's the code from Random2.as:

```
package {
    import flash.display.Sprite;

    public class Random2 extends Sprite
    {
        private var numDots:uint = 300;

        public function Random2()
        {
            init();
        }

        private function init():void
        {
            for(var i:uint = 0; i < numDots; i++)
            {
                var dot:Ball = new Ball(1, 0);
                dot.x = stage.stageWidth / 2 +
                        Math.random() * 100 - 50;
                dot.y = stage.stageHeight / 2 +
                        Math.random() * 100 - 50;
                addChild(dot);
```

```
                    }
                }
            }
        }
    }
```

And Figure 19-4 shows what you get.

Figure 19-4. This method starts to form a square. Not so random looking anymore.

As you see, the dots are starting to form a square. Maybe that's OK, but if you are trying to make some kind of explosion or star system or something of the sort, a square doesn't look too natural. If a square distribution is not exactly what you are looking for, try moving on to the next technique.

Circular distribution

While slightly more complex than a square distribution, circular distribution really isn't too hard to do. First you need to know the radius of your circle. Let's keep it at 50, to match the last example. This will be the maximum radius that a dot can be placed from the center. You'll take a random number from zero to that number to use as the radius for each dot. Then you'll choose a random angle from 0 to PI * 2 radians (360 degrees), and use a quick bit of trig to find the x and y position of the dot. Here's the code from Random3.as:

```
package {
    import flash.display.Sprite;

    public class Random3 extends Sprite
    {
        private var numDots:uint = 300;
        private var maxRadius:Number = 50;
```

```
public function Random3()
{
    init();
}

private function init():void
{
    for(var i:uint = 0; i < numDots; i++)
    {
        var dot:Ball = new Ball(1, 0);
        var radius:Number = Math.random() * maxRadius;
        var angle:Number = Math.random() *
                        (Math.PI * 2);
        dot.x = stage.stageWidth / 2 +
                Math.cos(angle) * radius;
        dot.y = stage.stageHeight / 2 +
                Math.sin(angle) * radius;
        addChild(dot);
    }
}
}
```

And that gives you a picture like the one in Figure 19-5.

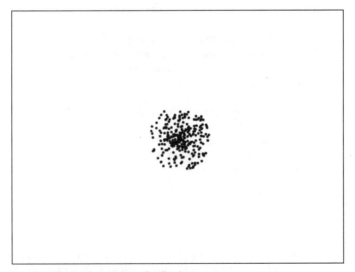

Figure 19-5. Circular random distribution

This is much more natural for most of the types of applications I mentioned earlier. However, you might notice that the dots seem to be even more clumped around the center of the circle. This is because an even distribution exists along the radius, meaning there are as many dots in the center as near the edge. But because the center has less space, they are more crowded.

Again, this may be fine for some applications, but Sean O'Shell (www.pixelwit.com) once challenged me to come up with a way of making the dots appear more uniformly distributed throughout the circle. I have to admit I was stumped, and the solutions I tried were pretty complex. Finally, he gave me a very simple solution, as you can see in Random4.as:

```
package {
    import flash.display.Sprite;

    public class Random4 extends Sprite
    {
        private var numDots:uint = 300;
        private var maxRadius:Number = 50;

        public function Random4()
        {
            init();
        }

        private function init():void
        {
            for(var i:uint = 0; i < numDots; i++)
            {
                var dot:Ball = new Ball(1, 0);
                var radius:Number = Math.sqrt(Math.random()) *
                                    maxRadius;
                var angle:Number = Math.random() *
                                    (Math.PI * 2);
                dot.x = stage.stageWidth / 2 +
                        Math.cos(angle) * radius;
                dot.y = stage.stageHeight / 2 +
                        Math.sin(angle) * radius;
                addChild(dot);
            }
        }
    }
}
```

By taking the square root of the random number, it has a bias toward 1 and away from 0, which is just enough to smooth out the distribution. You can see the result in Figure 19-6. Nice one, Sean!

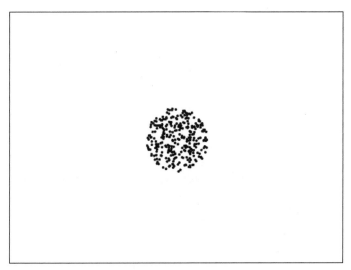

Figure 19-6. A smoother distribution

Biased distribution

Finally, you may want to give the random objects free range over the entire stage, but have them tend to show up in the middle area. You'd find some out on the edges, but the closer to the center you got, the more there would be. This would be somewhat like the first circular example, but applied to a rectangular area.

You do this by generating multiple random numbers for each position, and then averaging them to get the final value. For example, say the stage is 500 pixels wide. If you generate an x position for each object with just one random number, each object has an equal chance of being anywhere in that range. But if you generate two random numbers from 0 to 500, and take the average, there's a bit higher chance that it will be somewhere in the middle rather than out toward the edges.

Let's look at that in a little more depth. There is some chance that both numbers might be in a "high" range, say from 300 to 500. There's about the same chance that both might be in a low range, from 0 to 200. But there's a higher chance that one will be high and one low, or one middle and one high or low, or even both in the middle. All of these possibilities will average out to place most dots a bit closer to the middle.

OK, let's see it in code. As usual, you'll start on one dimension. Here's the code (which you'll also find in Random5.as):

```
package {
    import flash.display.Sprite;

    public class Random5 extends Sprite
    {
        private var numDots:uint = 300;
```

```
public function Random5()
{
    init();
}

private function init():void
{
    for(var i:uint = 0; i < numDots; i++)
    {
        var dot:Ball = new Ball(1, 0);
        var x1:Number = Math.random() * stage.stageWidth;
        var x2:Number = Math.random() * stage.stageWidth;
        dot.x = (x1 + x2) / 2;
        dot.y = stage.stageHeight / 2 +
                Math.random() * 50 - 25;
        addChild(dot);
    }
}
}
}
```

Here you are generating two random numbers, x1 and x2, and setting the dot's x position to the average of them. The y position is simply randomly near the center. This gives you something like what you see in Figure 19-7.

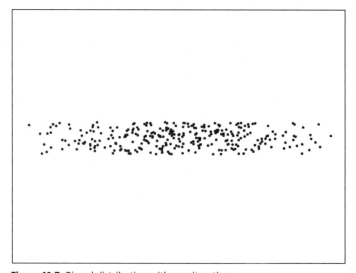

Figure 19-7. Biased distribution with one iteration

The effect isn't too pronounced here, but you can see that there is a bit more clumping in the center, and more space at the edges. Creating more random numbers and averaging them will make it more obvious. You'll move this into a for loop to make it dynamic (Random6.as):

```
package {
    import flash.display.Sprite;

    public class Random6 extends Sprite
    {
        private var numDots:uint = 300;
        private var maxRadius:Number = 50;
        private var iterations:uint = 6;

        public function Random6()
        {
            init();
        }

        private function init():void
        {
            for(var i:uint = 0; i < numDots; i++)
            {
                var dot:Ball = new Ball(1, 0);
                var xpos:Number = 0;
                for(var j:uint = 0; j < iterations; j++)
                {
                    xpos += Math.random() * stage.stageWidth;
                }
                dot.x = xpos / iterations;
                dot.y = stage.stageHeight / 2 +
                        Math.random() * 50 - 25;
                addChild(dot);
            }
        }
    }
}
```

Here the iterations variable controls how many numbers you will average. You start out with the variable xpos equal to zero, and add each random number to it. Finally, you divide that by the number of iterations for the final value. This gives you a picture like the one in Figure 19-8.

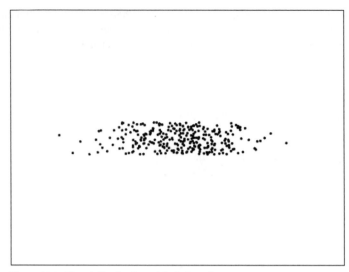

Figure 19-8. Biased distribution with six iterations

It is now easy to do the same thing for the y axis, and Random7.as does just that:

```
package {
    import flash.display.Sprite;

    public class Random7 extends Sprite
    {
        private var numDots:uint = 300;
        private var maxRadius:Number = 50;
        private var iterations:uint = 6;

        public function Random7()
        {
            init();
        }

        private function init():void
        {
            for(var i:uint = 0; i < numDots; i++)
            {
                var dot:Ball = new Ball(1, 0);
                var xpos:Number = 0;
                for(var j:uint = 0; j < iterations; j++)
                {
                    xpos += Math.random() * stage.stageWidth;
                }
                dot.x = xpos / iterations;
```

```
        var ypos:Number = 0;
        for(j = 0; j < iterations; j++)
        {
            ypos += Math.random() * stage.stageHeight;
        }
        dot.y = ypos / iterations;
        addChild(dot);
    }
  }
 }
}
```

This gives you a distribution like the one in Figure 19-9.

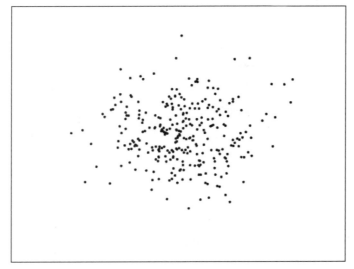

Figure 19-9. Two-dimensional biased distribution

To me, this is the most random, explosive, star system–like distribution of them all, though it is also the most intensive to generate. At any rate, you now have at least four ways to generate random positions.

Timer- and time-based animation

In all the examples in the book so far, animation has been done by placing motion code inside an onEnterFrame method and assigning that as the handler to the enterFrame event. I've always found this to be the simplest method, as the concept of frames is so deeply ingrained in Flash, it's sitting right there ready for you to use; and I guess most of all, it's just an old habit.

However, a lot of people, particularly those coming from non-Flash programming environments, are not so comfortable with this model. To them, a timer-based animation model (using intervals or timers) seems to offer more precise control over the speed of the animation. So we'll take a look at that.

Then we'll look at what I'll call "time-based animation," a technique that can be used with either frames or timers.

Timer-based animation

The key class used for timer-based animation is, not surprisingly, the flash.utils.Timer class. Along with that, you'll need the flash.events.TimerEvent class.

Using a timer for animation really isn't any different from using enterFrame. It just requires that you create a timer, tell it how fast to "tick," and listen for the TimerEvent.TIMER event, just like you would listen for the Event.ENTER_FRAME event. Oh, you'll also want to tell the timer to start! From there on out, the timer will broadcast a timer event at regular intervals, which will wind up calling whatever method you assigned to handle it. The interval at which the timer fires is specified in milliseconds, usually when you create the timer. Let's take a look at a simple example (which you can also find in Timer1.as):

```
package {
    import flash.display.Sprite;
    import flash.utils.Timer;
    import flash.events.TimerEvent;

    public class Timer1 extends Sprite
    {
        private var timer:Timer;

        public function Timer1()
        {
            init();
        }

        private function init():void
        {
            timer = new Timer(30);
            timer.addEventListener(TimerEvent.TIMER, onTimer);
            timer.start();
        }

        private function onTimer(timer:TimerEvent):void
        {
            trace("timer!");
        }
    }
}
```

The important parts are in bold. You create the timer, telling it to fire every 30 milliseconds, which means it will fire roughly 33 times per second. You add an event listener and tell it to start. The onTimer method is analogous to the onEnterFrame you've been using throughout the book.

That's most of what you need to know about timers. There are a couple other neat features. One is that when you create a timer you can tell it to run only a certain number of times, with the second parameter, repeatCount. Say you wanted a timer to run once per second for a total of five seconds. You'd do something like this:

```
timer = new Timer(1000, 5);
```

If you don't specify a repeat count, or pass 0, the timer will run indefinitely.

The other cool thing you can do with timers is stop and start them at any point, just by calling timer.stop and timer.start. In some cases, this might be easier than removing and readding your event listener.

Now, one reason that many people prefer timers over enterFrame is that, theoretically, timers give you millisecond-level control over the speed of your animation—a vast improvement over frames, which are notoriously inaccurate. However, I say "theoretically," because there are several things to be aware of.

First is that timers are in fact tied to frame rate. The other is that the time that the code in your timer's event handler takes to run gets added to the overall interval of your timer. I'll explain that second one shortly. For now, let's see how timers are connected to frame rate. The following is document class Timer2.as, which uses our now famous Ball class.

```
package {
    import flash.display.Sprite;
    import flash.utils.Timer;
    import flash.events.TimerEvent;

    public class Timer2 extends Sprite
    {
        private var timer:Timer;
        private var ball:Ball;

        public function Timer2()
        {
            init();
        }

        private function init():void
        {
            stage.frameRate = 1;
            ball = new Ball();
            ball.y = stage.stageHeight / 2;
            ball.vx = 5;
            addChild(ball);
            timer = new Timer(20);
            timer.addEventListener(TimerEvent.TIMER, onTimer);
            timer.start();
        }
    }
```

```
        private function onTimer(event:TimerEvent):void
        {
            ball.x += ball.vx;
        }
    }
}
```

Here we have a ball created and put on the left side of the stage. It moves across the stage with a vx of 5. We set a timer to run at 20 milliseconds, or about 50 times per second. We also set the movie's frame rate to 1 just to see whether the frame rate has anything to do with the timer.

When you run this, you'll see that instead of moving smoothly across the screen, the ball is jumping about once per second—the frame rate. And each jump is much more than 5 pixels. What's going on?

Well, if you think back to Chapters 1 and 2, where I talked about basic animation, you may remember that the model needs to be updated, and then the screen needs to be refreshed based on the new model. Here, the interval function is reliably updating the model and moving the ball 5 pixels every time it runs, but still the screen is only being refreshed when Flash enters a new frame. Simply running a function does not force Flash to redraw.

Fortunately, the good people at Macromedia (now Adobe) saw this coming and gave you another little tool to use: updateAfterEvent. Originally introduced in Flash MX, this is now a method of the TimerEvent object that gets passed to your timer event handler. As its name implies, it *updates* the screen *after* an *event*. Of course, since it is a method of the TimerEvent class, it can only be called from events that receive one of those. (Actually, it is also a method of KeyboardEvent and MouseEvent, so it can be called from those handlers, too.)

So, we can fix up our onTimer event to look like this:

```
        private function onTimer(event:TimerEvent):void
        {
            ball.x += ball.vx;
            event.updateAfterEvent();
        }
```

Now things are definitely better. Much smoother. But if you realize that the ball should be updated 50 times per second, you are basically looking at what should be a 50 fps movie. This means that the ball should be moving quite a bit more smoothly than the types of examples we were creating back Chapter 4, which were based on enterFrame events, and probably at a much lower rate than 50 fps. But it's actually moving more slowly.

The problem, it turns out, is that timers *are* actually somewhat tied to frame rate. By my measurements, at a frame rate of 1 fps, the fastest you will get timers to run are about every 100 milliseconds. This jibes with figures I've heard that you will only get 10 intervals per frame for timers. So, try upping the frame rate to 5. This should allow for 50 updates per second. For me, this still looks jumpy. It doesn't seem to really smooth out until you get up to about 10 frames per second. So, you can see that using timers doesn't totally free you from the shackles of frame rate.

The next issue with timers has to do with how they work internally, and this affects how accurate the timing will be. What actually happens is that as soon as timer.start() is called, Flash waits the specified amount of time and then broadcasts the event, which runs any handlers connected to that timer.

Only when all of those handlers have finished executing does the timer start timing its next interval. As an example, say you have the timer set to run every 20 milliseconds. But say there is so much code in its event handler that it takes 30 milliseconds to execute it all. The next round of timing won't begin until all that code has finished running. In this case, your function will actually run about every 50 milliseconds. As there is no way to accurately determine how fast code will run on the end user's machine, in many cases, interval-based animation winds up being no more accurate than frame-based animation.

If you really need accuracy, time-based animation is the way to go.

Time-based animation

Time-based animation is the method to use if the speed of objects in your movie needs to be consistent. This might be the case in many types of games. As you've seen, neither frame- nor timer-based animation can be counted on for a specific rate of playback. A complex movie on an older, slower computer may run at a much lower speed than it was designed for. As you'll see shortly, when you use a time-based animation, you'll get speed you can count on, no matter what frame rate the final movie ends up running at.

The first thing you need to do is change the way you think about velocity. Up to now, when I said, for example, vx = 5, the units you were using were *pixels per frame*. In other words, the object would move 5 pixels on the x axis each time a new frame was encountered. In timer-based animation, of course, it would be 5 pixels per timer interval.

For time-based animation, you'll actually start using real measurements of time, like seconds. Since you are dealing with a whole second, rather than a small fraction of one, the value needs to be much higher. If you had something moving at 10 pixels per frame at 30 frames per second, that is roughly 300 pixels per second. For the next example, I hijacked the Bouncing2.as document class from Chapter 6 and made a few changes, which you can see here in bold (and can also find in TimeBased.as):

```
package
{
    import flash.display.Sprite;
    import flash.events.Event;
    import flash.utils.getTimer;

    public class TimeBased extends Sprite
    {
        private var ball:Ball;
        private var vx:Number;
        private var vy:Number;
        private var bounce:Number = -0.7;
        private var time:Number;

        public function TimeBased()
        {
            init();
        }
```

```
private function init():void
{
    stage.frameRate = 10;
    ball = new Ball();
    ball.x = stage.stageWidth / 2;
    ball.y = stage.stageHeight / 2;
    vx = 300;
    vy = -300;
    addChild(ball);
    time = getTimer();
    addEventListener(Event.ENTER_FRAME, onEnterFrame);
}

private function onEnterFrame(event:Event):void
{
    var elapsed:Number = getTimer() - time;
    time = getTimer();
    ball.x += vx * elapsed / 1000;
    ball.y += vy * elapsed / 1000;
    var left:Number = 0;
    var right:Number = stage.stageWidth;
    var top:Number = 0;
    var bottom:Number = stage.stageHeight;

    if(ball.x + ball.radius > right)
    {
        ball.x = right - ball.radius;
        vx *= bounce;
    }
    else if(ball.x - ball.radius < left)
    {
        ball.x = left + ball.radius;
        vx *= bounce;
    }
    if(ball.y + ball.radius > bottom)
    {
        ball.y = bottom - ball.radius;
        vy *= bounce;
    }
    else if(ball.y - ball.radius < top)
    {
        ball.y = top + ball.radius;
        vy *= bounce;
    }
}
}
}
```

I bumped up the velocities, as described previously, and left them at hard-coded values, rather than randomly determined. I then created a variable called time, and set it to the result of the function flash.utils.getTimer. The getTimer function is quite simple. It returns the number of milliseconds the movie has been running—that's all it does. There is no way to clear it, reset it, change it, or anything else. It's just a counter.

Now, that might seem rather useless, but if you call getTimer once and store its value, and then call it again later and subtract the two values, you will know exactly—down to the millisecond—how much time elapsed between the two.

So here is the strategy: you call getTimer at the beginning of each frame and see how many milliseconds elapsed since the last frame. If you divide that by 1,000, you'll have what fraction of a second elapsed. Since your vx and vy are now in terms of pixels per second, you can multiply them by this fraction and know how much to move the object. Also, don't forget to reset the value of the time variable so you can measure the next frame.

Test it out, and you'll see that the ball moves at about the same speed as the original. But the really amazing thing is that you can publish the movie at any frame rate you want, and it will still move at the same speed! Try as high as 1,000 fps, or as low as 10 fps, by changing the stage.frameRate value, and you'll see that the speed of the ball is the same. Of course, the higher rates make for a much smoother movie, and the lower ones are quite jumpy, but the velocity itself should be consistent.

You can apply this technique to any example in the book that contains velocity. In doing so, you'll also need to apply a similar technique to any acceleration or repeated forces, such as gravity, as these are also time based. Values for acceleration actually have to be much larger when converted to this type of animation, because acceleration is defined as distance per time interval per time interval. For example, gravity is approximately 32 feet per second per second.

So where gravity might be something like 0.5 in a frame-based movie of around 30 fps, it would have to be more like 450 here. That's 0.5 * 30 * 30. Then you would apply it like so:

```
vy += gravity * elapsed / 1000;
```

Go ahead and try gravity applied like this to the last example, with a value of 450. You should find it just about equal to the same frame-based movie with a gravity of 0.5.

One tactic with this kind of technique is to set the movie's frame rate to something very high, like 100. Although nobody's machine will likely meet that actual frame rate, it will guarantee that anybody viewing the movie will see it at the smoothest playback possible.

Collisions between same-mass objects

Remember good old Chapter 11 and conservation of momentum? That was some pretty serious code. It happens you can make it a little bit simpler when two objects of the same mass collide. Basically, along the line of collision, such objects simply swap their velocities. While you still have coordinate rotation to determine that line of collision, as well as the object's velocities on it, this wipes out the complex conservation of momentum stuff. To see how it works, let's go back to file MultiBilliard2.as, which we'll use as the base for the next example, SameMass.as. I'm not going to list all of the code from the original here, as it's quite a big file. But let's take a look at the for loop that created all the balls:

```
for(var i:uint = 0; i < numBalls; i++)
{
    var radius:Number = Math.random() * 50 + 20;
    var ball:Ball = new Ball(radius);
    ball.mass = radius;
    ball.x = Math.random() * stage.stageWidth;
    ball.y = Math.random() * stage.stageHeight;
    ball.vx = Math.random() * 10 - 5;
    ball.vy = Math.random() * 10 - 5;
    addChild(ball);
    balls.push(ball);
}
```

For the new file, you'll start by changing that line shown in bold to the following:

```
var radius:Number = 30;
```

This will make all the balls the same size and remove the notion of mass, effectively giving them all the same mass.

Next you want to go down to the checkCollision function. Find the section that reads like this:

```
// rotate ball0's velocity
var vel0:Point = rotate(ball0.vx,
                        ball0.vy,
                        sin,
                        cos,
                        true);

// rotate ball1's velocity
var vel1:Point = rotate(ball1.vx,
                        ball1.vy,
                        sin,
                        cos,
                        true);

// collision reaction
var vxTotal:Number = vel0.x - vel1.x;
vel0.x = ((ball0.mass - ball1.mass) * vel0.x +
        2 * ball1.mass * vel1.x) /
        (ball0.mass + ball1.mass);
vel1.x = vxTotal + vel0.x;
```

This is the part that finds the velocities along the line of collision, and, along with their masses, figures out the result of the collision. The part labeled "collision reaction" is the part that factors in the conservation of momentum, and this is the part you can get rid of. You can replace that portion with code that simply swaps vel0 and vel1. This makes the whole section just shown look like this:

```
// rotate ball0's velocity
var vel0:Point = rotate(ball0.vx,
                        ball0.vy,
                        sin,
                        cos,
                        true);

// rotate ball1's velocity
var vel1:Point = rotate(ball1.vx,
                        ball1.vy,
                        sin,
                        cos,
                        true);

// swap the two velocities
var temp:Point = vel0;
vel0 = vel1;
vel1 = temp;
```

This could be even further optimized, but I'll leave it like this for clarity's sake. Here you've gotten rid of a good bit of math, and if you test the file before and after, you should be seeing the same thing.

Integrating sound

One thing that has been conspicuously absent from this book has been the use of sound. While sound is not directly a part of animation, well-done sound effects can go a long way to making a Flash movie more immersive and realistic.

You can use sound in Flash in different ways. There are specific ways to use sound in the Flash IDE that date back to the earliest versions of the program—importing sounds into the library and assigning them to frames. I'm not going to cover that aspect of using sound. Instead, I'll just cover some basics of sound in AS 3.

A lot has changed with the Sound class in AS 3, and there are several additional classes that help to customize your sound experience. There is not room to cover this in much depth, but there is one aspect that I think would be useful to what we've covered so far in the book. This would be sounds that play when a certain event happens in a movie. The most obvious would be a collision. A ball hits a wall or another ball, and you hear "bang" or "boing" or "splat" or whatever. For this, you need the ability to start the sound via ActionScript.

In this example, I'm again going back to Bouncing2.as, with the ball bouncing off the walls. Each time it hits a wall, I want it to make a sound. The new class is SoundEvents.as.

First, you are going to need a sound effect to use. There are many sources of free sound effects on the Web. One of the most popular sites for sound for Flash is good old FlashKit. In addition to their loops section, which are musical files, they have a sound effect library at www.flashkit.com/soundfx/. The effects are organized by categories such as Cartoon, Interfaces, Mechanical, and so on, and the site has well over 6,000 sound effect files to date, so you should be able to find something there to suit your needs. You can preview the effects right on the page, and when you find one you like, download it in MP3 format. Save it to your hard disk in the same directory you are publishing your final movie to.

It sometimes helps to rename the file to something a little more concise. For this example, I downloaded a "boing" sound, so I just renamed it boing.mp3.

The basic use of sound in AS 3 is actually a bit simpler than it was in AS 2.

First, you need to create a Sound object. Say you already declared a variable called boing in the class:

```
private var boing:Sound;
```

Creating the sound object is as simple as saying something like

```
boing = new Sound();
```

Of course, like most classes in AS 3, Sound is now part of a package, the flash.media package, so be sure to import flash.media.Sound first.

The easiest way to link a sound object to an external sound file is to pass in a request for it in the constructor. Like loading external images (see Chapter 4), you can't just pass in the URL to the external sound file. You need to wrap it in a URLRequest (which is actually flash.net.URLRequest, so import that). So this looks something like the following:

```
boing = new Sound(new URLRequest("boing.mp3"));
```

That's all there is to it. Now your sound is ready to play at your command. All you have to do is say

```
mySound.play();
```

at any point and the sound effect will play. There are optional parameters to play, such as the milliseconds to offset the sound, and how many times to play the sound, but the default use as shown will play the sound once from the beginning, which usually serves the purpose. Here is the full code for SoundEvents.as, showing the creation of the Sound object, and you can see that whenever the ball hits a wall, it plays that sound.

```
package
{
    import flash.display.Sprite;
    import flash.events.Event;
    import flash.media.Sound;
    import flash.net.URLRequest;

    public class SoundEvents extends Sprite
    {
        private var ball:Ball;
        private var vx:Number;
        private var vy:Number;
        private var bounce:Number = -0.7;
        private var boing:Sound;
```

```
public function SoundEvents()
{
    init();
}

private function init():void
{
    boing = new Sound(new URLRequest("boing.mp3"));

    ball = new Ball();
    ball.x = stage.stageWidth / 2;
    ball.y = stage.stageHeight / 2;
    vx = Math.random() * 10 - 5;
    vy = -10;
    addChild(ball);
    addEventListener(Event.ENTER_FRAME, onEnterFrame);
}

private function onEnterFrame(event:Event):void
{
    ball.x += vx;
    ball.y += vy;
    var left:Number = 0;
    var right:Number = stage.stageWidth;
    var top:Number = 0;
    var bottom:Number = stage.stageHeight;

    if(ball.x + ball.radius > right)
    {
        boing.play();
        ball.x = right - ball.radius;
        vx *= bounce;
    }
    else if(ball.x - ball.radius < left)
    {
        boing.play();
        ball.x = left + ball.radius;
        vx *= bounce;
    }
    if(ball.y + ball.radius > bottom)
    {
        boing.play();
        ball.y = bottom - ball.radius;
        vy *= bounce;
    }
    else if(ball.y - ball.radius < top)
    {
        boing.play();
        ball.y = top + ball.radius;
```

```
                    vy *= bounce;
                }
            }
        }
    }
```

Test the movie and see . . . hear the difference that sound can make. Of course, finding the *right* sounds to use in the right circumstances, and not overdoing it, is an art in itself.

Useful formulas

Throughout the book, I've presented various formulas relating to the different motion and effects you've been creating. I've tried to distill the most useful, and most used, formulas, equations, and code snippets, and list these at the end of each chapter. I also thought it would be useful to have these all in one place, so I've gathered them all together here as a one-shot reference to those things I think you'll need to use the most. I know that I, for one, will have a bookmark on this page.

Chapter 3

Calculate basic trigonometric functions:

```
sine of angle = opposite / hypotenuse
cosine of angle = adjacent / hypotenuse
tangent of angle = opposite / adjacent
```

Convert radians to degrees and degrees to radians:

```
radians = degrees * Math.PI / 180
degrees = radians * 180 / Math.PI
```

Rotate to the mouse (or any point):

```
// substitute mouseX, mouseY with the x, y point to rotate to
dx = mouseX - sprite.x;
dy = mouseY - sprite.y;
sprite.rotation = Math.atan2(dy, dx) * 180 / Math.PI;
```

Create waves:

```
// assign value to x, y or other property of sprite or movie clip,
// use as drawing coordinates, etc.
public function onEnterFrame(event:Event){
    value = center + Math.sin(angle) * range;
    angle += speed;
}
```

Create circles:

```
// assign position to x and y of sprite or movie clip,
// use as drawing coordinates, etc.
public function onEnterFrame(event:Event){
    xposition = centerX + Math.cos(angle) * radius;
    yposition = centerY + Math.sin(angle) * radius;
    angle += speed;
}
```

Create ovals:

```
// assign position to x and y of sprite or movie clip,
// use as drawing coordinates, etc.
public function onEnterFrame(event:Event){
    xposition = centerX + Math.cos(angle) * radiusX;
    yposition = centerY + Math.sin(angle) * radiusY;
    angle += speed;
}
```

Get the distance between two points:

```
// points are x1, y1 and x2, y2
// can be sprite / movie clip positions, mouse coordinates, etc.
dx = x2 - x1;
dy = y2 - y1;
dist = Math.sqrt(dx*dx + dy*dy);
```

Chapter 4

Convert hex to decimal:

```
trace(hexValue);
```

Convert decimal to hex:

```
trace(decimalValue.toString(16));
```

Combine component colors:

```
color24 = red << 16 | green << 8 | blue;
color32 = alpha << 24 | red << 16 | green << 8 | blue;
```

Extract component colors:

```
red = color24 >> 16;
green = color24 >> 8 & 0xFF;
blue = color24 & 0xFF;
```

```
alpha = color32 >> 24;
red = color32 >> 16 & 0xFF;
green = color32 >> 8 & 0xFF;
blue = color232 & 0xFF;
```

Draw a curve through a point:

```
// xt, yt is the point you want to draw through
// x0, y0 and x2, y2 are the end points of the curve
x1 = xt * 2 - (x0 + x2) / 2;
y1 = yt * 2 - (y0 + y2) / 2;
moveTo(x0, y0);
curveTo(x1, y1, x2, y2);
```

Chapter 5

Convert angular velocity to x, y velocity:

```
vx = speed * Math.cos(angle);
vy = speed * Math.sin(angle);
```

Convert angular acceleration (any force acting on an object) to x, y acceleration:

```
ax = force * Math.cos(angle);
ay = force * Math.sin(angle);
```

Add acceleration to velocity:

```
vx += ax;
vy += ay;
```

Add velocity to position:

```
movieclip._x += vx;
sprite.y += vy;
```

Chapter 6

Remove an out-of-bounds object:

```
if(sprite.x - sprite.width / 2 > right ||
   sprite.x + sprite.width / 2 < left ||
   sprite.y - sprite.height / 2 > bottom ||
   sprite.y + sprite.height / 2 < top)
{
    // code to remove sprite
}
```

Regenerate an out-of-bounds object:

```
if(sprite.x - sprite.width / 2 > right ||
   sprite.x + sprite.width / 2 < left ||
   sprite.y - sprite.height / 2 > bottom ||
   sprite.y + sprite.height / 2 < top)
{
     // reset sprite position and velocity.
}
```

Screen wrapping for an out-of-bounds object:

```
if(sprite.x - sprite.width / 2 > right)
{
   sprite.x = left - sprite.width / 2;
}
else if(sprite.x + sprite.width / 2 < left)
{
   sprite.x = right + sprite.width / 2;
}
if(sprite.y - sprite.height / 2 > bottom)
{
   sprite.y = top - sprite.height / 2;
}
else if(sprite.y + sprite.height / 2 < top)
{
   sprite.y = bottom + sprite.height / 2;
}
```

Apply friction (the correct way):

```
speed = Math.sqrt(vx * vx + vy * vy);
angle = Math.atan2(vy, vx);
if(speed > friction)
{
   speed -= friction;
}
else
{
   speed = 0;
}
vx = Math.cos(angle) * speed;
vy = Math.sin(angle) * speed;
```

Apply friction (the easy way):

```
vx *= friction;
vy *= friction;
```

Chapter 8

Simple easing, long form:

```
var dx:Number = targetX - sprite.x;
var dy:Number = targetY - sprite.y;
vx = dx * easing;
vy = dy * easing;
sprite.x += vx;
sprite.y += vy;
```

Simple easing, abbreviated form:

```
vx = (targetX - sprite.x) * easing;
vy = (targetY - sprite.y) * easing;
sprite.x += vx;
sprite.y += vy;
```

Simple easing, short form:

```
sprite.x += (targetX - sprite.x) * easing;
sprite.y += (targetY - sprite.y) * easing;
```

Simple spring, long form:

```
var ax:Number = (targetX - sprite.x) * spring;
var ay:Number = (targetY - sprite.y) * spring;
vx += ax;
vy += ay;
vx *= friction;
vy *= friction;
sprite.x += vx;
sprite.y += vy;
```

Simple spring, abbreviated form:

```
vx += (targetX - sprite.x) * spring;
vy += (targetY - sprite.y) * spring;
vx *= friction;
vy *= friction;
sprite.x += vx;
sprite.y += vy;
```

Simple spring, short form:

```
vx += (targetX - sprite.x) * spring;
vy += (targetY - sprite.y) * spring;
sprite.x += (vx *= friction);
sprite.y += (vy *= friction);
```

Offset spring:

```
var dx:Number = sprite.x - fixedX;
var dy:Number = sprite.y - fixedY;
var angle:Number = Math.atan2(dy, dx);
var targetX:Number = fixedX + Math.cos(angle) * springLength;
var targetY:Number = fixedX + Math.sin(angle) * springLength;
// spring to targetX, targetY as above
```

Chapter 9

Distance-based collision detection:

```
// starting with spriteA and spriteB
// if using a plain sprite, or object without a radius property,
// you can use width or height divided by 2
var dx:Number = spriteB.x - spriteA.x;
var dy:Number = spriteB.y - spriteA.y;
var dist:Number = Math.sqrt(dx * dx + dy * dy);
if(dist < spriteA.radius + spriteB.radius)
{
    // handle collision
}
```

Multiple-object collision detection:

```
var numObjects:uint = 10; // for example
for(var i:uint = 0; i < numObjects - 1; i++)
{
    // evaluate reference using variable i. For example:
    var objectA = objects[i];

    for(var j:uint = i+1; j<numObjects;j++)
    {
        // evaluate reference using j. For example:
        var objectB = objects[j];

        // perform collision detection
        // between objectA and objectB
    }
}
```

Chapter 10

Coordinate rotation:

```
x1 = Math.cos(angle) * x - Math.sin(angle) * y;
y1 = Math.cos(angle) * y + Math.sin(angle) * x;
```

Reverse coordinate rotation:

```
x1 = Math.cos(angle) * x + Math.sin(angle) * ;y
y1 = Math.cos(angle) * y - Math.sin(angle) * x;
```

Chapter 11

Conservation of momentum, in straight mathematical terms:

$$v0Final = \frac{(m0 - m1) * v0 + 2 * m1 * v1}{m0 + m1}$$

$$v1Final = \frac{(m1 - m0) * v1 + 2 * m0 * v0}{m0 + m1}$$

Conservation of momentum in ActionScript, with a shortcut:

```
var vxTotal:Number = vx0 - vx1;
vx0 = ((ball0.mass - ball1.mass) * vx0 +
    2 * ball1.mass * vx1) /
    (ball0.mass + ball1.mass);
vx1 = vxTotal + vx0;
```

Chapter 12

Basic gravity:

$$force = G * m1 * m2 / distance^2$$

ActionScript-friendly gravity implementation:

```
function gravitate(partA:Ball, partB:Ball):void
{
    var dx:Number = partB.x - partA.x;
    var dy:Number = partB.y - partA.y;
    var distSQ:Number = dx * dx + dy * dy;
    var dist:Number = Math.sqrt(distSQ);
    var force:Number = partA.mass * partB.mass / distSQ;
    var ax:Number = force * dx / dist;
    var ay:Number = force * dy / dist;
    partA.vx += ax / partA.mass;
    partA.vy += ay / partA.mass;
    partB.vx -= ax / partB.mass;
    partB.vy -= ay / partB.mass;
}
```

Chapter 14

Law of cosines:

$$a^2 = b^2 + c^2 - 2 * b * c * \cos A$$
$$b^2 = a^2 + c^2 - 2 * a * c * \cos B$$
$$c^2 = a^2 + b^2 - 2 * a * b * \cos C$$

Law of cosines in ActionScript:

```
A = Math.acos((b * b + c * c - a * a) / (2 * b * c));
B = Math.acos((a * a + c * c - b * b) / (2 * a * c));
C = Math.acos((a * a + b * b - c * c) / (2 * a * b));
```

Chapter 15

Basic perspective:

```
scale = fl / (fl + zpos);
sprite.scaleX = sprite.scaleY = scale;
sprite.alpha = scale;      // optional
sprite.x = vanishingPointX + xpos * scale;
sprite.y = vanishingPointY + ypos * scale;
```

Z-sorting:

```
// assumes an array of 3D objects with a zpos property
objectArray.sortOn("zpos", Array.DESCENDING | Array.NUMERIC);
for(var i:uint = 0; i < numObjects; i++)
{
    setChildIndex(objectArray[i], i);
}
```

Coordinate rotation:

```
x1 = cos(angleZ) * xpos - sin(angleZ) * ypos;
y1 = cos(angleZ) * ypos + sin(angleZ) * xpos;

x1 = cos(angleY) * xpos - sin(angleY) * zpos;
z1 = cos(angleY) * zpos + sin(angleY) * xpos;

y1 = cos(angleX) * ypos - sin(angleX) * zpos;
z1 = cos(angleX) * zpos + sin(angleX) * ypos;
```

3D distance:

```
dist = Math.sqrt(dx * dx + dy * dy + dz * dz);
```

519

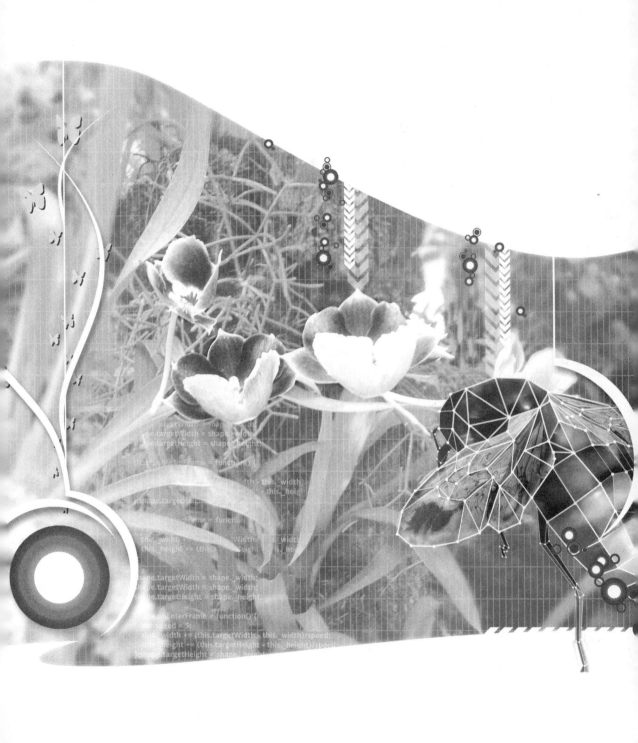

INDEX

B

N